iPhoto '11

the missing manual®

The book that should have been in the box®

iPhoto '11

the missing manual®

The book that should have been in the box®

David Pogue & Lesa Snider

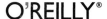

O'REILLY®

Beijing | Cambridge | Farnham | Köln | Sebastopol | Tokyo

iPhoto '11: The Missing Manual

by David Pogue & Lesa Snider

Printed in Canada.

Published by O'Reilly Media, Inc., 1005 Gravenstein Highway North, Sebastopol, CA 95472.

O'Reilly Media books may be purchased for educational, business, or sales promotional use. Online editions are also available for most titles: *http://my.safaribooksonline.com*. For more information, contact our corporate/institutional sales department: 800-998-9938 or *corporate@oreilly.com*.

Printing History:

March 2011:   First Edition.

ISBN: 978-1-449-3-9323-6

[TI]   [2012-01-13]

Table of Contents

The Missing Credits

About the Authors

David Pogue (original author, editor) is the weekly tech columnist for the *New York Times*, an Emmy-winning correspondent for *CBS News Sunday Morning*, a weekly CNBC contributor, and the creator of the Missing Manual series. He's the author or coauthor of 53 books, including 26 in this series, six in the *For Dummies* line (including *Macs, Magic, Opera*, and *Classical Music*), and a novel for middle schoolers called *Abby Carnelia's One and Only Magical Power*. In his other life, David is a former Broadway show conductor, a piano player, and a magician. He lives in Connecticut with his three awesome children.

Links to his columns and weekly videos await at *www.davidpogue.com*. He welcomes feedback about his books by email at *david@pogueman.com*.

Lesa Snider is an internationally acclaimed speaker and the author of *Photoshop CS5: The Missing Manual*. She writes a monthly column for *Photoshop User, Photoshop Elements Techniques*, and *Macworld* magazines. In addition, Lesa is a stock photographer and chief evangelist for iStockphoto.com, and founder of the creative tutorial site *www.GraphicReporter.com*. Lesa has recorded many training videos including "From Photo to Graphic Art," "Practical Photoshop Elements," "Photoshop Elements for Photographers" (all at *www.KelbyTraining.com*), and "Graphic Secrets for Business Professionals" (*www.Lynda.com*).

She teaches in the Denver/Boulder area for Mike's Camera (*www.mikescamera.com*) and hosts her own European River Cruise workshop, "Digital Photography on the Danube" (*www.photocruisewithlesa.com*). She also speaks at conferences such as Photoshop World, Mac Computer Expo, Macworld Expo, Geek Girl Boot Camp, Santa Fe Workshops, and a slew of Mac User Groups (she's a proud member of CO-MUG.com and NCMUG.org). You can email her at *lesa@graphicreporter.com*.

About the Creative Team

Dawn Mann (editor) is associate editor for the Missing Manual series. When not working, she plays soccer, beads, and causes trouble. Email: *dawn@oreilly.com*.

Holly Bauer (production editor) lives in Ye Olde Cambridge, MA. She's a production editor by day and an avid home cook, DIYer, and mid-century modern design enthusiast by night/weekend. Email: *holly@oreilly.com*.

Douglas Bergère (tech reviewer) lives in Rendon, Texas. When not working, he enjoys foreign travel and photography. He has been programming for over 20 years, most recently creating database-driven dynamic web pages. *http://xevio.us*

Acknowledgments

The Missing Manual series is a joint venture between Pogue Press (the dream team introduced on these pages) and O'Reilly Media (a dream publishing partner). I'm indebted, as always, to Tim O'Reilly, Laurie Petrycki, Peter Meyers, and the rest of the gang.

I also owe a debt of gratitude to my old Yale roommate Joe Schorr, who coauthored the first two editions of this book and wound up, years later, working at Apple, where he eventually became the product manager for Aperture and—how's this for irony?—iPhoto. Some of his prose and his humor live on in this edition.

Various editions of this book have also enjoyed the prose stylings of professional photographer/writer Derrick Story and fellow *New York Times* tech columnist Jude Biersdorfer. Above all, it was my pleasure to welcome Lesa Snider, who cheerfully undertook the challenge of updating this book to reflect the changes in iPhoto '11 without making it sound like two different authors were at work. She did a sensational job.

Above all, thanks to Kelly, Tia, and Jeffrey, whose patience and sacrifices make these books—and everything else—possible.

—David Pogue

What a huge treat it was to update this book! While I served as photographer/production assistant on previous editions, as coauthor I was able to pore over every word, feature, and figure in order to create a bright and cheery (yet comprehensive) book. And in doing so, I'm continually amazed at the ease of use, organizational, and editing power of iPhoto. I'm really proud of the way the book turned out, and I hope you'll enjoy it, too. (FYI, all the photography in this edition came from my trusty Canon 40D and Canon PowerShot S90.)

Of course, a million thanks go to David Pogue for teaching me how to make every figure a work of art, as well as how to write in an entertaining yet informative manner. His guidance has been the foundation for my career in more ways than I can count.

Thanks also to my editor, Dawn Mann, for her amazing attention to detail, and also to Douglas Bergère, who tech-edited this edition.

Last but not least, I owe a galactic debt of gratitude to my husband, Jay Nelson, for being incredibly supportive during this project and for keeping me, and our two loving cats, fed and watered.

—Lesa Snider

The Missing Manual Series

Missing Manuals are witty, superbly written guides to computer products that don't come with printed manuals (which is just about all of them). Each book features a handcrafted index; cross-references to specific pages (not just chapters); and Rep-Kover, a detached-spine binding that lets the book lie perfectly flat without the assistance of weights or cinder blocks.

Introduction

In case you haven't heard, the digital camera market is exploding. At this point, a staggering 98 percent of cameras sold are digital cameras. It's taken a few decades—the underlying technology used in most digital cameras was invented in 1969—but film photography has been reduced to a niche activity.

And why not? The appeal of digital photography is huge. When you shoot digitally, you don't pay a cent for film or photo processing. You get instant results, viewing your photos just moments after shooting them, making even Polaroids seem painfully slow by comparison. As a digital photographer, you can even be your own darkroom technician—without the darkroom. You can retouch and enhance photos, make enlargements, and print out greeting cards using your home computer. Sharing your pictures with others is far easier, too, since you can burn them to CD or DVD, email them to friends, or post them on the Web. As one fan puts it, "There are no 'negatives' in digital photography."

But there is one problem. When most people try to *do* all this cool stuff, they find themselves drowning in a sea of technical details: JPEG compression, EXIF tags, file format compatibility, image resolutions, FTP clients, and so on. It isn't pretty.

The cold reality is that while digital photography is full of promise, it's also been full of headaches. During the early years of digital cameras, just making the camera-to-computer connection was a nightmare. You had to mess with serial or USB cables; install device drivers; and use proprietary software to transfer, open, and convert camera images into a standard file format. If you handled all these tasks perfectly—and sacrificed a young male goat during the spring equinox—you ended up with good digital pictures.

iPhoto Arrives

Apple recognized this mess and decided to do something about it. When Steve Jobs gave his keynote address at Macworld Expo in January 2002, he referred to the "chain of pain" that ordinary people experienced when attempting to download, store, edit, and share their digital photos.

He also focused on another growing problem among digital photographers: Once you start shooting free, filmless photos, they pile up quickly. Before you know it, you have 10,000 pictures of your kid playing soccer. Just organizing and keeping track of all those photos is enough to drive you insane.

Apple's answer to all these problems was iPhoto, a simple and uncluttered program designed to organize, edit, and distribute digital photos without the nightmarish hassles. Successive versions added features and better speed. (There was no iPhoto 3 or 10, oddly enough. Keep that in mind if someone tries to sell you a copy on eBay!)

To be sure, iPhoto isn't the most powerful image-management software in the world. Like Apple's other iProducts (iMovie, iTunes, iDVD, and so on), its design subscribes to its own little 80/20 rule: 80 percent of us really don't need more than about 20 percent of the features you'd find in a full-blown, $200 digital asset management program like, say, Apple's own Aperture or Adobe Photoshop Lightroom.

Today, millions of Mac fans use iPhoto. Evidently, there were a lot of digital camera buffs out there, feeling the pain and hoping that iPhoto would provide some much-needed relief.

What's New in iPhoto '11

On the surface, iPhoto '11 looks much more polished and grown-up than iPhoto '09, and it now takes advantage of Apple's Core Animation technology (the brains behind moving graphics in Mac OS X). It also harbors new features designed to make it easier to share your photos with the world:

- **Full Screen view**. The most talked-about feature in iPhoto '11 is the new Full Screen view, which lets iPhoto commandeer each and every pixel on your screen. Enter this mode and everything else on your monitor disappears, including the menu bar. It's great for eliminating distractions and encourages you to concentrate more fully on the task at hand. The new views are simply gorgeous, whether you're browsing Events, peering at all the faces you've tagged (they appear as Polaroids tacked on a corkboard), or gawking at a full-screen map of all the places you've been. If you're viewing Albums, they appear as stacks just like they do on the iPad, and a beautiful new, pine-paneled Project Bookshelf holds the cards and calendars you've created.

- **Online sharing**. iPhoto '09 brought online sharing to the masses, and iPhoto '11 fine-tunes the process. In this version, you can easily upload photos to an existing Facebook album, Flickr set, or MobileMe gallery, or create a new one on the fly. If you've spent time tagging faces or adding descriptions in iPhoto, that info now travels with your photos to Facebook. You can also update your Facebook profile photo from *within* iPhoto, as well as view the comments your buddies have made about your "My Summer in Maui" pics (you'll see them in the Info panel).

- **Emailing photos**. Emailing photos from within iPhoto got a big overhaul. Instead of handing the task off to your email program, iPhoto now handles everything itself, without even opening your email program. Instead of simply attaching photos to an email (yawn!), you can choose from eight templates that display up to 10 photos in full splendor, complete with brief captions, right in the body of the message. This feature even keeps track of the photo-emails you've sent so you can easily edit and resend them to someone new.

    (The old way still works, too. iPhoto can still send out photo files as email attachments in whatever email program you use.)

- **New slideshow themes**. The beloved slideshow feature sports six new themes that build on the animated visual styles from iPhoto '09. The new goodies include Holiday Mobile, in which photos dangle in midair before the viewer's eyes (crib not included), Reflections, Vintage Prints, Places, and Origami. Each new theme takes advantage of iPhoto's ability to recognize faces, centering each face it finds. The themes even come with their own soundtracks, and the export option is now optimized for the iPad.

- **Better project design**. Apple revamped the way you design books, cards, and calendars, making the process easier and more visually pleasing. Here again, iPhoto takes advantage of its face-detecting skills to center people automatically in the frame, and it even groups photos according to when they were taken. You can still tweak the layout of individual pages, but the smarter-than-ever Autoflow feature works so well that you probably won't have to do much rearranging.

- **Letterpress cards**. These cards are top-of-the-line in every way, from their elegant templates to the super high-quality paper they're printed on. The sheer joy of holding—not to mention receiving—such a tactile treat is nothing short of extravagant, and it's a wonderful way to combine Ye Olde Print World with your digital photos.

- **View and trim videos**. At long last, you can watch videos captured with your digital camera right in iPhoto. (In previous versions, double-clicking a video opened it up in QuickTime Player for playback.) You can also trim footage from the beginning and end of your clips and then share them to your Facebook wall or MobileMe gallery.

There are other, more subtle changes, too. For example, new menu commands let you rescan photos for faces and places info, and you can copy edits from one photo to another using a keyboard shortcut. The icons at the bottom of the iPhoto window are now a sleek, charcoal gray, and the details about your photo—like the shutter speed and ISO, date taken, Faces and Places info, and so on—are tucked inside a collapsible panel (the Extended Photo Info panel no longer exists). Overall, the entire program looks and feels more streamlined.

In short, there are quite a few changes, so you'll definitely need a book to keep track—and you're holding it right now.

About This Book

Don't let the rumors fool you. iPhoto may be simple, but it's far from simplistic. It offers a wide range of tools, shortcuts, and database-like features; a complete arsenal of photo-presentation tools; and sophisticated multimedia and Internet hooks. Unfortunately, many of the best techniques aren't covered in the only "manual" you get with iPhoto—its slow, sparse electronic help screens and videos.

This book was born to serve as the iPhoto manual—the book that should have been in the box. It explores each of the program's features in depth, offers shortcuts and workarounds, and unearths features that the online help doesn't even mention.

And to make it all go down easier, this book has been printed in full color. Kind of makes sense for a book about photography, doesn't it?

About the Outline

This book is divided into four parts, each containing several chapters:

- Part 1, **iPhoto Basics**, covers the fundamentals of getting your photos into iPhoto. This includes organizing and filing them, tagging them with a face or a place, searching them, and editing them to compensate for weak lighting (or weak photography).

- Part 2, **Meet Your Public**, is all about the payoff, the moment you've been waiting for since you snapped the shots—showing them off. It covers the many ways iPhoto can present those photos to other people: on Facebook or Flickr; as a slideshow; as prints you order online or make yourself; as a professionally printed card or gift book; on a web page; by email; or as a QuickTime slideshow that you post on the Web, send to your iPhone, or distribute on DVD. It also covers sharing your iPhoto collection across an office network with other Macs and with other account holders on the same Mac.

- Part 3, **iPhoto Stunts**, takes you way beyond the basics. It covers a potpourri of additional iPhoto features, including turning photos into screensavers or desktop pictures on your Mac, exporting the photos in various formats, using iPhoto plug-ins and accessory programs, managing (or even switching) iPhoto libraries, backing up your photos by burning them to a CD or DVD, and even getting photos to and from smartphones.

- Part 4, **Appendixes**, brings up the rear, but gives you a chance to move forward. Appendix A offers troubleshooting guidance, Appendix B lists some websites that will help fuel your growing addiction to digital photography, and Appendix C (available online at *www.missingmanuals.com/cds*) goes through iPhoto's menus one by one to make sure that every last feature has been covered.

About→These→Arrows

Throughout this book, and throughout the Missing Manual series, you'll find sentences like this one: "Open the System folder→Libraries→Fonts folder." That's shorthand for a much longer instruction that directs you to open three nested folders in sequence. That instruction might read: "On your hard drive, you'll find a folder called System. Open it. Inside the System folder window is a folder called Libraries. Open that. Inside *that* folder is yet another one called Fonts. Double-click to open it, too."

Similarly, this kind of arrow shorthand helps to simplify the business of choosing commands in menus. The instruction "Choose Photos→Duplicate" means, "Open the Photos menu at the top of your monitor, and then choose the Duplicate command."

About the Online Resources

As the owner of a Missing Manual, you've got more than just a book to read. At the Missing Manuals website, you'll find tips, articles, and other useful info. You can also communicate with the Missing Manual team and tell us what you love (or hate) about this book. Head over to *www.missingmanuals.com*, or go directly to one of the following sections.

Missing CD

This book doesn't have a physical CD pasted inside the back cover, but you're not missing out on anything. Go to *www.missingmanuals.com/cds* to find a list of all the shareware and websites mentioned in this book as well as Appendix C.

Registration

If you register this book at oreilly.com, you'll be eligible for special offers—like discounts on future editions. Registering takes only a few clicks. To get started, type *http://tinyurl.com/registerbook* into your browser to hop directly to the registration page.

Feedback

Got questions? Need more info? Fancy yourself a book reviewer? On our Feedback page, you can get expert answers to questions that come to you while reading, share your thoughts on this Missing Manual, and find groups for folks who share your interest in iPhoto. To have your say, go to *www.missingmanuals.com/feedback*.

Errata

In an effort to keep this book as up to date and accurate as possible, each time we print more copies, we'll make any confirmed corrections you've suggested. We also note such changes on the book's website, so you can mark important corrections in your own copy of the book, if you like. Go to *http://tinyurl.com/iphotoerrata* to report an error and view existing corrections.

The Very Basics

You'll find very little jargon or nerd terminology in this book. You will, however, encounter a few terms and concepts that you'll see frequently in your Macintosh life. Here are the essentials:

- **Clicking**. To *click* means to point the arrow cursor at something onscreen and then—without moving the cursor at all—press and release the clicker button on the mouse or trackpad. To *double-click*, of course, means to click twice in rapid succession, again without moving the cursor at all. And to *drag* means to move the cursor while keeping the button continuously pressed.

   When you're told to ⌘-click something, you click while pressing the ⌘ key (next to the space bar). *Shift-clicking*, *Option-clicking*, and *Control-clicking* work the same way—just click while pressing the corresponding key on your keyboard. (On non-U.S. Mac keyboards, the Option key may be labeled "Alt" instead, and the ⌘ key may have a Windows logo on it.)

Note: On Windows PCs, the mouse has two buttons. The left one is for clicking normally; the right one produces a tiny shortcut menu of useful commands (see the note below). But new Macs come with Apple's Magic Mouse, a mouse that looks like it has only one button but can actually detect which side of its rounded front you're pressing. If you've turned on the feature in System Preferences, then you too can right-click things on the screen by clicking the right side of the mouse or by clicking with *two* fingers instead of one.

That's why, all through this book, you'll see the phrase, "Control-click the photo (or right-click it)." That's telling you that Control-clicking will do the job—but if you've got a two-button mouse or you've turned on the two-button feature of the Magic Mouse, right-clicking might be more efficient.

- **Keyboard shortcuts**. Every time you take your hand off the keyboard to move the mouse, you lose time and potentially disrupt your creative flow. That's why many experienced Mac fans use keystroke combinations instead of menu commands wherever possible. ⌘-P opens the Print dialog box, for example, and ⌘-M minimizes the current window to the Dock.

   When you see a shortcut like ⌘-Q (which quits the current program), it's telling you to hold down the ⌘ key, and, while it's down, type the letter Q, and then release both keys. And if you forget a keyboard shortcut, don't panic. Just look at the menu item and you'll see its keyboard shortcut listed to its right. (To see a list of *all* the keyboard shortcuts in iPhoto '11, choose Help→Keyboard Shortcuts.)

If you've mastered this much information, you have all the technical background you need to enjoy *iPhoto '11: The Missing Manual.*

Note: Apple has officially changed what it calls the little menu that pops up when you Control-click (or right-click) something on the screen. It's still a *contextual* menu, in that the menu choices depend on the context of what you click—but it's now called a *shortcut* menu. That term not only matches what it's called in Windows, but it's slightly more descriptive about its function. "Shortcut menu" is the term you'll find in this book.

Safari® Books Online

 Safari Books Online is an on-demand digital library that lets you easily search over 7,500 technology and creative reference books and videos to find the answers you need quickly.

With a subscription, you can read any page and watch any video from our library online. Read books on your cell phone and mobile devices. Access new titles before they are available for print, and get exclusive access to manuscripts in development and post feedback for the authors. Copy and paste code samples, organize your favorites, download chapters, bookmark key sections, create notes, print out pages, and benefit from tons of other time-saving features.

O'Reilly Media has uploaded this book to the Safari Books Online service. To have full digital access to this book and others on similar topics from O'Reilly and other publishers, sign up for free at *http://my.safaribooksonline.com.*

Camera Meets Mac

Your digital camera is brimming with photos. You've snapped the perfect graduation portrait, captured that jaw-dropping sunset over the Pacific, or compiled an unforgettable photo essay of your 2-year-old attempting to eat a bowl of spaghetti. It's time to use your Mac to gather, organize, and tweak all these photos so you can share them with the rest of the world.

That's the core of this book—compiling, organizing, and adjusting your pictures using iPhoto, and then transforming this collection of digital photos into a professional-looking slideshow, set of prints, movie, web page, email, desktop picture, calendar, or bound book.

But before you start organizing and publishing these pictures using iPhoto, they have to find their way from your camera to your Mac. This chapter explains how to get pictures from camera to computer and introduces you to iPhoto.

iPhoto: The Application

iPhoto approaches digital photo management as a four-step process:

- **Import**. Working with iPhoto begins with feeding your digital pictures (and videos) into the program, either from a camera or from somewhere else on your Mac. In general, importing is literally a one-click process. This is the part of iPhoto covered in this chapter.

- **Organize**. This step is about sorting and categorizing your chaotic jumble of pictures so you can easily find them and arrange them into logical groups. You can add searchable keywords like Vacation or Kids to make pictures easier to find. You can change the order of images, and group them into folders called albums. You can group your pictures based on *who's* in them, and have iPhoto help match names to faces. You can pin your photos to a virtual map that shows your travels around the globe. Chapter 2 and Chapter 3 cover all of iPhoto's organization tools, and Chapter 4 explains the Faces and Places features.

- **Edit**. This is where you fine-tune your photos to make them look as good as possible. iPhoto provides everything you need for rotating, retouching, resizing, cropping, color-balancing, straightening, and brightening your pictures. (More significant image adjustments—like editing out an ex-spouse—require a different program, like Photoshop Elements.) Editing your photos is the focus of Chapter 5.

- **Share**. iPhoto's best features have to do with sharing your photos, either onscreen or on paper. In fact, iPhoto offers nine different ways of publishing your pictures. In addition to printing pictures on your own printer (in a variety of interesting layouts and book styles), you can display images as an onscreen slideshow, turn the slideshow into a QuickTime movie, order professional-quality prints or a professionally bound book, email them, apply one to your desktop as a backdrop, select a batch to become your Mac OS X screensaver, post them online as a web page, and so on. Chapters 8–13 explain how to undertake these self-publishing tasks.

Note: Although much of this book focuses on using digital cameras, remember this: You don't have to shoot digital photos to use iPhoto. You can just as easily use it to organize and publish pictures you've shot with a traditional film camera and then digitized using a scanner (or had your local camera store convert into a photo CD). Importing scanned photos is covered later in this chapter.

---

iPhoto Requirements

To run iPhoto '11, Apple recommends a Mac that has an Intel chip, Mac OS X 10.6.3 (that's Snow Leopard) or later, and 1 gigabyte of memory or more.

The truth is, iPhoto may be among the most memory-dependent programs on your Mac. It *loves* memory. Memory is even more important to iPhoto than your Mac's processor speed. It makes the difference between tolerable speed and sluggishness. So the more memory and horsepower your Mac has, the happier you'll be.

Finally, of course, you'll need a lot of hard drive space—not just several gigabytes for iPhoto and the other iLife programs, but also lots of gigabytes for all the photos you'll be transferring to your Mac. (Apple recommends at least 5 gigabytes free.)

Getting iPhoto

A free version of iPhoto has been included on every Mac sold since January 2002. If your Mac falls into that category, then you'll find iPhoto in your Applications folder. (To open this folder, press Shift-⌘-A or, in the Finder, choose Go→Applications.)

You can tell which version you have by single-clicking its icon—the little camera superimposed on the palm tree—and then choosing File→Get Info. In the resulting info window, you'll see the version number. (Confusingly, iPhoto '11 is actually version 9 of the program.)

If you bought your Mac after October 2010, you probably have iPhoto '11 installed. Otherwise, it's available only as part of Apple's iLife '11 software suite—a $49 DVD that includes GarageBand, iMovie, iPhoto, iDVD, and iWeb. You can get the iLife box from *www.apple.com/store*, mail-order websites, or local computer stores.

Note: You can also purchase iPhoto '11 (all by itself) for $15 from Apple's Mac App Store. If you're using Mac OS 10.6.6 or later, the Mac App icon (it looks like a round, blue button with a white A in the middle) probably appears in your Dock, or for sure in your Applications folder.

When you run the iLife installer, you're offered a choice of programs to install. Install all five programs, if you like, or just iPhoto. (The other programs in iLife can access your iPhoto library, too.)

When the installation process is over, you'll find the iPhoto icon in your Applications folder and in your Dock, so you'll be able to open it more conveniently from now on.

Note: If you installed iPhoto '11 from the iLife DVD, *do not* launch iPhoto '11 yet! There was a serious bug in the initial release, capable, in some cases, of deleting your photo library (that's why backups are so important!). The fix is to run Software Update and download the iPhoto 9.1.1 update (or a higher-numbered one) first. That is, choose →System Preferences, and then click the Software Update icon (it looks like a tiny globe encircled by two arrows). Click Check Now; your dutiful Mac connects to Apple.com and downloads the update. Once it's finished downloading, click the Install button. It's now safe to install iPhoto from the DVD.

Upgrading from earlier versions

If you've used an earlier version of iPhoto, then you'd be wise to make a backup of your *iPhoto library*—your database of photos—before running iPhoto '11. That's because iPhoto's first bit of business is converting that library into a new, more efficient format that's incompatible with earlier iPhotos (see Figure 1-1, bottom).

Ordinarily, the upgrade process is seamless: iPhoto smoothly converts and displays your existing photos, comments, titles, and albums. But lightning does strike, fuses do blow, and the technology gods have a cruel sense of humor—so making a backup copy before iPhoto converts your old library is very, very smart.

To perform this safety measure, open your Home→Pictures folder, and then copy or duplicate the iPhoto Library icon. (This folder may be huge, since it contains copies of all the photos you've imported into iPhoto. This is a solid argument for copying it onto a second hard drive, an iPod classic, or a bunch of burnable DVDs; see page 329.) Now, if anything should go wrong with the conversion process, you'll still have a clean, uncorrupted copy of your iPhoto library files.

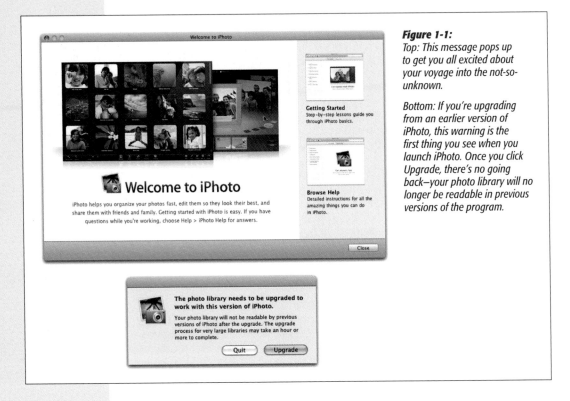

Figure 1-1:
Top: This message pops up to get you all excited about your voyage into the not-so-unknown.

Bottom: If you're upgrading from an earlier version of iPhoto, this warning is the first thing you see when you launch iPhoto. Once you click Upgrade, there's no going back—your photo library will no longer be readable in previous versions of the program.

Running iPhoto for the First Time

Click the iPhoto icon in your Dock to open the program. After you dismiss the "Welcome to iPhoto" dialog box (Figure 1-1, top), iPhoto checks to see if you have an older version and, if so, offers to convert its photo library (Figure 1-1, bottom). (If you've got a lot of photos, you'll have time to fetch a snack—or possibly get a graduate degree—while iPhoto does the conversion.)

Finally, you arrive at the program's main window, the basic elements of which are shown in Figure 1-2.

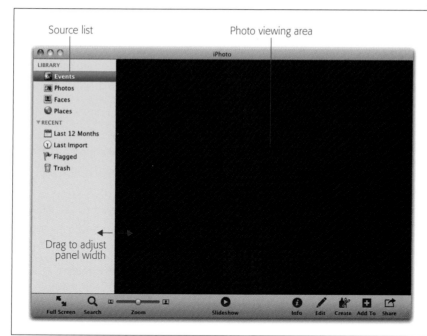

Source list   Photo viewing area

Drag to adjust panel width

Full Screen   Search   Zoom   Slideshow   Info   Edit   Create Add To Share

Figure 1-2:
Here's what iPhoto looks like when you first open it. The large photo-viewing area is where thumbnails of your imported photos will appear. The sleek, charcoal gray icons at the bottom of the window, new in iPhoto '11, represent all the cool stuff you can do with your photos. (If you've never used iPhoto before, you see a big yellow sticky note prompting you to connect a camera or memory card to get started.)

Note: When you first run iPhoto '11, the program also asks if you'd like it to look up photo locations on Apple's servers so your photos can be placed on a map. This is part of the Places feature, explained in Chapter 4.

Getting Your Pictures into iPhoto

With iPhoto installed and ready to run, it's time for you to import your own pictures into the program—a process that's remarkably easy, especially if your photos are going directly from your camera into iPhoto.

Of course, if you've been taking digital photos for some time, you probably have a lot of photo files already crammed into folders on your hard drive, on flash drives, or on CD/DVDs. If you shoot pictures with a traditional film camera and use a scanner to digitize them, you've probably got piles of JPEG or TIFF images stashed away on disk already, waiting to be cataloged using iPhoto.

This section explains how to transfer files into iPhoto from each of these sources.

Connecting with a USB Camera

Every digital camera can connect to a Mac's USB port. If your Mac has more than one USB jack, any of them will do.

Plugging a USB-compatible camera, iPhone, or camera-equipped iPod into your Mac is the easiest way to transfer pictures from your camera into iPhoto.

The whole process practically happens by itself:

1. **Connect the camera to one of your Mac's USB jacks, and then turn the camera on.**

   To make this camera-to-Mac USB connection, you need what is usually called an *A-to-B* USB cable; your camera probably came with one. The "A" end—the part you plug into your camera—has a small, flat-bottomed plug whose shape varies by manufacturer. The Mac end of the cable has a larger, flatter, rectangular, standard USB plug. Make sure both ends of the cable are plugged in firmly.

   If iPhoto isn't already running when you make this connection, the program opens and springs into action as soon as you switch on the camera.

Note: If this is the first time you've ever run iPhoto, it asks if you always want it to run when you plug in the camera. If you value your time, say yes. Why is it even asking? Because, believe it or not, your Mac came with another program, called Image Capture, that can import photos from a camera. It's in your Applications folder, and you can use iPhoto's Preferences to specify which program you want to open automatically when you connect your camera. (Choose iPhoto→Preferences, click the General tab, and then use the "Connecting camera opens" pop-up menu.)

A wonderful thing happens when you connect the camera: After a pause, you get to see thumbnails (miniature images) of all the photos on your camera's memory card, as shown in Figure 1-3.

Tip: If, for some reason, iPhoto doesn't "see" your camera after you connect it, try turning the camera off, then on again.

How is this wonderful? Let us count the ways. First, it means that you can see right away what's on the card. You don't have to sit through the time-consuming importing process just to discover, when it's all over, that you grabbed the wrong card or the wrong camera.

Second, you can choose to import only *some* of the pictures. (To choose the photos you want to import, use any of the photo-selection techniques described on page 49.)

The option to import only some of the photos opens up a whole new workflow possibility: You can *leave all the photos on your memory card*, all the time. You can take new photos each day, and import only those onto your Mac each night. If your memory card is big enough, this routine means that you always have a backup of your photos.

Something else happens when you connect the camera, too: Its name and icon appear in the *Source list* (the list on the left side of the iPhoto window) and at the top of the iPhoto window. That's handy, because it means that you can switch back and forth between the importing mode (click the camera's icon) and the regular working-in-iPhoto mode (click any other icon in the Source list), even while the time-consuming importing is under way.

(Here's an idea for Apple: As long as the camera's appearing in the Source list, wouldn't it be cool if you could drag photos *onto* the camera, too?)

Tip: If you've decided to work this way, then you can save yourself some time and worry by turning on the Hide Photos Already Imported checkbox at the bottom of the screen. Now, each time you connect the camera, you'll be shown only the new photos, the ones you haven't imported yet. One quick click on the Import All button (step 3) brings in only the latest shots, without your having to pick through the whole collection on the card, trying to remember which pictures you've already downloaded to your Mac.

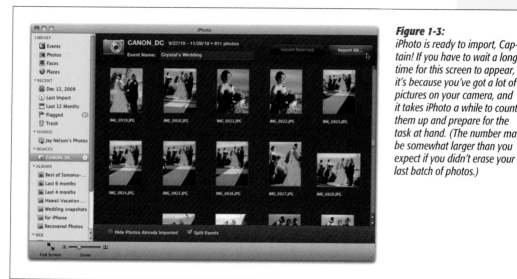

Figure 1-3:
iPhoto is ready to import, Captain! If you have to wait a long time for this screen to appear, it's because you've got a lot of pictures on your camera, and it takes iPhoto a while to count them up and prepare for the task at hand. (The number may be somewhat larger than you expect if you didn't erase your last batch of photos.)

2. **Type an *Event name* and description for the pictures you're about to import.**

   An Event, in iPhoto's little head, is "something you photographed within a certain time period" (for example, on a certain day or during a certain week).

   See, in the old days, iPhoto just imported everything on your memory card and displayed all of those pictures in one gigantic clump—even if they included photos from several different events, shot weeks apart.

   Now, during the importing, iPhoto automatically analyzes the time stamps on the incoming photos and puts them into individually named groups according to when you took them.

You can read much more about Events on page 38. In the meantime, your job here is to type a name for the event whose photos you're about to import. It could be *Disney Trip, Casey's Birthday,* or *Baby Meets Lasagna,* for example—anything that will help you organize and find your pictures later.

Tip: See the Split Events checkbox at the bottom of the iPhoto window? If you turn it on, iPhoto will automatically group the imported pictures into Events, as described above; you won't, however, be offered the chance to *name* the Events (except for the first one) until after the importing is over.

If this option is turned off, then all the photos will end up in one giant Event. (You can split up this one giant batch into several Events later.)

---

3. **Click the appropriate button: Import Selected or Import All.**

    If you selected just *some* of the photos in step 1, then the Import Selected button springs to life. Clicking it brings only the highlighted photos onto your Mac, and ignores the rest of the camera's photos.

    If you click Import All, well, you'll get all of the photos on the card, even if only some are selected.

Note: At this point, you might see a special message if you're about to import photos you've already imported (Figure 1-4, top).

In any case, iPhoto swings into action, copying each photo from your camera to your hard drive. You get to see them as they parade by (Figure 1-4, bottom).

When the process is complete and the photos are safe on your hard drive, iPhoto has another question for you: Do you want to delete the transferred pictures from the memory card?

If you click Delete Photos, iPhoto deletes the transferred photos from the memory card (either all the photos or just the selected ones, depending on the button you clicked at the beginning of step 3). The photos are gone forever, but your memory card will have that much more free space for another exciting photo safari.

If you click Keep Photos, then iPhoto leaves the memory card untouched. You might opt for this approach if you've adopted the "use the card as a backup" lifestyle described on page 14. (You can always use the camera's own menus to erase its memory card.)

4. **"Eject" the camera by clicking the ⏏ button next to its name in the Source list.**

    Or, if the ⏏ button doesn't appear, just drag the camera's icon directly onto the Trash icon in the Source list (you can also Control- or right-click the icon and choose Unmount from the shortcut menu). You're not actually throwing the camera away, of course, or even the photos on it—you're just saying, "Eject this." Even if the camera's still attached to your Mac, its icon disappears from the Source list.

At last, your freshly imported photos appear in the main iPhoto window, awaiting your organizational talents.

5. **Turn off the camera, and then unplug it from the USB cable.**

   You're ready to start having fun with your new pictures.

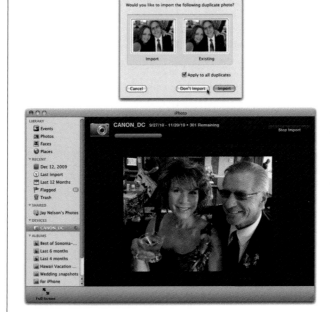

Figure 1-4:
Top: You may sometimes see the "Duplicate Photo" message. iPhoto notices the arrival of duplicates (even if you've edited or rotated the first copy) and offers you the option of downloading them again, resulting in duplicates on your Mac, or ignoring them and importing only the new photos from your camera.

Bottom: As the pictures get slurped into your Mac, iPhoto shows them to you, nice and big, as a sort of slideshow. You can see right away which ones were your hits, which were your misses, and which you'll want to delete the instant the importing process is complete.

USB Card Readers

A USB *memory card reader* offers another convenient way to transfer photos into iPhoto. Most of these card readers, which look like tiny disk drives, are under $20, and some can read more than one kind of memory card.

Note: New iMacs and many Mac laptop models have a memory-card slot built right in. It fits the SD cards used in the huge majority of digital cameras. (A few SLR models use Compact Flash cards, and some older Sony and Olympus cameras accept only Memory Stick and xD cards, respectively; in those cases, the Mac's built-in card slot won't help you.)

If you have a reader, then instead of connecting the camera to the Mac, simply remove the camera's memory card and insert it into the reader (which you can leave permanently connected to the Mac). iPhoto recognizes the reader as though it's a camera and offers to import the photos—all of them or some of them—just as described on the previous pages.

This method offers several advantages over the camera-connection method. First, it's faster and eliminates the battery drain involved in pumping the photos straight off the camera. Second, it's less hassle to pull a memory card out of your camera and slip it into your card reader (which is always plugged in) than it is to constantly plug and unplug camera cables. Finally, this method lets you use almost *any* digital camera with iPhoto, even those too old to include a USB cable connector.

Tip: iPhoto doesn't recognize most camcorders, even though most models can take still pictures. Some camcorders also have a "memory card" connection option that makes the camcorder act like, well, a *memory card* when it's attached to your Mac. If that doesn't work, many camcorders store their stills on a memory card just as digital cameras do, so a memory card reader is exactly what you need to get those pictures into iPhoto.

Connecting a USB card reader is almost identical to connecting a camera. Here's how:

1. **Pop the memory card out of your camera, and then insert it into the reader.**

   Of course, the card reader should already be plugged into the Mac's USB jack.

   As when you connect a camera, iPhoto displays the thumbnails of all the photos on the card, and offers you a chance to type an Event name and description.

2. **Click Import All (or Import Selected).**

   iPhoto swings into action, copying the photos off the card. When you're asked how you want iPhoto to deal with the originals on the memory card, click either Delete Photos or Keep Photos.

3. **Click the Eject button (⏏) next to the card's name in the Source list, and then remove the card from the reader.**

   Put the card back into the camera, so it's ready for more action. There's nothing worse than grabbing your camera to capture a prize-winning shot and finding that you forgot to put the memory card back in.

Importing Photos from Really Old Cameras

If your camera doesn't have a USB connection *and* you don't have a memory card reader, you're still not out of luck.

First, copy the photos from your camera/memory card onto your hard drive (or other disk) using whatever software or hardware came with your camera. Then bring them into iPhoto as you would any other graphics files, as described next.

Tip: If your camera or memory card appears on the Mac desktop like any other removable disk, you can also drag its photo icons, folder icons, or even the "disk" icon itself directly into iPhoto. Your folder names will become Event names once they're in iPhoto.

Importing Existing Graphics Files

iPhoto is also delighted to help you organize digital photos—or any other kinds of graphics files—that are already on your computer, like in a folder somewhere.

For years, Mac fans complained about the way iPhoto handled photos that were already on the hard drive: When you imported them into iPhoto, the program *duplicated* them. So you wound up with one set inside iPhoto's proprietary library package (page 30) in *addition* to the original folder full of photos. Disk space got eaten up rather quickly as a result. This system also meant that iPhoto couldn't simultaneously track photos that resided on more than one hard drive.

But today's iPhoto can track, organize, edit, and process photos on your hard drive(s) *right in the folders that contain them*. The program doesn't have to copy them into the iPhoto library, meaning it doesn't have to double their disk-space consumption.

This is a blessing if you already have folders filled with photos. You can drag them directly into iPhoto's Source list (or the main viewing area). iPhoto acts like it's importing them, but doesn't really. Yet you can work with them exactly like the ones iPhoto socked away into its own library.

GEM IN THE ROUGH

The Memory Card's Back Door

When you connect most cameras to a Mac, the memory card shows up as a disk icon at the upper-right corner of your desktop, as shown here.

You get the same effect when you insert a memory card into a card reader attached to your Mac.

In the disk window, you'll usually find several folders, each cryptically named by the camera's software. One contains your photos; another may contain movies.

In the iPhotos of years gone by, you could perform a sneaky trick with this icon. By opening this "disk" icon, you could *selectively* delete

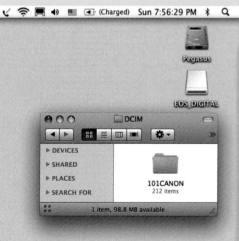

or copy photos from the card. But since iPhoto now offers that feature right within the program, there's no need to muck around with the desktop card icon.

Except in one situation.

Finding the folder that contains the memory card's photos is still the only way to copy photos from your hard drive to your camera (if you like keeping photos on your camera in order to show them off, for example). Just drag photos to the "disk" icon in the Finder, either from another Finder window or even right out of the iPhoto window.

If you choose to go this route, here are a few tips and notes:

- Very ugly things will happen in iPhoto if you *delete* a photo "behind its back," in the Finder (meaning you also emptied your Mac's trash). When you try to open or edit one of the deleted photos in iPhoto, an error message will appear, offering you the chance to locate the photo manually. And if you can't find it, then the photo opens up as a huge, empty, gray rectangle filled with an exclamation point. (You kind of know what the program means.)

- On the other hand, iPhoto is pretty smart if you *rename* a photo in the Finder, or even drag it to a different folder.

  Apple doesn't really want this feature publicized, hopes you won't try it, and won't say how iPhoto manages to track pictures that you move around even when the program isn't running.

  But it works. Moved or renamed photos still appear in iPhoto, and you can still open, edit, and export them. However, you may have to do a lot of manual reorganizing.

- If you delete a photo within iPhoto, you're not actually deleting it from your Mac. It's still sitting there in the Finder, in the folder where it's always been. You've just told iPhoto not to track that photo any more.

- Using this feature, you can use iPhoto to catalog and edit photos that reside on multiple hard drives—even *other computers on the network*. Just make sure those other disks are "mounted" (visible on your screen) before you attempt to work with them in iPhoto.

- On the other hand, iPhoto's offline smarts don't make it a good choice for managing photos on CDs, DVDs, or other disks that aren't actually connected to, or inserted in, your Mac.

Internal or External?

Now, it's nice that iPhoto can track external photos without having to make its own private copies. But the old way had some advantages, too. When iPhoto copies photos into its own library, they're safer. For example, you can back up your iPhoto library, content in the knowledge that you've really backed up all your photos (instead of leaving some behind because they're not *actually* in the library).

Tip: Time Machine, Apple's automated back-up program, backs up your main hard drive, too—yet another reason why it's safer to store your photos internally than externally.

Fortunately, how iPhoto behaves when you import graphics files is entirely up to you. It can *either* copy them into its own library *or* it can track photos in whatever Finder folders they're already in. You make this choice for future imports in iPhoto's Preferences (Figure 1-5, top); choose iPhoto→Preferences to open it.

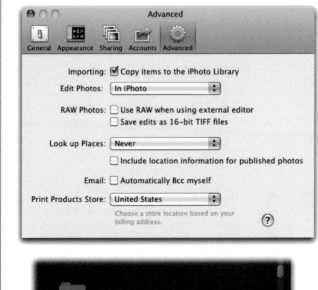

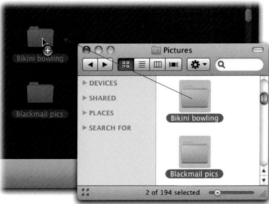

Figure 1-5:

Top: In the Preferences dialog box, click the Advanced button. Here's where you specify whether or not you want iPhoto to duplicate imported photos from your hard drive so that it has its own library copy. (If you turn off this checkbox, iPhoto simply tracks the photos in their current Finder folders.)

Bottom: When you drop a folder into iPhoto, the program automatically scans all the folders inside it, looking for pictures to catalog. Depending on your Preferences settings, it may create a new Event (Chapter 5) for each folder it finds. iPhoto ignores irrelevant files and stores only the pictures that are in formats it can read.

Dragging into iPhoto

No matter what choice you make in the Preferences dialog box, the easiest way to import photos from your hard drive is to drag them into the main iPhoto window. You can choose from two methods:

- **Drag the files directly into the main iPhoto window**, which automatically starts the import process. You can also drop an entire *folder* of images into iPhoto to import the contents of the whole folder, as shown at the bottom of Figure 1-5. You can even drag a *bunch* of folders at once.

- **Choose File→Import to Library** (or press Shift-⌘-I) in iPhoto and then select a file or folder in the Import Photos dialog box, shown in Figure 1-6.

These techniques also let you select and import files from other hard drives, CDs, DVDs, iPods, flash drives, or other disks on the network.

Tip: Take the time to name your folders intelligently before dragging them into iPhoto, because the program retains their names. If you drag a folder directly into the main photo area, then you get a new Event named for the folder; if you drag the folder into the Source list on the left side of the screen, then you get a new *album* named for the folder. And if there are folders inside folders, then they too become new Events or albums. Details on all this reside in Chapter 2.

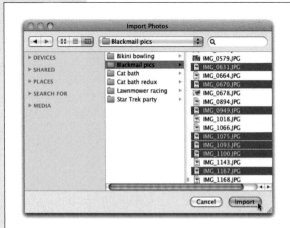

Figure 1-6:
When the Import Photos dialog box appears, navigate to and select any graphics files you want to bring into iPhoto. You can ⌘-click individual graphics to select more than one simultaneously, as shown here. You can also click one, then Shift-click another one, to highlight both files and everything in the list in between.

Side Doors into iPhoto

Don't look now, but Apple has been quietly creating other ways to get photos into iPhoto, directly from other programs on your Mac.

For example, if you use the Mail program of Mac OS X 10.6 (Snow Leopard) and someone sends you a photo, you can pop it directly into iPhoto from within the email message. Just click the little Save button that appears above the body of the message. From the pop-up menu, choose Add to iPhoto.

You can also send pictures to iPhoto right from the Finder. Highlight some icons and then press the space bar to open the Quick Look preview. Once the preview opens, you see a couple of icons at the bottom of the window: Full Screen and Add to iPhoto. In fact, the same button appears anywhere *slideshows* are found in Mac OS X, including Preview and Mail—once a slideshow is under way, wiggle your mouse to summon the slideshow control bar.

Both of those handy buttons deposit a copy of the photo directly into your iPhoto collection, even if iPhoto isn't open at the time. (Actually, there's a folder named Auto Import lurking deep inside iPhoto that automatically imports any photos you drag into it. Skip to page 321 for details.)

The File Format Factor

iPhoto can't import digital pictures unless it understands their file formats, but that rarely poses a problem. Every digital camera on earth can save its photos as JPEG files—and iPhoto handles this format beautifully. (JPEG is the world's most popular file format for photos because, even though it's compressed to occupy a lot less disk space, the visual quality is still very high.)

Note: The terms JPEG, JFIF, JPEG JFIF, and JPEG 2000 all mean the same thing.

But iPhoto '11 imports and recognizes some very useful additional formats.

GEM IN THE ROUGH

Saving Everyday Documents into iPhoto

Most people think of iPhoto as a photo-management program. But thanks to a sneaky command that Apple has added to every program, iPhoto can now serve as a *document*-management program, too.

Thanks to this command, iPhoto has become a convenient, centralized, well-organized database of documents. You can keep drafts or final copies of all your work, ready to be searched, sorted, emailed, printed, cropped, even laid out and custom published as a hardcover book. (Are you listening, authors, lawyers, and real estate agents?)

The key to all this magic is the "Save PDF to iPhoto" command. It's sitting there even now, in almost every program on your Mac. So why haven't you seen it? Because it's hidden.

Start in the program where you've done the work: a word

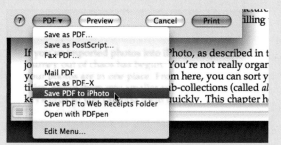

processor, database, layout program, sheet-music program, web design program, whatever. Choose File→Print. In the Print dialog box, click the PDF button. From the pop-up menu, choose "Save PDF to iPhoto."

In a moment, a funny little dialog box appears, asking which iPhoto album you want this PDF document stored in. Choose an existing album or create a new one, and then click OK.

Now you arrive in iPhoto, where your newly hatched PDF document is ready to inspect. Open it for editing just as you would any photo (see Chapter 2). Now you can page through it using the Previous and Next controls; print or send it using the toolbar controls; edit it like a graphic; apply searchable keywords, description text, or ratings to it; and so on. The only limit is your imagination.

Raw Files

Most digital cameras work like this: When you press the shutter button, the camera studies the data picked up by its sensors. The circuitry then makes decisions pertaining to sharpening level, contrast and saturation settings, color "temperature," and so on—and then saves the resulting processed image as a compressed JPEG file on your memory card.

For millions of people, the resulting picture quality is just fine, even terrific. But all that in-camera processing drives professional photographers nuts. They'd much rather preserve *every last iota* of original picture information, no matter how huge the resulting file on the memory card—and then process the file *by hand* once it's been safely transferred to their Macs.

That's the idea behind Raw, which is an option in many pricier digital cameras. (Raw stands for nothing in particular, so there's no good explanation for why it's so often written in all capitals.)

A Raw image isn't processed at all; it's a complete record of all the data passed along by the camera's sensors. As a result, each Raw photo takes up much more space on your memory card. For example, on a 6-megapixel camera, a JPEG photo is around 2 MB, but the same picture is over 8 MB when saved as a Raw file. Most cameras take longer to store Raw photos on the card, too.

But for image-manipulation nerds, the beauty of Raw files is that once you open them up on your Mac, you can perform astounding acts of editing on them. You can actually change the lighting of the scene—retroactively! And you don't lose a single speck of image quality along the way.

Until recently, most people used a program like Camera Raw (which comes with Photoshop and Photoshop Elements), Lightroom, or Aperture to do this kind of editing. But amazingly enough, humble, cheap little iPhoto '11 can edit Raw files, too. For the full scoop, see Chapter 5.

Note: Not every camera offers an option to save your photos as Raw files. And among those that do, not all are iPhoto compatible. Apple maintains a partial list of compatible cameras at *http://support.apple. com/kb/HT3825*. (Why are only some cameras compatible? Because Raw is a concept, not a file format. Each camera company stores its photo data in a different way, so in fact, there are dozens of different file formats in the Raw world. Programs like iPhoto must be upgraded periodically to accommodate new camera models' emerging flavors of Raw.)

Movies

In addition to still photos, today's digital cameras can also capture digital *movies*. These are no longer jittery, silent affairs the size of a Wheat Thin; modern cameras capture full-blown, 30-frames-per-second, fill-your-screen movies—even high-definition movies.

Movies eat up a memory card fast, but you can't beat the convenience, and the quality comes breathtakingly close to camcorder quality. (Recent camera models can even zoom and change focus while "filming," just like a camcorder.)

Fortunately, iPhoto can import and organize them. The program recognizes .mov files, .avi files, and many other movie formats. In fact, it can import any format that QuickTime Player (the program on your Mac that actually plays these movies) recognizes, which is a very long list indeed.

You don't have to do anything special to import movies; they get slurped in automatically. You can even *play* them without leaving iPhoto, as Figure 1-7 shows.

Tip: iPhoto '11 also lets you trim footage from the beginning and end of your movie clips. Page 292 tells you how.

Other graphics formats

Of course, iPhoto also lets you load pictures that have been saved in a number of other file formats, too—including a few unusual ones. Here's what it can handle:

- **TIFF**. Most digital cameras capture photos in a graphics file format called JPEG. Some cameras, though, offer you the chance to leave your photos *uncompressed* on the camera, in what's called TIFF format. These files are huge—in fact, you'll be lucky if you can fit one TIFF file on the memory card that came with the camera. Fortunately, they retain 100 percent of the picture's original quality.

  Note, however, that the instant you *edit* a TIFF-format photo (Chapter 5), iPhoto converts it into JPEG.

  That's fine if you plan to order prints or a photo book (Chapter 9) from iPhoto, since JPEG files are required for those purposes. But if you took that once-in-a-lifetime, priceless shot as a TIFF file, then don't do any editing in iPhoto—don't even rotate it—if you hope to maintain its perfect, pristine quality.

- **GIF** is the most common format used for non-photographic images on web pages. The borders, backgrounds, and logos you typically encounter on websites are usually GIF files—as well as 98 percent of those blinking, flashing banner ads that drive you insane.

- **PNG** and **FlashPix** are also used in web design, though not nearly as often as JPEG and GIF. They often display more complex graphic elements.

- **BMP** is a popular graphics file format in Windows.

- **PICT** was the original graphics file format of the Macintosh before Mac OS X. When you take a screenshot from Mac OS 9, paste a picture from the Clipboard, or copy an image from the Scrapbook, you're using a PICT file.

- **Photoshop** refers to Adobe Photoshop, the world's most popular image-editing and photo-retouching program. iPhoto can even recognize and import *layered*

Photoshop files—those in which different image adjustments or graphic elements are stored in sandwiched-together layers. (If you want to learn more, there's a Missing Manual on Photoshop, too.)

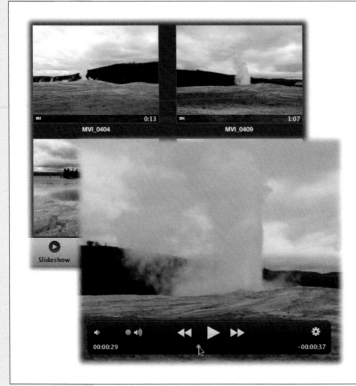

Figure 1-7:
Top: The first frame of each video clip shows up as though it's a photo in your library; only a little camera icon and the total running time let you know that it's a movie and not a still image.

Bottom: Double-click a movie in iPhoto '11 to open it up at full size and play it. iPhoto is no iMovie, though; you can view and trim the length of the movie, but that's it (you can't rotate movies or edit specific scenes, for example). See Chapter 10 for details on editing them in iMovie, or trimming them with iPhoto and QuickTime Player X.

It's nice to see Old Faithful is still being faithful!

- **MacPaint** is the ancient file format of Apple's very first graphics program from the mid-1980s. No, you probably won't be working with any MacPaint files in iPhoto, but isn't it nice to know that if one of these old, black-and-white, 8 × 10 pictures, generated on a vintage Mac SE happens to slip through a wormhole in the fabric of time and land on your desk, you'll be ready?

- **SGI** and **Targa** are specialized graphics formats used on high-end Silicon Graphics workstations and Truevision video-editing systems.

- **PDF** files are Portable Document Format files that open up in Preview. They might be user's manuals, brochures, or Read Me files that you downloaded or received on a disc.

  As of version '09, iPhoto is a better PDF reader than ever. You can open a PDF document at full-screen size, page through it, and even crop or edit it as though it were a photo. In fact, Mac OS X makes it extra easy to create PDFs and stash them in iPhoto all in one step, as described in the box on page 23.

If you try to import a file that iPhoto doesn't understand, you see the message shown in Figure 1-8.

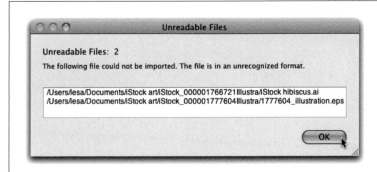

Figure 1-8:
Here's iPhoto's way of telling you that you just tried to feed it a file that it can't digest: an EPS file, an Adobe Illustrator drawing, or a PowerPoint file, for example.

The Post-Import Inspection

Once you've imported a batch of pictures into iPhoto, what's the first thing you want to do? If you're like most people, this is the first opportunity you have to see, at full-screen size, the masterpieces you and your camera created. After all, until this moment, the only sight you've had of your photos was on the little screen on the back of the camera.

There's a great way to go about inspecting your pictures after you've imported them: the old "double-click to magnify" trick.

Once you've imported some pictures, click the Last Import icon in the Source list. In the main iPhoto window, you're now treated to a soon-to-be-familiar display: a grid of thumbnails. In this case, they represent the pictures you just imported.

Double-click the first one. If all goes well, it swells to fill the main part of the iPhoto window. If you're feeling frisky, click the new ▣ button at the bottom left of the iPhoto window; your photo commandeers every last pixel on your monitor, as shown in Figure 1-9.

After the shock of seeing the giant-sized version of your photo has worn off, press the ◄ key on your keyboard to bring the second one into view. Press it again to continue walking through your imported photos.

This is the perfect opportunity to throw away lousy shots, fix the rotation, and linger on certain photos for more study. You can even apply a rating with a keyboard shortcut; later, you can use these ratings to sort your pictures or create *smart albums*. See Chapters 2, 3, and 4 for full details on smart albums and ratings.

Here's the full list of things you can do as you walk through the magnified pictures, whether you opted for Full Screen view or not:

- Double-click the photo to demagnify it. You return to the window full of thumbnails. (Double-click another one to magnify *it* and return to the inspection process.)

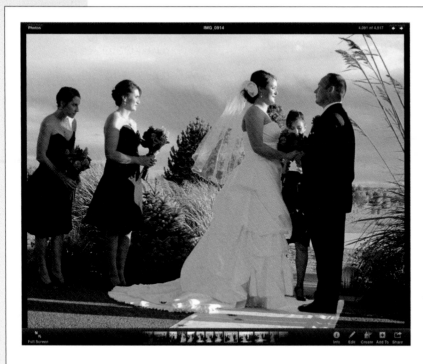

Figure 1-9:
iPhoto's new Full Screen view is available anywhere within iPhoto, whether you're browsing Events or Albums, editing your photos, or creating a project. While you're in this view, you can walk through your new photos using the arrow keys on your keyboard or by clicking images in the new filmstrip at the bottom of your screen.

To bring back the iPhoto menu system, just mouse up to the top of your monitor. To exit Full Screen view, click the Full Screen button again or press the Esc key.

- Press the ◄ and ► keys on your keyboard to browse back and forth through your photos, or use the new filmstrip at the bottom of the iPhoto window.

- Press the Delete key on your keyboard to send a photo to iPhoto's Trash can.

- Give each photo a star rating, from 1 (terrible) to 5 (terrific). To do that, press ⌘-1 through ⌘-5 (or press ⌘-0 to remove the rating). Chapter 3, which explains how to find and flag photos, also tells you how add star ratings in a variety of ways (page 90).

Tip: You don't actually see the stars appear unless you open the Info panel by clicking the little Info button at the bottom right of the iPhoto window.

Control-clicking a photo displays a shortcut menu that gives you access to more goodies:

- Click the Rotate button to flip a photo counterclockwise, 90 degrees at a time. (Option-click the button to rotate the photo clockwise instead.)

- Click the Hide button to *hide* a photo, which isn't the same as deleting it. The photo's out of your way, but it's still in your library, and you can always bring it back. You can accomplish the same thing (without Control-clicking first) by pressing ⌘-L. Either way, the now-hidden photo disappears from the filmstrip at the bottom of your iPhoto window, but it stays onscreen (sigh). More on hiding photos appears on page 51.

- Click the Trash button to throw your photo into iPhoto's very own Trash can (page 71).

- Edit the image in iPhoto by choosing "Edit in iPhoto," or open it in another program (say, Photoshop Elements) by choosing "Edit in External Editor" (see page 122).

- If you Control-clicked a photo while viewing an Event, you can make this photo the key photo (the icon thumbnail) for the Event by choosing Make Key Photo. You'll learn all about key photos on page 40.

The other buttons on the bottom-edge toolbar offer ways to view info about your pictures; edit photos; create projects; add photos to an album, slideshow, or project; and share photos in myriad ways. You'll learn about *all* your options in the coming chapters.

Where iPhoto Keeps Your Files

Having entrusted your vast collection of digital photos to iPhoto, you may find yourself wondering, "Where the heck is iPhoto putting all those files, anyway?"

Most people slog through life, eyes to the road, without ever knowing the answer. After all, you can preview, open, edit, rotate, copy, export, and print all your photos right in iPhoto, without actually opening a folder or double-clicking a single JPEG file.

Even so, it's worthwhile to know where iPhoto keeps your pictures on your hard drive. Armed with this information, you can keep those valuable files backed up and avoid the chance of accidentally throwing them away 6 months from now when you're doing a little digital spring cleaning.

A Trip to the Library

As you now know, when you import pictures into iPhoto, the program generally makes *copies* of them, leaving your original files untouched. (Of course, if you tell iPhoto to erase your camera's memory card after importing, then the originals aren't untouched—they're obliterated. But you get the point.)

The question is: Where do they all go?

iPhoto stores its copies of your pictures in a special folder called iPhoto Library, which you can find in your Home→Pictures folder. If the short name you use to log into Mac OS X is *mozart*, then the full path to your iPhoto Library folder from the main hard drive window would be Macintosh HD→Users→mozart→Pictures→ iPhoto Library.

Now, if you're following along in the comfort of your own living room, you might be objecting to the description of the iPhoto Library. "Hey," you might be saying, "that's not a folder! In old versions of iPhoto, it *was* a folder. But I can't open this one to see what's inside. So it's *not* a folder."

OK, you' re right—it's not an ordinary folder. It's a package.

In Mac OS X, *packages* or *bundles* are folders that *behave* like single files. For example, every properly written Mac OS X *program* looks like a single, double-clickable application icon. Yet to the Mac, it's actually a folder that contains both the actual application icon and all of its hidden support files. (Even *documents* can be packages, including iDVD project files, iMovie files, and some TextEdit documents.)

As it turns out, iPhoto '11's library is a package, too. It may look like a single icon called iPhoto Library, sitting in your Home→Pictures folder. But it's actually a folder, and it's absolutely teeming with the individual JPEG files that represent your photos.

If you'd like to prove this to yourself, try this experiment: Choose Go→Home. Double-click the Pictures folder. See the iPhoto Library icon? Control-click it or right-click it. From the shortcut menu, choose Show Package Contents. (You're asking Mac OS X to show you what's inside the iPhoto Library.) Voilà! The iPhoto Library package window opens.

Tip: You should back up your iPhoto Library regularly—using the Share→Burn command to save it onto a CD or DVD, for example. After all, it contains all the photos you import into iPhoto, which, essentially, is your entire photography collection. Chapter 13 offers much more on this important file-management topic.

What all those numbers mean

Within the iPhoto Library, you'll find a set of mysteriously numbered files and folders. At first glance, this setup may look bizarre, but there's a method to iPhoto's madness. It turns out that iPhoto meticulously arranges your photos within these numbered folders according to the *creation dates* of the originals, as explained in Figure 1-10.

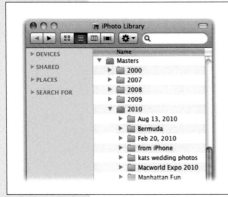

Figure 1-10:
Behold the mysteries of the iPhoto Library. Once you know the secret, this seemingly cryptic folder structure actually makes sense, with all the photos in the library organized by their creation dates.

Other folders in the iPhoto Library

In addition to the numbered folders, you'll find several other items nested in the iPhoto Library window, most of which you can ignore:

- **AlbumData.xml**. Here's where iPhoto stores access permissions for the various *photo albums* you've created within iPhoto. (Albums, which are like folders for organizing photos, are described in Chapter 2.) For example, it's where iPhoto keeps information on which albums are available for sharing across the network (or among accounts on a single machine). Details on sharing are in Chapter 8.

- **Library.data, Library.iPhoto, Library6.iPhoto**. These are iPhoto's for-internal-use-only documents. They store information about your iPhoto Library, such as which keywords you've used, along with the image dimensions, file size, rating, and modification date for each photo.

- **Masters**. This folder (called Originals in previous versions of iPhoto) is the real deal: It's the folder that stores your entire photo collection. Inside, you'll find nested folders organized in the year/month/day structure illustrated in Figure 1-10.

  This folder is also the key to one of iPhoto's most remarkable features: the "Revert to Original" command.

  Whenever it applies any potentially destructive operations to your photos—like cropping, red-eye removal, brightening, or black-and-white conversion—iPhoto *duplicates* the files and stuffs the edited copies in the Previews folder. The pristine, unedited versions remain safe in the Masters folder. If you later decide to scrap your changes to a photo using the "Revert to Original" command (page 126)—even months or years later—then iPhoto ditches the duplicate. What you see in iPhoto is the original version, preserved in its originally imported state.

- **Previews**. In earlier iPhotos, this folder was named Modified. It's where the program keeps the latest versions of your pictures, as edited. (Remember, behind the scenes, iPhoto actually duplicates a photo when you edit it.)

- **Thumbnails**. This folder contains index card-sized previews of your pictures—jumbo thumbnails, in effect—organized in the year/month/day structure shown in Figure 1-10.

Look, but don't touch

While it's enlightening to wander through the iPhoto Library window to see how iPhoto keeps itself organized, *don't rename or move any of the folders or files in it*.

You should do *all* your photo organizing within the iPhoto program, not behind its back in the library. Making changes in the Finder will confuse iPhoto to the point where it will either be unable to display some of your photos or it'll just crash.

And that, by the way, is precisely why the iPhoto Library is now a package (which takes some effort and knowledge to open) instead of a regular folder. Apple Tech Support evidently got one too many phone calls from clueless Mac users who'd opened the iPhoto Library manually and wound up deleting or damaging their photo collections.

FREQUENTLY ASKED QUESTION

Moving the iPhoto Library

Do I have to keep my iPhoto Library in my Pictures folder? What if I want it stored somewhere else?

No problemo! iPhoto has come a long way since the days when it had to keep its library in your Pictures folder.

Just quit iPhoto. Then move the whole iPhoto Library (currently in your Home→Pictures folder) to another location— even onto another hard drive.

Now open iPhoto again. It proclaims that it can't find your iPhoto Library. Click the Choose Library button to show the program where you put it. Done deal!

You can also press and hold the Option key when you launch iPhoto to summon the Choose Library dialog box; see page 239.

The Digital Shoebox

When you get right down to it, working in iPhoto takes place at three different zoom levels. You begin fully zoomed out, looking at *piles* of photos—your *Events* (called Spring Break, Robin's Graduation, and so on). Then you drill down into one of the piles; in the main Photos view, every picture appears as an individual thumbnail. Finally, you can zoom in even more, filling the iPhoto window (or your entire monitor) with just one photo.

If you've imported photos into iPhoto, as described in the previous chapter, your journey out of chaos has begun. You're not really organized yet, but at least all your photos are in one place. From here, you can sort your photos, give them titles, group them into smaller subcollections (called *albums*), and tag them with keywords so you can find them quickly. This chapter helps you tackle each of these organizing tasks as painlessly as possible.

The Source List

Even before you start naming your photos, assigning them keywords, or organizing them into albums, iPhoto imposes an order of its own upon your digital shoebox.

The key to understanding it is the *Source list* at the left side of the iPhoto window. This list grows as you import more pictures and organize them—but right off the bat, you'll find categories such as Library, Recent, and Albums, each containing icons you can click for fast access to particular photos (Last Import, Last 12 Months, and so on). This section explains each category in detail.

If you're enjoying Full Screen view, you can use the big Event, Faces, Places, Albums, and Projects buttons at the bottom of your monitor to see what's in your Source list. That said, it might be easier to remain in standard view while you're poring over this chapter.

Library

The first four icons in the Source list are under a heading called Library. This is a very reassuring little heading, because no matter how confused you may get in working with subsets of photos later in your iPhoto life, clicking one of the first two Library icons (Events or Photos) returns you to your entire picture collection. It makes *all* of your photos appear in the viewing area. Clicking the Faces or Places icons (Chapter 4) shows the photos you've tagged based on who's in them or where they were taken.

- **Events**. When you click Events in the Source list, each thumbnail represents one pile (or shoebox, or envelope) of pictures. (Figure 2-1 shows the effect.) Each pile is one *Event*, a clump of pictures that were all taken at about the same time—all on someone's birthday or wedding weekend, for example.

    You can open up one of these "shoeboxes" by double-clicking it, or you can flick through the thumbnails within an Event by passing your cursor slowly across its thumbnail, left to right. Details on Events begin on page 38.

- **Photos**. Click Photos, on the other hand, to see *all* the photos' thumbnails displayed; not just summary Event thumbnails, but one thumbnail per photo on a massive, scrolling display (Figure 2-1, bottom). Happily, you can still see which photos were taken at which Event, thanks to the headings that separate the batches.

- **Faces**. If you've taken the time to introduce iPhoto to your friends and family as described on page 94, you can click Faces to see everyone grouped into neat little albums on a virtual corkboard. (In Full Screen view, it's a very large corkboard indeed.)

- **Places**. Miraculously, iPhoto '11 can link your photos to specific places on a map. Click Places in the Source list to see your world in your own pictures. Unless your camera or smartphone is GPS-enabled, this doesn't happen automatically, however; you need to tag your photos in a special way to get them on the map. Page 108 has the scoop.

Recent

Since an iPhoto library can grow to 250,000 pictures, it's a smart assumption that what you want to see most often are the photos you've worked with *recently*. That's why the items in this list change over time to reflect what you've been doing lately. For example:

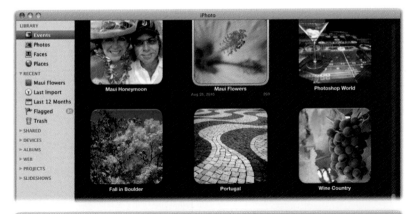

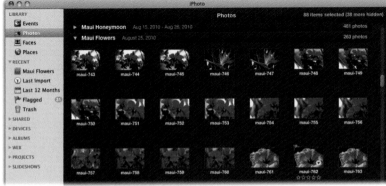

Figure 2-1:
Top: Each Event is a clump of photos all taken at about the same time. Events are iPhoto '11's primary organizing structure, like it or not. (The Library heading doesn't even list your photos by year anymore.)

Bottom: You can also view your entire collection as Photos, meaning that every single photo has its own thumbnail in a huge scrolling list. They're still grouped by Event, though, as indicated by the collapsible headings. In iPhoto '11, these headings become slightly opaque and "float" to the top of the window as you scroll through your photos. That way, you always know which Event the photos belong to.

- **[Most recently viewed Event]**. The first icon here identifies the Event you most recently opened in the Events list. You can think of it as a handy shortcut for when the Event you want to work with this morning is the same one you were editing last night. If the Event has a name, you see it here; if not, you see a date instead.

- **Last Import**. Another group of photos you'll probably want to access quickly are the photos you just liberated from your camera. That's the purpose of this icon. With one click, iPhoto displays only your most recently downloaded photos, hiding all the others. This feature can save you a lot of time, especially as your library grows.

- **Last 12 Months**. The Last 12 Months icon puts the most recent photos at your fingertips. The idea, of course, is that the freshest photos are often the most interesting to you.

Actually, it doesn't even have to say "Last 12 Months." You can specify how *many* months' worth of photos appear in this heap—anywhere from one month to a year and a half—by choosing iPhoto→Preferences and going to the General panel (Figure 2-2).

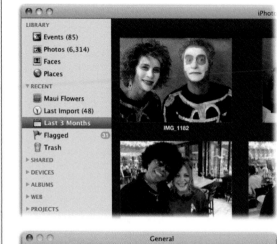

Figure 2-2:
Top: You can specify how far back the "Last___ Months" album goes in the General panel of iPhoto Preferences (bottom).

Don't forget, by the way, that iPhoto isn't limited to grouping your pictures by year. It can also show you the photos you took on a certain day, in a certain week, or during a certain month. See page 81 for details.

Bottom: While you're in Preferences, don't miss the "Show item counts" option. It places a number in parentheses after each album name in the Source panel (except for smart albums and the "Last_ Months" album), representing how many pictures are inside. By turning on this checkbox, you can find out whether you're certifiably snap happy.

- **Flagged**. As noted on page 78, *flagging* a photo marks it for your attention later. You can flag all the good ones, or all the ones that need editing, or all the ones you want to round up to use in a calendar project. Click this icon to see all the photos you've flagged, no matter which albums or Events they're in.

- **Trash**. Click this icon to see all the photos, albums, folders, books, and other items you've targeted for deletion. They're not really gone until you *empty* iPhoto's Trash, though. See page 71 for details.

Shared

Under this heading, you'll see the names of all the other iPhoto libraries that people on your home or office network have *shared*, so that you can view them (or copy them) from the comfort of your own desk. See Chapter 8 for details on sharing. (If you don't see a Shared heading, then there aren't any other Macs on your network with iPhoto running that are sharing their photos.)

Later in this book, you'll find out how to dump photos onto CDs or DVDs—and then load them back into iPhoto whenever you darned well feel like it. CD icons and DVD icons show up under Shared, too.

Subscriptions

It's one of iPhoto's coolest features: Once somebody has published a set of photos on the Web (say, on a Flickr page, described in Chapter 8), you can *subscribe* to it. You wind up with a special kind of album, listed as a Subscription, that's automatically updated and synchronized with the online album as it changes. (Think grandparents and grandkids, and you'll see the possibilities.)

Devices

As soon as you plug a camera or memory card reader into a USB port, its name appears here. If you plug your iPhone or iPod Touch into your Mac, it shows up here, too.

Albums

Later in this chapter, you'll find out how to create your own arbitrary subsets of pictures, called *albums*, and even how to stick a bunch of related albums into an enclosing entity called a *folder*. You can even have iPhoto create an album for you, based on criteria like "highest rated" or "taken with my Canon" (a *smart album*).

Your folders, albums, and smart albums appear here.

Web

Once you've published a set of photos as a Web-based picture gallery in MobileMe, Flickr, or even Facebook (Chapter 8), its icon appears here. Click it to remind yourself what's in that gallery or, if it's a Facebook album, to update the comments and tags—and, if you've permitted your fans to upload photos of their own to MobileMe, to download *their* pictures into *your* copy of iPhoto.

FREQUENTLY ASKED QUESTION

Your Own Personal Sorting Order

I want to put my photos in my own order. I tried using View→Sort Photos→Manually, but the command is dimmed out! Did Apple accidentally forget to turn this on?

No, the command works—but only when viewing the contents of an Event or an album. You can't manually sort the thumbnails in Photos view. If you create a new photo album (as explained later in this chapter) and fill it with photos, you can then drag them into any order you want.

Projects

Under this heading, you'll find the icons for any of Apple's custom-publishing goodies that you've assembled: photo books, photo calendars, or photo greeting cards. Open the iPhoto window wide to see separate icons for Book, Calendar, and Cards. Chapter 9 has details.

Slideshows

Saved slideshows (Chapter 6) get their own icons in the Source list, too.

Tip: Saved slideshows and custom-publishing projects can be filed in folders, too, right alongside albums. (You might not expect that, since slideshows and projects begin life under separate headings in the Source list.)

As you go, though, remember this key point: Photos listed under the Library and Recent headings are the *real* photos. Delete a picture from one of these collections, and it's gone forever. However, that's *not* true of albums, which store only aliases— phantom duplicates—of the real photos.

All About Events

The primary photo-organizing concept in iPhoto '11 is the Event: a group of photos that were all taken at about the same time. It certainly makes a lot more sense than the *film roll*, the organizing construct of earlier versions of the program. (A film roll consisted of all the photos you imported at once, no matter how many months apart you took them.)

Note: If you upgraded to iPhoto '11 from an earlier version, then your old film rolls were automatically converted into Events.

---

iPhoto does this autosplitting whenever you bring new pictures in from your camera or memory card, *if* you've told it to do so by turning on the "Autosplit events after importing" checkbox shown in Figure 1-3 (page 15). If you don't, then all the pictures you import in a single batch get clumped into a single Event, regardless of when they were taken. If you're importing photos from your hard drive, they get dumped into a single Event, too.

That said, you can always have iPhoto autosplit your events after you've imported them. It's an easy process and is covered later in this chapter on page 45.

The Events List

When you click Events at the top of the Source list, you see an array of big, rounded thumbnails, as shown in Figure 2-1, top. They represent your Events. To save space, iPhoto shows only *one* picture from each Event; you can think of it as the top photo on the pile. Using that sample photo, along with the Event's name and date, you should be able to figure out which pile of photos each Event contains.

Tip: You can make the Event thumbnails bigger or smaller; just drag the Zoom slider in the lower-left of the toolbar.

The Events page is a zoomed-out, big-picture view of your entire photo collection. Thanks to that "piles" concept, a single screenful of thumbnails might represent thousands of individual photos.

Here's what you can do when you're looking at the Events thumbnails:

- **Scan through a pile**. Here's a tricky move that's relatively new to the Macintosh skill set: Move your cursor sideways across an Event thumbnail *without clicking*. As you go, the photo on the face of the thumbnail changes, as all the pictures within flicker by. It's a good, quick way to get a look at the other pictures in the virtual heap.

UP TO SPEED

Defining an Event

When you import photos, either from a camera or from your hard drive, you're given the opportunity to have iPhoto autosplit them into Events. When the importing is over, you might wind up with two, five, or 10 "piles" of photos on the Events screen shown in Figure 2-1, depending on how long it's been since the last time you downloaded pictures.

Right out of the box, iPhoto defines an Event as one day. If you took pictures on June 1, 2, and 3, then you wind up with three Events.

You might consider that breakdown too rigid, though. It's not an especially logical grouping if, for example, you were away for a wedding weekend, a three-day trip to a theme park, or a week-long cruise. In those cases, you'd probably consider all the photos from that trip to be one Event.

In other, less common situations, you might consider one day to be too long a window. If you're a school photographer who conducts two shooting sessions a day—morning and afternoon, for example—you might want iPhoto to split up the incoming photos into smaller time chunks, like a new Event every four hours. (Also, some photo-sharing websites limit the number of pictures that can go in a single album.)

In any case, iPhoto can accommodate you. Choose iPhoto→Preferences and then click the General button. From the "Autosplit into Events" pop-up menu shown at the bottom of Figure 2-2, take your pick: "One event per day," "One event per week," "Two-hour gaps," or "Eight-hour gaps." (Those "gap" options are iPhoto's way of saying, "If more than that many hours have elapsed since the last batch you took, then I'll call it a new Event.")

Of course, it's extremely easy to split, merge, slice, and dice Events, move photos around between Events, and so on; details appear later in this chapter. But you may as well let iPhoto do the bulk of the grunt work the moment you import the pictures.

(If there are lots of photos in the Event, then every fraction of a millimeter of mouse movement triggers the appearance of the next photo, which makes it very hard to have much control. Making the thumbnails bigger may help. Remembering that this technique is just supposed to give you an *idea* of what's in the Event—it isn't supposed to be a real slideshow—may also help.)

- **Sort the Events**. Ordinarily, iPhoto presents the Event thumbnails in chronological order; in effect, it chooses View→Sort Events→By Date for you. But you can also sort them alphabetically by choosing View→Sort Events→By Title. In either case, you can also reverse the sorting by choosing View→Sort Events→Descending (or Ascending).

- **Rearrange the Event thumbnails**. You can drag one thumbnail between two others to rearrange them. When you do that, iPhoto chooses View→Sort Events→Manually for you, because your thumbnails are no longer sorted alphabetically or chronologically.

- **Change the key photo**. The *key* photo is the one on top of the pile; the one that represents the Event itself. As it turns out, iPhoto suggests one at random. Typically you'll want to rummage through your pictures and choose a better one to represent the whole batch. For a birthday party, for example, you might choose the candle-blowing-out shot to be the one on top of the pile.

  To change the key photo, scan through the pile using the cursor trick described above. When you see the picture you want to be the new key photo, tap the space bar. You can also Control-click (or right-click) the thumbnail—and then, from the shortcut menu, choose Make Key Photo.

Note: You can designate a key photo while you're surveying the photos *within* an Event, too. See the Tip on page 41.

- **Rename an Event**. To rename an Event, just click its existing name and then type away. Press Return, or click somewhere else, when you're finished.

- **Merge Events**. You can combine two (or more) Events into one simply by dragging one Event thumbnail onto another. iPhoto instantly combines the two sets of photos. (The one you dragged vanishes; the combined pile assumes the name and key photo of the one you dragged *onto*.)

- **Delete an Event**. If you're quite sure you want to ditch an entire batch of pictures, click its icon and then press ⌘-Delete. (Or drag the Event's thumbnail onto the Trash icon in the Source list.) Later, you can empty iPhoto's Trash as described on page 71.

Note: There are other ways to merge, split, create, delete, rename, and move photos between Events—but you do all that in Photos view, described later in this chapter.

Opening an Event

And then there's the one thing you'll do most often on the Events page: *Open* an Event.

Double-clicking an Event thumbnail opens the Photos view (shown in Figure 2-1, bottom), where the main part of the iPhoto window is filled with the *individual* thumbnails of all the pictures in that Event. From here, you can search, sort, edit, and otherwise work with your photos.

You can always return to the Events screen by clicking Events in the Source list, clicking the All Events arrow button at the top left of the iPhoto window, or pressing ⌘-left arrow.

Tip: Once you've opened an Event into Photos view, you have another, even better chance to choose a key photo for it (the one that appears "on top of the pile" in Events view). Just click the thumbnail of the photo you want to exalt to that special position, and then choose Events→Make Key Photo.

Photos View

When you click Photos in the Source list, or when you double-click an Event, you arrive at the main iPhoto display. It's called, for want of a better term, Photos view.

This is your lightbox, your slide sorter. Here, every photo has its own thumbnail. You can scroll through this list, looking over your pictures or marking them with keywords, ratings, and descriptions. Here's where you choose photos for inclusion in slideshows, prints, books, and calendars.

In short, this is the view where you'll be spending most of your organizational time.

Size Control

You can make the thumbnails in iPhoto grow or shrink using the Zoom slider in the iPhoto toolbar, just under the photo-viewing area. Drag the slider all the way to the left, and you get micro-thumbnails so small that you can fit hundreds of them in the iPhoto window. Drag it all the way to the right, and you end up with larger thumbnails, though they're not as big as they were in previous versions of the program.

FREQUENTLY ASKED QUESTION

The Missing Events Preferences Pane

iPhoto used to magnify a photo when I double-clicked an Event. Now I can't find the Events pane in Preferences to fix it. What gives?

Apple giveth, and Apple taketh away.

Apple figures you'll be spending most of your time in the new Full Screen view, where it's not necessary to magnify a photo manually. That's why they zapped the Events Preferences pane and, along with it, the ability to tell iPhoto to magnify a photo when you double-click an Event.

To make your photo large enough to fill the iPhoto window, give the image a double-click. To get out of this "super zoom" view and back to your thumbnails, click the left-pointing arrow button at the top left of the main viewing area, or press ⌘-left arrow.

Tip: You don't have to drag the Zoom slider; just click anywhere along the slider to make it jump to a new setting. You can also scale all the thumbnails to their minimum or maximum size by clicking the tiny icons at either end of the slider.

By the way, you might notice that this Zoom slider performs different functions depending on which mode iPhoto is in. When you're editing a photo, it zooms in and out of an individual image; when you're designing a photo-book layout or any other project (Chapter 9), it magnifies or shrinks the book, calendar, or card's page.

Tip: Because iPhoto '11 takes advantage of Core Animation—the programming magic responsible for all moving graphics on your Mac—you'll notice that iPhoto magnifies and shrinks your photos much faster than it used to.

Sorting Photos

iPhoto starts out sorting your photos chronologically, with the oldest ones at the top of the window. Your main iPhoto window may look like a broad, featureless expanse of pictures, but they're actually in a logical order.

Tip: If you'd prefer that the most recent items appear at the top of the iPhoto window instead of the bottom, choose View→Sort Photos→Descending.

Using the View→Sort Photos submenu, you can make iPhoto sort all the thumbnails in the main window in a number of useful ways:

- **By date**. This sort order reflects the *dates* the photos were taken.
- **By keyword**. This option sorts your photos alphabetically by the *keywords* you've assigned to them (page 83).
- **By title**. This arrangement is alphabetical by the photos' *names*. (To name your photos, see page 67.)
- **By rating**. If you'd like your masterpieces at the top of the window, with the losers way down below, choose this option. (To rate your photos, see page 90.)
- **Manually**. If you choose this option, you can drag the thumbnails around freely within the window, placing them in any order that suits your fancy. To conserve your Advil supply, however, make no attempt to choose this option when you're viewing an *Event's* contents—do so only in an *album*. See the box on page 37 for details.

Renaming Photos

To make every photo's name appear beneath its thumbnail, choose View→Titles. That works just great—as long as you don't mind referring to your pictures as IMG_09231.JPG or DSC_0082.JPG.

Page 68 explains how to rename a whole batch of photos at once (Yellowstone 1, Yellowstone 2, and so on).

But if you're inclined to rename each photo *individually*, you'll find that task really easy in iPhoto '11. You can rename just about anything by double-clicking its existing name and typing over it: Events, albums, slideshows, projects—and photos. See Figure 2-3.

You can make a photo's name as long as you want, but it's smart to keep it short (about 10 characters or so). That way, you can see all or most of the name in the Title field (or under the thumbnails).

You can find a faster method for renaming photos at the bottom of page 67. It's handy if you're plowing through an album, renaming a ton of photos at once.

Displaying Event Names

When you enter Photos view by opening an Event, you see *only* the photos associated with that Event. All the others are hidden.

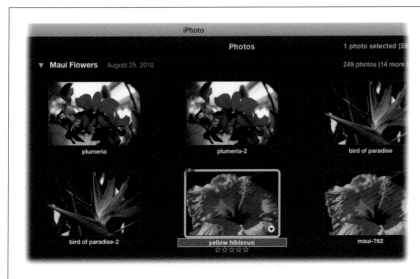

Figure 2-3:
iPhoto doesn't display photo names automatically, but you can turn them on by choosing View→Titles.

To rename a photo, double-click its thumbnail and type away. To rename the next one, press Tab to highlight its name. Proceed this way (Tab, type; Tab, type) until you've renamed everything in the batch. The great part is that you never have to lift your hands off the keyboard!

If, however, you click Photos in the Source list, then you see *all* your photos. At the top of the window, a dark bar appears, identifying the photos' Event, date, and quantity (see Figure 2-4). (You can press Shift-⌘-F to hide or show this dark bar.)

As your collection grows, these groupings become excellent visual aids to help you locate a certain photo—even months or years after the fact.

Furthermore, as your library becomes increasingly massive, you can use these Event groupings to preserve your sanity. By collapsing the flippy triangles next to the groups you're *not* looking at right now (Figure 2-4), you speed up iPhoto considerably. Otherwise, iPhoto may grind almost to a halt as it tries to scroll through ever more photos. (About 250,000 pictures is its realistic limit for a single library on everyday Macs. Of course, you can always start new libraries, as described in Chapter 13.)

Tip: You can rename an Event even in this Photos view. Just click the Event's name in the dark gray bar to open its editing box, then type away.

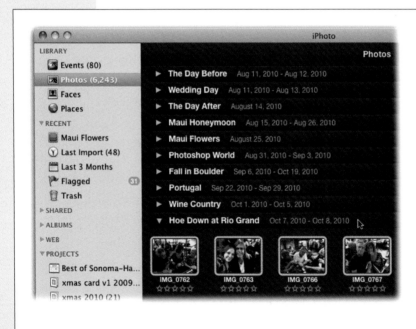

Figure 2-4:
This tidy arrangement is the fastest way to use iPhoto: Display the photos grouped by Event, and then hide the photo batches you're not working with. Click the flippy triangle beside each header to expand or collapse the Event, just like a folder in the Finder's list view.

You can click anywhere on an Event's dividing line—on the Event's name, for example—to select all the photos in that Event. You might do that before dragging them into a book or calendar project, for example.

Collapsing Events En Masse

On a related note, here's one of the best tips in this entire chapter: *Option-click* an Event's flippy triangle to hide or show the contents of *all* your Events in one fell swoop. When all your photos are visible, scrolling can be slowish if you have a bazillion photos, but at least you can see everything. By contrast, when all your Events are collapsed, you see nothing but their names (as shown in Figure 2-4), and scrolling is almost instantaneous no matter how many photos you have.

Creating Events Manually

Events are such a convenient way of organizing your pictures that Apple even lets you create Events manually, out of any pictures you choose.

This feature violates the sanctity of the original Event concept: that all the photos taken in a certain time period are one Event. Still, in this case, usefulness trumps concept—and that's a good thing.

You just select any bunch of pictures in your library (using any of the techniques described on page 49) and then choose Events→Create Event. iPhoto creates and highlights the new Event, like any normal Event. It then gives the newborn Event a generic name, "untitled event." You can always rename it as described on page 40.

Tip: If you've *flagged* photos in your collection (page 78), you can also choose Events→Create Event From Flagged Photos. That's a great way to round up pictures that currently sit in different Events—but nonetheless belong together. (iPhoto removes them from the old Event.)

Alternatively, you can gather up all those flagged photos and add them to an existing Event. To do that, click Events in the Source list. Next, click the desired Event's thumbnail, and then choose Events→Add Flagged Photos to Selected Event.

Splitting Events

Here's yet another way to create a new Event: Split off a bunch of photos from another one. You can either ask iPhoto to do that automatically, based on when the pictures were taken, or you can do it manually:

- **The automatic way**. Suppose you didn't turn on the "Autosplit events after importing" checkbox (page 38) when you imported some photos, and now you're having second thoughts. You wound up importing hundreds of pictures taken over the course of several weeks, and now you decide that it *would* be sort of handy if they were broken up by day or by week.

   First, make sure you've told iPhoto what time period you want to serve as the cutoff point for Event groups (a day, a week, two hours, or eight hours; see the box on page 39).

   Then click Events in the Source list. Highlight the Event or Events that you want to split using any of the selection techniques on page 49. Finally, choose Events→Autosplit Selected Events.

   iPhoto automatically breaks up the selected Events into more Events, as necessary, to put the photos into your desired groupings.

- **The manual way**. You can also chop an Event in two, subdividing it at any point that feels right. For example, iPhoto may have grouped 24 hours' worth of photos into a single Event, even though you actually got five hours' sleep in the middle and would prefer the subsequent photos to appear in their own Event. Figure 2-5 has the details.

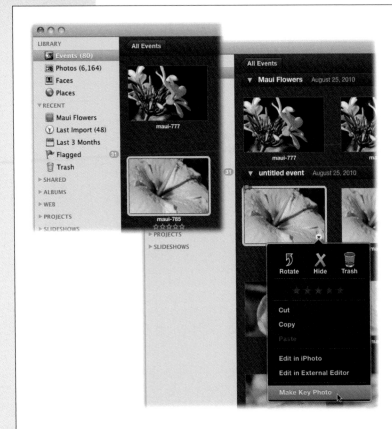

Figure 2-5:
Left: To split an existing Event in two, click Events in the Source list, and then open the Event you want to split. Scan through the thumbnails and then click the photo that marks the beginning of what you'd like to become the new, separate Event. Finally, choose Events→Split Event, or press the S key on your keyboard.

Right: iPhoto creates a second Event out of the photo you clicked and all the ones after it, and names it "untitled event" (just click the Event's name and type to rename it). While you're here, you can pick a key photo (a representative thumbnail) for your new Event. Point to the Event's thumbnail, click the ▼ at its bottom right, and then choose Make Key Photo, as shown here.

Moving Photos Between Events

The fact that iPhoto offers to group photos into Events by time period is a handy starting point. But it's *only* a starting point. You can, and should, freely drag photos among your Events according to any logic that suits you.

In Photos view, select any photos you want to move and then drag them directly onto another Event's name. The deed is done.

Note: When you're dragging photos between Events, it's easy to plop them into the wrong one accidentally. Because iPhoto doesn't indicate which Event they're headed for (hello, Apple?!), be mindful of where your cursor is positioned before releasing your mouse button. If you make a mistake, don't panic—just press ⌘-Z to undo the move.

Merging Events

You can *merge* Events with one quick swipe—a great technique when your collections start to get enormous.

Start in Events view (click Events in your Source list), then proceed as shown in Figure 2-6.

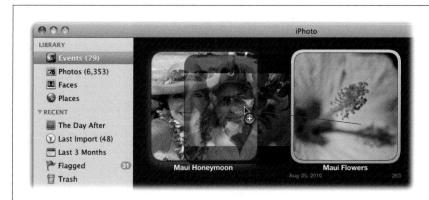

Figure 2-6:
You can combine two existing Events by dragging the key photo of one Event on top of another, as shown here. The Event you moved disappears into the other one instantly. If you change your mind about merging the Events, you can undo it by pressing ⌘-Z.

Renaming and Dating Events

As you know from Chapter 1, iPhoto gives you the opportunity to name each Event as it's created—that is, at the joyous moment when a new set of photos becomes one with your iPhoto library.

If you don't type anything into the Event Name box that appears at that time, though, iPhoto just labels each Event with "untitled event" or a date. Fortunately, you can easily change any Event's name at any time anywhere it appears—in Events or Photos view. To rename an Event, click its existing name and then start typing.

To change an Event's date, make sure you're in Events view and then click the Event you want to change. Then choose Photos→"Adjust Date and Time." In the resulting dialog box, the existing date and time appear, along with a text box where you can enter a new one, as shown in Figure 2-7.

Scrolling Through Your Photos

Enough learning about iPhoto already—now it's time to start *using* it!

Happily, browsing, selecting, and opening photos is straightforward. In fact, here's everything you need to know:

- You can use the vertical scroll bar on the right side of the iPhoto window to navigate through your photo thumbnails.

If you have a laptop, Apple Magic Mouse, or Magic Trackpad, you can also scroll by swiping up or down with two fingers. Using the Page Up and Page Down keys works, too (they scroll one screenful at a time). If your mouse has a scroll wheel on top (or a scroll pea, like Apple's old Mighty Mouse), you can also use that to scroll.

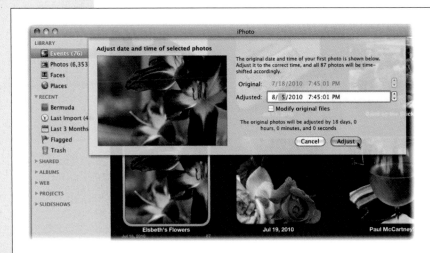

Figure 2-7:
Feel like changing history? As long as you don't turn on "Modify original files," the real shot date of your photos remains intact as part of its metadata (see the Tip on page 80). Changing an Event's date can help your Events appear in the correct chronological order.

Tip: iPhoto can display a large, translucent "heads-up display" that shows, chronologically or alphabetically, where you are as you scroll. See page 75 to turn it on.

- Even though iPhoto '11 is faster than ever, scrolling can still take awhile if you have a huge library, especially if you haven't collapsed the Events you're not viewing. But you can use this standard Mac OS X trick for faster navigation: Instead of dragging the scroll box or clicking the scroll bar arrows, *Option-click* the spot on the scroll bar that corresponds to the location you want in your library. If you want to jump to the bottom of the library, Option-click near the bottom of the scroll bar. To find photos in the middle of your collection, Option-click the middle portion of the scroll bar, and so on.

Note: By turning on "Jump to the spot that's clicked" in the Appearance pane of your System Preferences, you can make this the standard behavior for all Mac OS X scroll bars—that is, you won't need the Option key. If you *do* use the Option key, you'll jump to the next page instead.

- Press Home to jump to the very top of your photo collection, or End to leap to the bottom. (You have to hold down the Function [fn] key *plus* Home or End on some MacBooks.)

- You can't hide the Source list at the left side of the window, but you can adjust its width. To do so, drag the thin, black divider bar (between the Source list and the main photo-viewing area) sideways. When your cursor's in the right place for dragging, it turns into a double-headed arrow. If you're in Full Screen view, you can access your Source list by using the Events, Faces, Places, Albums, and Project buttons at the bottom of your monitor.

Selecting Photos

To highlight a single picture in preparation for dragging, opening, duplicating, deleting, and so on, you click its thumbnail once.

That much may seem obvious. But many Mac novices have no idea how to manipulate *more* than one icon at a time—an essential survival skill.

To highlight multiple photo (or Event) thumbnails in preparation for doing anything with them, use one of these techniques:

- **Select all the photos in the window**. To select all the pictures in the Event or album you're viewing, press ⌘-A. (That's the equivalent of the Edit→Select All command.)

Tip: In Photos view, you can select all the photos *in one Event* by clicking its name or its key photo, as shown on page 44.

- **Select several photos by dragging**. You can drag diagonally to highlight a group of nearby photos. You don't even have to enclose the thumbnails completely; your cursor can touch any part of any icon to highlight it. In fact, if you keep dragging past the edge of the window, iPhoto scrolls the window automatically.

Tip: If you include a particular thumbnail in your dragged group by mistake, ⌘-click it to remove it from the selected cluster.

- **Select consecutive photos**. Click the first thumbnail you want to highlight, and then Shift-click the last one. All the files in between are automatically selected, along with the two photos you clicked (Figure 2-8, top). This trick mirrors the way Shift-clicking works in a word processor, the Finder, and many other programs.
- **Pick and choose photos**. If you want to highlight, for example, only the first, third, and seventh photos in a window, start by clicking the first photo's thumbnail. Then ⌘-click each of the others. Each thumbnail sprouts a yellow border to indicate that you've selected it (Figure 2-8, bottom).
- **Deselect a photo**. If you're highlighting a long string of photos and then click one by mistake, you don't have to start over. Instead, just ⌘-click it, and the yellow

border disappears. (If you do want to start over from the beginning, then just deselect all the photos by clicking in any empty part of the window.)

The ⌘-click trick is especially handy if you want to select *almost* all the photos in a window. Simply press ⌘-A to select everything in the folder, and then ⌘-click any unwanted photos to deselect them. You'll save a lot of time and clicking.

Tip: You can also combine the ⌘-clicking business with the Shift-clicking trick. For instance, you could click the first photo, then Shift-click the tenth, to highlight the first 10. Next, you could ⌘-click photos 2, 5, and 9 to remove them from the selection.

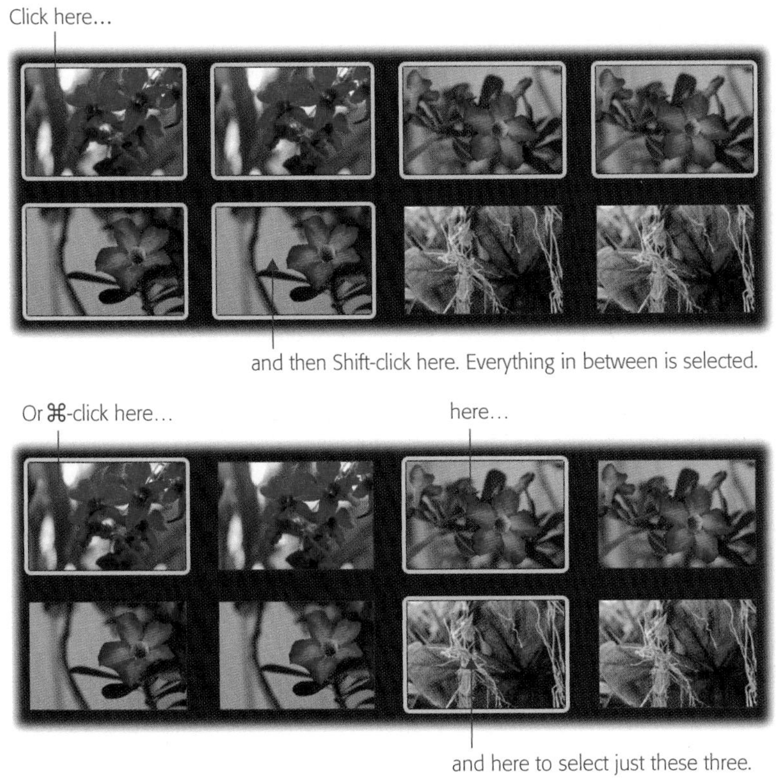

Click here...

and then Shift-click here. Everything in between is selected.

Or ⌘-click here...   here...

and here to select just these three.

Figure 2-8:
Top: To select a block of photos (as indicated by the yellow border on each one), click the first one and then Shift-click the last one. iPhoto selects all the files in between your clicks.

Bottom: To select nonadjacent photos, ⌘-click them. To remove one of the photos from your selection, ⌘-click it again.

Once you've highlighted multiple photos, you can manipulate them all at once. For example, you can drag them en masse out of the window and onto your desktop—a quick way to export them. (Actually, you may want to drag them into a *folder* in the Finder to avoid spraying their icons all over your desktop.) You might also drag them onto your email program's icon to send them as attachments. Or you can drag them into an album at the left side of the iPhoto window. Just drag any *one* of the highlighted photos; all the other highlighted thumbnails go along for the ride.

In addition, when multiple photos are selected, the commands in the File, Edit, Photos, and Share menus—including Duplicate, Print, Revert to Original, and Email—apply to all of them simultaneously.

Hiding Photos

For years, you had only two choices when confronting a so-so photo in iPhoto: Keep it or delete it.

Keeping it isn't a satisfying solution, because it's not one of your best, but you're still stuck with it. You have to look at it every time you open iPhoto, skip over it every time you're making a photo book or slideshow, and so on.

But deleting it isn't such a great solution, either. You just never know when you might need *exactly* that photo again, years later.

Now there's a happy solution to this quandary: You can *hide* a photo. It's still there behind the scenes, and you can always bring it back into view should the need arise. In the meantime, you can pare your *visible* collection down to the really good shots, without being burdened every day by the ghosts of your less impressive work.

To hide some photos, select them as explained in the previous section, and then take one of these steps:

- Press ⌘-L, or choose Photos→Hide Photos.
- Control-click (or right-click) one of the selected photos; in the shortcut menu, click the big orange X.

The selected photos sprout little Xs in their upper-right corners—and then they vanish. Of course, they're still taking up disk space. But they no longer bog down iPhoto when you're scrolling or depress you when they stare out at you every day.

FREQUENTLY ASKED QUESTION

The Blurry-Photo Effect

Hey, what's the deal? When I double-click a photo to open it for editing, it appears momentarily in a coarse, low-resolution version. It takes a couple of seconds to fill the window so I can get to work. Do I need to send my copy of iPhoto in for servicing?

No, not exactly.

Today's digital photos are pretty big, especially if you've got one of those cameras that takes giant-sized photos (12 megapixels, for example).

Now, as it turns out, that's a lot more pixels than even the biggest computer screen has. So your Mac must not only "read" all the photo information off your hard drive, but

it also must then compute a scaled-down version that's exactly the size of your iPhoto window. Naturally, all this computation takes time.

Apple has tried to disguise this moment of computation by first displaying a full-sized but blurry, low-resolution photo, filling in the sharpened details a moment later. You can't begin editing until the full-window computation is complete. On the other hand, you do get to see, clearly enough, which photo you've opened. And if you've opened the wrong one, you don't have to wait any longer; you can click over to a different photo, having wasted no more time than necessary.

But don't worry: iPhoto doesn't let you forget that they're there. Whenever you open an Event, the words "(7 more hidden)"—or whatever the number is—appear in the title bar; you can see it in Figure 2-9. This notation also appears in Photos view.

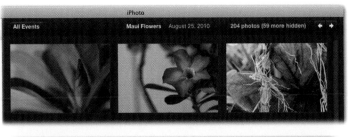
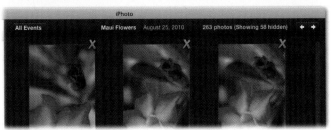

Figure 2-9:
Top: When you open an Event, iPhoto reminds you of the hidden photos it contains, no matter whether you're in Events or Photos view.

Bottom: When you choose View→Hidden Photos, the hidden pictures reappear.

Seeing Hidden Photos

To bring all your hidden photos back into view for a moment, do one of these things:

- Choose View→Hidden Photos.
- Press Shift-⌘-H.

Either way, all the hidden photos reappear, bearing those little Xs on their corners (Figure 2-9, bottom). This is your chance to reconsider—either to delete them for good, or to welcome them back into society.

Of course, you can rehide the hidden photos whenever it's convenient by choosing View→Hidden Photos again.

Unhiding Photos

Just marking a photo as hidden doesn't mean you can't change your mind. At any time, you can unhide a hidden photo, turning it back into a full-fledged photographic citizen.

To do that, first make your hidden photos visible, as described above. Then select any photos you want to unhide, and repeat whatever step you took to hide them in the first place. For example:

- Press ⌘-L, or choose Photos→Unhide Photos.

- Control-click (or right-click) one of the selected photos; then, from the shortcut menu, choose Unhide Photo.

Note: In iPhoto '11, you can't click the phrase "(# more hidden)" (shown at the top of Figure 2-9) to make your hidden photos reappear, as you could in iPhoto '09.

Three Ways to Open a Photo

iPhoto wouldn't be a terribly useful program if it let you view only postage-stamp versions of your photos (unless, of course, you like to take pictures of postage stamps). Fortunately, iPhoto offers three ways to view your pictures at something much closer to actual size.

You'll use these methods frequently when you start editing your photos, as described in Chapter 5. For the moment, though, it's useful to know about these techniques simply for the more common act of viewing the pictures at larger sizes.

Method 1: Right in the Window

The easiest way to open a photo is simply to double-click its thumbnail. The photo opens in the main iPhoto window, scaled to fit into the viewing area (Figure 2-10).

Whenever you've opened a photo this way, the bottom of the window displays a parade of all the *other* photos' thumbnails. This is the iPhoto '11 *filmstrip* or *thumbnail browser*. You can use it to jump to a different photo, as described in Figure 2-10.

Tip: iPhoto '11 only lets you see one photo at a time in this view. To see multiple sections simultaneously, you have to be in Edit mode, as explained at the bottom of page 123.

Method 2: Full Screen View

Here's another way to take a gander at a photo: Full Screen view. (You could get this view in previous versions, but it involved tweaking iPhoto's preferences.) In Full Screen view (Figure 2-11), a selected photo fills your *entire* monitor, edge to edge. There's no Source list stacked with icons down the left side—everything you need shrinks down to the smallest possible size at the top and bottom of your monitor, letting you focus on your glorious photo, blown up as big as it can go. Figure 2-11 tells how to display images in this view.

Note: You no longer have the option of opening a photo into a floating window of its own, as in previous versions of iPhoto.

This mode is fantastic when you're *editing* photos, which is why it's described and illustrated in greater length in Chapter 7. To exit Full Screen mode, click the Full Screen icon again, or tap the Esc key on your keyboard.

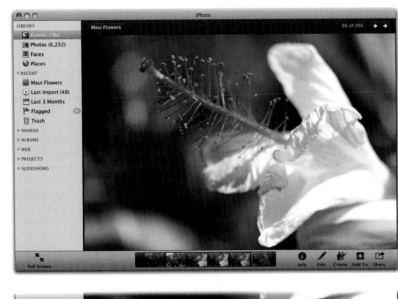

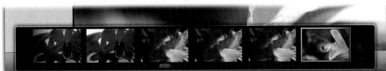

Figure 2-10:
Top: Here's how most people open pictures, at least at first. It's comforting to see landmarks like the Source list and toolbar. The downside is that those other screen elements limit the size of the enlarged photo; that's why you might want to consider the new Full Screen view.

Bottom: The filmstrip at the bottom of the window is new in iPhoto '11. Point to it without clicking to enlarge it so you can see the other photos in that Event or album. A little scroll bar appears underneath it so you can pick another photo to view at close range.

Note: You can't tweak iPhoto '11's settings so that a double-click switches you to Edit mode (as you could in previous versions). Apple figures you'll do most of your editing in Full Screen view.

Method 3: In Another Program

Apple knows there's other software out there—big, burly photo-editing programs like Adobe Photoshop or Apple's Aperture. That's why you can tell iPhoto that you'd rather use a different program for manipulating the finer points of your photos. To do so, choose iPhoto→Preferences→Advanced→Edit Photos→"In application" and then pick another program installed on your Mac. Chapter 5 has more information.

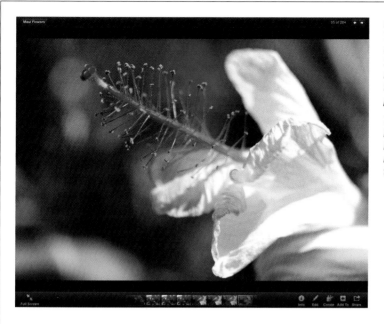

Figure 2-11:
The ■ at the lower left of the iPhoto window opens Full Screen view, which is down-right glorious. The filmstrip at the bottom expands when you point to it.

To go back to viewing the individual thumbnails in your Event, press ⌘-left arrow. To return to All Events view, press ⌘-left arrow again.

Albums

In the olden days of film cameras and drugstore prints, most people kept their pictures in the paper envelopes they were in when they came from the drugstore. You might have put a photo in an album or physically mailed it to somebody—but then the photo was no longer in the envelope and couldn't be used for anything else.

But you're digital now, baby. You can use a single photo in a million different ways, without ever removing it from its original "envelope" (that is, its Event).

In iPhoto terminology, an *album* is a collection of your pictures—drawn from a single Event or many different ones—that you group together for easy access and viewing. Represented by a little album-book icon in the Source list at the left side of the screen, an album can consist of any photos you select. It can even be a *smart album* that iPhoto assembles automatically by matching certain criteria you set up—all pictures that you took in 2011, for example, or all photos that you've rated four stars or higher.

While your iPhoto library as a whole might contain thousands of photos from a hodgepodge of unrelated family events, trips, and time periods, a photo album has a single focus: Cutest Cat Pics, City Skylines, and so on.

As you probably know, mounting snapshots in a *real* photo album is a pain—that's why so many people still have stacks of Kodak prints stuffed in envelopes and shoeboxes. But with iPhoto, you don't need mounting corners, double-sided tape, or scissors to create an album. In the digital world, there's no excuse for leaving your photos in hopeless disarray.

Of course, you're not *required* to group your digital photos in albums with iPhoto, but consider the advantages of doing so:

- **You can find specific photos faster**. By opening only the relevant album, you can avoid scrolling through thousands of thumbnails in the library to find a picture you want—a factor that takes on added importance as your collection expands.

- **Only in a photo album can you drag your photos into a different order**. To change the order of photos displayed in a slideshow or iPhoto hardbound book, for example, you need to start with a photo album (see Chapters 6 and 9).

Creating an Empty Album

In iPhoto '11, there's only one way to create a new, completely empty photo album: Press ⌘-N. Even choosing File→New Album grabs some—or all—of your photos (depending upon what's active in your Source list).

When you create an album this way, the new album appears at the bottom of the Albums section of the Source list with its name highlighted—"untitled album"—so you can type a new one (*Best of Bermuda, Marching Band Mayhem, Road Trips 2011*, or whatever). You can see several albums on display in Figure 2-12.

You can add photos to your newly spawned album by dragging thumbnails into it from your library (also shown in Figure 2-12). There's no limit to the number of albums you can add, so make as many as you need to satisfactorily organize all the photos in your library.

Tip: New albums always appear at the bottom of the Source list's Albums section, but you can drag them up or down in the list. You can also make iPhoto put them in alphabetical order by Control-clicking (or right-clicking) any album and choosing Sort Albums from the shortcut menu.

Creating an Album by Dragging

Creating a new, empty album isn't always the best way to start. Usually it's easier to create an album *and* fill it with pictures in one fell swoop.

Here are a couple of ways you can create a new album by clicking and dragging:

- Drag a thumbnail (or a batch of them) from the Photos area directly into an empty portion of the Source list. In a flash—well, in about 2 seconds—iPhoto creates a new album for you, named "untitled album." The photos you dragged are automatically dumped inside.

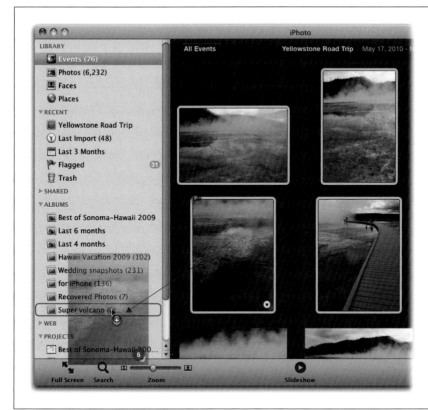

Figure 2-12:
When you drag multiple photos into an album, a little red numeric badge appears near the pointer, telling you exactly how many items you've got selected. In this example, six pictures are being dragged en masse into a photo album.

- Similarly, you can drag a bunch of graphics files from the *Finder* (the desktop behind iPhoto) directly into the Source list. In one step, iPhoto imports the photos, creates a new album, names it after the folder you dragged in, and puts the newly imported photos into that album.

Tip: You can also drag photos directly from the Finder onto an *existing* album icon in the Source list, forcing iPhoto to file them there in the process of importing.

Creating an Album by Selecting

For the quickest album creation-and-filling in the West, first select some photos using the methods described on page 49. (If you're cruising through Photos view, the images don't have to be from the same Event, or even the same year.) Then, you can:

- **Choose File→New→Album.** iPhoto adds the photos to the album and highlights the album's name so you can change it.
- **Click the Add To icon** at the bottom right of the iPhoto window, as shown in Figure 2-13.

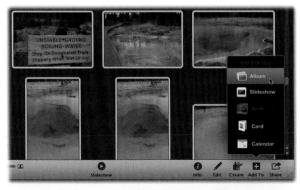

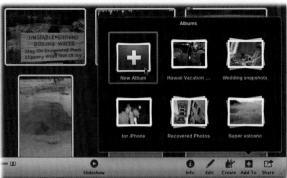

Figure 2-13:
Top: When you click the new Add To icon at the bottom of your iPhoto window, a menu opens that lets you add the selected photos (or Event) to an album, slideshow, project, and so on.

Bottom: When you click Album, another menu appears that lets you create a new album or choose an existing one to hold the photos.

- **Click the Create button** in iPhoto's toolbar and choose Album.

You can also create an album from *flagged* photos. Flag the images you want to include in your new album (page 78) and then click the Flagged icon in your Source list (it's in the Recent category). Press ⌘-A to select all and then choose File→New Album. Of course, if you've previously flagged photos for another project, they'll end up in your new album, too.

Tip: To rename an existing album, double-click its name (not its icon) in the Source list. A renaming rectangle appears around the album's name, with the text highlighted and ready to be edited.

Adding More Photos

To add photos to an existing album, just drag them onto its icon. Figure 2-12 illustrates how you can select multiple photos and drop them into an album in one batch. (If you're paid by the hour, you can also select some photos, then use the Add To pop-up menu in the lower-right of the iPhone window; click Album; then click the name of the album you want.)

The single most important point about adding photos to an album is this: Putting photos in an album doesn't really *move* or *copy* them. It makes no difference where the thumbnails start out—whether it's the library or another album. You're just creating *references*, or pointers, back to the photos in your master photo library.

This feature works a lot like Macintosh aliases; in fact, behind the scenes, iPhoto actually creates aliases of the photos you're dragging. (It stashes them in the appropriate album folders within the iPhoto library.)

What this means is that you don't have to commit a picture to just one album when organizing; one photo can appear in as many different albums as you want. So, if you've got a killer shot of Grandma surfing in Hawaii and you can't decide whether to drop it into the Hawaiian Vacation album or the Grandma & Grandpa album, the answer is easy: Put it in both. iPhoto just creates two references to the same original photo in your library.

Viewing an Album

To view the contents of an album, click its name or icon in the Source list. All the photos included in the selected album appear in the photo-viewing area, while the ones in your library are hidden.

You can even browse more than one album at a time by highlighting their icons:

- To view the contents of several adjacent albums in the list, click the first one, then Shift-click the last one.
- To view the contents of albums that aren't consecutive in the list, ⌘-click each of them.

Tip: Viewing multiple albums at once can be extremely useful when it's time to share your photos. For example, you can make prints or burn an iPhoto CD or DVD archive (as explained in Chapters 7 and 13) containing the contents of multiple albums.

To return to All Albums view, click the arrow button at the top left of the main viewing area or press ⌘-left arrow.

Remember, adding photos to albums doesn't remove them from the original Events where they started out. So if you lose track of which album contains a particular photo, just click the Events icon in the Source list to return to the overview of your *entire* photo collection.

Moving Photos Between Albums

There are two ways to transfer photos from one album to another:

- To *move* a photo between albums, select it and then choose Edit→Cut (or press ⌘-X), removing the photo from the album. Next, click the destination album's name or icon, and then choose Edit→Paste (or press ⌘-V). The photo is now a part of the second album.

- To *copy* a photo into another album, drag it onto the destination album's icon in the Source list. Now the photo belongs to *both* albums.

Removing Photos from an Album

If you change your mind about the way you've organized your photos and want to remove a photo from an album, first open the album and select the photo. (Caution: Check your Source list to be sure you're viewing the contents of a photo *album* and not the main library, the Last 12 Months collection, or the Last Import collection. Deleting a photo from those sources really does move it to iPhoto's Trash.)

Now do one of the following:

- Choose Edit→Cut (or press ⌘-X). With this method, the photo remains on your Mac's Clipboard, giving you the opportunity to *paste* the photo into another album if you'd like (choose Edit→Paste or press ⌘-V).
- Drag the photo's thumbnail onto the little Trash icon in your Source list.
- Press the Delete key.
- Press the Del (forward delete) key.
- Control-click (or right-click) the photo, and then, in the shortcut menu, click the Trash icon.

In all but the last option, iPhoto asks if you're sure you want to remove the photo (notice it doesn't say "delete"). Click OK. The thumbnail disappears from the album, but of course it's not really gone from iPhoto; it's still in your library. (If you don't see the confirmation message, you or someone else probably turned on the "Don't show this message again" checkbox.)

Duplicating a Photo

iPhoto doesn't let you drag the same photo into an album twice. When you try, the thumbnail simply *leaps* stubbornly back into its original location, as though to say, "Nyah, nyah, you can't drag the same photo into an album twice!"

It's often useful to have two copies of a picture, though. As you'll discover in Chapter 7, a photo whose dimensions are appropriate for a slideshow or photo book (that is, a 4:3 proportion) is inappropriate for ordering prints (4 × 6, 8 × 10, or whatever). To use the same photo for both purposes, you really need to crop two copies independently.

In this case, the old adding-to-album trick isn't going to help you. Instead, you truly have to duplicate the file and consume a little more hard drive space behind the scenes. To do this, highlight the photo, and then choose Photos→Duplicate (⌘-D). iPhoto switches briefly into Import mode, copies the file, and then returns to your previous mode. The copy appears next to the original, bearing the same name plus the words "Version 2." (If you don't see the name, choose View→Titles.)

Note: If you duplicate a photo in an album, you'll see the duplicate in the album *and* in the library. If you duplicate a photo in the library, that's the only place you'll see the twin.

Putting Photos in Order

If you plan to turn your album into a slideshow, a series of web pages, or a printed book, then you'll have to tinker with the order of the pictures, arranging them in the most logical and compelling sequence. Sure, photos in an Event or a smart album (page 62) are locked into a strict sort order—either by creation date, rating, or name—but once they're in a photo album, you can shuffle them manually by dragging. Figure 2-14 explains all.

Duplicating an Album

It stands to reason that if you have several favorite photos, you might want to use them in more than one iPhoto slideshow, book, or what have you. That's why it's often convenient to *duplicate an entire album* so you can create two different sequences for the photos inside.

Just highlight an album, and then choose Photos→Duplicate. iPhoto does the duplicating in a flash—after all, it's just copying a bunch of tiny aliases and not chewing up precious hard drive space. Now you're free to rearrange the order of the photos inside, to add or delete photos, and so on, independently of the original album.

Tip: For quick duplication, you can Control-click (or right-click) an album in the Source list and then choose Duplicate from the shortcut menu.

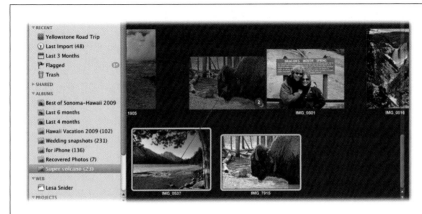

Figure 2-14:
Arrange photos any way you like by dragging them to a new spot within an album. Here, two photos from the bottom-left corner are being dragged to a new location in the row above (the red circle indicates the number of photos being moved).

Instead of a black vertical bar indicating where your photos will land when you release your mouse button, the thumbnails in iPhoto '11 temporarily scoot apart—and even hang off the edge of the window—to make room for the ones you're dragging.

Merging Albums

Suppose you have three albums that contain photos from different trips to the beach, called Spring Break at the Beach, Summer Beach Party, and October Coast Trip. Wouldn't it make sense to merge them into a single album called Beach Trips 2011?

To do that, select all three albums in your Source list (⌘-click each, for example) and the photos from each appear in the photo-viewing area. Next, create a new, *fourth* album, using any of the usual methods. Finally, select all of the visible thumbnails by pressing ⌘-A, and then drag them into the new album.

You now have one big album containing the photos from all three original albums. You can delete the three source albums, if you like, or keep all four hanging around. Remember, albums contain only references to your photos—not the photos themselves—so you're not wasting space by keeping the extra albums. The only penalty you pay is that you have a longer list of albums to scroll through.

Deleting an Album

To delete an album, just click its icon in your Source list and then press the Delete key. You can also Control-click (right-click) an album and then choose Delete Album from the shortcut menu. Either way, iPhoto asks you to confirm your intention. If you really want it gone, then click Delete.

Deleting an album doesn't delete any photos—just the references to those photos. So even if you delete *all* your albums, your library remains intact.

Smart Albums

Albums, as you now realize, are a primary organizational tool in iPhoto. Since the dawn of iPhoto, you've had to create them yourself, one at a time, using the methods described in the previous section.

But thanks to *smart albums*, iPhoto can fill up albums *for* you. Smart albums are self-updating folders that always display pictures according to criteria you set up—all pictures with "Aunt Edna" in the comments, for example, or all the photos that you've rated four stars or higher. (If you've ever used smart playlists in iTunes, you'll recognize the idea immediately.)

Tip: Smart albums can take advantage of Faces, Places, and keyword tags, too. For example, by using Faces tags, you could quickly create a smart album containing photos of all three of your kids. Page 102 in Chapter 4 tells you how.

To create a smart album, choose File→New→Smart Album, press Option-⌘-N, or Option-click the Create button in your toolbar and choose Smart Album from the pop-up menu. Whichever method you use, the Smart Album sheet slides down from the top of the window (Figure 2-15).

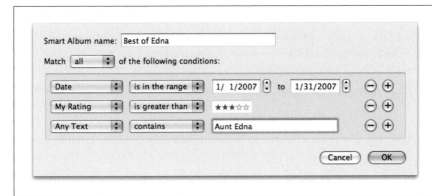

Figure 2-15:
The Smart Album dialog box is really just a powerful search command, because iPhoto is really just a powerful database. You can set up certain criteria, like this hunt for photos taken during a certain time period.

The controls here are designed to set up a search of your photo library. Figure 2-15 illustrates how to find pictures that you took in the first month of 2007—but only those that have four- or five-star ratings and mention your Aunt Edna in their titles or comments.

Click the **+** button to add a new criterion row and be even more specific about which photos you want iPhoto to include in the smart album. Use the first pop-up menu to choose a type of photo feature (keyword or date, for example) and the second pop-up menu to tell iPhoto whether you want to match it ("is"), eliminate it ("is not"), and so on. The third part of the criterion row is another pop-up menu or a search field where you finally tell iPhoto what to look for. Here's how to use it:

- You can limit the smart album's reach by limiting it to a certain **Album**. Or, by choosing "is not" from the second pop-up menu, you can *eliminate* an album from consideration. All your albums are listed in the third pop-up menu.

Tip: You can also use a smart album to find all the photos that you haven't put into an album (a great way to rediscover forgotten photos or to find candidates for deletion). To do so, create a new smart album and name it something like "Not in any album." Then set the pop-up menus to "Album," "is not," and "Any." Who knew?

- **Any Text** searches your library for words or letters that appear in the title, comments, or keywords that you've assigned to your photos.

If you can't remember how you spelled a word or whether you put it in the Description or Title field, choose "Any Text," select "contains" from the second pop-up menu, and type just the first few letters of the word ("am" for Amsterdam, for example) in the search field. You're bound to find some windmills now!

- **Description, Filename, Keyword, and Title** work the same way, except that they search *only* that part of the photo's information. Search for "Keyword" "is" "Family" (type "Family" into the text field where the third pop-up menu used to be), for example, to find only those pictures to which you specifically assigned the keyword Family, and not just any old photos where you've typed the word *family* somewhere in the comments.

- **Date** was once one of iPhoto's most powerful search criteria. By choosing "is in the range" from the second pop-up menu, you can use it to create an album containing, for example, only the pictures you took on December 24 and 25 of last year, or for that five-day stretch two summers ago when your best friends were in town. In iPhoto '11, however, the Calendar's date search serves this function much more conveniently (see page 81).

- **Event** lets you make iPhoto look only in, for example, the last five Events (choose "is in the last" from the second pop-up menu and type 5 in the box). Or, if you're creating an album of old shots, you can eliminate the latest few Events from consideration by choosing "is not in the last."

- If you've tagged photos in Faces or Places (Chapter 4), then **Face** and **Place** let you make smart albums based on who's in the photos or where they were taken.

Tip: Once you dig into Chapter 4 and start tagging Faces, you can create a smart album on the fly by dragging a Faces snapshot from your corkboard onto an empty spot in your Source list. iPhoto adds a new smart album bearing that person's name. If you want to add another buddy to the same smart album, just drag his Faces snapshot onto it!

- The **My Rating** option in the first pop-up menu really puts the fun into smart albums. Let's suppose you've been dutifully giving your pictures star ratings from 1 to 5, as described on page 90. It's payoff time! You can now use this smart album feature to collect, say, only those with five stars to create a quick slideshow of just the highlights. Another option is to choose "is greater than" two stars for a more inclusive slideshow that leaves out only the real duds.

- **Photo** lets you include (or exclude) photos according to whether they're hidden, flagged, or edited. When you choose this option, the third pop-up menu lets you pinpoint Raw photos, digital movies, or geotagged images. These are fantastically useful options; everyone should have a smart album just for movies, at the very least.

- **Aperture, Camera Model, Flash, Focal Length, ISO,** and **Shutter Speed** are behind-the-scenes data bits that your camera automatically records with each shot, and even embeds in the resulting photo file. Thanks to these options, you can use a smart album to round up all your flash photos, all photos taken with an ISO (light sensitivity) setting of 800 or higher, all pictures with a certain shutter speed, all the ones you took with your Canon Powershot S95, and so on. (If you choose Camera Model from the first pop-up menu, the third pop-up menu conveniently lists every camera you've ever used to take photos.)

- Click the — button next to a criterion to take it out of the running. For example, if you decide that date shouldn't be a factor, delete any criterion row that tells iPhoto to look for certain dates.

When you click OK, your smart album is ready to show off. When you click its name in the Source list (it has a little ✿ icon), the main window displays thumbnails of the photos that match your criteria. The best part is that iPhoto keeps this album updated whenever your collection changes—as you change your ratings, take new photos, tag more Faces, and so on.

Tip: To change or review a smart album's parameters, click its icon in the Source list and then choose File→Edit Smart Album or press ⌘-I. (You can also Control- or right-click its icon and choose Edit Smart Album from the shortcut menu.) In each case, the Smart Album sheet dutifully reappears.

Folders

Obviously, Apple hit a home run when it invented the album concept. Let's face it: If there were a Billboard Top Software-Features Hits chart, iPhoto's albums feature would have been number one for months on end.

Albums may have become *too* popular, however. It wasn't long before iPhoto fans discovered that their long list of albums had outgrown the height of their Source lists. As a result, people grew desperate for some way to organize albums *within* albums.

Apple's response consisted of one word: *folders*.

If you choose File→New→Folder, iPhoto promptly creates a new, folder-shaped icon in the Source list called "untitled folder" (type a name for it, and then press Return). Its sole purpose in life is to contain *other* Source list icons—albums, smart albums, saved slideshows, book layouts, and so on.

What's really nice about folders is that they can contain *other* folders. That is, iPhoto is capable of more than a two-level hierarchy; you can actually create folders within folders within folders within folders, as shown in Figure 2-16.

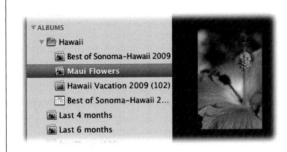

Figure 2-16:
A folder is a convenient container for other kinds of Source list icons. Once you've created a folder, you can drag related albums, saved slideshows, projects, and so on, into it. Thereafter, you can make your Source list tidier by collapsing the folder, thereby hiding its contents. To collapse or expand a folder, click the flippy triangle to its left.

Otherwise, folders work exactly like albums. You rename them the same way, drag them up and down the Source list the same way, delete them the same way, and duplicate them the same way.

Clearly, the people have spoken.

Tip: If you've put something into a folder by accident, no problem; you can easily drag it back out again. Just drag it upward directly onto the Albums heading in the Source list, and then release your mouse button. And if you'd rather keep your Hawaii calendar under the Projects category (instead of in a folder), you can drag it back there, too.

The Info Panel

At the bottom right of your iPhoto window, you'll find a set of five buttons. The first one, the ❶, hides or shows the *Info panel*, which displays general data about a photo, album, Event, or whatever else you've selected. (This button used to live beneath the Source list.)

When the Info panel is visible, you may see any number of different displays (Figure 2-17):

- When a single photo is selected, iPhoto displays that picture's name, rating, creation time and date, dimensions (in pixels), file size, camera settings, the description you've typed, as well as Faces or Places tags (if you've added any).

  If you've published the photo to your Facebook, Flickr, or MobileMe account, or sent an email from within iPhoto (page 195), you see that info here, too. If someone leaves a comment on a photo you published to Facebook, it shows up here the next time the albums are synced (which happens automatically when you double-click to view a published album).

- When multiple photos are selected, you see the *range* of their creation dates, plus how many photos are selected, how much disk space they occupy, as well as Faces and Places tags.

- When no photos are selected, the Info panel displays information about whatever *container* is selected in the Source list—the current album or Event, for example. You get to see the name of the container, the range of dates of its photos, the number of photos, and their total file size on your hard drive.

- When your MobileMe, Flickr, or Facebook icon is selected (Chapter 8), you get to see the number of albums or sets you've published, the date range, the number of photos, and their total file size.

To close the Info panel, click the ❶ icon again. The panel slides out of sight.

Note: In iPhoto '11, there's no Info panel for Projects or Slideshows.

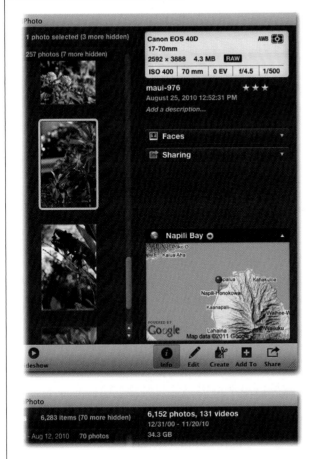

Figure 2-17:
Top: When you open the Info panel with a photo selected, you see all manner of details at the top right. If you select a photo with Faces or Places tags, you see those here, too. If the photo has been published to Facebook, Flickr, MobileMe, or emailed from inside iPhoto, a Sharing section appears. Click any section's name—Faces, Sharing, or Places—to expand or collapse it.

Bottom: If you click Events or Photos in your Source list, but have no single Event selected, the date-range statistic shown here is pretty cool. It amounts to a stopwatch measuring the span of your interest in digital photography (in the iPhoto era, anyway).

Similarly, the file-size info can be extremely useful when creating backups, copying photos to another disk, or burning CDs or DVDs. One glance and iPhoto tells you exactly how much disk space you'll need to fit the current album, folder, or Event. (That said, iPhoto is perfectly capable of splitting your library across a number of CD/DVDs. You'll learn about that in Chapter 13.)

Renaming Photos

Just about everything in iPhoto has its own title: every photo, album, folder, Event, photo book, slideshow, and so on. You can rename most of them very easily—just by double-clicking the existing name.

To rename photos, make sure their titles are turned on (choose View→Titles). Single-click the title you want to edit and type a new name, then press Return, Enter, or Tab, or click somewhere else.

If you want to rename a whole slew of photos (like a batch you've just imported), rename one and then press the Tab key on your keyboard. iPhoto not only highlights the next picture, but also highlights all the text in its title box so you don't need to click anything before typing a new name for it. (Pressing Shift-Tab takes you back one photo instead.)

Changing Titles, Dates, or Comments En Masse

The trouble with naming photos is that hardly anybody takes the time. Yes, the keystroke described above certainly makes it easier to assign every photo its own name with reasonable speed—but are you really going to sit there and make up individual names for 25,000 photos?

Mercifully, iPhoto lets you change the names of your photos all at once, thanks to a "batch processing" command. No, each photo won't have a unique, descriptive name, but at least they can have titles like *Spring Vacation 2* and *Spring Vacation 3* instead of *IMG_1345* and *IMG_1346*.

To use it, select an Event or album and then choose Photos→Batch Change (Shift-⌘-B). The Batch Change sheet drops down from the top of the iPhoto window, as shown in Figure 2-18. To create the kind of naming scheme mentioned above, change the first pop-up menu to Title and the second one to Text, and then turn on "Append a number of each photo."

Tip: Don't be fooled by the command name *Batch Change*. iPhoto still can't edit a batch of photos. You can't, for example, apply the Enhance filter to all of them at once. (Though you can copy and paste edits from one photo to another; see Chapter 5.)

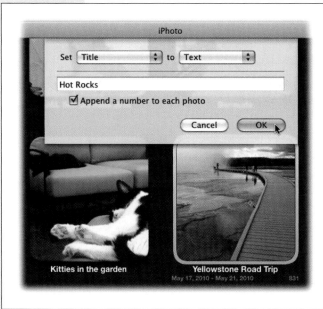

Figure 2-18:
iPhoto's batch-processing feature lets you specify titles, dates, and description for any number of photos you select. When you title a batch of pictures, turn on "Append a number to each photo" to number them in sequence, too.

While Title is selected in the first Batch Change pop-up menu, peek inside the *second* pop-up menu for these options:

- **Empty**. Set the titles to Empty if you want to unname the selected photos so they're all blank. You might appreciate this option when, for example, you're working on a photo book (Chapter 9) and you've opted for titles to appear with each photo, but you really want only a few pictures to appear with names under them.

- **Text**. This option produces an empty text box into which you can type, for example, *Ski Trip*. When you click OK, iPhoto names all of the selected pictures to match.

   If you turn on the "Append a number to each photo" checkbox, then iPhoto adds digits after whatever base name you choose—for example, *Ski Trip 1, Ski Trip 2*, and so on.

- **Event Name**. Choose this command to name all the selected photos after the Event they're part of—"Grand Canyon 2011," for example. iPhoto automatically adds the photo number after this base name.

- **Filename**. If you've been fooling around with naming your photos and now decide that you want their original, camera-blessed file names to return (*IMG_1345* and so on), then use this command.

- **Date/Time**. Here's another approach: Name each photo for the exact time it was taken. The dialog box gives you a wide variety of formatting options: long date, short date, time of day, and so on.

Photo Dates

You can also use the Batch Change command to rewrite history, resetting the dates of a group of photos all at once.

Choose Date from the first Batch Change pop-up menu and turn on "Add 1 Minute between each photo" to give each one a unique time stamp, which could come in handy later when you're sorting them. iPhoto changes only its internal time stamps; it doesn't actually modify the photo files on your hard drive unless you also turn on "Modify original files."

We trust you won't use this feature for nefarious ends, such as "proving" to the jury that you were actually in Disney World on the day of the office robbery.

Note: Actually, if you just want to fix the date and time stamps on some photos, or a whole Event, the Photos→"Adjust Date and Time" command is more direct. It opens the "Adjust date and time of selected photos" dialog box, where you can choose a new date and time of the *first* selected photo. Any other selected photos are adjusted, too, by proportional amounts. For example, if you change the first photo's time stamp to make it 10 minutes later, then all other selected photos are shifted by 10 minutes. You can see it in action back in Figure 2-7 (page 48).

Description

Sometimes you need more than a one- or two-word title to describe the contents of a photo, album, folder, book, slideshow, or Event. If you want to add a lengthier description, you can type it in the Description field in the Info panel, as shown in Figure 2-19.

Even if you don't write full-blown captions for your pictures, you can use the Description field to store details such as the names, places, dates, and events associated with your photos.

The best thing about adding comments is that they're searchable. After you've entered all this free-form data, you can use it to quickly locate a photo using iPhoto's Search command.

Tip: If you speak a non-English language, iPhoto makes your life easier. As you're typing comments, you can choose Edit→Special Characters. Mac OS X's Characters palette opens, where you can add international letters like É, ø, and ß. Of course, it's also ideal for classic phrases like "I ♥ my cat."

Keep the following in mind as you squirrel away all those bits and scraps of photo information:

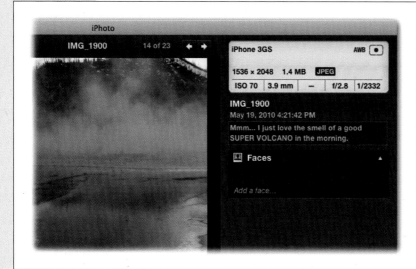

Figure 2-19:
Got a picture that's worth a thousand words? Well, the Description field can handle it, but you won't see more than a sentence because iPhoto '11's Info panel isn't expandable like it was in previous versions. To add a description, click below the photo's date, where it says "Add a description," and start typing.

- You don't have to manually *type* to enter data into the Description field. You can paste information in using the standard Paste command, or even drag selected text from another program (like Microsoft Word) right into the Description box.
- If no photos, or several photos, are selected, then the notes you type into the Description box get attached to the current *album*, rather than to pictures.

- You can add the same comment to a group of photos using iPhoto's Batch Change command. For example, ⌘-click all the pictures of your soccer team. Next, choose Photos→Batch Change, choose Description from the first pop-up menu, and then type a list of your teammates' names in the Description field. Years later, you'll have a quick reminder of everyone's names.

You can just as easily add comments for an album, folder, slideshow icon, book, or Event whose name you've highlighted.

Description as captions

While the Description field is useful for storing little scraps of background information about your photos, you can also use it to store the *captions* that you want to appear with your photos. In fact, some of the book layouts included with iPhoto's book-creation tools (Chapter 9) automatically use the text in the Description field to generate a caption for each photo.

(On the other hand, you don't *have* to use the Description box text for captions. You can always add different captions when you're editing the book.)

Deleting Photos

As every photographer knows—well, every *good* photographer—not every photo is a keeper. So at some point, you'll want to take a deep breath and prune your photo collection. Read on.

The iPhoto Trash

iPhoto has a private Trash can that works just like the Finder's Trash. It's sitting there in the Source list (under the Recent heading, for some reason). When you delete a picture, iPhoto puts it into the Trash "folder," awaiting permanent disposal via the Empty Trash command. This feature gives you a layer of protection against accidentally deleting a precious picture.

In the main Photos view, you can relegate items to the Trash by selecting one or more photo thumbnails within your Library (not in an album, but in Events or Photos view), and then doing one of the following:

- Dragging the thumbnails into the Trash.
- Control-clicking (or right-clicking) a photo, and then clicking the Trash icon on the shortcut menu.
- Pressing the Delete key, or choosing Photos→Move to Trash.

Tip: Pressing the Delete key also works when you've opened a photo for editing. But to delete a photo from a smart album, you have to press Option-⌘-Delete instead.

To view the photos that you've sentenced to the great shredder in the sky, click the Trash icon, as shown in Figure 2-20. If you suddenly decide you don't really want to get rid of some of these trashed photos, it's easy to resurrect them, using one of these techniques:

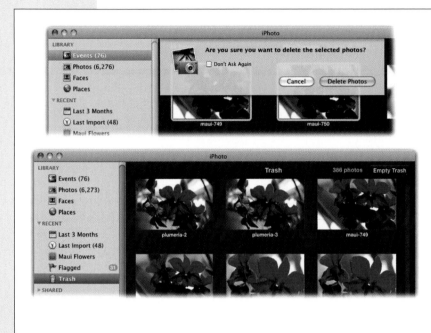

Figure 2-20:
Top: When you try to delete a picture, iPhoto asks for confirmation.

Bottom: Even if you toss a photo into the Trash, it's not really gone—it's just relocated to iPhoto's Trash folder. Clicking the Trash icon in the Source list shows you all the photos awaiting obliteration, and displays the total number of files at the top right of the iPhoto window. If you really want to delete them from your hard drive, click the Empty Trash button (also at the upper right).

MEMORY LANE

Goodbye, Extended Photo Info Window

Previous versions of iPhoto included Extended Photo Info that you could summon by choosing Photos→Show Extended Photo Info. iPhoto would then display a complete dossier of details about your photo: the make and model of the camera used to take it, the exposure, and a slew of other settings.

Apple has retired the Extended Photo Info window in iPhoto '11, but most (if not all) of these details appear in the Info panel described on page 66.

How does iPhoto know so much about how your photos were taken, anyway? Most digital cameras embed a wealth of image, camera, lens, and exposure information in the photo files they create, using a standard data format called *EXIF* (Exchangeable Image Format). iPhoto simply scans photos for EXIF data as it imports them.

Some cameras do a better job than others of embedding EXIF data in photo files. iPhoto can extract this information only if it was properly stored by the camera when the digital photo was created. Of course, this information is missing altogether if your photos didn't come from a digital camera (if they were scanned, for example).

- Highlight them and then press ⌘-Delete (or choose Photos→"Restore to Photo Library"). Think of this as the un-Trash command.
- Drag the thumbnails out of the Trash and onto the Photos icon in the Source list.
- Control-click (or right-click) the photo or photos and, from the shortcut menu, choose "Restore to Photo Library."

You've just rescued them from photo-reject limbo and put them back into your main photo collection.

To *permanently* delete what's in the Trash, choose iPhoto→Empty iPhoto Trash, or Control-click (right-click) the Trash icon to access the Empty Trash command via a shortcut menu. iPhoto then displays an alert message, warning you that emptying the Trash removes these photos permanently and irreversibly. Only when you click OK does your iPhoto library actually shrink in size.

(Of course, if you imported the photos from files on disk or haven't deleted them from your camera, you can still recover the original files and reimport them.)

Whatever pictures you throw out by emptying the Trash also disappear from any albums you've created.

Note: If you use iPhoto to track photos that aren't actually in iPhoto (they remain "out there" in folders on your hard drive), deleting them in iPhoto doesn't do much. They no longer show up in iPhoto, but they're still on your hard drive, right where they always were. See page 19 for more on this external photo-tracking feature.

Customizing the Shoebox

iPhoto's Photos view starts out looking just the way you probably see it now, with each picture displayed as a small thumbnail against a dark gray background. This view makes it easy to browse through photos and work with iPhoto's various tools.

But, hey, this is *your* digital shoebox. With a little tweaking and fine-tuning, you can completely customize the way iPhoto displays your photos.

Start with a visit to iPhoto→Preferences, and then click the Appearance button.

Tip: You can open the iPhoto Preferences window anytime by pressing ⌘-comma. This keystroke is blissfully consistent across all the iLife programs, and indeed most Mac programs.

Changing the View

The controls in the Preferences window's Appearance panel (Figure 2-21) let you make some pretty significant changes to the overall look of your library.

Here are your options:

- **Add or remove an outline or a shadow**. The factory setting, Outline, puts a thin black or white frame around your photos (whichever contrasts best with the screen background). Your other choice, "Drop shadow," puts a soft black shadow behind each thumbnail in the photo-viewing pane, a subtle touch that gives your library an elegant 3-D look.

  As pretty as this effect is, however, there are those who say that on slow Macs, it can bog iPhoto down slightly, as the program has to continually redraw or resize those fancy shadows behind each thumbnail whenever you scroll or zoom. In that case, turning off the drop shadow might grant you slightly faster scrolling.

- **Change the background color**. The Background slider lets you adjust the background color of the photo-viewing pane. Actually, the term "color" is a bit of an overstatement, since your choices include only white, black, or any shade of gray in between.

- **Show reflections when viewing Events**. Turn on the "Show reflections" checkbox if you want the key photos of your Events to look like they're reflecting off a shiny surface, as shown in Figure 2-21 (bottom).

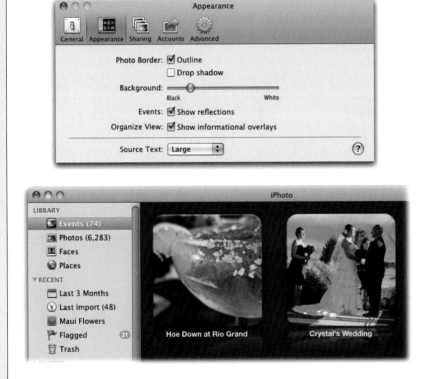

Figure 2-21:
Top: Oh sure you can revert to the look of iPhotos of yore by changing the background color to light gray (it remains dark gray in Events view), but would you really want to? If you're tempted, consider that Apple gave iPhoto '11 a dark gray background for a reason—it's easier on your eyes and it gives you a more accurate sense of color (by eliminating other distracting colors).

Bottom: If you turn on the "Show reflections" checkbox, your Events look like they're sitting atop a glassy surface.

- **Show informational overlays**. This option is well worth turning on. It makes a big, see-through "heads-up display" appear whenever you're scrolling through, well, anything. Apple used to call it the Scroll Guide, and it shows where you are, chronologically or alphabetically, as you scroll. Figure 2-22 should make this idea clearer.

- **Source Text**. Use this pop-up menu to control the size of the text in your Source list. Your choices are Large or Small.

Note: The heads-up display doesn't appear when you've chosen Manual sorting mode for an album.

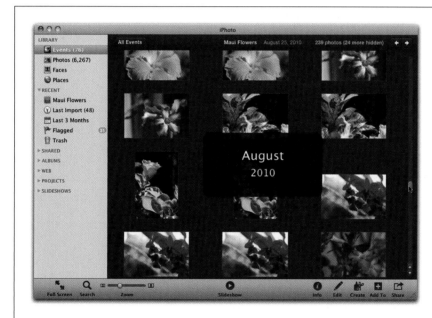

Figure 2-22:
As you drag the vertical scroll bar, this heads-up display shows where you are in the collection. What you see here depends on the current sorting method. For example, if you've sorted by name, you see letters of the alphabet as you scroll. If you've sorted by rating, you see stars, showing you where you are in your scroll through the ratings, and so on.

Showing/Hiding Titles, Ratings, and Keywords

If you want your thumbnails to appear with their titles, ratings, and keywords, or all three, then choose View→Titles (Shift-⌘-T), View→Ratings (Shift-⌘-R), or View→Keywords (Shift-⌘-K). Titles, ratings, and keywords appear under each thumbnail. (See Chapter 3 for more on keywords.) To show or hide Event titles, choose View→Event Titles or press Shift-⌘-F.

As with most of iPhoto, your formatting options are limited. You can't control the font, style, color, or size of this text. Your only choice is to either display the title and keywords or to keep them hidden.

Five Ways to Flag and Find Photos

The more you get into digital photography, the more pictures you'll probably store in iPhoto. And the more pictures you store in iPhoto, the more urgently you'll need ways to *find* them again—to pluck certain pictures out of this gigantic, seething haystack of digital files.

Fortunately, iPhoto is equally seething with search mechanisms. You can find pictures by the text associated with them (name, location, description, Event, and so on); by the date you took them; by the keywords you've tagged them with; or by the ratings you've given them. You can also use iPhoto's *flagging* feature to find, and later round up, any arbitrary photos you like.

This chapter covers all five methods.

Note: You can easily track down photos by tagging them with Faces and Places, too. Those features are covered in Chapter 4.

Flagging Photos

Here's a simple, sweet iPhoto feature: You can *flag*, or mark, a photo.

So what does the flag mean? Anything you want it to mean; it's open to a multitude of personal interpretations. The bottom line, though, is that you'll find this marker extremely useful for temporary organizational tasks.

For example, you might want to cull only the most appropriate images from a photo album for use in a printed book or slideshow. As you browse through the images, flag each shot you want. Later, you can round up all of the images you flagged so you can drag them all into a new album en masse.

How to Flag a Photo

Unlike in previous versions of the program, there's no flag button at the bottom of the iPhoto '11 window. But you still have a couple of ways to flag photos.

You can flag a selected photo, or a bunch of selected photos, by choosing Photos→Flag Photo (or pressing ⌘-period). You can also flag a photo by pointing to its thumbnail and clicking the pennant that appears on its top left corner.

Either way, a little orange flag appears on the upper-left corner of the photo's thumbnail, as shown in Figure 3-1.

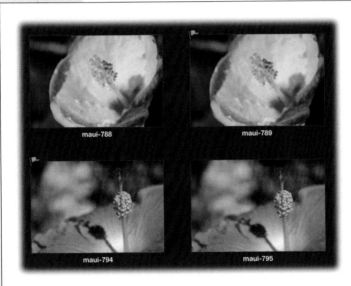

Figure 3-1:
When you flag a photo, you're adding a temporary, orange pennant badge to its thumbnail. It's like you're setting this photo aside so you can make it part of a grouping of like-minded pictures later.

How to Unflag Photos

You can remove photos' flags by highlighting their thumbnails and then choosing Photos→Unflag Photos (or pressing ⌘-period again). You can also click the pennant that appears at the top left of the photo's thumbnail.

Tip: You can also remove the flags from *all your photos at once*, everywhere in your library, by using a secret command. Open the Photos menu, hold down the Option key, and marvel as the new Clear All Flags command appears. You can also click the number to the right of Flagged in your Source list; the number turns into a clickable, albeit microscopic, ✕.

How to Use Flagged Photos

Suppose you've worked through all your photos for some purpose, carefully flagging them as you go. Here's the payoff: rounding them up so that you can delete them all, hide them all, incorporate them into a slideshow, finally sit down and geotag them (page 107), use them in a book, export them as a batch, and so on.

See them all at once

If you click the Flagged icon in the Source list, then iPhoto shows you all flagged photos in your entire library. You can select them all and drag them into a *regular* album (not a smart album), if you like, in readiness for making a slideshow, a book, or anything else where you'd like the freedom to rearrange their sequence.

Put them into an Event

iPhoto can generate a new Event that contains only the photos you've flagged in all your *other* Events. This method isolates the flagged photos instantly into a single, handy subset, and removes them from their original Events (photos can only live inside one Event at a time).

All you have to do is choose Events→Create Event From Flagged Photos. A box appears to warn you that you're about to remove the photos from their *original* Events; nod understandingly and click Create. In a flash, your new Event appears, filled with flagged photos and ready to rename.

Tip: You don't have to create a *new* Event to hold your flagged photos, either. If you click Events in the Source list and then click an Event, you can then choose Events→Add Flagged Photos To Selected Event. That way, you add the flagged photos to an *existing* Event—a handy option when you've put all the flagged photos into an Event and later added flags to *more* photos that really belong with their brethren.

Create a smart album

You can easily set up a *smart album* (page 62) to round up all the flagged photos in your entire collection. Choose File→New→Smart Album, and in the dialog box that appears, set up the pop-up menus to say "Photo" "is" "Flagged." (Since a Flagged icon is already in the Source list, you'll generally want to do this only if you want a smart album that incorporates some *additional* criteria, like "Rating is greater than 4 stars.")

Hide them all at once

Here's another sneaky hidden iPhoto command. Open the Photos menu and then hold down your Control key. The new Hide Flagged Photos command appears. When you choose it (or just press Control-⌘-L), iPhoto designates all of your flagged photos as hidden (page 51).

Move them all to the Trash

The parade of sneaky hidden iPhoto commands never stops. If you open the Photos menu and hold down the Control key, you also get the "Move Flagged to Trash" command, which does just what it says.

Searching for Photos by Text

The flagging mechanism described above is an adequate way to *tag* photos, but there are other ways, too. For example, the name you give a picture might be significant; its original file name on the hard drive might be important; and maybe you've typed some helpful clues into its Description field or given its Event a meaningful name.

Finding that kind of information is the purpose of the Search icon (Q) at the bottom left of the iPhoto toolbar. Start by selecting the container you want to search—the Event, album, folder, or whatever—and then proceed as shown in Figure 3-2.

Tip: iPhoto can search your photos' *metadata*, too–the photographic details like camera manufacturer, f-stop, flash status, exposure settings, and so on. But you don't use the Search box for that; you have to create a smart album instead, as described on page 62.

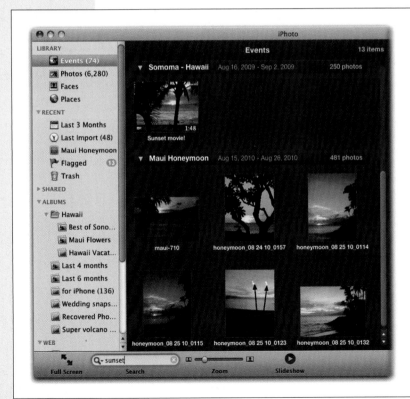

Figure 3-2:
Click the Q at the bottom of the iPhoto window to open the Search box. As you type, iPhoto hides all pictures except the ones that have your typed phrase somewhere in their titles, keywords, descriptions, Faces, Places, file names, or Event titles. In this case, the word "sunset" appears somewhere in every photo. (To cancel your search and reveal all the pictures again, click the ❸ at the right end of the Search box.)

Keep in mind that iPhoto restricts the search to the currently selected container. For example, if you want to search all your Events, make sure you don't have any Events selected when you trigger the search.

The Calendar

iPhoto offers a long list of ways to find certain photos: visually, by Event, by album, by searching for text in their names or comments, and so on. But it also offers what seems like an obvious and very natural method of finding specific pictures: by consulting a calendar.

After all, you might not know the file names of the pictures you took during your February 2010 trip to Poughkeepsie, and you might not have filed them away in an album. But one thing's for sure: You know darn well you were there in February of 2010 because it was cold! The iPhoto calendar can help you find those pictures fast.

To use the calendar, start by selecting the container you want the calendar to search: an album or folder, for example, or one of the Library or Recent icons.

Next, click the ९ icon and then make the calendar appear by clicking the tiny ९ button at the left edge of the Search box. From the pop-up menu, choose Date (Figure 3-3).

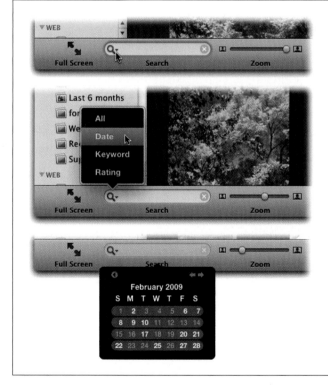

Figure 3-3:
Top: If you click the ९ in iPhoto '11's toolbar, you'll see the Search field shown here, and its little pop-up menu.

Middle: To make the calendar appear, choose Date.

Bottom: Click a day, week, month, or year on the calendar to round up only the photos taken in those time intervals.

The little calendar may look small and simple, but it holds a lot of power—and, if you look closely, a lot of different places to click.

For example, the calendar offers both a Year view (showing 12 month buttons) and a Month view (showing 28 to 31 date squares). Click the tiny triangle in the calendar's upper-left corner to switch between these two views. You can also use the tiny ← and → buttons in the upper-right corner to move through months or years (depending upon which view you've chosen). And you can double-click a month's name (in Year view) to open the month, or double-click the month title in Month view ("March 2011") to return to Year view.

Here's how you can use the calendar to pinpoint photos taken in a certain time period:

- **Photos in a certain month**. See the names of the months in Year view? The names in bold white type are the months when you took some photos. Click a boldfaced month to see the thumbnails of those photos; they appear in the main viewing area. (To scroll to a different year, click ← and → buttons at the top right of the calendar, as shown in Figure 3-3.)

- **Photos on a certain date**. In Year view, the calendar changes to show you the individual dates within each month. As you scroll through the months, bold white type lets you know that photos are waiting. Click a date square to see the photos you took that day. (Here again, the arrows above the calendar let you scroll to different months.)

- **Photos in a certain week**. Once you've drilled down into Month view, as described above, you can round up the photos taken during an entire week: Just double-click the week in question. iPhoto highlights the horizontal week bar of the calendar, and the photos taken during any of those seven days appear in the main viewing area.

It's possible to develop some fancy footwork when you work with this calendar, since, as it turns out, you can select more than one week, month, or day at a time. In fact, you do that using exactly the same keyboard shortcuts that you would use to select individual photo thumbnails. For example:

- You can select **multiple adjacent time units** by clicking the first and then Shift-clicking the last. For example, in Year view, you can select all the photos from June through August by first clicking June, and then Shift-clicking August. (You can use the same trick to select a series of days or weeks in Month view.)

Tip: Alternatively, you can just drag the mouse across the dates in Month view or the months in Year view to select consecutive time periods.

- You can select **multiple time units that *aren't* adjacent** by ⌘-clicking them. For example, in Month view, you can select November 1, 5, 12, 20, and 30 by ⌘-clicking those days. In the photo-viewing area, you see all the photos taken on all of those days combined.

- Here's an offbeat shortcut that might actually be useful someday: You can round up all the photos taken during a specific month, week, or day *from every year in your collection* by holding down the Option key as you select.

  For example, you can round up six years' worth of Christmas shots by Option-clicking the December button in Year view. Or you can find the pictures taken every year on your birthday (from all years combined) by Option-clicking that date in Month view.

Apple really went the extra mile on behalf of shortcut freaks when it designed the calendar. Here are a few more techniques that you probably wouldn't stumble upon by accident:

- In Year view, select all the days in a month by double-clicking the month's name. In Month view, you can do the same by triple-clicking any date.

- Return to Year view by quadruple-clicking any date, or by clicking the month's name.

- Skip ahead to the next month or year (or the previous month or year) by turning the scroll wheel on your mouse, if you have one.

- Deselect anything that's selected in the calendar by clicking any empty spot in the calendar.

Once you've made a date selection, faint gray type in the Search box reminds you of the date range you've selected.

Tip: Once you've made an initial date selection, you can reopen the calendar by clicking inside the Search box; you don't have to fuss with the little pop-up menu beside it.

In any case, you can close the calendar and return to seeing *all* your pictures by clicking the ✖ at the right end of the Search box.

Keywords

Keywords are descriptive words—like Family, Vacation, or Fido—that you can use to label and categorize your photos, regardless of which album or Event they're in.

The beauty of keywords in iPhoto is that they're searchable. Want to comb through all the photos in your library to find every closeup taken of your children during summer vacation? Instead of browsing through multiple photo albums, just perform an iPhoto search for photos containing the keywords Kids, Vacation, Closeup, and Summer. You'll have the results in seconds.

Note: The next chapter explains how to tag your photos with the names of the people in them or the locations where the photos were taken. Needless to say, you can also search for names and places in iPhoto '11.

Editing Keywords

Apple offers you a few sample entries in the Keywords list to get you rolling: Favorite, Family, Kids, and so on. But these are intended only as a starting point. You can add as many new keywords as you want—or delete any of Apple's—to create a meaningful, customized list.

Start by popping into Photos view—either click Photos in your Source list or double-click an Event. Then choose Window→Manage My Keywords, or just press ⌘-K. The weird and wonderful Keywords window shown in Figure 3-4 appears.

Then, to add, delete, or rename keywords, click Edit Keywords. Proceed as shown in Figure 3-4.

Note: As usual in iPhoto, you can select multiple keywords for deletion by Shift-clicking or (for nonconsecutive selections) ⌘-clicking them in the list before clicking the minus sign at the bottom of the dialog box to remove them. When you remove a keyword from the list, iPhoto also removes that keyword from any pictures you've applied it to.

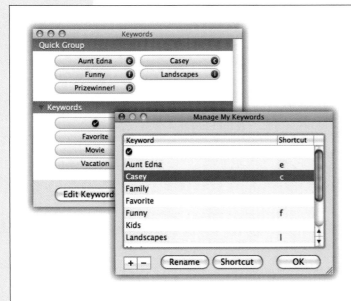

Figure 3-4:
Left: Behold the Keywords window, with clickable buttons for applying keywords. The first time you open this window, you won't see anything in the Quick Group section at the top, but as soon as you add keywords of your own, they'll appear there automatically.

Right: This window appears when you click Edit Keywords. Click + to create a new list entry called "untitled," ready to be edited. Type your new keyword name, and then press Return. iPhoto automatically chooses a one-letter keyboard shortcut for the new keyword (usually the first letter of the word), which lets you apply that keyword without having to fuss with the Keywords window.

Double-click an existing keyword to rename it. Click in the Shortcut column to designate or change a keyword's keystroke.

Be careful about renaming keywords after you've started using them; the results can be messy. If you've already applied the keyword Fishing to a batch of photos but later decide to replace it with Romantic in your keyword list, all the Fishing photos automatically inherit the keyword Romantic. Depending on you and your interests, this may not be what you intended.

It may take some time to develop a really good master set of keywords. The idea is to assign labels that are general enough to apply across your entire photo collection—but specific enough to be meaningful when you conduct searches. You might find it helpful to think of adding keywords as attaching who, what, or where info to your photos. (iPhoto knows the "when" because that info is captured by your camera.)

Here's a general rule of thumb: Use *albums* to group pictures for specific projects—a book, a slideshow, or a web page, for example. Use *Events* to group pictures by time or event. And use *keywords* to focus on general characteristics that are likely to appear throughout your entire photo collection—words like Concerts, Humor, Soccer, Motorcycling, Beaches, and Sci-Fi Conventions.

Note: In previous versions of iPhoto, keywords were a great way to track people. These days, the Faces feature does a much better job of that, so it's redundant to assign keywords that essentially do the same thing.

Suppose your photo collection includes a bunch of photos that you shot during a once-in-a-lifetime trip to Rome last summer. You might be tempted to assign *Rome* as a keyword—don't. Why? Because you probably won't use it on anything other than that one set of photos. It would be smarter to use Places to create a smart album called "Trip to Rome" to hold all those Rome pictures. Then use your keywords to tag the same pictures with descriptors like Travel or Ancient Ruins.

It also might be useful to apply keywords that describe attributes of the photos themselves, such as Closeup, Landscape, Portrait, or Sunsets.

Note: iPhoto automatically creates the checkmark keyword. It's just a little checkmark that, when applied to your thumbnails, can mean anything you want. In fact, it works *exactly* like the flag feature described earlier in this chapter.

The only reason the checkmark keyword still exists, in fact, is to provide compatibility with previous versions of iPhoto, to accommodate people who used to use the checkmark keyword for purposes now much better served by the flag.

Assigning and Unassigning Keywords

You can apply as many keywords as you like to an individual photo. So a picture of your cousin Rachel at a hot-dog-eating contest in London might bear all these keywords: Relatives, Travel, Food, Humor, and Medical Crises. Later, you'll be able to find that photo no matter which of these categories you use for hunting.

iPhoto offers three ways to apply keywords: the mouse way, the keyboard way, and the *other* keyboard way.

- **Mouse method**. Open the Keywords window by pressing ⌘-K. Highlight the photo(s) you want to bless with a keyword, and then click the appropriate keyword-button in the Keywords window.

- **Keyboard method, with Keywords window**. Open the Keywords window by pressing ⌘-K. Highlight the photo(s) you want to bless with a keyword, and then press the keyboard shortcut letter for the keyword you want to apply (V for Vacation, for example).

Note: When you use the two methods listed above, you get visual feedback that the keyword was actually applied—it appears briefly in the center of the photo-viewing area, like the informational overlays described on page 75.

- **Keyboard method, with Info panel**. Choose View→Keywords and then open the Info panel by clicking the Info icon in iPhoto's toolbar. Then proceed as shown in Figure 3-5.

Note: If you import photos from your hard drive into iPhoto, they may come with keywords you didn't assign. The additional blurbs came from the program you used to import the photos from your camera to your computer. For example, both Adobe Lightroom and Photoshop Elements automatically assign keywords (like Raw, Blurry, Closeup, Longshots, and so on) when they're importing and analyzing images. Since that info is stored inside your photo as part of its EXIF data (see the box on page 72), those keywords come along for the ride into iPhoto '11.

To unassign a keyword you've applied, just repeat the steps you used to assign it, or open the Info panel, click the keyword, and then press the Delete key. If you've got the Keyword window open, you see the keyword appear in red in your photo-viewing area. It even "explodes" with the same graphical animation you see when you remove an icon from your Mac's Dock.

Keyboard Shortcuts

The business of applying keywords using keyboard shortcuts makes the whole keyword business a lot faster and easier.

You can let iPhoto choose one-letter keystrokes for your keywords automatically, or you can make them up yourself:

- **To have iPhoto assign shortcuts:** In the Keywords window, drag your most frequently used keywords up into the Quick Group. As you can see at left in Figure 3-4, iPhoto automatically assigns each one to a letter key. (It uses the first letter of the keyword. If that's already assigned to another keyword, it uses the *second* letter. And so on.)
- **To assign shortcuts yourself:** For more control, open the Keywords window, and then click Edit Keywords. Double-click in the Shortcut column and then press the letter key you want to assign. (iPhoto lets you know if you pick a key that's already in use.)

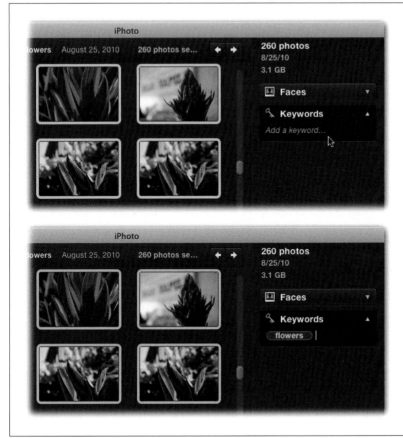

Figure 3-5:
Top: To add a keyword in the Info panel, first select a photo (or photos). Next, click the flippy triangle to the right of the word Keywords to expand that section (if it's not already expanded) and then click "Add a keyword."

Bottom: Begin typing the keyword you want to assign or press its keyboard shortcut; iPhoto completes the typing for you. Press Return to accept the suggestion. If you like, you can type the beginning of another keyword to assign more than one.

Warning: There's a keyboard shortcut for splitting Events while you're in Events view, and it's the letter S. That means if you (or iPhoto) assigns S as a keyword keyboard shortcut (say, for the keyword "sunset"), you need to make sure the Keywords window is open, or you'll wreak Event-splitting havoc.

Viewing Keyword Assignments

Once you've tagged a few pictures with keywords, you can see those keywords in either of two ways:

- **Open the Keywords window**. When you select a photo, its assigned keyword checkboxes light up in the Keywords list.

- **Choose View→Keywords, or press Shift-⌘-K, and then open the Info panel**. Click the little triangle to the right of the word Keywords to expand that section (if it isn't already expanded) and iPhoto lists the keywords you've assigned. (You can see the result in Figure 3-5, bottom.)

There's no way to view keywords below the photo thumbnails in iPhoto '11. If you used that feature in previous versions as a way to spot photos that didn't have keywords, you can use a smart album instead. This technique is explained in the box at the bottom of this page.

Using Keywords

After you've tagged photos with keywords, the big payoff for your diligence arrives when you need to get your hands on a specific set of photos, because iPhoto lets you *isolate* them with one quick click.

Start by clicking the ⚲ icon at the bottom of the iPhoto window, and then click the tiny magnifying glass inside the search field. (This icon usually looks like this: ⚲.) In the list that appears, click Keyword.

A little palette of all your keywords appears, and here's where the fun begins. When you click one of the keyword buttons, iPhoto immediately rounds up all the photos labeled with that keyword, displays them in the photo-viewing area, and hides all your other images.

Tip: If you point to one of these buttons without clicking, a pop-up balloon tells you *how many* photos have been assigned that keyword.

WORKAROUND WORKSHOP

Finding Photos That Don't Have Keywords

In previous versions of iPhoto, you could choose View→Keywords to make keywords appear below their thumbnails. To the dismay of many, that feature isn't in iPhoto '11, which makes it tough to find photos that don't have keywords.

The good news is that there's a workaround.

To find all the photos that don't have keywords, choose File→New→Smart Album and name it "No keywords." Then set the pop-up menus to "Keyword," "is," and "None," and then click OK. iPhoto scours your entire library for photos that don't have any keywords applied and plops them into your new smart album. The next time you've got a hankering to go keywordin', those photos will be waiting for you. And as soon as you add a keyword, they'll dutifully remove themselves from the Smart Album.

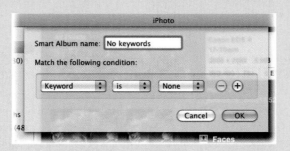

Here are the important points to remember when using iPhoto's keyword searches:

- To find photos that match multiple keywords, click additional keyword buttons. For example, if you click Travel and then click Holidays, iPhoto reveals all the pictures that have *both* of those keywords. To find photos that have *either* keyword (but not necessarily both), Shift-click the keyword buttons instead.

  Every button stays "clicked" until you click it a second time; you can see two keyword buttons "lit up" in Figure 3-6.

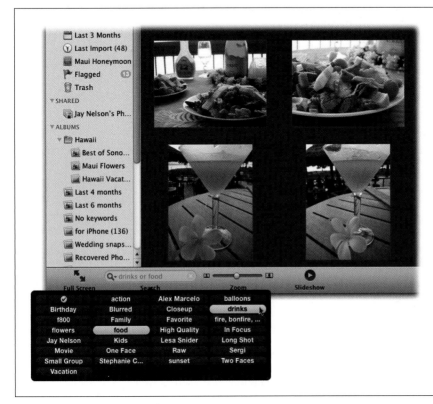

Figure 3-6:
As you click keyword buttons, iPhoto hides all photos except the ones that match. The gray lettering in the Search box identifies, in words, what you're seeing. In this example, the keyword Food was clicked first, and then Drinks was Shift-clicked, which is why the search field says "drinks or food."

- Suppose you've rounded up all your family pictures by clicking the Family keyword. The trouble is, your ex-spouse is in half of them, and you'd really rather keep your collection pure.

  No problem: *Option*-click the Ex-Spouse keyword button. iPhoto obliges by removing all photos with that keyword from whatever is currently displayed. In other words, Option-clicking a keyword button means "Find photos that don't contain this keyword." (In that case, the Search box says, in faint gray lettering, "Vacation and *not* Casey," or whatever.)

- You can confine your search to a single album by selecting it before searching. Similarly, clicking the Event (or Recent) icon in the Source list before searching means you want to search that photo collection. You can even select multiple albums and search only in those.

- In the Search box, click ✖ to restore the view to whatever you had visible before you performed the search.

Tip: Want even more flexibility when it comes to assigning and managing keywords? Check out Keyword Manager, a plug-in that uses iPhoto's internal keyword system, but gives you faster ways of assigning them. You also get the ability to create sub-keywords (for example, Boulder could be a sub-keyword for Colorado, and so on). You can download it at *www.bullstorm.se*. (Plug-ins are described in Chapter 12.)

Ratings

iPhoto offers another great way to categorize your pictures: by how great they are! You can assign each picture a rating of one to five stars and then use the ratings to sort your library, or gather only the cream of the crop into a slideshow, a smart album, or a photo book.

Note: Why, you might ask, would you bother to rate your photos if you just spent hours giving them all keywords? To give yourself another level of filtering. By using a smart album, you can filter your photos by keyword *and* rating find the best photos of a subject or place even faster.

Here's how you can rate your digital masterpieces:

- Select a photo (or several) and then choose Photos→My Rating; from the submenu, choose from one through five stars. You can even do this while you're editing a single photo.

- If you're not a mousy sort of person, you can perform the same stunt entirely from the keyboard, which is handy in iPhoto '11's new Full Screen view (page 53). Press ⌘-1 to assign a rating of one star, ⌘-2 for two stars, and so on. Press ⌘-0 to strip away any existing ratings.

- Choose View→Ratings and then hover your cursor over a photo's thumbnail; you see little hollow stars appear beneath it. Figure 3-7 (top) explains how to assign ratings this way.

- Click the ▼ in the lower-right corner of any photo to summon the shortcut menu shown in Figure 3-7, bottom. Under the Rotate, Hide, and Trash icons, click the star for the rating you want to apply.

- To remove a rating, select the photo and then choose Photos→My Rating→None. You're saying, in effect, "This photo has not yet been rated." Keyboard shortcut: ⌘-0.

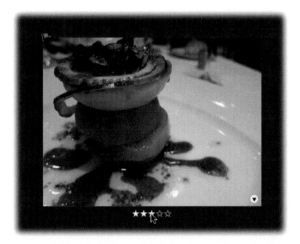

Figure 3-7:
*Top: By choosing
View→Ratings, you
can see the star rat-
ings you've assigned
to each photo and, if
you point to a thumb-
nail without clicking,
iPhoto produces a
row of hollow stars
you can use to rate
that photo. Click the
star that represents
the rating you'd like
to bequeath. For
example, to apply a
three-star rating, click
the third star (you
don't have to click
each individual star).
To remove the rating,
click just left of the
first star.*

*Bottom: The stars in
this shortcut menu
work the same way—
just click the star for
the rating you want
to apply, or click to
the left of the stars to
take the rating away.*

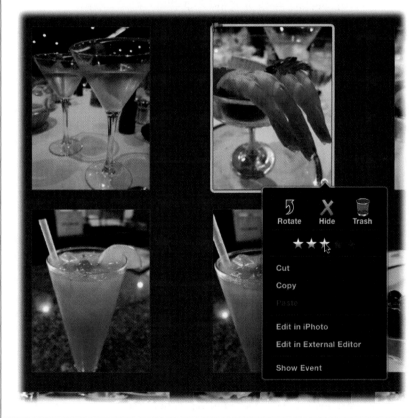

Once you've rated your photos, you can make that effort pay off in any number of ways:

- **Sort by ratings.** Choose View→Sort Photos→By Rating. iPhoto displays all of the thumbnails in the current Event in ratings order. If the View→Sort Photos→Ascending option is checked, then the worst photos (no stars or one star) appear at the top, and the best ones (five stars) at the bottom. Choose View→Sort Photos→Descending to put the five-star prize-winners at the top.

- **Find by ratings.** You can round up all of the five-star photos in the current container (Event, album, whatever) by clicking the Search box at the bottom of the window, using the ۹ pop-up menu to choose Rating, and then clicking the fifth star. All your photos except the ones with five stars are temporarily hidden. (Of course, you can use the same technique to find the one-, two-, three-, or four-star photos.) Click the ✖ button to unhide all photos.

- **Create a smart album of the best.** You can easily create a living, self-updating smart album that contains your best work at all times. After all, you never know when the Popular Photography contest-committee judges might come ringing your doorbell. Page 63 has the details.

Faces and Places

i Photo gives you plenty of ways to organize your pictures into neat little collections. But until the '09 version came along, the only way to organize everything was manually. Manually apply keywords. Manually drag things into albums. Drag, drag, drag.

Now it's all different. iPhoto comes with two features that organize your photos *automatically*. You'd call it artificial intelligence if it didn't seem so much like *real* intelligence.

One of them uses face recognition to group your photos based on who's in them. It can be extremely handy when, say, you need to quickly round up a bunch of pictures of Chris for that last-minute, surprise-party slideshow. This isn't the crude sort of face recognition that you find in lesser photo programs or even in digital cameras, which can tell you only *if* there's a face in the picture. iPhoto attempts to go a step further and tell you *whose* face it is.

You can also round up photos based on *where* they were taken. You can compare various trips to Paris, for example, or show friends what else you did in Chicago besides go to a White Sox game.

Meet Faces and Places, two iPhoto features that have become favorites of people who really want to get to the who and the where of their photos.

Faces

Here's the Faces feature in a nutshell: By analyzing the unique properties of each face in each photo—distance between the eyes, nose, mouth, hair color, lack of hair, and so on—iPhoto attempts to distinguish among the people in the photos of your library and group them into piles. (Once the setup process is complete, you'll see these piles when you click the Faces icon in your Source list.)

iPhoto makes a first pass at this automatically, which is pretty amazing.

It's not a perfect process, however; after its initial pass, iPhoto requires you to review each photo and confirm its subject's identity. (It's easy and fun!)

Thereafter, you can click the Faces icon in the Source list to see that iPhoto has grouped your photos by *the people in them*.

Step 1: Analysis

When you upgrade from an earlier version, iPhoto '11 doesn't waste any time. The first time you run it, the program upgrades your photo library (page 11)—and gets to work searching all your images for human faces.

Note: Depending on the number of photos you're importing, iPhoto may take quite some time to perform its initial face hunt.

This part of the Faces setup doesn't require any effort from you, and it happens each time you import photos.

After completing its scan, iPhoto has a good idea of what your social circle looks like. But it still has no idea what those people's names are, as you can see in Figure 4-1.

Note: If iPhoto doesn't detect any faces in your photos, you see an empty corkboard with a note about getting started. If you've been using Faces in the previous version of iPhoto, you see a corkboard with a slew of Polaroid-style headshots with names underneath (shown in Figure 4-3).

Tagging Faces Automatically

Now that iPhoto has done its face-detection dance, it's time to introduce it to your friends and family. Once you label a face, the program looks around and tries to match it up with other similar faces in the library. The whole face-tagging process is incredibly simple:

1. **Click Faces in your Source list.**

   iPhoto displays thumbnails of a few faces it found in your library.

2. **Click the "unnamed" label below a thumbnail and type the person's name, and then press Return.**

   While you can type any name you want—like *Dad* or *Uncle Robin*—it's a good idea to stick with the person's real name, as iPhoto automatically tries to match it with the contents of your Address Book, as shown in Figure 4-2. This is especially important in iPhoto '11 because it makes emailing from *within* iPhoto fast and easy (Chapter 8).

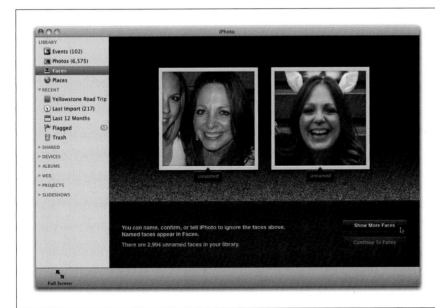

Figure 4-1:
If you've never used Faces before, this is the first screen you'll see. Now that iPhoto has plowed through your photo library detecting faces in your pictures, you can start telling it to whom those faces belong... all 2,994 of 'em.

Tip: To enter names more quickly, skip the mouse and just use your keyboard. Name one thumbnail and then press the Tab key to move to the next one's naming area. (To go backwards—say, if you accidentally skipped a thumbnail or you named it incorrectly—press Shift-Tab instead.) Enter another name and then press Tab to highlight the Show More Faces button, and then press Return to move on to the next set of thumbnails.

You can also use the keyboard to confirm names: Press Tab to highlight the naming area and then press Return to confirm the name (the ✓ has a little blue circle around it). To tell iPhoto it made a mistake, press Tab again, and when you see a little blue circle around the ✗, press Return.

Here are a few things to remember as you're naming faces:

- **Focus on naming photos that have a clear, frontal view of the person**. iPhoto will try to match other pictures in the library with this initial one, and it works best when there's plenty of face to recognize.

- **Name faces in profile, too**. While it's important to name full-face photos, naming profile shots helps iPhoto recognize those, too.

- **Name faces of different ages**. If you've got several years worth of photos in your library, chances are that you'll have photos of the same person at a variety of ages.

- **Don't waste time naming blurry or poorly lit photos, or those with microscopic faces**. Each time you name a photo, iPhoto broadens its range of suggested photos for that person. Naming bad shots makes it harder for iPhoto to recognize people.

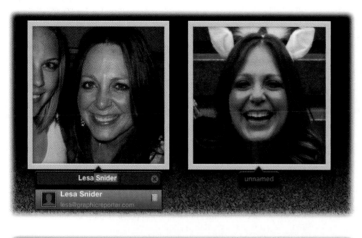

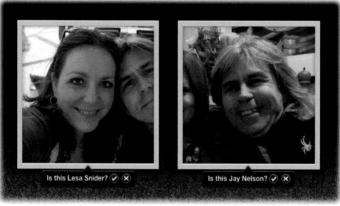

Figure 4-2:
Top: As soon as you begin typing a name, iPhoto tries to match it with the names in your Address Book. If the person isn't in your Address Book, feel free to type anything you want.

Bottom: As soon as you start tagging faces, iPhoto begins making suggestions for you. If iPhoto guesses correctly, click the ✓; if not, click the ✗ and enter a new name. The more faces you confirm, the better iPhoto will be at tagging them in other photos.

Note: iPhoto sometimes gets a little overzealous. It may tag faces in paintings, framed photos, statues, *Star Trek* action figures, or shadows on drapery. In these cases, point the cursor at the top-left corner of the thumbnail and click the ✗ to delete it, so you can go on tagging the actual humans in the shot. The thumbnail doesn't disappear, it just dims slightly. Theoretically, it won't show up as a face the next time you go tagging.

When you've had your fill of naming faces, click Continue to Faces at the bottom right of the iPhoto window. As shown in Figure 4-3, you now see a corkboard with Polaroid-style shots of each person you've tagged so far, labeled with the names you just assigned. It's like being the casting director in the movie of your life.

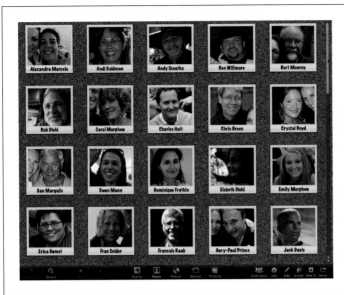

Figure 4-3:
As your list of names grows, more head-shots appear on your Faces corkboard. You can click the ▣ at the bottom left of your iPhoto window to make the corkboard take over your monitor, as shown here.

To see your pictures of each person, double-click a face. You can also use the slider near the bottom-left corner of the iPhoto window to increase or decrease the size and number of headshots in a row. To return to your Faces corkboard, press ⌘-left arrow or click All Faces at the top left of the main viewing area.

To continue naming and confirming faces, click the Find Faces icon at the bottom of the iPhoto window.

Tagging Faces Manually

If iPhoto fails to detect a face during import or rescan (see the box below)—a fairly rare occurrence—you can always tag it yourself. Start by selecting the photo and then opening the Info panel. In the panel, click the word Faces to expand that section and then click "Add a face," as shown in Figure 4-4.

Rescanning Photos for Missing Faces

New in iPhoto '11 is the ability to rescan photos for faces it may have missed during the import process. To do so, select the offending photo(s) using one of the techniques described on page 49, and then choose Photos→Detect Missing Faces. Over in your Source list, you see a tiny spinning ○ icon appear to the right of the word Faces to let you know that iPhoto is taking another look at your photos. To find more faces, iPhoto uses looser facial-recognition criteria, so you may end up with more objects tagged than people.

Once iPhoto is finished processing, you can see if it found anything by selecting one photo at a time, and then clicking the Info icon at the bottom of the iPhoto window. (If you only had one photo selected, the Info panel opens automatically.) If the search was successful, you see the additional names listed in the Faces portion of the Info panel, along with other detected-but-unknown faces labeled "unnamed"—just click to add a name.

If iPhoto *still* didn't find a face, you can point it out manually as shown in Figure 4-4.

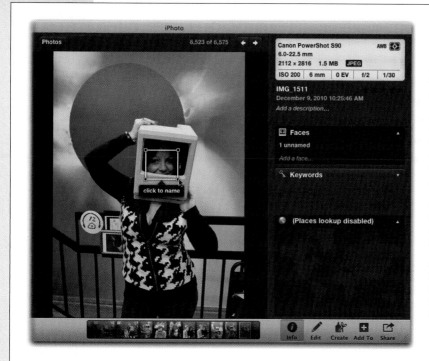

Figure 4-4:
If iPhoto can't find a face—say, because you've got an old Mac 512k box on your head!—click "Add a face" in the Info panel. When you do, iPhoto displays a little white square that you can resize and position around your subject's face. When you get it just right, click the text field below the square and type the person's name.

And yes, this kind of silliness really does take place at Mac User Group parties worldwide.

A fresh white square appears, which you can drag over onto that poor, undetected face. Drag the corners of the box to resize it. (Dragging a corner causes both sides of the box to change size, making it a little awkward to get perfectly centered over the face. To better control your box resizing, hold down the Option key as you drag a corner. This stops both sides of the box from moving around and lets you manipulate the size from just the corner you're dragging.)

When you've got the white square right where you want it, click the "click to name" balloon and type the real name of the person. Repeat as necessary with any other people you know in the picture.

Note: While it's not quite as sophisticated as the software the FBI and Interpol are using these days, the face-detection feature generally gets better the more you work with it. But there are still some cases when you'll have to plod through manually.

For example, the program may not recognize shaggy dogs as actually having faces, but you can sail through those pictures of Skipper and use the Info panel's "Add a face" link to add your pet to the Faces wall. Babies, identical twins, and people wearing sunglasses (or posing at odd angles) may also require manual intervention.

Adding More Pictures to a Name

Once you've put at least one name to a face, iPhoto's powers of recognition really kick in. Here's how to help it match up the rest of the names and faces:

1. **Double-click a person on the Faces corkboard.**

   iPhoto displays all the photos you've already tagged with this person's name. At the bottom of the window, you see a note telling you how many *other* pictures iPhoto thinks contain this same person.

2. **Just above the iPhoto toolbar, click Confirm Additional Faces.**

   The program now displays a screen full of tiles. Each tile contains a closeup of the lucky person's face, each culled from a different photo. The caption "click to confirm" appears beneath each one (Figure 4-5). This is your chance to tell iPhoto's face-detection software how it did.

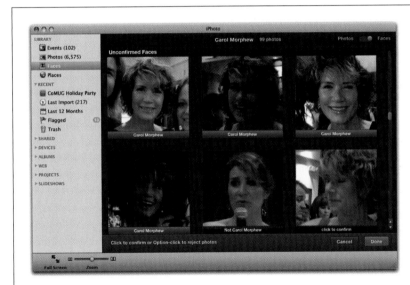

Figure 4-5:
You can give iPhoto a hand by confirming its correct guesses and rejecting its wrong ones. Photos above the gray bar (not shown) are confirmed pictures of this Face; photos below it are ones that iPhoto wants you to confirm (iPhoto lists them in order of certainty). Click a picture to confirm it, or Option-click to reject it. The more you work with iPhoto here, the better it gets at identifying people. However, if you come to a point where you're seeing more misses than hits, click Done and move on to confirming someone else's face.

3. **Click a photo once to confirm that iPhoto has correctly matched this face with the name.**

   When you click a face, the "click to confirm" bar turns green and displays the *name* of the person—for example, Chris. Behind the scenes, iPhoto learns from your selection. "Ah, OK—that's Chris," it says to itself. You've just helped it refine its recognition smarts for next time.

Tip: If most of the tiles contain the correct person, you can accept them all at once: Just drag the mouse over a whole batch of photos to select them and their captions will turn green.

---

4. **When you encounter a tile that shows somebody else—iPhoto has picked the wrong person—either Option-click it or double-click it.**

   The "click to confirm" banner turns red, and the text says, "Not Chris" (or whoever).

Tip: Here again, you can reject a whole bunch of tiles at once. This time, hold down the Option key as you drag the cursor over the faces.

---

5. **When you're finished accepting or rejecting tiles, click Done.**

   The more guidance you give iPhoto in identifying people in your photos, the more accurate it gets at recognizing them in new images. With enough input from you, the program has a better chance of telling babies and bald men apart, and even differentiating among your various bald friends.

Tip: To see the whole photo instead of a closeup of the face in question, drag the little slider in the upper-right corner of the iPhoto window to Photos; to switch back to viewing closeups, drag the slider to Faces.

Naming faces anytime

Any time you select Faces in your Source list, the Find Faces button appears on the iPhoto toolbar, even after your initial burst of face tagging. Click it to see the faces iPhoto has identified in your library, and then set about the task of naming them.

Even as you stroll around your photo library in Events or Photos view and come upon photos or people you want to add, the "Add a face" link awaits you in the Info panel, as shown on page 98. iPhoto is always trying to guess who the people in your life are. For example, if you open up a snapshot from that family reunion and click the Info button and then take a peek at the Faces pane, iPhoto will offer a guess if the face looks familiar.

You see the customary white square around the face, but instead of "unnamed" under it, you get a polite question like, "Is this Leroy?" (Figure 4-6).

If it is indeed Cousin Leroy, then click ✓ to confirm and add the picture to Leroy's Faces album. If iPhoto has guessed wrong, then click the ✗ and type in the name that does go with the face.

As you add more and more names to your Faces library, iPhoto tracks your typing and offers a drop-down list of potential, previously typed names (as well as names that are in your Mac OS X Address Book) that you can select from to save keystrokes. The top of Figure 4-7 shows an example.

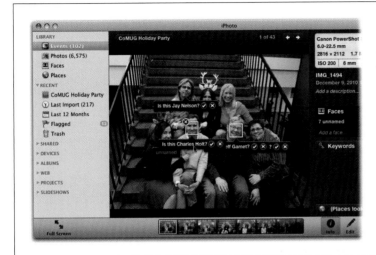

Figure 4-6:
If iPhoto recognizes someone it's seen before, it asks you to verify the person's identity. Click ✓ if iPhoto guessed the right name. Click the ✗ if iPhoto missed, and then type in the correct name for the person.

Tip: When naming or confirming names using the Info panel in Events or Photos view, you can click the ❯ next to the name on any face tag (Figure 4-7, bottom) to jump into that person's Faces album.

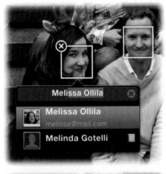

Figure 4-7:
Top: Once you tag a few faces, iPhoto builds a library of names. When you start typing to identify a face, the program cheerfully offers a list of past names as well as those from your Mac OS X Address Book. Click the correct name or hit the ▼ key until you get to it, and then press Return to select it.

Bottom: The ❯ after the name is your shortcut to the rest of this person's Faces album. Click it to jump there. Once you land, you can always confirm the name on a few more photos iPhoto thinks this person is in (page 99).

The Payoff

Between iPhoto's own analysis and your patient confirmation of faces, you gradually refine the Faces feature.

Eventually, you wind up with a whole array of mugshots on the Faces corkboard (click Faces in the Source list), as shown back in Figure 4-3 (page 97). The next time you need to gather pictures of Suzy, just double-click her Polaroid on your Faces corkboard; iPhoto displays closeups of all the photos she's in. (To see the whole photo instead of her face, drag the little slider at the top right of your window to Photos instead of Faces.) This kind of thing is a real time-saver when you need to, say, make that monthly book of grandchild pictures for your parents or a slideshow of your hubby's ever-evolving facial hair for his 50th birthday blowout.

To return to the corkboard array of faces, click All Faces at the top left of your iPhoto window.

You can also drag a corkboard snapshot directly into your Source list to create a smart album (see Figure 4-8). This album will eternally update itself, auto-adding any confirmed photos of the person that may enter your collection in the future. You can also drag a snapshot onto an existing Face-based smart album to make one that updates with *both* people—very convenient for corralling all those pics of the kids or the bowling team into one convenient place.

Deleting Faces

OK, you got a little excited by iPhoto's face-detection technology and tagged your annoying coworker Madge. Look, there she is on the Faces corkboard next to pictures of Mom. Yikes! Don't panic—if you want to remove a face from the wall, select it and press ⌘-Delete. iPhoto asks if you're sure you want to remove this person from Faces. If you are, then click Delete Face and wave goodbye.

If you want to zap multiple people off the wall at once, ⌘-click each undesired person, and then press ⌘-Delete. Again, iPhoto asks you to confirm your action. (If you want to delete a whole row of people, Shift-click the first and last faces in the row to select them *and* everyone in between.)

Note: Deleting a face from the Faces corkboard never deletes any pictures from your iPhoto library.

Adding More Details to a Face

In addition to neatly lining up mugshots of all your family and friends, the iPhoto Faces album helps you keep track of your pictures (and the people in them) in several other ways.

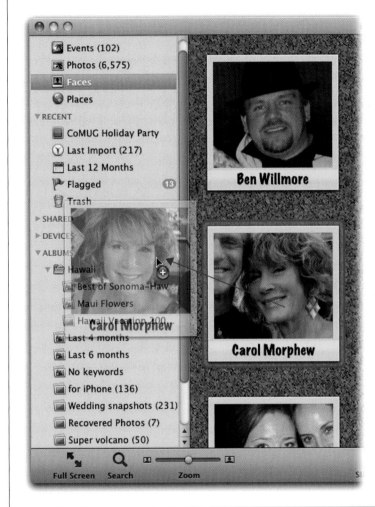

Figure 4-8:
Drag any snapshot onto a blank spot in your Source list, as shown here, to make a new smart album for that person. You can also drag a snapshot onto an existing smart album icon to make one that corrals photos of both people, which is handy for creating gift projects like books or calendars.

Click any face on the corkboard and then click the Info button on the iPhoto toolbar to open the Info panel. As Figure 4-9 shows, you see the number of photos (and range of photo dates) you have for this person, a spot to type the person's full name and email address, a map of where those photos were taken (if you've added that info), and how many photos might contain this person, should you decide to confirm them.

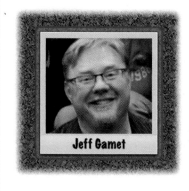

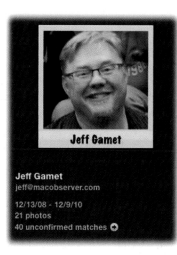

Figure 4-9:
Top: By selecting a face and then opening the Info panel, you can edit your buddy's name and email address.

Bottom: If you take the time enter the person's full name and email address here, any future photos you confirm in iPhoto and upload to Facebook will carry along the same tags. This gives you more time to do other stuff on Facebook, like SuperPoking your buddies.

Now, why would you want to add the person's email address here? No, it doesn't automatically add the photo to the appropriate entry in the Mac's Address Book program, or stick that photo onto incoming messages in Mail (although it would be very nice if Apple made that happen…*hint, hint*).

No, by giving you a place to add your friend's email address, you get to use iPhoto '11's new graphic email option that lets you send emails from *inside* iPhoto. The program is also banking that this same name and address are also used for your friend's account on Facebook, the social-networking site that is a gigantic time vacuum for over 500 million people. Later, when you post iPhoto pictures on your Facebook page, the name tags you've so carefully assigned go along for the ride, saving you the trouble of tagging them all over again in Facebook.

For more on merging your iPhoto and Facebook lives, skip to Chapter 8.

Organizing the Faces Album

Seeing your friends and family all lined up in Faces view gives you a glorious sense of organization. (A few years ago, those pictures would have been falling out of physical photo albums—or still in their envelopes from the drugstore and shoved into the back of a desk drawer!) But even on the corkboard, you can organize the faces still further.

Change the key photo

The key photo is the one that represents a person on your Faces corkboard; it's typically the first one you tagged (Figure 4-10). If that photo doesn't do your friend justice, there are at least three easy ways to change it:

- Click Faces in your Source list. As you slowly move the mouse pointer (don't click) over a face on the corkboard, all the tagged pictures of that person flit by in the frame. When you see the one you want to use, tap the space bar to set it as the key photo.

- Double-click the face to open up the album. Scroll through and select a photo you like better, and then choose Events→Make Key Photo. Even if it's a group shot from a distance, iPhoto is savvy enough to zoom in on the person's face.

- If you have a face-tagged photo selected, Control-click (or right-click) it, and then choose Make Key Photo from the shortcut menu shown in Figure 4-10.

UP TO SPEED

Smart Albums and Happy Faces

iPhoto's smart albums (page 62) are a terrific way to round up all the photos that meet a certain set of conditions—for example, all the ones you shot with a particular camera, or on a particular date. The names you apply to Faces can be smart albums conditions, too.

Say you're planning the Embarrassing Slideshow portion of your friend's birthday dinner. You need to find all the photos in your library that contain either Jeff or Erica, *and* photos with both Jeff and Erica together.

Choose File→New Smart Album (or press Option-⌘-N on the keyboard). Give the album a name, and then set up the pop-up menus to say "Face" and "is" and "Jeff." Click the + button to add another row, and then repeat the steps to add "Erica" as the name on the second line. Finally, choose Any from the Match pop-up menu near the top of the

dialog box (this option becomes available after you set at least two conditions).

When you click OK, a new smart album appears in your Source list containing all the photos you've ever tagged of Jeff and Erica, either together or apart, in one handy place. (Later, when you've *geotagged* your photos—see page 107—and want to add Place as a condition, too, you can even make an album of all the times you went skiing *in Colorado* with Jeff and Erica.)

You can also set up a smart album to corral all the pictures you haven't gotten around to face-tagging yet. Just choose File→New→Smart Album and call it something memorable, like "Untagged photos." Set up the pop-up menus to say "Face" and "is." In the last box, pick "Unnamed" and click OK to create a smart album of the great untagged.

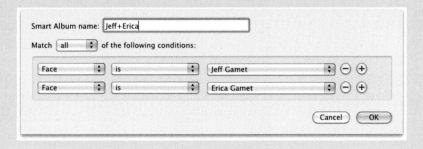

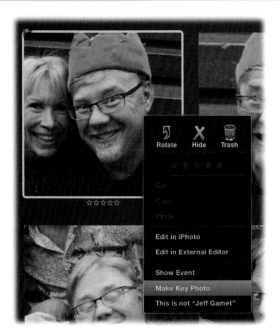

Figure 4-10:
The key photo represents the person on your Faces corkboard. One easy way to change it is to Control-click (or right-click) the photo you want to use and then choose Make Key Photo from the shortcut menu, as shown here.

An even faster method is to wave your mouse over their album to see what other pictures have been tagged to that name, and then tap the space bar when you see the one you want to use instead.

Rearrange the order

Would you like to put Mom and Dad together on the board, or get all your soccer team pals in a row? No problem; you can drag the Faces snapshots around on your corkboard, as Figure 4-11 illustrates.

Be careful where you drop that face, though. If you accidentally drop the person on somebody *else's* snapshot, you *merge* their two sets of photos, and iPhoto applies the wrong name to all of the faces in the pile you dropped. (If that happens, press ⌘-Z, the Undo command.)

Tip: Just as you can merge Events (page 40), you can merge Faces, too. Why would you want to? Well, say you make a typo in someone's name when tagging photos and inadvertently create two Faces for the same person. You can merge the two by dragging the snapshot of the Typo Name right onto the snapshot of the Correct Name and not have to rename a thing!

If it's too late for ⌘-Z, double-click the merged pile. Then click the Confirm Name button and reject (and eject) the wrong face out of the photo collection, as described on page 99. (Or Control-click each unwanted photo and choose "This is not [Name]" from the shortcut menu.)

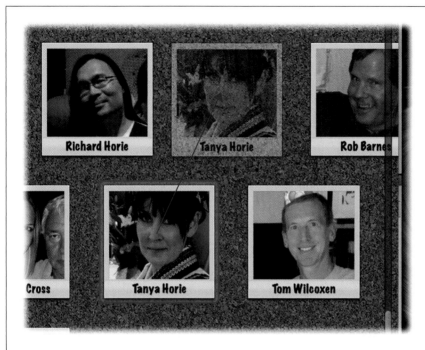

Figure 4-11:
Rearranging albums on your Faces board is a drag—literally. To move someone, drag their album to a new place on your corkboard and the other faces politely slide over to make room.

Tip: You can also organize the faces alphabetically, though by first name only. Choose View→Sort Photos→By Name. (That creates an A to Z order. You can also be contrary and go from Z to A; use the same menu and choose Descending.) Switching to name sorting, however, means you can't drag your pals around manually. At least not until you choose View→Sort Photos→Manually.

Edit names

Want to change the spelling or fix a typo in the name displayed on the corkboard key photo? Just click the name, and the gray box reappears, letting you type whatever you want. Clicking the ⊗ at the right of the little box automatically clears the existing text, but since clicking the name selects it anyway, you can just start typing right over the old name.

Places

Geotagging is the latest hot feature of digital photography. That's when your camera buries longitude and latitude coordinates into each picture it takes (invisibly, the same way it stamps the time and date) so you'll always be able to pinpoint where a picture was taken.

There are only two problems with this scenario.

First, very few cameras actually contain the necessary GPS circuitry to geotag your photos. Second, what happens after you geotag your photos? What are you going to do, say, "Oh, yes, I remember that romantic evening at +41° 30' 18.48" N, -81° 41' 55.08" W"?

iPhoto solves the second problem, at least. It translates those coordinates to the much more recognizable "Cleveland," or even more precisely, a street address, like "100 Alfred Lerner Way, Cleveland, Ohio" (which happens to be the address of Cleveland Browns Stadium)—and shows that spot with a red pin on a map right in iPhoto.

This can be really convenient if you've made several trips to London and want to see *all* the pictures taken there over the years, and not just ones from a particular album or Event. It's also a great way to learn geography—slideshows, books, and calendars take advantage of this info, and include themes that make a quick map of your trip.

Automatically Geotagging Photos

Your photos are probably geotagged when you shoot them if you're using one of the following gadgets:

- A digital camera with a built-in GPS chip, like the Nikon Coolpix P6000.

- A GPS-enabled cellphone, like a recent iPhone.

- The Eye-Fi Geo Card. It's a remarkable SD memory card, the kind you put into most camera models, with built-in wireless networking and a pseudo-GPS feature ($70 for a 4 GB card). See *www.eye.fi* for details.

- A small GPS-enabled box like the $90 ATP PhotoFinder that tracks the time and your coordinates as you snap photos—and marries them up with the time stamps on your pictures when you insert the camera's memory card. See *http://photofinder.atpinc.com* for more information.

If that's your situation, then all you have to do is import the pictures into iPhoto (page 13) and smile smugly. When the images appear in the viewing window, you can check the location by clicking the Info button on the iPhoto toolbar to open the Info panel shown in Figure 4-12.

In the Places section of the Info panel, you can see the location's name and a pin on a miniature Google map; if the map is generally correct, then iPhoto has done its job.

However, GPS coordinates can sometimes be off by yards. Or, if the place is wrong and you know it (because you forgot to turn on the Location Services function of your iPhone, for example), don't worry; You can *manually* assign the photo to a place, as described in the next section.

Manually Geotagging Photos

But what about photos that don't have geographical information embedded—like the 300 billion photos that have been taken with non-GPS cameras?

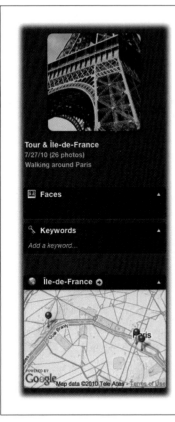

Figure 4-12:
Various tidbits appear in the Info panel's Places section, including the photo's name (probably something creative like IMG_4576.JPG), the date it was taken, and the place where the photo was snapped. Just click the little globe icon to see a tiny Google map bearing a red pin marking the spot where you took the photo. Neat!

If all the photos in an Event have been geotagged, you get a map with multiple pins showing the various locations, as shown here.

In that case, you can geotag them manually.

1. **Select a photo (or an Event) and then click the Info button on the iPhoto toolbar.**

    The Info panel opens to reveal several bits of information, including the name of the picture.

2. **Click "Assign a Place" and start typing the name of the town, city, or landmark (like *Washington Monument*) where the picture was taken.**

    As shown in Figure 4-13, a pop-up menu appears; iPhoto is trying to guess what you're typing, to save you some effort (and spelling). If you see the location in the list, use the arrow keys on the keyboard to select it and then press Return to confirm your choice, or just click the correct location in the list.

Tip: If, by some bizarre occurrence, you have the latitude and longitude of your location, you can enter those numbers instead of a name. Click "Assign a Place" and then type the coordinates separated by a comma, such as *38, −9* (the latitude always goes first). A pop-up menu appears with iPhoto's guess as to where on the map those coordinates actually are.

---

3. **If the place you're typing doesn't appear on the list, pick one that's close and then move the marker pin.**

   Unlike the previous version of the program, iPhoto '11 doesn't have a "Find on Map" option, mainly because you don't need it. In the off chance that iPhoto *and* Google can't find your location, just pick a spot that's close. Then, click the red pin on the little map and drag it to the correct location, as Figure 4-14 shows.

Note: You can only move marker pins using the tiny map in the Info panel; you can't move them when you're looking at the big map in Places view.

When You Don't Feel Like Sharing

I'm all for having machines do things for me automatically, but what if I don't want iPhoto revealing where my iPhone pictures were snapped?

These days, privacy concerns run deep; sometimes, you may not want iPhoto blabbing about where you've been.

If this is the case, you have a couple of options. The first one—if you remember to do it in time—is to turn off the GPS feature on your camera or camera-phone. On the iPhone, for example, go to the Home screen and tap your way through Settings→General→Location Services→Off. (Just remember to turn Location Services back on again the next time you want to use Maps or another location-aware app.)

Second, you can tell iPhoto itself not to look up the GPS coordinates embedded in the file. Choose iPhoto→Preferences (or press ⌘-comma) and then click the Advanced icon. In

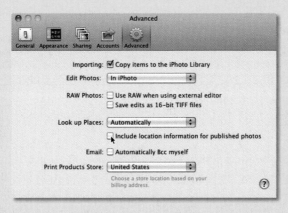

the "Look up Places" pop-up menu, change Automatically to Never, and then click OK.

Also, new in iPhoto '11 is the option to have iPhoto keep locations secret for *published* photos only (those you send off to photo-sharing websites like Facebook, Flickr, and so on). If that sounds more agreeable, you can leave the "Look up Places" menu set to Automatically and then turn off "Include location information for published photos" underneath it.

However, if you're part of the Witness Protection Program, you might want to *delete* location information that's already been added to a photo or Event. Just click the Info icon in the iPhoto toolbar to summon the Info panel and then click Places to expand that section. Then click the location tag and click the ⊗ to its right, shown in Figure 4-14. To delete location info for multiple photos or Events, just select them using the techniques described on page 49 first.

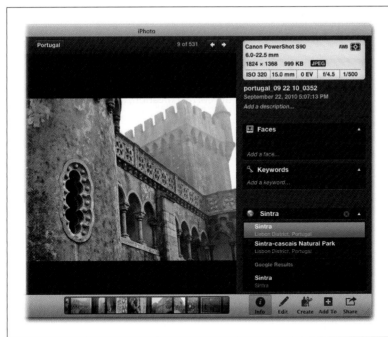

Figure 4-13:
As you type, iPhoto tries to guess where you're going.

If iPhoto can't find the location on its own maps, it tries to find the location using a Google search (which is why there's a Google Results entry in the list).

Tip: If you've accidentally relocated a photo taken in Paris, France to Paris, Texas, you can revert to the photo's original location by choosing Photos→Rescan for Location. This forgiving little menu item is new in iPhoto '11.

---

4. **When the pin is in the right spot, click the ⊘ next to the location tag to confirm it.**

   You can also refine and/or delete locations by choosing Window→Manage My Places. This command summons a list of all the places you've tagged in iPhoto—or captured by your GPS-enabled phone or camera—with a handy map that lets you move location pins to and fro, as well as reduce or widen the region of a particular pin using tiny left and right triangles that automatically appear to its right.

Renaming Places

The Geotagging photos approach is usually enough for most people. But if you want to add a personal touch to your locations, you can rename them in the Info panel.

Once iPhoto finds your location (or you find it yourself), click the marker pin to summon the location tag (the marker pin turns yellow). Once the tag appears, highlight it and then type a new name, such as *Grandma's House*. Click the ⊘ to confirm the new name (or just press Return). Later, you'll be able to use iPhoto's Search box to round up all the pictures that were taken at Grandma's House, just by typing *grandm*.

Tip: Once you've pinpointed the right location for a photo, you can copy that info to *other* photos. Just select the photo with the correct locale and then choose Edit→Copy. Next, select the photo(s) you want to copy the location to and then choose Edit→Paste Location. That's all there is to it.

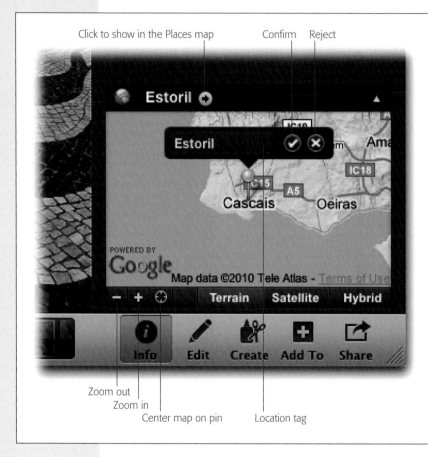

Click to show in the Places map   Confirm   Reject

Zoom out
Zoom in
Center map on pin   Location tag

Figure 4-14:
If you don't see your locale on the list, pick a place that's close and then fine-tune it by moving the pin on the map. Drag the pin to the correct location and then click the pin to rename it (it turns yellow). If you're lucky, iPhoto updates the location tag itself (in this example, iPhoto changed the location to Estoril), though in most cases you have to type the info in yourself.

You can zoom in and out of the map as needed with the buttons labeled here. You can also drag the map itself to see another area.

Adding Additional Info to a Photo or Event

As you may have noticed, the Info panel has room for more facts than just a photo's spot on the map. Here's a quick roundup of what the other controls shown in Figure 4-15 can do for you:

- **Rename the photo**. If you're tired of all your pictures being called IMG_this or DSC_that, then click the Name field near the top of the Info panel (below the white box) and type in a better title, like *Baby's first Jell-O parfait* or *Bath time!*

- **Rate the photo**. See those dark stars next to the photo's name? Drag your cursor mouse along them to add the number of stars you think the picture deserves. (See page 90 for details on ratings.)

- **Add a description**. Along with a better title, you can also add details about what's in the photo: "Stevie's first at-bat in the T-ball game" or "Toboggan accident Day 3." Just click where it says "Add a description" and start typing.

- **Zoom the map**. Just below the map, click the **+** and **−** buttons to zoom in and out of the image, anywhere from a closeup street view to a world map. (These controls appear when your cursor is on the map.)

- **View on the Places map**. Next to the location tag is a tiny arrow ➡ that you can click to see the location on iPhoto's Places map. (This tiny arrow is labeled back in Figure 4-14.)

- **Change the look of the map**. When you point to the tiny map, a row of labeled buttons appears near the bottom. They let you see the location three different ways: a cartographical Terrain view that shows street names and elevations, a Satellite view with an overhead photo of the area, or Hybrid—a combination of both.

Tip: Once you've geotagged your photos, you can use iPhoto's Search box to find them. First, click Events or a particular album in the Source list. Then, at the bottom of the iPhoto window, click the Search icon (🔍) and type what you're looking for, like *San Francisco* or *Wrigley Field*. Press Return to see your results.

Going Places with Places

Now that your photos are geotagged, detailed, and ready, it's time to see how they look in iPhoto's Places view. In the Source list, click Places. Or, if the Info panel is open, click ➡ in your photo's location tag (labeled back in Figure 4-14).

Tip: Once iPhoto knows where your pictures were taken—because you've geotagged them—that information is preserved if you upload the pictures to Flickr (page 205). That means your admirers will be able to see where you took those photos using Flickr's geotag maps—*if* you haven't turned off the new location privacy option in iPhoto '11's preferences, that is (see the box on page 110).

Map view

In the Places map view shown in Figure 4-16, a global map fills your screen, festooned with little red pins representing all the pictures you've geotagged. (If you click iPhoto '11's new Full Screen button, the map takes over your whole monitor!) To see the photos attached to a pin, point to that pin and click the ◉ next to the place's name.

Here are some ways to navigate the map:

- **Zoom in** by double-clicking a pin until you get as close as you want.

- **Zoom out** of the map by Control-clicking (or right-clicking) twice.

- **Zoom in or out** by dragging the slider near the bottom-left of the iPhoto toolbar.

- **If you want to travel more incrementally,** drag the map itself with the mouse to get to the part you want to see.

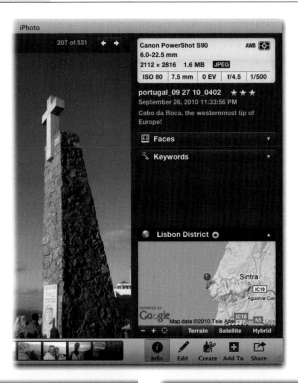

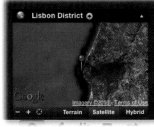

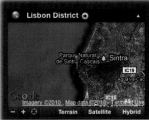

Figure 4-15:
Top: A photo's Info panel can store quite a bit of information about it—like names, dates, and ratings—which you can use for searching or making smart albums.

Bottom: You also get a choice of map styles, as shown here. The left image shows Satellite view, and the right Hybrid view (the top image shows Terrain view).

- **See all your pins on the map at once** by clicking the Home button at the top left of the iPhoto window (it looks like a little house).

- **See all the countries, states, cities, and places you've visited** by clicking the floating lists at the top of the map. These lists are new in iPhoto '11; they let you view photos by region, as discussed in the next section.

Along the top-right edge of the iPhoto window are buttons for the same three map types you can see in the Info panel's mini-map: Terrain, Satellite, and Hybrid (see Figure 4-15).

To see all the photos you've mapped, click the Show Photos button at the bottom of the iPhoto window.

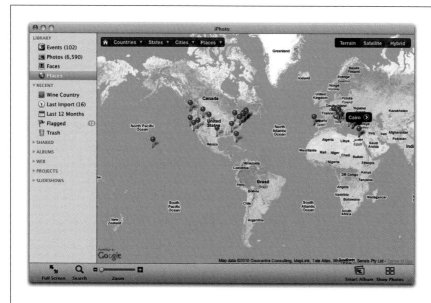

Figure 4-16:
Click the Home icon to see all your tagged locations in Places map view. Red pins mark every place on the map where you've got geotagged photos. Point to a pin to see the name of the location, and click the arrow next to it to see the photos themselves.

Tip: iPhoto '11 now understands *gestures*, those little motions you make atop your trackpad or Magic Mouse. For example, you can use two-finger zooming to zoom into iPhoto's maps, just as you can with (for example) Google Maps online. If your mouse has a scroll wheel, you can use it for zooming, too.

View photos by region

The map view is fun and all, but sometimes you want to see all your Places information grouped together in a good, old-fashioned list. Easy: Use the new floating lists at the top of the Places map, shown in Figure 4-17.

Note: These floating lists replace iPhoto '09's Browser view.

Longtime fans of iTunes should instantly recognize this look: a series of lists in the top part of the window, and the locations (countries, states, cities, or places—not songs) in each list underneath. Four columns appear in the top part of the window, breaking down each location into smaller and smaller subcategories.

As shown in Figure 4-17 (top), the left-hand column has the big overall location: the individual countries where you've tagged photos. As you move to the right, countries get divided into states or provinces, which get narrowed down to cities or towns (Figure 4-17, middle). It can get as specific as a street address or a landmark, if you've gone that far in your geotagging frenzy.

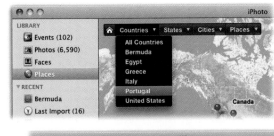

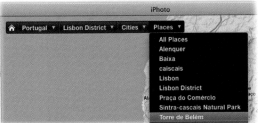

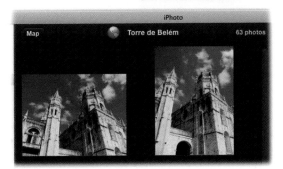

Figure 4-17:
It's like iTunes for pictures! These new floating lists let you see Places information by country, state/province, town, and even down to a landmark, making it easy to pull out all the photos from a certain location.

To see all the places you've pinned in Portugal, for example, click Portugal in the Countries column. To drill down to see all the photos taken in a particular city, click the city's name in the Cities column. Keep clicking across the columns to get to just the markers pinned in a certain town or location.

To see the photos pinned to a certain spot, click the pin and then click the tiny right-pointing arrow to its right (or click the Show Photos button in the iPhoto toolbar).

Places for Your Smart Albums

Want a self-updating album of all the photos in a certain state or city? Smart albums (page 62) play nice with Places, too. Setting up a location-aware smart album is easier than ever in iPhoto '11, as long as you have an Internet connection to keep the map info flowing from Google.

To set up a smart album based on location, follow these steps:

1. **In your Source list, click Places and then click the Home button at the upper left of the map.**

    Your own personal map of the world appears, complete with a red pin for every location you've tagged in a photo.

2. **Find the location you want using the floating region columns, or drill down through the lists until you find a specific location. Then click its red pin.**

If you're making a smart album to contain all the photos you've ever taken in Italy, choose it from the Country list (Figure 4-18).

If you're making a smart album based on Florence, you can drill down through the other region lists until you find a marker pin for Florence, and then click it. In a big blast of colorful contrast, the red pin turns yellow.

3. **Click the Smart Album icon at the bottom of the window.**

   A fresh, new smart album appears in the Source list based on the pins shown on your map, sporting the name of the location you just chose.

Tip: To make a smart album based on multiple locations, zoom in until the map shows all the pinned places you want to include. Then click the Smart Album button in the iPhoto toolbar to make a self-updating album that includes photos from all those places. It appears in the Source list under an unwieldy name like "United Kingdom, France and more" but you can click to rename it something a little catchier, like "Europe."

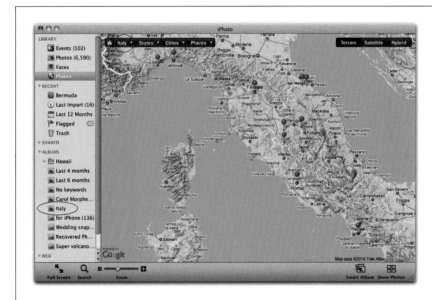

Figure 4-18:
To make a smart album based on a country, you can use iPhoto '11's new floating region lists. Simply choose a country (or state, or city) and then click the Smart Album button in the iPhoto toolbar.

Over in your Source list, you'll find a new smart album named after the country you chose.

If you don't happen to be online at the time (*the horror!*), you can still set up a smart album without looking at the map:

1. **Option-click the Create button in the iPhoto toolbar. From the shortcut menu, choose Smart Album.**

   The Smart Album sheet slides down from the top of the iPhoto window.

2. **Type a name for the album. Set up the pop-up menus to say "Place" and "contains." In the remaining box, type the location you want to use, like *Texas* or *Grand Canyon*, and then click OK.**

Your new smart album rounds up all the photos that match the Place criteria you entered. It also keeps an eye out for photos with matching geotags that may arrive in the future.

Tip: You can commemorate all this geotagging work with a custom map that can be added to a book of your photos. Page 252 has the details.

Editing Your Shots

S traight from the camera, digital snapshots often need a little bit of help. A photo may be too dark or too light. The colors may be too bluish or too yellowish. The focus may be a little blurry, the camera may have been tilted slightly, or the composition may be somewhat off.

Fortunately, one of the amazing things about digital photography is that you can fine-tune images in ways that, in the world of traditional photography, would require a fully equipped darkroom, several bottles of smelly chemicals, and an X-Acto knife.

OK, iPhoto isn't a full-blown photo-editing program like Adobe Photoshop, but it's respectable nonetheless. This chapter shows you how to use each of the tools in iPhoto's digital darkroom to spruce up your photos—and how to edit your photos in other programs if more radical image enhancement is needed.

Editing in iPhoto

You can't add text, make collages, or apply 50 different special effects filters with iPhoto, as you can with more expensive editing programs like Photoshop or Photoshop Elements. But iPhoto is well-equipped to handle basic (and not-so-basic) photo fix-up tasks like rotating, cropping, straightening, fixing red-eye, color correction, special effects (like black and white or sepia tone), edge vignetting (adding a soft white or black oval fade around the photo's edge), and tweaking brightness, contrast, saturation, color tint, exposure, shadows, highlights, and sharpness.

In iPhoto '11, all the editing tools are gathered together in a panel on the right side of the window in a new Edit view. In hopes of accommodating every conceivable working style, Apple has designed iPhoto to offer three different editing-window styles, three different ways to get there, and two different degrees of directness.

Choosing an Editing Setup

iPhoto '11 gives you three different ways to edit your photos:

- **Right in the iPhoto window, in Edit view**. *Pros*: You don't lose your bearings; all of the familiar landmarks, including the Source list, remain visible. Simple and reassuring. *Cons*: The picture isn't very big, since it has to fit inside the main iPhoto window.

- **In Full Screen view**. *Pros*: The photo fills your entire monitor, as big and dramatic as you can possibly see it (at least without upgrading to a bigger screen). Elements like the menu bar and Source list are temporarily hidden. *Cons*: You can navigate only to another photo in the same album or Event.

- **In another program**. It's one of iPhoto's slickest tricks: You can set things up so that double-clicking a photo in iPhoto (or clicking the Edit button) opens it up in a totally different program, like Photoshop Elements. You edit, you save your changes, you return to iPhoto—and presto, the changes you made, apparently behind iPhoto's back, are reflected right there in iPhoto. You can even use the "Revert to Original" command (page 126) to bring back the original photo later, if necessary.

  Pros: Other programs have a lot more editing power than iPhoto. For example, the Auto Levels command in Photoshop and Photoshop Elements is a better color fixer than iPhoto's Enhance button. And you need a Photoshop-type program if you want to scale a photo up or down to specific pixel dimensions, add text to a photo, combine several photos into one (a collage), do some head-swapping, whiten teeth, or adjust colors in just a *portion* of a photo.

  Cons: Well, you're using two programs instead of one. And nobody ever said Photoshop was cheap (although Photoshop Elements has most of the power with a *much* lower price tag). Also, iPhoto '11 *duplicates* your photo—whether it's a JPEG or a Raw file—meaning you end up with two copies of the same document. That chews up a lot of hard drive space (especially if you're editing Raw files), but it preserves your original photo no matter *what* you do to it in the other program.

Note: iPhoto veterans may notice that Apple retired a fourth way of opening a photo for editing–in a floating window of its own. Enough was enough.

Getting into Edit view

When you switch to Edit view in iPhoto '11, you see three clickable editing tabs at the top right of your window with a series of buttons underneath, as Figure 5-1 shows. To use Edit view, select one or more photos and then do one of the following:

- **Click the Edit button at the bottom right of the iPhoto window.**

- **Press Return (pressing Return *again* spits you out of Edit view).**

- **Choose Photo→Edit Photo or press ⌘-E.**

- **Control-click (or right-click) a thumbnail or a photo** and, from the shortcut menu, choose "Edit in iPhoto" or "Edit in External Editor" (discussed later in this section).

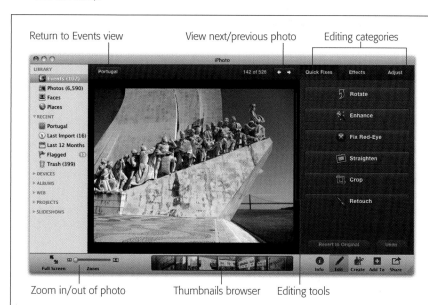

Return to Events view

View next/previous photo

Editing categories

Zoom in/out of photo

Thumbnails browser

Editing tools

Figure 5-1:
iPhoto '11's fancy new Edit view.

To exit Edit view and return to Events or Photos view, click the Edit button on iPhoto's toolbar again, press Return, or click the arrow-shaped button near the top left of the iPhoto window.

Using Full Screen view

Mac screens come in all sizes and resolutions these days, but one thing is for sure: Even the biggest ones usually can't show you an entire digital photo at full size. A 5-megapixel photo (2784 × 1856), for example, is still too big to fit entirely on Apple's 30-inch Cinema Display (2560 × 1600 pixels) without shrinking the photo.

The bottom line: For most of your iPhoto career, you'll be working with scaled-down versions of your photos. That's a particular shame when it comes to *editing* those photos, when you need as much clarity and detail as possible. That's why the invention of full-screen mode in iPhoto '09 was such a big deal, and it's a whole lot better in iPhoto '11. In this view, the selected photo is magnified to fill your entire screen. As Figure 5-2 illustrates, it's *awesome*.

Note: There were some problems with editing photos in iPhoto '09's full-screen mode. For example, the editing tools and thumbnail browser would hide themselves automatically. While this made for a gloriously clean view of your photo, many people were left wondering where the heck their tools went. In iPhoto '11, the editing tools and the thumbnail browser remain visible in Full Screen view. The menu bar disappears, but you can temporarily bring it back by moving the cursor to the very top of your screen.

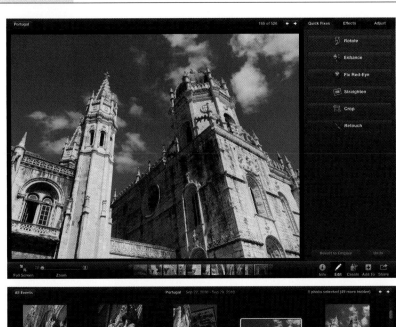

Figure 5-2:
Top: Editing photos in Full Screen view makes them as big as they can possibly be.

Bottom: You can jump back to Events or Photos view by double-clicking the photo you're editing, clicking the arrow button at the top left, or by pressing ⌘-left arrow.

Go back two views and you see big Source icons at the bottom of your monitor for Events, Places, Faces, Albums, and Projects.

To use Full Screen view when you're already in Edit view, click the Full Screen button at the bottom left of the iPhoto toolbar (or press ⌘-Option-F); your photo takes over your monitor. (If you're not in Edit view already, click the Full Screen button *and then* click Edit at the bottom of your screen.) To exit Full Screen view, just click the button again or tap the Esc key.

Editing in another program

If you own another image-editing program such as Photoshop or Photoshop Elements, you can have iPhoto open your masterpieces *there* anytime you enter Edit view. However, this requires a bit of prep work in iPhoto.

Choose iPhoto→Preferences and then click the Advanced button at the top of the resulting dialog box. From the Edit Photos pop-up menu, choose "In application…," as shown in Figure 5-3.

Note: In previous versions of iPhoto, you got to tweak the program's Preferences to control what happened when you double-clicked a photo's thumbnail. In iPhoto '11, double-clicking zooms in on the photo so you can take a closer look—period.

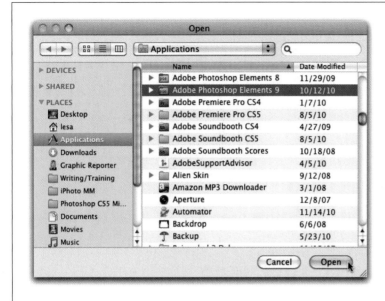

Figure 5-3:
In the Advanced pane of iPhoto's Preferences, you can use the Edit Photos pop-up menu to specify your favorite editor: "In iPhoto" or "In application…" Clicking the latter summons the Open dialog box shown here, where you can navigate to the other program (in this case, Photoshop Elements). Once you pick the application, iPhoto chooses it for you in the pop-up menu.

From now on, entering Edit view will launch the other program (if it's not already running) and open your photo as a new document in that program. iPhoto also creates a copy of your original photo for safekeeping.

Using the Thumbnail Browser

Another useful feature in Edit view is the *thumbnail browser* parked at the bottom of your window or monitor (it appears in both Standard and Full Screen views). You can use it to move to another photo for editing, or to choose *multiple* versions of the same shot to compare them and pick which one to edit.

Tip: If your camera is set to burst mode (consult your camera's manual to learn how to turn it on), it fires off several shots each time you depress the shutter button. This is handy for making sure at least *one* photo is nice and sharp, because the very act of pressing and releasing the shutter button can jiggle the camera. Unfortunately, shooting in burst mode also means several versions of the same photo in your library. That's why the ability to compare different versions in iPhoto *while you're editing* is so useful.

Using the thumbnail browser is easy, as Figure 5-4 explains. To choose another photo to edit, click its thumbnail. To compare the original photo with a different shot, ⌘-click the comparison shot in the thumbnail browser; iPhoto opens it alongside the photo you were originally editing. (You have to be in Edit mode to compare photos.)

You're not limited to comparing *two* photos side by side. You can compare three, four, or however many your screen can hold. If you're the kind of person who thinks ahead, you can select a batch of pictures (using the techniques described on page 49) and *then* go into Edit view. You'll see all those photos displayed.

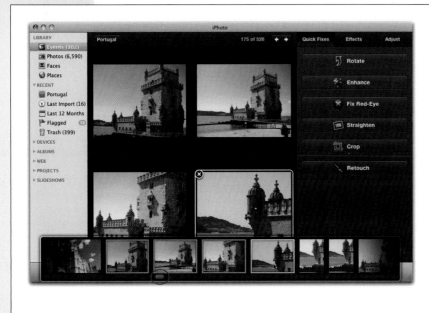

Figure 5-4:
Worried that you can't see the tiny thumbnails to pick one to click? Don't panic—the thumbnail browser enlarges when you mouse over it, as shown here. You can use the scroll bar (circled) to move forward or backward through the thumbnails.

When you're done comparing photos, you can restore the single-photo view by ⌘-clicking the comparison shot's thumbnail again, or by clicking the photo you want to dismiss and then clicking the ✗ in its top-left corner.

If you're *already* in Edit view, just ⌘-click or Shift-click to select additional photos in the thumbnails browser, and iPhoto makes room for all of them. (To remove a photo from the comparison, ⌘-click its thumbnail again.)

Notes on Zooming and Scrolling

Before you get deeply immersed in the editing process, it's well worth knowing how to zoom and scroll around, since chances are you'll be doing quite a bit of it.

By now, you know that double-clicking an image gives you a closer look, and that you can then use the Zoom slider in the toolbar to go deeper. However, there are many other ways to adjust your point of view. The following methods work in both standard and full-screen Edit views.

Note: iPhoto '11 is fully gesture-aware, meaning you can use a Magic Mouse, Magic Trackpad, or Macbook Trackpad to pinch (move two fingers together) to zoom out of your photo, or spread (move two fingers apart) to zoom in.

Using the Navigator

The biggest problem with zooming way in on a photo is that it's tough to know *where* you are in the photo. That's where the Navigator comes in—it's a little window that appears the minute you use the Zoom slider, or when you use the numeric shortcuts described below. The Navigator lets you change your position in the enlarged photo. Figure 5-5 has the details.

Note: The Navigator in iPhoto '11 no longer has a Size slider at the bottom of its window; you have to use the Zoom slider on the iPhoto toolbar instead.

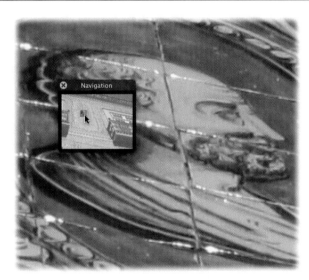

Figure 5-5:
As soon as you begin using the Zoom slider in iPhoto's toolbar, the Navigator window appears to help you find your way around your photo. You can move to different areas of the image by dragging the tiny "You are here" rectangle within the Navigator. (You can move the Navigator window itself by clicking and dragging near its name.)

Zooming Numerically

Touch typists will love this one: In Edit view, you can press the number keys on your keyboard—0, 1, and 2—to zoom in or out of your photos. Hit 1 to zoom in so far that you're viewing every single pixel (colored dot) in the photo; that is, one pixel of the photo occupies one pixel of your screen. The photo is usually bigger than your screen at this point, so you're now viewing only a portion of the whole—but it's great for detail work.

Hit 2 to double that magnification level. Now each pixel of the original picture consumes *four* pixels of your screen, a handy superzoom level when you're trying to edit individual skin cells.

Finally, when you've had quite enough of superzooming, tap your zero (0) key to zoom out again so the whole photo fits in the window.

Note that these numeric zooming tricks work in Edit view only; they do different things in Events and Photos view. For a secret decoder list of keyboard shortcuts, choose Help→Keyboard Shortcuts.

Scrolling Tricks

Once you've zoomed in on it, you can scroll a photo in any direction by pressing the space bar as you drag the mouse (your cursor turns into a tiny hand). That's more direct than fussing with two independent scroll bars.

If your mouse has a scroll wheel on top (or a scroll pea, like Apple's old Mighty Mouse), you can scroll images up and down while zoomed in on them by turning that wheel. To scroll the zoomed area *horizontally*, press Shift while turning.

Tip: If you're using a laptop trackpad, an Apple Magic Mouse, or a Magic Trackpad, you can swipe to the left or right with one finger to scroll from side to side while you're zoomed into a photo. Swiping *two* fingers to the left or right moves you back and forth through the thumbnails browser in Edit view.

The "Before and After" Keystroke

After making any kind of edit, it's incredibly useful to compare the "before" and "after" versions of your photo. So useful, in fact, that Apple has dedicated one whole key (OK, two of the same) to that function: the Shift key on your keyboard.

Hold it down to see your unenhanced "before" photo; release it to see the "after" image.

By pressing and releasing the Shift key, you can switch between the two versions of the photo to assess the results of the enhancement. This keyboard shortcut is well worth memorizing.

Backing Out

As long as you remain in Edit view, you can back out of your changes, one by one, no matter how many of them you've made. For example, if you've cropped a photo, you can uncrop it by choosing the Edit→Undo Crop command (or by pressing ⌘-Z).

The only catch is that you have to back out of the changes one at a time. In other words, if you rotate a photo, crop it, and then change its contrast, you must use the Undo command three times—first to undo the contrast change, then to uncrop, and finally to unrotate.

But once you leave Edit view—either by closing the photo's window, by choosing another photo in your thumbnail browser, or by returning to Events or Photos view—you lose the ability to undo *individual* edits one at a time. At this point, the only way to restore your photo is to click "Revert to Original" in Edit view or choose

Photos→Revert to Original. Either way, iPhoto removes all the edits you've made to the photo since you imported it.

The Quick Fixes

In iPhoto '11, the editing tools are divided into three categories: Quick Fixes, Effects, and Adjust.

The Quick Fixes category contains the most commonly used editing tools. To see all your Quick Fix options, pop into Edit view and then click the Quick Fixes tab in the upper right of the iPhoto window.

Tip: You can also display the Quick Fixes panel by tapping the Q key while you're in Edit view.

The Rotate Button

Unless your digital camera has a built-in orientation sensor, iPhoto imports all photos in landscape orientation (wider than they are tall). The program has no way of knowing if you turned the camera 90 degrees when you took your pictures. To get all your photos right-side up (if you didn't do so during your first perusal of them, as described in Chapter 1), just select the sideways ones and rotate them into position by clicking the Rotate button in the Quick Fixes panel.

Remember, you don't have to be in Edit view to rotate photos. You can also use one of the following methods to turn them right-side up:

- Choose Photos→Rotate Counterclockwise (or Rotate Clockwise).

- Press ⌘-R to rotate selected photos counterclockwise, or Option-⌘-R to rotate them clockwise.

- Control-click (or right-click) a photo in Edit view and choose Rotate Clockwise (or Rotate Counter Clockwise) from the shortcut menu. (If you're in any other view, you'll see a Rotate button instead.)

Tip: If you're in any other view, clicking Rotate in a photo's shortcut menu (or pressing ⌘-R) generally rotates photos *counterclockwise*, while Option-clicking that button (Option-⌘-R) generally rotates them clockwise. Think about how you hold your camera when you take a vertical shot—do you rotate the camera to the right or to the left? If the answer is to the right, you can swap these directions by choosing iPhoto→Preferences and changing the Rotate setting on the General pane of the dialog box.

After importing a batch of photos, you can save a lot of time and mousing if you select all the thumbnails that need rotating first (by ⌘-clicking each, for example). Then use one of the rotation commands above to fix all the selected photos in one fell swoop.

The Enhance Button

The Enhance button gives you a simple way to improve the appearance of less-than-perfect digital photos. You click this one button to make colors brighter, skin tones warmer, and details sharper (see Figure 5-6). It's a lot like the Auto Levels command in Photoshop.

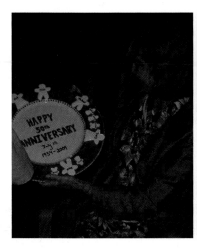 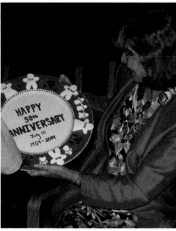

Figure 5-6:
The Enhance command works particularly well on photos that are slightly dark and lack contrast, like the original photo on the left.

Back in iPhoto '09, Apple seriously enhanced the Enhance button by borrowing some of the voodoo behind its professional photo editor, Aperture. In iPhoto '11, this button is almost magic.

Clicking Enhance makes iPhoto analyze the relative brightness of all the pixels in your photo and attempt to "balance" the image by dialing the brightness or contrast up or down and intensifying dull or grayish-looking areas. In addition to this overall adjustment of brightness, contrast, and color, the program makes a particular effort to identify and bring out the subject of the photo. Usually, this makes pictures look somewhat richer and more vivid than they did originally.

You'll see the effects of your Enhance button–clicking in the histogram (page 140)—a great way to learn about what, exactly, the Enhance button is doing.

Tip: If clicking Enhance improves your photo, but just not enough, then you can click it repeatedly to amplify its effect. However, applying Enhance more than three times or so risks turning your photo into digital mush. If you go too far, remember that you can press ⌘-Z (or choose Edit→Undo) to backtrack as many steps as you like, all the way back to the original photo.

---

iPhoto's image-correcting algorithms are just guesses at what your photo is supposed to look like. The program has no way of knowing whether you've shot an overexposed, washed-out picture of a vividly colored sailboat or a perfectly exposed picture of a pale-colored sailboat on an overcast day. So you may find that Enhance has no real effect on some photos and only minimally improves others. Remember, too, that you can't enhance just one part of a photo—it's all or nothing. If you want to *selectively* adjust specific portions of a picture, you need a true pixel-editing program like Aperture, Lightroom, or Photoshop Elements.

In some cases, you'll need to do more than just click the Enhance button to coax the best possible results from your digital photos; you may have to use the Adjust panel instead, as described on page 138.

Fixing Red Eye

Let's say you snap a near-perfect family portrait: The focus is sharp, the composition is balanced, and everyone is smiling. And then you notice that Uncle Bob, dead center in the picture, has glowing red eyes.

You're the victim of *red eye*, a common problem in flash photography (especially with older cameras). This creepy, possessed look has ruined many an otherwise-great photo (see Figure 5-7).

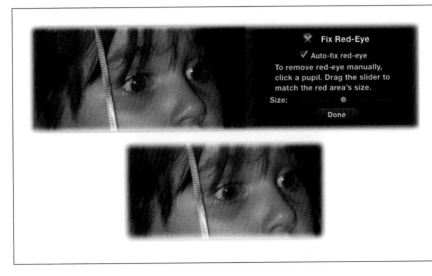

Figure 5-7:
Top: When you click the Quick Fix panel's Fix Red-Eye button, instructions appear telling you what to do: Click carefully inside each affected pupil.

Bottom: Friends and family members look more attractive—and less like Star Trek characters—after you touch up their phosphorescent red eyes with iPhoto.

Red-eye is caused by light reflected back from your subjects' eyes. The bright light of your camera's flash illuminates the blood-red retinal tissue at the back of their eyes. That's why red-eye problems are worse when you shoot pictures in a dim room: Your subjects' pupils are dilated, allowing even *more* light from your flash to reach their retinas. Turning up the room's lights or using the camera's red-eye reduction setting (if it has one) can help prevent devil eyes. But if it's too late for that, there's always iPhoto's Fix Red-Eye button, which digitally removes the offending red pixels. (It won't fix pet's eye problems, because animal eyes reflect white light instead.)

Truth be told, the red-eye tool doesn't know an eyeball from a pinkie toe. It just turns any red pixels black, regardless of what body part they're associated with. So your job is to tell iPhoto exactly what needs fixing. Start by opening your photo and zooming in, if necessary, so that you have a closeup view of the eye with the crimson problem. Then click the Fix Red-Eye button.

Most of the time, you can leave the Auto-fix checkbox turned on and, if iPhoto senses a face in the photo, it zaps the red eye for you. If it doesn't, then use the cross-hair cursor to click inside each red-tinted eye; with each click, iPhoto neutralizes the red pixels, painting the pupils solid black. To adjust the size of the cursor, drag the Size slider. When everything looks good, click Done.

Straightening

Many a photographer has remarked that it's harder to keep the horizon straight when composing images on a digital camera's LCD screen than when looking through an optical (eyepiece) viewfinder. Whether that's true or not, off-axis, tilted photos are a fact of photography, and especially of scanning—and iPhoto makes fixing them incredibly easy. Figure 5-8 shows the secrets of the Straighten slider.

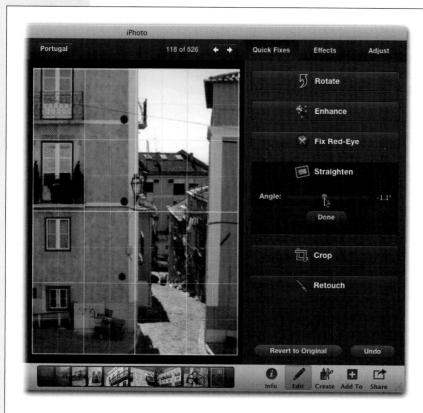

Figure 5-8:
The minute you click the Straighten button, iPhoto superimposes a yellow grid on your picture, as shown here. By moving the Angle slider in either direction, you rotate the image.

You can use the yellow grid to help you align the horizontal or vertical lines in your photo.

If you think about it, you can't rotate a rectangular photo without introducing skinny empty triangles at the corners of its "frame." Fortunately, iPhoto sneakily eliminates that problem by very slightly magnifying the photo as you straighten it. Now you're *losing* skinny triangles at the corners, but at least you don't see empty triangular gaps when the straightening is over.

In other words, the straightening tool isn't a free lunch. Straightening an image decreases the picture quality slightly (by blowing up the picture, thus lowering the resolution) and clips off tiny scraps at the corners. You have to view the before and after pictures side by side at high magnification to see the difference, but it's there.

So, as cool as the straightening tool is, it's not a substitute for careful composition with your camera. However, it can help you salvage an otherwise wonderful image that's skewed. (And besides—if you lose a tiny bit of clarity in the straightening process, you can always apply a little sharpening afterward. Read on to learn how.)

Cropping

Think of iPhoto's cropping tool as a digital paper cutter. It neatly shaves off unnecessary portions of a photo, leaving behind only the part you really want.

You'd be surprised at how many photographs can benefit from selective cropping. For example:

- **Eliminate parts of a photo you just don't want**. This is a great way to chop your brother's ex-girlfriend out of an otherwise perfect family portrait, say (provided she was standing at the end of the lineup).

- **Improve a photo's composition**. Trimming a photo allows you to adjust where your subject matter appears within the frame of the picture. If you inspect the professionally shot photos in magazines or books, you'll discover that many pros get more impact from a picture by cropping tightly around the subject, especially in portraits.

- **Get rid of wasted space**. Huge expanses of background sky that add nothing to a photo can be eliminated, keeping the focus on your subject.

- **Fit a photo to specific proportions**. If you're going to place your photos in a book layout (Chapter 9) or turn them into standard-size prints (Chapter 7), you may need to adjust their proportions. That's because there's a substantial discrepancy between the *aspect ratio* (length-to-width proportions) of your digital camera's photos and those of film cameras—a difference that will come back to haunt you if you order prints.

How to crop a photo

Here are the steps for cropping a photo:

1. **Open the photo for editing.**

   You can use any of the methods mentioned earlier in this chapter, like double-clicking a thumbnail and then pressing Return.

2. **In the Quick Fixes panel, click the Crop button, or press the C key on your keyboard.**

The Constrain pop-up menu appears on the right side of your iPhoto window, and a strange light gray rectangle superimposes itself on your photo (Figure 5-9).

When you click the Crop button, a light gray rectangle appears on your photo, which you can adjust by clicking and dragging its corners. You can also create a new rectangle, if you like, by dragging diagonally up or down.

As you drag, a tic-tac-toe grid appears, just in case you want to crop according to the Rule of Thirds. (The Rule of Thirds is a photographic guideline that imagines a photo frame divided into thirds, both horizontally and vertically. Better composition, the Rule contends, comes from putting the most interesting parts of the image at these four points.)

3. **Make a selection from the Constrain pop-up menu, if you like.**

The Constrain pop-up menu controls the behavior of the cropping tool. When the Constrain checkbox it turned off, you can draw a cropping rectangle of any size and proportions, in essence going freehand.

When you choose one of the other options in the pop-up menu, however, iPhoto constrains the rectangle you draw to preset proportions. It prevents you from coloring outside the lines, so to speak.

The Constrain feature is especially important if you plan to order prints of your photos (Chapter 7). Prints come only in standard photo sizes: 4 × 6, 5 × 7, 8 × 10, and so on. You may recall, however, that most digital cameras produce photos whose proportions are 4:3 (width to height). This size is ideal for DVDs and iPhoto books, because standard television and iPhoto book layouts use 4:3 dimensions, too—but it doesn't divide evenly into standard print photograph sizes.

That's why the Constrain pop-up menu offers you canned choices like 4 × 6, 5 × 7, and so on. Limiting your cropping to one of these preset sizes guarantees that your cropped photos will fit perfectly into Kodak prints. (If you don't constrain your cropping this way, Kodak—not you—will decide how to crop them to fit.)

Another crop-to-fit option in the Constrain menu lets you crop photos for use as a desktop picture; this option is named something like "1024 × 768 (Display)" (or whatever your actual monitor's dimensions are). You'll also find an "Original" option here (which maintains the proportions of the original photo even as you make it smaller), and a Square option.

Tip: Here's a bonus feature: the item in the Constrain pop-up menu called Custom. Inside the two text boxes that appear, you can type any proportions you want: 4 × 7, 15 × 32, or whatever your eccentric design needs call for.

As soon as you make a selection from this pop-up menu, iPhoto draws a preliminary cropping rectangle—of the proper dimensions—on the photo, turning everything outside it darker.

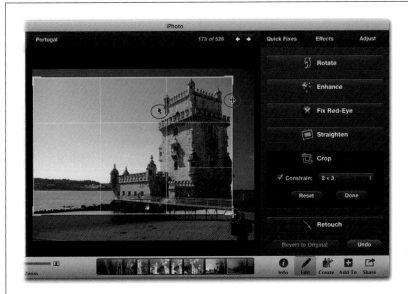

Figure 5-9:
Top: Here, in this improbable illustration, are the three different cursor shapes you may see, depending on where you move the pointer: the + crosshair for the initial drag, the double arrow for reshaping when you're near a boundary, and the arrow pointer for sliding the entire rectangle around the photo.

Bottom: Once you click Done, the excess margin falls to the digital cutting-room floor, thus enlarging your subject. (You can always get it back by clicking "Revert to Original.")

By the way, iPhoto thinks hard about how to display this rectangle—that is, whether it starts out in either landscape (horizontal) or portrait (vertical) orientation. The rectangle always starts out matching the photo itself: landscape for landscape photos, portrait for portrait photos. You can, however, reopen the Constrain pop-up menu and choose "Constrain as landscape" or "Constrain as portrait" to flop the selection rectangle 90 degrees.

Tip: Actually, there's a quicker way to rotate the selection from horizontal to vertical (or vice versa): Starting at a point outside the current crop box, Option-drag across the photo to draw a new selection rectangle. The selection rectangle crisply turns 90 degrees.

There are three situations when these selection-rectangle rotation tricks don't work. You can't change the rectangle's orientation if you've selected the "Original" option, because its whole point is to preserve the photo's original shape. The "4 × 3 (DVD)" and "16 × 9 (HD)" options, furthermore, are hard-coded in landscape mode, because they're intended to be shown on a TV set, and most people's TVs don't rotate.

At this point, the cropping area that iPhoto suggests with its dark-margin rectangle may, as far as you're concerned, be just right. In that case, skip to step 6. More often, though, you'll probably want to give the cropping job the benefit of your years of training and artistic sensibility by *redrawing* the cropping area.

4. **Drag the corners of the cropping rectangle to adjust its size and shape. Or just create a new cropping rectangle by starting at a point outside the current crop box and dragging diagonally across the portion of the picture that you want to *keep*.**

As you drag across your photo, the part of the photo that iPhoto will eventually trim away is dimmed out once again (Figure 5-9).

Tip: Even if you turned on one of the Constrain options in step 3, you can override the constraining by pressing the Shift key after you begin dragging.

Don't worry about getting your selection perfect, since iPhoto doesn't actually trim the photo until you click the Done button.

5. **Adjust the cropping, if necessary.**

   If the shape and size of your selection area are OK, but you want to adjust which part of the image is selected, then you can move the selection area without re-drawing it. Position your mouse inside the selection so that the pointer turns into an arrow. Then drag the existing rectangle where you want it.

   You can also change the rectangle's size. Move your cursor close to any edge or corner so that it changes to a + shape (near the corner) or a double-headed arrow (near the edge). Now you can drag the edge or corner to reshape the rectangle.

   If you get cold feet, you can cancel the operation by tapping the Esc key or clicking Reset.

UP TO SPEED

When Cropping Problems Crop Up

Remember that cropping always shrinks your photos. Remove too many pixels, and your photo may end up too small (that is, with a resolution too low to print or display properly).

Here's an example: You start with a 1600 × 1200-pixel photo. Ordinarily, that's large enough to be printed as a high-quality, standard 8 × 10 portrait.

Then you go in and crop the shot. Now the composition is perfect, but your photo measures only 800 × 640 pixels. You've tossed out nearly a million and a half pixels!

The photo no longer has a resolution (pixels per inch) high enough to produce a top-quality 8 × 10 print. The printer is forced to blow up the photo to fill the specified paper size, producing visible, jagged-edged pixels in the printout. The 800 × 640 pixel version of your photo would make a

great 4 × 5 print (if that were even a standard-size print), but pushing the print's size up further noticeably degrades the quality.

Therein lies a significant advantage of using a high-resolution digital camera (at least 10 megapixels, for example). Because each shot starts out with such a high resolution, you can afford to shave away a few hundred thousand pixels and still have enough left over for good-sized, high-resolution prints. And if your camera has a digital zoom option, don't use it. If you do, your photo is cropped in-camera before it's saved to the memory card—you'll get better results by cropping in iPhoto yourself.

Moral of the story: Know your photo's size and intended use—and don't crop out more photo than you can spare.

(Despite its elaborate control over the relative dimensions of your cropping rectangle, iPhoto doesn't tell you the size, in pixels, of your selection. If you want to crop a photo to precise pixel dimensions, you have to use another program, like Photoshop Elements. Page 122 explains how to open photos in a different editing program.)

6. **When the cropping rectangle is just the way you want it, click Done, or just press Return.**

   If throwing away all those cropped-out pixels makes you nervous, relax. If you realize immediately that you've made a cropping mistake, then you can click the Undo or "Revert to Original" button, or choose Edit→Undo to go back one editing step. If you have regrets *weeks* later, on the other hand, then you can always select the photo and choose Photos→"Revert to Original." After asking if you're sure, iPhoto promptly reinstates the original photo from its backup, discarding every change you've ever made to it.

Note: When you crop a photo, you're changing it in all the albums in which it appears (page 55). If you want a photo to appear cropped in one album but not in another, you have to duplicate it (highlight it and then choose Photos→Duplicate), and then edit each version separately.

Retouching Blemishes, Scratches, and Hairs

Sometimes an otherwise perfect portrait is spoiled by the tiniest of imperfections—a stray hair or an unsightly blemish, for example. Professional photographers, whether working digitally or in a traditional darkroom, routinely remove such minor imperfections from their final prints—a process known as *retouching*, for clients known as *self-conscious* or *vain*. (Kidding!)

iPhoto's Retouch brush lets you do the same thing with your own digital photos. You can paint away scratches, spots, hairs, or any other small flaws in your photos with a few quick strokes.

The operative word here is *small*. The Retouch brush can't completely erase somebody's mustache. It's intended for tiny touch-ups that don't involve repainting whole sections of a photo. (For that kind of photo overhaul, you need a pixel-editing program like Photoshop Elements.)

The Retouch brush works its magic by blending the colors in the tiny area that you're fixing. It doesn't cover the imperfections you're trying to remove, but *blurs* them out by softly blending them into a small radius of surrounding pixels (in other words, you can't use it to whiten teeth). You can see the effect in Figure 5-10.

Tip: The Retouch brush is particularly useful if your photo library contains pictures that you've scanned in. In that case, you can use it to wipe away the dust specks and scratches that often appear on film negatives and prints, or those that are introduced by the scanner itself.

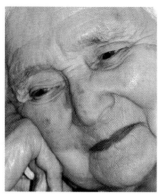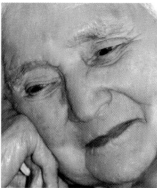

Figure 5-10:
Most of the time, the Retouch brush works like magic; but sometimes, it creates bizarre artifacts. In those cases, press ⌘-Z to undo your latest stroke.

Overall, though, you can see how the Retouch brush can help an original photo (left) by softening wrinkles and hiding blemishes (right), like an application of digital Botox.

Using the Retouch brush

Once you've clicked Retouch in the Quick Fixes panel, your cursor turns into a circle with a dotted outline. Find the imperfection and "paint" over it, either by dabbing or dragging to blend it with the surrounding portion of the photo. You can also use the Size slider to make the Retouch brush's size match the size of the unfortunate feature.

Tip: You can adjust the size of the Retouch brush the keyboard, too: Press the left bracket key ([) repeatedly to make it smaller, or the right bracket key (]) to make it bigger.

Don't overdo it: If you apply too much retouching, the area you're working on starts to look noticeably blurry and unnatural, as if someone smeared Vaseline on it. (Fortunately, you can use the Edit→Undo command [⌘-Z] to take back individual brush strokes as necessary.) When you're finished, click the Done button. If you don't like the results, click the "Revert to Original" or Undo button instead.

If you've used the Retouch brush in previous iPhoto versions, you'll be amazed at how well it works in '11. Here again, Apple cannibalized its own professional software (Aperture) to give the iPhoto tools a huge upgrade; the Retouch brush in iPhoto is now very powerful indeed. You can paint out not just zits and wrinkles, but even entire shirt stains.

Note: On high-resolution photos (especially Raw files), it can take a moment or two for iPhoto to process each individual stroke of the Retouch brush. If you don't see any results, wait a second for iPhoto to catch up with you.

The Effects Panel

iPhoto '11 offers three lighting effects, six color effects, three effects that soften a photo's borders, and three effects that alter color intensity. These effects can be incredibly useful for creating artistic effects or saving photos with terrible color that you can't fix any other way.

To open this panel, click the Effects tab or tap the E key on your keyboard. No matter which editing view you're in (normal or full-screen), the Effects panel appears (Figure 5-11).

Tip: In most cases, you can click an Effects button repeatedly to intensify that particular effect. Some effects (Antique, Matte, Vignette, Edge Blur, Fade, and Boost) even display a number to let you know how many times you've applied it. You can use the left and right arrows on either side of the digit to increase or decrease the effect, respectively. You don't see anything like that when you click the first two rows of buttons, but clicking them repeatedly still adds to the effect (watch your photo to see the change).

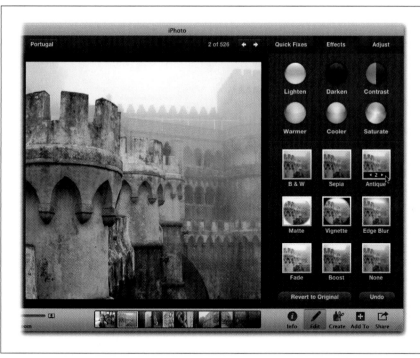

Figure 5-11:
By clicking the Effects tab in Edit view, you summon a panel filled with 14 different clickable effects (up from 8 in iPhoto '09), good for a solid 10 minutes of photo-editing fun.

The Antique effect is shown here.

Applying these effects is probably the easiest thing you'll ever do in iPhoto: Just click a button to apply the appropriate effect to the photo you're viewing. Here's what each one does:

- **Lighten.** Brightens photos that are too dark (underexposed).
- **Darken.** Darkens a photo that's too light (overexposed).

- **Contrast.** If your photo looks flat, use this effect to bring out details. It makes the dark parts of your photo a little darker, and the light parts a little lighter.

- **Warmer.** If your photo looks too blue (cold), use this effect to add golden tones and warm it up.

- **Cooler.** Introduces more blue tones if your photo is riddled with red or gold.

- **Saturate.** Want to make the colors in your flower photos pop off the page? Give this button a few clicks to intensify the color. Try not to use this effect on photos with people, though—it can turn their skin a very unflattering hot pink.

- **B & W (Black and White), Sepia.** These effects drain the color from your photos. B & W converts them into moody grayscale images (a great technique if you're going for that Ansel Adams look); Sepia repaints them entirely in shades of antique brown (as though they were 1865 daguerreotypes). Click once to apply the effect; click again to remove it.

- **Antique**. A heck of a lot like Sepia, but not quite as severe. Still gets light brownish, but preserves some of the original color—like, say, a photo from the 1940s.

- **Matte**. This effect whites out the outer portion of the photo, creating an oval-shaped frame around the center.

- **Vignette**. Same idea as Matte, except that iPhoto darkens the outer edges instead of lightening them.

- **Edge Blur**. Same idea again, except the outer edges lose focus rather than changing color. The central portion of the photo stays in focus.

- **Fade Color**. The colors get quite a bit faded, like a photo from the 1960s.

- **Boost Color**. Increases the color saturation, making colors more vivid.

- **None**. Click this button to undo all the playing you've done so far, taking the photo back to the way it was when you first opened the Effects panel.

The Adjust Panel

For thousands of people, the handful of basic image-fixing tools described on the previous pages offer plenty of power. But power users don't like having to trot off to a program like Photoshop to make more advanced changes to their pictures, like fiddling with exposure (the intensity of light), adjusting shadows and highlights, sharpening, and so on.

That's where the Adjust panel comes in (Figure 5-12). To see it, click the Adjust tab in Edit view.

Before you let the following pages turn you into a tweak geek, here are some preliminary words of advice concerning the Adjust panel:

- **When to use it**. Plenty of photos need no help at all; they look fantastic right out of the camera. And others are ready for prime time after only a single click of the Enhance button, described earlier (page 128).

The beauty of the Adjust panel, though, is that it permits infinite *gradations* of the changes that the Enhance button makes. For example, if a photo looks too dark and murky, you can bring details out of the shadows without blowing out the highlights. If the snow in a skiing shot looks too bluish, you can de-blue it. If the colors don't pop quite enough in the winning-soccer-goal shot, you can boost their saturation levels.

In short, there are fixes the Adjust panel can make that no one-click magic button can touch.

- **How to play**. You can fiddle with the Adjust panel's sliders in two different ways, as illustrated in Figure 5-12.

- **Backing out**. You can always click the "Revert to Original" or Undo buttons (both are new in iPhoto '11). The first one takes you back to the original photo you shot, while Undo lets you take back individual changes you made with the Adjust panel.

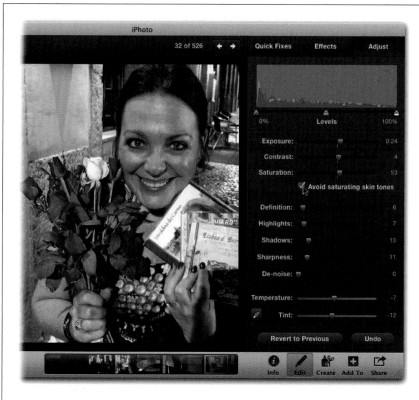

Figure 5-12:
When the Enhance button doesn't do what you want, it's time to summon the Adjust panel, which gives you finer control over many aspects of the photo.

There are two ways to manipulate the panel's sliders, depending on the degree of fine-tuning you need to do. You can drag a slider's handle, but that doesn't give you much accuracy. You can also click the slider, which makes the handle jump to that spot.

If you're working with people pictures and you decide to pump up the Saturation, be sure to turn on "Avoid saturating skin tones," as shown here.

(The "Revert to Original" button changes to read "Revert to Previous" if you've tweaked the photo in one panel [say, Quick Fixes] and then you tweak it in another panel [Adjust] during the same editing session. This is handy if you succumb to the temptation of using the Adjust panel on a photo a second time and then decide it looked just fine before. Essentially the "Revert to Previous" button means, "Undo all the Adjust-panel changes I've made during this session.")

Introduction to the Histogram

While you can certainly make a bad photo look good by dragging the Adjust panel's sliders to and fro, learning to use them *effectively* involves learning about its *histogram*: the colorful little graph at the top of the panel.

The histogram is the heart of the Adjust panel (it lives at the top of the panel—see Figure 5-12). It's a self-updating visual representation of the dark and light tones that make up your photograph. If you've never encountered a histogram before, this may sound complicated. But the Adjust panel's histogram is a terrific tool, and it'll make more sense the more you work with it.

Within each of the histogram's superimposed graphs (red, blue, green), the scheme is the same: The amount of the photo's darker shades appears toward the left side of the graph; the lighter tones are graphed on the right side.

Therefore, in a very dark photograph—a coal mine at midnight, say—you'll see big mountain peaks at the left side of the graph, trailing off to nothing toward the right. A shot of a brilliantly sunny snowscape, on the other hand, will show lots of information on the right and probably very little on the left.

Those peaks represent the areas in the photo where there's a lot of information. Histograms showing peaks throughout the graph reflect a photo that's balanced, with no super-dark or blown-out light areas making steep peaks stacked against the left or right sides. These middle mountains are fine, as long as you have some visual information in other parts of the histogram, too.

The histogram for a *bad* photo, on the other hand—a severely under- or overexposed one—has mountains all bunched at one end or the other. Rescuing those pictures involves spreading the mountains across the entire spectrum, which is what the Adjust panel is all about.

Three Channels

As noted above, the histogram actually displays three superimposed graphs at once. These layers—red, green, and blue—represent the three "channels" of a color photo.

When you make adjustments to a photo's brightness values—for example, when you drag the Exposure slider just below the histogram—you'll see the graphs in all three channels move in unison. Despite changing shape, they essentially stick together. Later, when you make color adjustments using, say, the Temperature slider, you'll see those individual channels move in different directions.

Adjusting the Levels

If the mountains of your graph seem to cover all the territory from left to right, you already have a roughly even distribution of dark and light tones in your picture, so you're probably in good shape. But if the graph comes up short on either the left (darks) or the right (lights) side of the histogram, you might want to make an adjustment.

To do so, drag the right or left pointer on the Levels slider *inward*, toward the base of the "mountain" (Figure 5-13). If you're moving the *right* pointer inward, for example, you'll notice that the whites become brighter, but the dark areas stay pretty much the same; if you drag the *left* pointer inward, the dark tones change, but the highlights remain steady.

Tip: Instead of dragging these handles inward, you can click the slider track itself at the outer base of the mountain. That's faster and gives you better control of the handle's landing point.

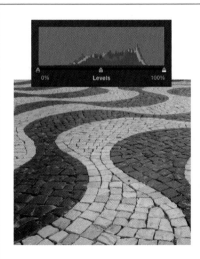 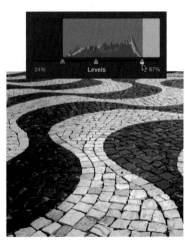

Figure 5-13:
Left: One way to fix a photo that looks too "flat" is to use the Levels adjustment. Notice how the tonal information is bunched up in the middle of this histogram, meaning the photo has no true highlights or shadows.

Right: Move the left and right pointers in, toward the edges of the histogram data, to improve highlights and shadows.

In general, you should avoid moving these endpoint handles inward *beyond* the outer edges of the mountains. Doing so adds contrast, but it also throws away whatever data is outside the handles, which generally makes for a lower quality printout.

Once you have your endpoints set, turn your attention to the middle pointer. This adjustment controls the midtones. The general rule is that you *center* the midtone pointer between the shadow pointer on the left and the highlight pointer on the right. Often, the result is a pleasing rendition of the photo. But you can adjust to taste, too; inching the pointer to the left lightens the midtones; moving it to the right darkens them.

Exposure

In the simplest terms, the Exposure slider makes your picture lighter when you move it to the right and darker when you move it to the left. That said, its effects differ slightly depending on your photo's file format:

- When you're editing **JPEG** graphics (that is, most photos from most cameras), the Exposure slider primarily affects the middle tones (as opposed to the brightest highlights and darkest shadows). If you're used to Photoshop, you may recognize this effect as a relative of its *gamma* controls. ("Gamma" refers to the middle tones in a picture.)

- When you're working with **Raw** files, however (page 151), Exposure is even more interesting. It actually changes the way iPhoto *interprets* the dark and light information that your camera recorded when it took the picture. A photographer might say it's like changing the ISO setting (the camera's sensitivity to light) before taking the picture—except that now you can make this kind of change long *after* you snap the shutter.

  The Exposure slider demonstrates one of the advantages of Raw. In a Raw file, iPhoto has a lot more image information to work with than in a JPEG. As a result, you can make exposure adjustments without sacrificing the overall quality of the photograph.

Watch the data on the histogram as you move the Exposure slider. Make sure you don't wind up shoving any of the "mountain peaks" beyond the edges of the histogram box. If that happens, then you're discarding precious image data; when you print, you'll see a loss of detail in the darks and lights.

If you've already adjusted your image using the Levels controls, then you probably won't need to play with Exposure and Contrast. Most images can be fine-tuned with either set of controls (the three pointers in Levels, or the dynamic duo of Exposure and Contrast). But very few pictures require both approaches.

Contrast

The Contrast slider changes the shape of the histogram by pushing the data out in both directions. Contrast is the difference between the darkest and lightest tones in your picture. If you increase the contrast, you "stretch out" the shape of the histogram, creating darker blacks and brighter whites (Figure 5-14). When you decrease the contrast, you're scrunching the shape of the histogram inward, shortening the distance between the dark and light endpoints. Since the image data now resides in the middle area of the graph, the overall tones in the picture are duller. Photographers might call this look "flat" or "muddy."

Contrast works especially well on "flat" shots because a single slider moves the histogram in two directions at once (outward toward the edges). You can create a similar effect in Levels by moving the endpoints inward toward the edges of the histogram.

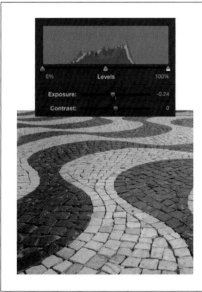 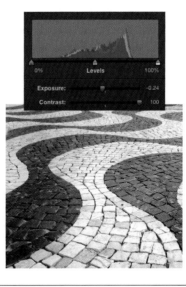

Figure 5-14:
Instead of working with Levels (Figure 5-13), you can use Exposure and Contrast to achieve a similar effect, as shown here.

Left: Use the Exposure slider to center the data in the middle of the histogram. In this case, the slider was dragged slightly to the left.

Right: Then use the Contrast slider to push the data toward both ends of the histogram.

Which approach is better? If the histogram data is centered in the middle of the graph, then Contrast is the easier adjustment because it pushes the data outward evenly. But if the histogram data is skewed to one side or the other, then Levels is the better choice because you can adjust the highlights and shadows independently.

Saturation

When you increase the saturation of a photo's colors, you make them more vivid; essentially, you make them "pop." You can also improve photos that have harsh, garish colors by dialing *down* the saturation so the colors end up looking a little less intense than they were in the original snapshot. That's a useful trick in photos whose *composition* is so strong that the colors are almost distracting (think super-bright objects, like ceramics or flowers). You can increase or decrease the intensity of a photo's colors by moving the Saturation slider right or left, respectively.

The Adjust panel can save you from yourself, at least when it comes to saturation. If you're trying to crank up the color of Cousin Jack's orange shirt—but want to avoid drenching Uncle Jack's face in hyped-up hues—then put a check in the box next to "Avoid saturating skin tones" under the Saturation slider.

Note: *iPhoto's Enhance button automatically adjusts saturation when "enhancing" your photos, but it provides no way to control the* degree *of its adjustment.*

Definition

The result of moving iPhoto's Definition slider is tough to describe. Dragging it to the right can make a hazy or muddy photo appear sharper, but it's not the same as using the Sharpness slider (page 145). The Definition slider has more in common with the Contrast slider, though it works more delicately; it adjusts contrast in the parts of your photo that contain small details. In doing so, it makes your photo look sharper.

You'd be hard-pressed to find a photo that doesn't benefit from at least a *little* extra definition. Try moving this slider up to 20 or so and see what you think.

Highlights and Shadows

The Highlights and Shadows sliders are designed to recover lost detail in the highlights and shadows of your photos, turning what once might have been unsalvageably overexposed or underexposed photos into usable shots (Figure 5-15).

Sure, you can find this kind of sophisticated adjustment in Adobe Camera Raw or Aperture—but in a program designed for regular folks?

Suppose you've got everything in the photo looking good, except that you don't have any detail in either the brightest parts of the shot or in murky, dark areas. All you have to do is drag the appropriate slider and marvel as the detail magically appears. Suddenly, you'll see texture in what was once a washed-out white wall or sky, or detail in what used to be nearly black (Figure 5-15).

Be a careful, though; if you drag either the Highlights or Shadows slider too far, then everything takes on a strange, radioactive sheen. But used in moderation, these sliders work real magic, especially if you're editing Raw files.

FREQUENTLY ASKED QUESTION

Battle of the Sliders

All right, first you said that I can create a well-balanced histogram with the Levels sliders. Then you said that the Exposure and Contrast sliders do pretty much the same thing. So which should I use?

Photography forums everywhere are overflowing with passionate comments advocating one approach over the other.

The bottom line is, for most normal JPEG photos, you can use whichever you prefer, as long as you wind up creating a histogram whose peaks generally span the entire graph.

If you have no preference, you may as well get into the habit of using the Levels sliders. One day, when you begin editing super-high-quality Raw files (page 151), you'll appreciate the clever way these controls interpret the data from the camera's sensors with virtually no loss of quality.

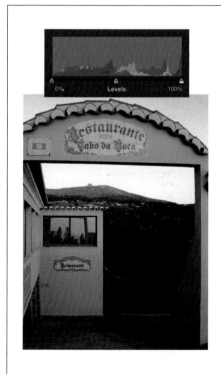

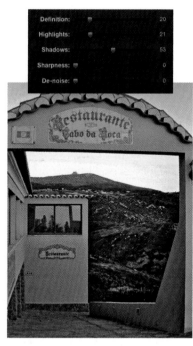

Figure 5-15:
The Highlights and Shadows sliders are just more examples of the power tucked into the Adjust panel.

Left: Even though the histogram for this photo looks pretty good—it has a full range of darks and lights—there's a lot of detail lost in the shadows.

Right: Drag the Shadows slider to the right and presto! A whole world of detail emerges. Drag the Highlights slider slightly to the right and a little more color comes back into the sky. (The Saturation slider was also boosted a tad.)

Sharpness

The Sharpness slider seems awfully tempting. Could technology really solve the problem of blurry, out-of-focus photos?

Well, no.

Instead, the Sharpness slider works by subtly increasing the contrast among pixels in your photo, which seems to enhance the crispness. In pro circles, adding a pinch of sharpening to a photo is a regular part of the routine.

To sharpen in iPhoto, drag the Sharpness slider to the right. If you don't like what you see, drag the slider back to the left to reduce the effect. (There's no way to remove sharpness captured in the original photo—in other words, there's no *Softness* slider.)

Too much sharpening can *ruin* a photo, since eventually the pixels become grainy and weird-looking. Fortunately, Apple has mostly protected you from this sort of disaster by keeping both the effects and the *side effects* of the Sharpness control to a minimum. You can help matters by moving the slider in small increments.

Generally speaking, sharpening should be the last Adjust-panel tweak you make to your photo. If you apply other corrections after sharpening, you may discover that you have to sharpen it *again*.

Note: Keep in mind that photos with a lot of hard lines–landscapes, architecture, or fur-filled pet photos–benefit from a stronger dose of sharpening than, say, portraits where a lot of sharpening makes imperfections practically *leap* out of the photo.

De-noise

In photographic terms, *noise* means graininess—colored speckles. Noise is a common problem in digital photography, especially in low-light shots taken with older cameras. Some cameras, for example, claim to have "anti-blur" features that turn out to be nothing more than goosed-up ISO (light-sensitivity) settings in low light. But over ISO 800 or so, the resulting digital noise can be truly hideous.

If a photo looks noisy (grainy), you can lessen the effect by moving the Adjust panel's De-noise slider to the right. To gauge how much, first zoom in on your image to 100 percent size (press the 1 key), then keep an eye on a dark area or the sky as you move the slider. Generally speaking, moving the slider more than halfway softens your image too much.

The De-noise slider can't work wonders. But by subtly smoothing neighboring pixels, it does a reasonable job of removing noise from low-light photos, which, on grainy shots, can be a definite improvement.

Tip: The De-noise slider is also handy to use if you've lightened shadows, as described in the previous section, which can introduce a little noise into the photo.

Color Balance

If all you ever shoot is black-and-white photos, then Levels or Exposure/Contrast may be all you ever need. But if you're like most people, you're also concerned about a little thing called color.

Truth is, digital cameras (and scanners) don't always capture color accurately. Digital photos sometimes have a slightly bluish or greenish tinge, producing dull colors, lower contrast, and sickly looking skin tones. In fact, the whole thing might have a faint green or magenta cast. Or perhaps you just want to take color adjustment into your own hands, not only to get the colors right, but also to create a specific mood. Maybe you want a snowy landscape to look icy blue so friends back home realize just how darned cold it was!

In addition to the Saturation slider (page 143), the Adjust panel offers two other sliders that wield power over this sort of thing: Temperature and Tint. And it offers two ways to apply such changes: the manual way and the automatic way.

Manual Color Adjustment

The sliders at the bottom of the Adjust panel provide plenty of color-adjustment power. The Tint and Temperature sliders govern the *white balance* of your photo. Different kinds of light—fluorescent lighting, overcast skies, and so on—lend different color casts to photographs. White balance is a setting that eliminates or adjusts the color cast according to the lighting.

For best results, start at the bottom slider and work your way upward:

- **Tint**. Like the tint control on a color TV, this slider adjusts the photo's overall tint along the red-green spectrum. Nudge the slider to the right for a greenish tint, left for red. As you go, watch the histogram to see how iPhoto is applying the color.

  Adjusting this slider is particularly helpful for correcting skin tones and compensating for difficult lighting situations, like fluorescent lighting.

- **Temperature**. This slider, on the other hand, adjusts the photo along the blue-orange spectrum. Move the slider to the left to make the image "cooler," or slightly bluish. Move the slider to the right to warm up the tones, making them more orangeish—a particularly handy technique for breathing life back into subjects who have been bleached white with a flash. A few notches to the right on the Temperature slider, and their skin tones look healthy once again!

  Professional photographers *love* having color-temperature control; in fact, many photographers can handle the bulk of their image correction with nothing but the Exposure and Temperature controls.

POWER USERS' CLINIC

Coping with Fluorescent Lighting

You can correct most pictures using the automatic gray-balance feature or the Tint, Temperature, and Saturation sliders described in this chapter. Some images, however, will drive you insane—no amount of tweaking will seem to make their colors look realistic. Pictures taken under fluorescent lighting can be particularly troublesome.

The problem with fluorescent bulbs is that they don't produce light across the entire color spectrum; there are, in effect, spectrum gaps in their radiance. Your best color-correction tool, the Temperature slider, works only on images where a full spectrum of light was captured, so it doesn't work well on fluorescently lit shots.

You'll have some luck moving the Tint slider to the left to remove the green cast of fluorescent lighting. But the overall color balance still won't be as pleasing as with pictures shot under full-spectrum lighting, such as outside on a sunny day.

The best time to fix fluorescent-light color-balance problems, therefore, is at the moment you take the picture. One solution is to use your camera's flash, and to ensure that it's the dominant light source where possible (its light helps to fill in the gaps in the fluorescent spectrum, making color correction much easier in iPhoto later). Another option is to change your camera's white balance (the setting that controls the color of light) to fluorescent light. Consult your owner's manual to learn how.

Automatic Color Correction

Dragging the Tint and Temperature sliders by hand is one way to address color imbalances in a picture. But there's an easier way: iPhoto also has a handy feature that adjusts both sliders *automatically*.

It relies on your ability to find, somewhere in your photo, an area of what *should* appear as medium gray or white (you can use either). Once you find the gray or white point, iPhoto takes it from there—it can adjust all the other colors in the photo accordingly, shifting color temperature and tint with a single click. This trick works amazingly well on some photos.

Before you use this feature, though, make sure you've already adjusted the overall *exposure* of the photo, using the techniques described on the previous pages.

Next, scan your photo for an area that should appear as a neutral gray or clean white (something that really *is* white, and not a white reflection). Slightly dark grays are better for this purpose than bright, overexposed grays.

Once you've found such a spot, click the eyedropper icon next to the Tint slider. Your mouse pointer becomes crosshairs that you can position over your gray or white sample, as shown in Figure 5-16 (left). Then simply click.

Instantly, iPhoto automatically adjusts the color-balance sliders to balance the photo's overall color (Figure 5-16, right). If you don't like the results, click the Undo button and then click a different neutral area. You can keep doing this until the photo looks good to you.

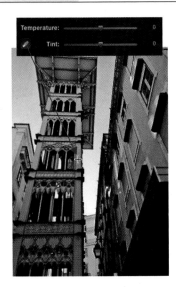 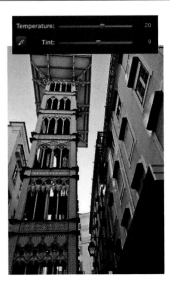

Figure 5-16:
Left: Click the eyedropper to activate Automatic Color Adjustment tool, and then position the crosshairs on a neutral gray or white area and click once.

Right: iPhoto adjusts the whole photo's color for you, as shown here.

Thankfully, there's an easy way to check how well iPhoto corrected the photo. Take a look at an area that should be plain white. If it's clean (no green or magenta tint), then you're probably in good shape; if not, then undo the adjustment and try again.

Tip: If you're a portrait photographer, here's a trick for magically correcting skin tones. The key is to plan ahead by stashing a photographer's gray card somewhere in the composition that can be cropped out of the final print. Make sure the card receives about the same amount of lighting as the subject.

Later, in iPhoto, click the gray card in the composition with the automatic color corrector, and presto: perfect skin tones! Now crop out the gray card and make your print, grateful for the time you've just saved.

Copy and Paste

Working an image into perfect shape can involve a lot of time and slider-tweaking. And sometimes, a whole batch of photos require the same fixes—photos you took all at the same time, for example.

Fortunately, you don't have to recreate your masterful slider work on each of 200 photos, spending hours performing repetitive work. You can copy the adjustment settings from one photo and paste them onto others. And in iPhoto '11, you can do it with a keyboard shortcut, making that even easier than before.

First, open a photo you've previously edited in Edit view (you don't have to open the Adjust panel). Then choose Edit→Copy Adjustments or press ⌘-Option-C. Now move to the next shot (using the thumbnails browser, for example) and then choose Edit→Paste Adjustment or press ⌘-Option-V. iPhoto applies all your corrections to the new picture. You can apply those copied settings to as many photos as you wish. This is a *gigantic* time-saver when you're correcting several photos shot in the same lighting conditions.

Beyond iPhoto

Thanks to the Adjust panel, iPhoto's editing tools have come a long, long way. There's a lot less reason now to invest in a dedicated editing program.

But that doesn't mean that there are *no* reasons left. The Auto Levels command (in Photoshop and Photoshop Elements) is still a better color-fixer than iPhoto's Enhance button, and some people really like the "I'm Feeling Lucky" button in Picasa. Photoshop-type programs are also necessary if you want to superimpose text on a photo, combine several photos into one (a collage or a montage), create partial-color effects (where everything but a single object is black and white)—the list goes on.

Adobe Photoshop is by far the most popular tool for the job, but at about $700, it's also one of the most expensive (not to mention complicated). Fortunately, you can save yourself a lot of money by buying Photoshop Elements instead. It's an easier to use, trimmed-down version of Photoshop with all the basic image-editing stuff and just enough of the high-end features. It costs less than $100, and a free trial version is available online at *www.adobe.com*.

The Official Way

As noted at the beginning of this chapter, iPhoto makes it very easy to open a photo in another program for editing: You can either use the Preferences dialog box to specify that you *always* want to edit photos in an external program, or you can Control-click (right-click) a thumbnail whenever the spirit moves you, and then choose "Edit in external editor" from the shortcut menu.

Either way, the external program opens the photo. When you make your changes, use the other program's Save command, and then return to iPhoto, you'll discover that iPhoto has duplicated your photo. Now the original and the edited version are side by side. (In previous versions of iPhoto, this duplication process happened only to Raw files; now it happens to photos in any format.)

The Quick-and-Dirty Way

If you don't want to bother with setting up an external editor in Preferences, then you can also open a photo in another program by dragging its thumbnail *right out of the iPhoto window* and onto the other program's Dock icon.

In fact, you can drag several thumbnails at once to open all of them simultaneously.

Either way, they open in that other program, and you can happily edit away.

Warning: When you edit a photo in another program the "quick-and-dirty" way, you're essentially going behind iPhoto's back; the program doesn't have a chance to make a safety copy of the original. Therefore, you're sacrificing your ability to use the "Revert to Original" command (described below) to restore your photo to its original state in case of disaster.

Reverting to the Original

iPhoto includes built-in protection against overzealous editing—a feature that can save you much grief. If you end up cropping a photo too much, cranking up the brightness of a picture until it seems washed out, or accidentally turning someone's lips black with the red-eye tool, you can undo all your edits at once with the "Revert to Original" command. This command strips away *every change you've ever made* since the picture arrived from the camera. It leaves you with your original, unedited photo.

The secret of the "Revert to Original" command: Whenever you use any editing tools, iPhoto—without prompting and without informing you—instantly makes a duplicate of your original file. With an original version safely tucked away, iPhoto lets you go wild on the copy. Consequently, you can remain secure in the knowledge that in a pinch, iPhoto can always restore an image to the state it was in when you first imported it.

To restore an original photo (undoing all cropping, rotation, brightness adjustments, and so on), select a thumbnail of a photo. Then choose Photos→"Revert to Original," or Control-click (right-click) a photo and choose "Revert to Original" from the short-cut menu. (When you're editing a photo, the command reads "Revert to Previous" instead.) Now iPhoto swaps in the original version of the photo—and you're back where you started.

As noted earlier, iPhoto does its automatic backup trick whenever you edit your pictures (a) within iPhoto or (b) using a program that you've set up to open when you edit a picture. It does *not* make a backup when you drag a thumbnail onto another program's Dock icon. In that event, the "Revert to Original" command is dimmed when you select the edited photo.

Note: The unedited originals are stored in an Originals folder inside the iPhoto Library package (page 30). The edited versions are in a folder called Modified. (The Modified folder doesn't exist until you edit at least one photo.)

Editing Raw Files

iPhoto can handle Raw—the special, unprocessed file type that takes up a lot of space on your memory card but offers astonishing amounts of control when editing later on your Mac. Raw is generally available on most newer cameras over $300, and all SLR cameras (those that can handle interchangeable lenses).

Tip: Don't know which photos are Raw files? You could pop open the Info panel to find out (page 66) or take a peek at the top right of your histogram in the Adjust panel, but there's a faster way. In fact, you can gather up *all* your Raw files by creating a smart album. Choose File→New→Smart Album and set the pop-up menus to Filename, Contains, and, in the text field, type *cr* (which stands for "camera raw"). Tada! All the Raw files in your iPhoto library have just been corralled into a single album.

Actually, iPhoto can do more than handle Raw files. It can even edit them…sort of.

iPhoto is, at its heart, a program designed to work with JPEG files. Therefore, when it grabs a Raw file from your camera, it instantly creates a JPEG version of it, which is what you actually see onscreen. The Raw file is there on your hard drive (deep within the labyrinth known as the iPhoto Library package).

But what you see *onscreen* is a JPEG interpretation of that Raw file. (This conversion to JPEG is one reason iPhoto takes longer to import Raw files from a camera than other kinds of files.)

This trick of using JPEG look-alikes as stand-ins for your actual Raw files has two important benefits. First, it lets you work with your photos at normal iPhoto speed, without the lumbering minutes of calculations you'd endure if you were working with the original Raw files. Second, remember that your iPhoto photos are also accessible from within iDVD, iMovie, iWeb, Pages, and so on—programs that don't recognize Raw files.

So the question naturally comes up: What happens if you try to *edit* one of these Raw-file stunt doubles?

No problem. iPhoto accepts any changes you make to the JPEG version of the photo. Then, behind the scenes, it reinterprets the original Raw file, applying your edits. Finally, it generates a new JPEG for you to view.

External Raw Editors

It's nice that iPhoto comes with more powerful editing tools, and that you can use them with your original Raw files. Nevertheless, iPhoto doesn't offer every conceivable editing tool. So what happens if you want to edit your Raw files in another program, while still using iPhoto to organize them? Here, life can get a little complicated.

First, choose iPhoto→Preferences and click the Advanced tab (Figure 5-17). Turn on "Use RAW when using external editor." You've just told iPhoto that you want to work with Raw files in a different program, which is probably Adobe Camera Raw (the Raw-file editor that comes with Photoshop and Photoshop Elements), Lightroom, Aperture, or the Raw editor that came with your camera.

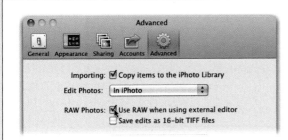

Figure 5-17:
You can now send an edited Raw file out of iPhoto for more sophisticated Raw editing, in a program like Adobe Camera Raw, with a quick double-click. The first step is to turn on the "Use RAW…" checkbox in iPhoto's Advanced preferences pane.

The Secret Recovery Slider

As Chapter 1 explains, photos captured in Raw format contain far more information than their JPEG brethren (page 151). And as you learned in this section, iPhoto was really built to handle JPEG files. Even so, a little more Raw editing power seems to sneak into the program now and then.

Case in point: If you open a Raw file in Edit view and then open the Adjust panel, you can hold down the Option key

and the Exposure slider changes to a *Recovery* slider. If you continue to hold down Option as you drag the slider to the right, you can recover hidden details in the highlights that weren't displayed by iPhoto in the first place (it doesn't work on shadows). Who knew?

Now, when you open a Raw file for editing, one of two things may happen:

- **If you've never edited the Raw file**. It opens up in Adobe Camera Raw (or whatever Raw-editing program you use), ready for editing.

- **If you have edited the file in iPhoto**. In this situation, iPhoto sends the edited *JPEG* file instead of the Raw file to Camera Raw! And that's probably not what you wanted.

  You can correct this case of mistaken identity by closing the photo and returning to iPhoto. Click the Raw file's thumbnail and then choose Photos→Reprocess RAW. (That's what the "Revert to Original" command becomes when you're working with Raw files.) iPhoto strips away your previous edits. Now you can double-click the picture to open it in your external Raw editor.

But beware! You can't just click the Save button and smile, confident that you'll see the edited version of the photo when you return to iPhoto. (That's how things work with JPEG files, as described earlier in this chapter, but not with Raw-format files.)

FREQUENTLY ASKED QUESTION

In iPhoto, Less is More

I just finished editing a batch of photos, cropping each picture to a much smaller size. But now my iPhoto Library file is taking up more space on my hard drive! How can making the photos smaller increase the size of my photo collection? Shouldn't throwing away all those pixels have the opposite effect—shrinking things down?

Your cropped photos do, in fact, take up much less space than they previously did. Remember, though, that iPhoto doesn't let you monkey with your photos without first stashing away a copy of each original photo, in case you ever want to use the "Revert to Original" command to restore a photo to its original condition.

So each time you crop a picture (or do any other editing) for the first time, you're actually creating a new, full-size copy on your hard drive, as iPhoto stores both the original and the edited versions of the photo. Therefore, the more photos you edit in iPhoto, the more hard drive space your photo collection will occupy.

Incidentally, it's worth noting that iPhoto may be a bit over-zealous when it comes to making backups of your originals. The simple act of rotating a photo, for example, creates a backup (which, considering how easy it is to re-rotate it, you might not consider strictly necessary). And if you've set up iPhoto to open a double-clicked photo in another program like Photoshop, then iPhoto creates a backup copy even if you don't end up changing it in that external program.

If you have The Library That Ate Cleveland, you can take matters into your own hands. But wading through your iPhoto library and manually tossing out dupes of your photos probably isn't your idea of a good time. Fortunately, you can get technology to do it for you if you have a spare $8. Yes, for less than the price of a movie ticket, Duplicate Annihilator from Brattoo Propaganda Software promises to comb through your collection and zap those needless copies hogging up your hard drive space. It works amazingly well, and you can snag it at *www.brattoo.com*.

Duplicate Annihilator methodically compares your images and detects duplicates with a set of algorithms. You can have the program slap a label on the copies or delete the duplicates as it finds them. And getting rid of all those unneeded files means a leaner and zippier iPhoto experience.

Instead, you have to use Camera Raw's Save As command to save the edited picture as a *new file* on your hard drive. You'll probably want to export it as a JPEG file, because that's the easiest format to work with in the iLife programs, email, on the Web, and so on. (Remember, your original Raw file is still tucked away safely in the iPhoto library if you want to revisit it. All you have to do is double-click its thumbnail again, and you're right back in Camera Raw.)

When you click Save, a JPEG version of your edited Raw file is waiting for you on the Desktop. Click Done in Adobe Camera Raw to make it go away.

Your last step, believe it or not, is to *reimport* the edited JPEG file back into iPhoto. First, though, you may want to make sure that the file number (say, IMG_6268.jpg) is the same as the original Raw version in iPhoto (IMG_6268.CR2). Why? Because you're going to wind up with the edited JPEG *and* the original Raw file side by side in your library.

This roundabout method of editing a Raw file is not, ahem, the height of convenience. However, if you want to use high-level image controls for your Raw files, then this is the path you must take, Grasshopper.

16-Bit TIFF Files Instead of JPEGs

For some time, high-end iPhotonauts bearing fancy cameras and memory cards full of Raw files have groused a bit about their choices. They could keep sending their Raw files on that clumsy round-trip to Photoshop, or they could work with iPhoto's converted, lower-quality JPEG files instead.

But since iPhoto '09, there's been a third option: They can tell iPhoto to convert those Raw files into TIFF files instead of JPEGs.

TIFF, of course, is an extremely high-quality graphics format that's frequently used in the professional printing business. (All of the illustrations in this book, for example, are TIFF files.) If you intend to print high-quality enlargements directly from iPhoto, then it might be worth telling iPhoto to convert your Raw files into TIFF instead of JPEG.

To make this switch, choose iPhoto→Preferences, click Advanced, and then turn on "Save edits as 16-bit TIFF files" (visible in Figure 5-17).

Making this switch involves a price, however.

First, if you've already edited some of your Raw files, then iPhoto has *already* converted them into the JPEG format. You'll have to strip away your edits by highlighting the thumbnails and choosing Photos→Reprocess RAW. *Now* when you open those files for editing, they'll turn into fully editable 16-bit TIFF files within iPhoto.

Second, you'll pay an enormous price in hard drive space.

Suppose that you start with a Raw file that takes up about 8 megabytes of space in your iPhoto library. You make a few edits; iPhoto generates a working JPEG that adds another 1.2 megs; fine.

But then you decide to reach for the brass ring of quality, so you instruct iPhoto to reprocess that Raw file and convert it into a TIFF instead. That TIFF version will add *62 megabytes* to your library, just for that one picture!

The moral: Save the TIFF-conversion business for your most prized photos, the ones that really merit that file format and all that quality.

And once you've finished working with them, return to the Preferences menu and turn off the checkbox.

The iPhoto Slideshow

iPhoto's slideshow feature offers one of the world's best ways to show off your digital photos (and videos, for that matter). Slideshows are easy to set up, they're free, and they make your photos look fantastic. And in iPhoto '11, they've been given a dose of steroids. You'll find six new themes that build on the flying, animated visual styles that debuted in iPhoto '09, and they even come with their own soundtracks so the animations and music match. All themes also take advantage of iPhoto's face-recognition smarts—they try to center your subjects' faces on the screen during the slideshow.

This chapter details not only how to put together an iPhoto slideshow, but also how to create presentations that make you *and* your photos look their absolute best.

About Slideshows

When you run an iPhoto slideshow, your Mac presents the pictures in Full Screen view—no windows, no menus, no borders—with your images filling every inch of your monitor. Professional transitions take you from one picture to the next, producing a smooth, cinematic effect. If you want, you can change or turn off the music that accompanies the presentation (each theme comes with its own soundtrack). The total effect is incredibly polished, yet creating a slideshow requires very little setup.

Note: If you're lucky enough to have more than one monitor—or you've got a laptop plugged into an external monitor or a TV—the slideshow plays on the monitor containing the iPhoto window. The other monitor displays solid black.

You always begin by selecting the pictures you want—by clicking an album or an Event header, for example. In iPhoto '11, you can also make slideshows based on a particular person on your Faces corkboard or a location in Places. Once you've done that, you can kick off a slideshow in two different ways:

- **Instant**. Click the Slideshow button in the middle of the iPhoto toolbar. Your screen goes black and the Themes panel appears, asking you to pick a visual animation style for your slideshow, as described below. Click a theme's thumbnail once to choose it. If you're feeling feisty, you can also change the music and other settings using the tabs at the top of the panel. But if you just want to see the show, click the Play button.

- **Saved**. In the early days of iPhoto, each album had its own associated slideshow settings. The album was, in essence, the container for the slideshow.

  That was a convenient approach, but not the most flexible. For example, it meant that if you wanted a slideshow that displayed only *half* the pictures in an album, then you had to make a new album just for that purpose. It also meant that you couldn't create different slideshow versions of the same album's worth of photos—a 2-seconds-per-shot version for neighbors, for example, and a 10-seconds-per-shot version for adoring grandparents.

  Now iPhoto offers something called a *saved* slideshow, an icon that appears in the Source list and is saved forever, independent of any album. It works a lot like an album in many ways. For example, the photos inside are only "pointers" to the real photos in the library, and you can drag them into any order you like. On the other hand, unlike an album, a saved slideshow contains special advanced controls for building a really sophisticated slideshow.

This chapter covers both of these techniques.

Slideshow Themes

One of iPhoto's most fun features is *themed slideshows*, and iPhoto '11 includes six new ones. Peppered with fancy graphics and animation, these visual presentation styles spice up your slideshows with a minimum of effort on your part. As shown in Figure 6-1, the first thing iPhoto wants you to do when you play an instant slideshow is to pick a theme from the Themes panel.

Your choices include:

- **Ken Burns**. If you like that slow pan-and-zoom approach that made the documentary filmmaker famous, you can use it yourself here. There's more on this man and his technique in the box on page 161.

- **Origami**. New in iPhoto '11, this theme displays your photos by folding them open into a variety of different sized squares and rectangles. It first debuted on the iPad, but here in iPhoto, any faces the program detects are centered within each shape instead of being clumsily cropped.

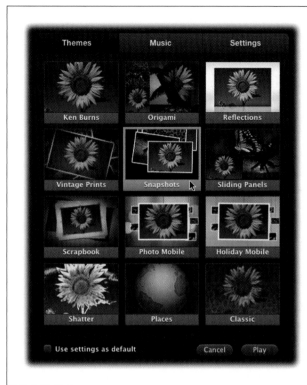

Figure 6-1:
Click the Slideshow button on the iPhoto toolbar, and the first thing it wants you to do is pick a theme for your show. To preview a theme, simply hover your cursor over its thumbnail.

Click a theme's thumbnail to select it, and then click the Play button if you want to see how your photos do against iPhoto's default music. You can also click the Music and Settings tabs in the panel to tinker before the first slide even plays.

- **Reflections**. This new theme pairs the Ken Burns zoom effect with photos (or groups of photos) on a white background. Look closely and you'll see a pretty little reflection near the bottom of your screen.

- **Vintage Prints**. One of the most beautiful and artistic themes, this new one displays your photos as if they were Polaroids (complete with thin white border) in a big messy stack on your coffee table. The photo on top appears in color and the rest are black and white. The stacks then zoom in, out, and rotate, à la Ken Burns.

- **Snapshots**. If you miss the white-bordered prints of yesteryear, this theme slides the old-style photos into the center of the screen. As the next photo arrives, it appears to land on top of the previous few shots, which fade to black-and-white in the background.

- **Sliding Panels**. Another motion-filled theme, Sliding Panels lives up to its name by slipping your photos onto the screen from several directions. It also displays several pictures at once, sort of like the average layout in a celebrity magazine or an episode of *24*.

- **Scrapbook**. Your photos are cleverly animated right into images of old-fashioned scrapbooks, just like Grandma used to make out of paper and glue. The unseen cameraman pans across these scrapbook pages, pausing to admire each photo.

- **Photo Mobile, Holiday Mobile**. These new, motion-packed themes have your photos swinging in and out of view, bobbing and dangling as if they were attached to a real mobile. The Holiday version even has snowflakes falling in the background.

- **Shatter**. This theme appears to colorfully smash apart your photos across the white expanse of screen—only to reassemble them into the next photo. This hyperkinetic theme works great for slideshows filled with action shots. For weddings or memorials? Not so much.

- **Places**. Perhaps the most animated of the new iPhoto '11 slideshow themes, this one begins with a huge, spinning, 3-D globe. Next, it zooms into a slightly tilted map displaying red marker pins and small thumbnails of the photos you took in those spots, and then zooms in on each photo. It's impressive, but if you haven't geotagged any of your photos (as described in Chapter 4), you'll see the slightly depressing message shown in Figure 6-2.

- **Classic**. It worked for Coca-Cola, so Apple has rebranded the old iPhoto slideshow style as "Classic." It's classic indeed: Each slide appears for a couple of seconds, filling the screen, then crossfades into the next. You have lots of control over transitions and other effects.

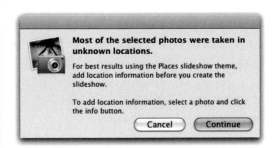

Figure 6-2:
iPhoto hates for you to be disappointed, so you see this message if you choose the Places theme and haven't yet geotagged the photos you've selected to show. Bummer!

Instant Slideshows

An *instant* slideshow, for the purposes of this book, is one that you begin by clicking the triangular Slideshow button in the iPhoto toolbar, as shown in Figure 6-3. Instant slideshows are not quite as instant as they used to be in past versions of the program, but with the built-in themes, you get a slick, fancy slideshow in just a couple of clicks.

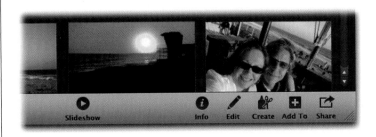

Figure 6-3:
The quickest way to kick off a slideshow in iPhoto is to click the Slideshow button in the toolbar at the bottom of your iPhoto window (or monitor if you're in Full Screen view).

Tip: While there's no keyboard shortcut for starting a slideshow, you can press the space bar to pause it, or use the arrow keys to move through the show manually, photo by photo. To stop a show once it's running, press the Esc key or wiggle your mouse so the slideshow controls appear and then click the ⊗.

Selecting a Slideshow Theme

After you click the Slideshow button on the main iPhoto window, the window expands to fill your monitor, turns black, and displays the Themes panel.

1. **Click to select one of the nine themes shown in Figure 6-1.**

FREQUENTLY ASKED QUESTION

The Ken Burns Effect

Who's this Ken Burns guy, and what's his effect?

Apple first introduced what it calls the "Ken Burns effect" in iMovie, not iPhoto. It's a special effect designed to address the core problem associated with using still photos in a movie—namely, that they're *still!* They just sit there without motion or sound, wasting much of the dynamic potential of video.

For years, professional videographers have addressed the problem by using special sliding camera rigs that produce gradual zooming, panning, or both, to bring photographs to life.

Among the most famous practitioners of this art is Ken Burns, the creator of PBS documentaries like *The Civil War,*

Baseball, and *The National Parks*—which is why Apple, with Burns' permission, named the feature after him.

And now your own humble slideshows can have that graceful, animated, fluid Ken Burns touch or even a whole Ken Burns theme. No photo ever just sits there motionless on the screen. Instead, each one flies gracefully inward or outward, sliding and zooming.

It's a great effect, but it can occasionally backfire, too. Every now and then, for example, the actual subject of the photo won't be centered, or the photo won't make it completely onto the screen before the next one begins to zoom on. (One of the virtues of the *saved* slideshow, described on page 170, is that *you* control where the Ken Burns panning and zooming begins and ends.)

Point to a theme's thumbnail without clicking to see a tiny preview of what it does. If you turn on "Use settings as default," then iPhoto saves these settings, but only for *this* slideshow—not for all your slideshows from here on out.

2. **Adjust the music and transitions by clicking the Music and Settings tabs.**

Each theme comes with its own soundtrack. In fact, Apple paid a lot of money for them, and they include such famous copyrighted tunes as "You've Got a Friend in Me" (Randy Newman) and the theme from "Peanuts" (Vince Guaraldi). In fact, iPhoto includes 14 songs scientifically engineered to work well with the animated themes. But if you don't care for the canned music or pre-selected transitions, click the appropriate tabs and make your own adjustments. The following sections explain how.

3. **Click the Play button.**

The slideshow starts, beginning with the title of the album. Sit back and enjoy the fruits of your clicking.

What to Do During a Slideshow

If you wiggle your mouse while the slideshow is playing, you get the control panel shown in Figure 6-4. Here's what you can do while this display is onscreen:

- Pause the show, or click the arrow buttons to skip forward or back.

- Click the slides icon to reopen the Themes panel shown in Figure 6-1, if the current theme isn't rocking your world.

- Click the musical-notes button to open the Music chooser, shown on page 164.

- Click the ✿ icon to open the Settings panel, where you can change the timing and transition settings for your slideshow (page 165).

- Finally, click ✖ to close Full Screen view, end the slideshow, and go back to the regular iPhoto window.

Note: It's not your imagination; buttons for Rotate, Ratings, and Delete This Photo are no longer part of the slideshow control bar. And in iPhoto '11, there's no slide browser either.

If you wait long enough without clicking anything, the control bar eventually disappears, returning the full glory to the slideshow in progress.

Music: Soundtrack Central

Perhaps more than any other single element, *music* transforms a slideshow, turning your ordinary photos into a cinematic event. When you pair the right music with the right pictures, you do more than just show off your photos; you create a mood that can stir the emotions of your audience. So if you really want your friends and family to be transfixed by your photos, then add a soundtrack.

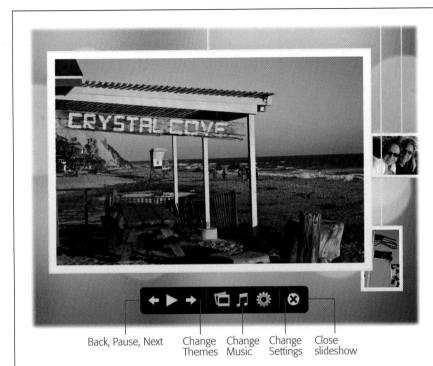

Figure 6-4:
As the slideshow progresses, you can pause the show, go backward, or get to the panel for Themes, Music, and Settings, all courtesy of this onscreen control bar.

The Photo Mobile theme was used here. Nifty, ain't it?

Back, Pause, Next   Change Themes   Change Music   Change Settings   Close slideshow

That's especially easy if, like many Mac OS X fans, you've assembled a collection of your favorite music in iTunes, the MP3-playing software that comes with every Mac.

For the background music of an iPhoto slideshow, you have the choice of an individual song from your iTunes library or an entire *playlist*. Gone are the days of listening to the same tune repeating over and over again during a lengthy slideshow—a sure way to go quietly insane (unless, of course, you *really* like that song).

The possibilities of this feature are endless, especially combined with iPhoto's smart albums feature (page 62). You can create a smart album that contains, say, only photos of your kids taken in December, choose the Holiday Mobile theme, give it a soundtrack composed of holiday tunes (created effortlessly using a smart playlist in iTunes), and you've got an instant holiday slideshow!

Your first iPhoto slideshow is born with several ready-to-use soundtracks—as noted earlier, they include expensively licensed songs from Randy Newman, Miles Davis, and Vince Guaraldi. And if you choose one of the animated themes, the song syncs perfectly with the animation (or, at least, it's supposed to).

iPhoto '11 includes 14 songs listed in the Theme Music folder, which is identified in the Source pop-up menu (Figure 6-5). In that same Source menu, you can also choose Sample Music, where you'll find 11 more slideshow-worthy tracks, including two hits from J.S. Bach and some other instrumentals from various musical genres.

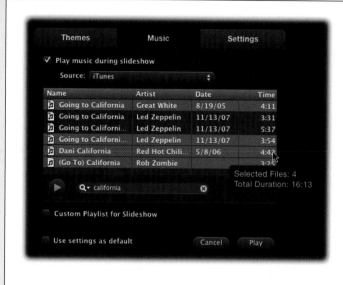

Figure 6-5:
The Music panel lets you choose a playlist or your entire iTunes library from the Source menu. By clicking the column headings, you can sort the song list by name, artist, date, or length. You can also use the Search box, as shown here, to pinpoint an individual song. To select several songs, ⌘-click each one. Hover your mouse over a song's length in the Time column and iPhoto tells you the duration of the songs you've chosen, as shown here.

If you have a long slideshow, you can use the Source menu to choose an iTunes playlist rather than a single song. iPhoto repeats the song (or playlist) for as long as your slideshow lasts. Inspired to make a playlist right here? Turn on the "Custom Playlist for Slideshow" checkbox and drag song titles from the list above into the space that appears.

Of course, you can also choose music from your own collection. If, from that Source pop-up menu, you choose GarageBand, you're offered any musical masterpieces you've created yourself, using the GarageBand music-recording software.

Most people, however, will be more inclined to choose iTunes from this list. At that point, every track and playlist in your iTunes library automatically appears here. You can search and sort through your songs and playlists, just as though you were in iTunes itself.

In other words, you can use this list either to select an entire playlist to use as your soundtrack, or to call up a playlist for the purpose of listing the individual songs in it, thereby narrowing your search for the one song you seek.

Here are a few other tricks you can use in the Music panel:

- To listen to a song before committing to it as a soundtrack, double-click it, or click its name in the list, and then click the Play button (▶). Click the same button, which turns blue during playback, when you've heard enough.

- To use an entire playlist as a soundtrack for your slideshow, select it from the list. At slideshow time, iPhoto begins the slideshow with the first tune in the playlist and continues through all the songs in the list before starting over.

- To use an individual song as a soundtrack, click its name in the list. That song will loop continuously for the duration of the slideshow.

- To use more than one song as a soundtrack, ⌘-click each one in the list.

- Rather than scroll through a huge list, you can locate the tracks you want by using the capsule-shaped Search box below the song list. Click the Search box, and then type a word (or part of a word) to filter your list. iPhoto searches the Artist, Name, and Album fields of the iTunes library and displays only the matching entries. To clear the search and view your whole list again, click the ⊗ in the Search box.

- Click one of the three headers—Artist, Name, or Time—to sort the iTunes music list by that header.

- You can also change the arrangement of the three columns by grabbing the headers and dragging them into a different order.

- The "Custom Playlist for Slideshow" checkbox lets you whip up a mini-playlist right here, right now. When you turn on this option, an empty list box appears below the list of songs. Scroll through the songs in the top part of the panel; when you find one you want to include in the slideshow, drag its tiny icon down into the lower part. Drag the tracks up and down within the playlist to rearrange them.

Once you've settled on (and clicked) an appropriate musical soundtrack for the current slideshow, you can turn on "Use settings as default" (to memorize that choice without starting the slideshow) or Play (to begin the slideshow). From now on, that song or playlist plays whenever you run an instant slideshow from that album.

Alternatively, if you decide you don't want any music to play, then turn off the "Play music during slideshow" checkbox at the top of the panel.

Different Shows, Different Albums

You can save different slideshow settings for each icon in your Source list.

To save settings for a specific photo album, for example, first choose the album from the Source list, and then click the Slideshow button on the iPhoto toolbar to open the Slideshow panel (Figure 6-1). On the Music and Settings tabs, you can pick the speed, order, repeat, and music settings you want; finally, turn on "Use settings as default." The settings you saved automatically kick in each time you launch a slideshow from that album.

Slideshow Settings

With Theme and Music taken care of, the third tab of the Slideshow panel handles just about everything else that makes a great presentation. On this tab, you can fiddle with the timing between slides, the Hollywood-style transitions between each shot, titles and captions, and other elements that influence the slideshow's look and feel. The options available depend on which theme you're using.

Slide Timing

If left to its own devices, iPhoto '11 advances through your pictures at the rate of one photo every 3–7 seconds, depending on the theme. Apple's slide durations are fine for most purposes, but you can change the rate.

On the Settings tab of the Slideshow panel, use the "Play each slide for a minimum of __ seconds" controls to specify a different interval, as shown in Figure 6-6. Or, if you want your slideshow to last exactly as long as the song or playlist you chose for the soundtrack, turn on "Fit slideshow to music."

Note: iPhoto '11 doesn't let you use the ◄ or ► keys on your keyboard to adjust slide speed during playback the way you could in previous versions.

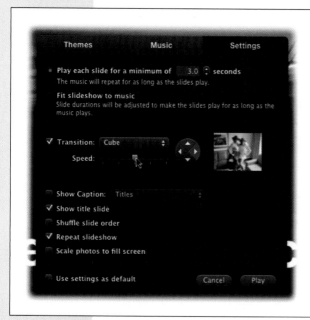

Figure 6-6:
The controls in the Settings panel let you fine-tune the timing and transition between slides. (Depending on your theme, you may not see all these options.) Turn on Transition and use the pop-up menu to test different effects (like Cube or Wipe) for getting from one slide to the next.

In the lower part of the panel, you can also choose to display the titles, locations, and descriptions you may (or may not) have spent hours adding to your photos.

Turn on "Use settings as default" if you want to save your tinkerings. "Default" here doesn't mean the default settings for all your iPhoto slideshows, though—just this one.

Transitions

Themes like Shatter and Sliding Panels use special transition (crossfade) styles between images. But if you're using the Classic or Ken Burns themes for your show, you can choose from 14 different types of transition effects between slides—for example, the classic crossfade or dissolve, in which one slide gradually fades away as the next "fades in" to take its place. Here's a summary:

- **Random.** A combination of the various transitions.
- **None.** An abrupt switch, or simple cut, to the following image.

- **Cube**. Imagine that your photos are pasted onto the sides of a box that rotates to reveal the next one. If you've ever used Mac OS X's Fast User Switching feature, you've got the idea.

- **Dissolve**. This is the classic crossfade.

- **Droplet**. This wild effect resembles animated, concentric ripples expanding from the center of a pond—except that a new image forms as the ripples spread.

- **Fade Through Black**. After each slide has strutted and fretted its time upon the stage, the screen fades momentarily to black before the next one fades into view. The effect is simple and clean, like an old-fashioned living-room slideshow. Along with Dissolve, this effect is one of the most natural and least distracting choices.

- **Flip**. The first photo seems to flip over, revealing the next photo pasted onto its back.

- **Mosaic Flip Large, Mosaic Flip Small**. The screen is divided into several squares, each of which rotates in turn to reveal part of the new image, like puzzle pieces turning over. (The two options refer to the size of the puzzle pieces.)

- **Move In**. Photos slide in un-dramatically from the edges of the screen.

- **Page Flip**. Apple's just showing off here. The first photo's lower-right corner peels up like a sheet of paper, revealing the next photo "page" beneath it.

- **Push, Reveal, Wipe**. Three variations of "new image sweeping onto the screen." In Push, Photo A gets shoved off the other side of the screen as Photo B slides on. In Reveal, Photo A slides off, revealing a stationary Photo B. And in Wipe, Photo A gets covered up as Photo B slides on.

- **Twirl**. Photo A appears to spin furiously, shrinking to a tiny dot in the middle of the screen—and then Photo B spins onscreen from that spot. The whole thing feels a little like the spinning-newspaper effect used to signify breaking news in old black-and-white movies.

In most cases, choosing a transition effect makes two additional controls "light up" just below the pop-up menu:

- **Speed**. Move the slider to the right for a speedy transition, or to the left for a leisurely one. Take into account your timing settings. The less time your photo is onscreen, the better off you are with a fast transition, so that your audience has time to see the picture before the next transition starts. However, moving the Speed slider *all* the way to the right produces a joltingly fast change.

- **Direction**. This arrow-covered wheel determines the direction the new image enters from. Click the corresponding arrow to choose right to left, top to bottom, or vice versa (left to right or bottom to top). As soon as you click, iPhoto shows you what the transition will look like in the preview area to the right of the wheel. (Most people find left to right the most comfortable way to experience a transition, but a slow top-to-bottom wipe is pleasant, too.)

Show Caption

Need some words to go with the music? Use this pop-up menu to show text like descriptions, places, dates, or titles.

As noted on page 67, every photo in your collection can have a name—a title, in other words. And if you want to show off your geotagged (page 107) pictures from your cross-country trip, it's easy to put all those place names and descriptions up on the big screen. If you turn on this option, iPhoto superimposes the selected text in big white text on the lower corner of the image, as shown in Figure 6-7.

Note: The Show Captions option works only with themes that *aren't* animated, meaning you can use it only on the Ken Burns and Classic themes. After all, rotated or bouncing text is pretty tough to read.

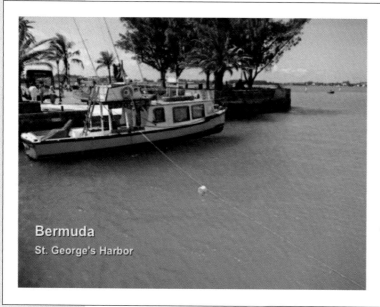

Figure 6-7:
If you don't feel like narrating your slideshow over and over, then fill in the name and description fields in the photo's Info panel (page 66).

When it comes time to set up the slideshow, turn on Show Caption in the Settings panel and then choose the text you want to display (titles and descriptions are turned on here). When you play the slideshow, iPhoto lets your viewers know what they're looking at. If your photo has a location (page 107), it appears in large white text.

Needless to say, the cryptic file names created by your digital camera (like *IMG_0034 .jpg*) usually don't add much to your slideshow. But if you've taken the time to give your photos helpful, explanatory names ("My dog, age 3 months"), then by all means turn on the Show Captions checkbox and choose the text you want to display.

Show Title Slide

Show titles? Sure—*Fiddler on the Roof! West Side Story! Cats!*

Just kidding.

Turn on "Show title slide" if you want the first slide in the show to display the name of the album, face, or place you're basing the slideshow on. (Try it before you chuck it; it's actually a great way to start the slideshow.)

Shuffle Slide Order

An iPhoto slideshow normally displays your pictures in the order they appear in the photo-viewing area. But if you'd like to add a dash of surprise and spontaneity to the proceedings, then turn on "Shuffle slide order." Now iPhoto displays the pictures in whatever random order it pleases.

Repeat Slideshow

When iPhoto is done running through all your photos in a slideshow, it ordinarily starts playing the whole sequence from the beginning again. If you want your photos to play just once through, then turn off "Repeat slideshow."

Scale Photos to Fill Screen

If any photos in your slideshow don't match your screen's proportions, then you may want to turn on "Scale photos to fill screen." For example, if your slideshow contains photos in portrait orientation—that is, pictures taken with the camera rotated—iPhoto normally fills up the unused screen space on each side with vertical black bars.

Turning on "Scale photos" makes iPhoto enlarge the picture so much that it completely fills the screen. This solution, however, comes at a cost: Now the top and bottom of the picture are lost beyond the edges of the monitor.

When the middle of the picture is the most important part, this option works fine. If it's not, and the black bars bother you, then the only other alternative is to crop the odd-sized pictures in the saved slideshow (or album) to match your monitor's shape. (See "Cropping" on page 131.)

Note: This option doesn't mean "Enlarge smaller photos to fill the screen"—iPhoto always does that. This option affects only photos whose *proportions* don't match the screen's.

Picking Photos for Instant Slideshows

Among the virtues of instant slideshows is the freedom you have to choose which pictures you want to see. For example:

- If no photos are selected, iPhoto exhibits all the pictures currently in the photo-viewing area, starting with the first photo in the album, Face, or Event.

Most people, most of the time, want to turn one *album* into a slideshow. That's easy: Just click the album before starting the slideshow. It can be any album you've created, a smart album, the Last Import album, or one of iPhoto's Recent collections. As long as no individual pictures are selected, iPhoto uses all the pictures in the album currently open.

Tip: You can also create an instant slideshow from multiple albums. That is, you can select more than one album simultaneously (by ⌘-clicking them). When you click Play, iPhoto creates a slideshow from all of their merged contents, in order.

- If *one* photo is selected, iPhoto uses that picture as its starting point for the show, ignoring any that come before it. Of course, if you've got the slideshow set to loop continuously, then iPhoto will eventually circle back to display the first photo in the window.
- If you've selected more than one picture, iPhoto includes *only* those pictures.

Photo Order

iPhoto displays your pictures in the same order you see them in the photo-viewing area. In other words, to rearrange your slides, drag the thumbnails around within their album. Just remember that you can't drag pictures around in an Event, a Face, a Place, a smart album, the Last 12 Months collection, or the Last Import folder—only within a regular album.

Note: If iPhoto appears to be shamelessly disregarding the order of your photos when running a slideshow, it's probably because you've got the "Shuffle slide order" option turned on in the Slideshow panel, as described on page 169.

Saved Slideshows

iPhoto also offers *saved* slideshows, each of which appears as an icon in your Source list. The beauty of this system is that you can tweak a slideshow to death—you can even set up different transition and speed settings for *each individual slide*—and then save all your work as an independent clickable icon, ready for playback whenever you've got company. Saved slideshows are also a snap to shuttle over to your iPad, iPhone, or iPod for musical memories on the go (page 284).

Here's how you create and fine-tune a saved slideshow, which is easier than ever in iPhoto '11:

1. **Select the photos you want to include.**

   You can select either a random batch of slides (using any of the techniques described on page 49) or an icon in the Source list (like an album, Place, or Face).

By Shift-clicking or ⌘-clicking, you can actually select several icons in the Source list simultaneously. When you proceed to step 2, iPhoto will intelligently merge their contents into one glorious slideshow.

2. **Choose File→New→Slideshow.**

Thunder rumbles, the lights flicker—and you wind up in the slideshow editing mode shown in Figure 6-8, which has some features of Edit view and some features of regular old thumbnail-organizing mode. The first thing you see is a title (beginning) slide filled with black containing the name of the Event or album.

Note: While the title of your slideshow initially appears on a solid black slide, that's not how it'll play back: it'll be superimposed atop your first slide instead. However, if you'd like to change the font, size, or the text itself, just highlight it and then press ⌘-T to summon OS X's Fonts dialog box.

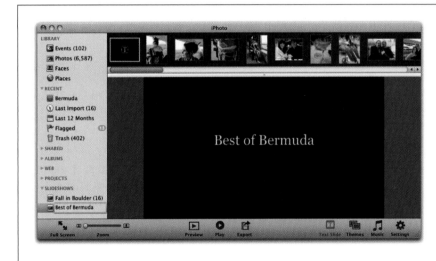

Figure 6-8:
In the slideshow editor, the window shape is designed to mimic your Mac's monitor shape (or whatever screen proportions you've specified in the Settings panel); that's why gray bars appear on the left and right sides. The Themes, Music, and Settings buttons in the lower right let you finesse the slideshow as you go. Click the Preview button to play the show in the iPhoto window.

At the same time, a new icon with the name of the Event or album appears in the Source list, highlighted so you can rename it. (The icon looks like a little pile of actual slides.)

3. **Choose a playback order for your pictures.**

The trick here is to drag the thumbnails at the top of the window horizontally. Don't forget that you can move these en masse, too. For example, click slide number 1, Shift-click slide number 3, and then drag the three selected thumbnails as a group to a different spot in the lineup.

4. **Click the Theme button to choose one of the 12 themes (page 158).**

Each theme's tiny thumbnail image gives the vaguest hint of what to expect; point to it without clicking to see an animated preview. If you don't like the theme, you can change it later.

5. **Click the Music and Settings buttons to set up the global playback options.**

That is, set up the preferences that affect *all* slides in the show (like timing and transitions), using the controls at the bottom of the window. You can read about what these controls do in the next section.

6. **If you like, walk through the slides one at a time, taking the opportunity to set up their individual characteristics.**

For example, you can choose to have one slide linger longer on the screen, have another dissolve (rather than wipe) into the next picture, and so on.

7. **Preview the show.**

If you click the Preview button, iPhoto plays a miniature version of the slideshow in the iPhoto window.

8. **Roll it!**

When everything looks ready, click the Play button (the big one, next to Preview) to play the actual slideshow in Full Screen view.

When it's over, you can do all the usual things with the slideshow icon that now resides in your Source list:

- **Delete it**. Drag it onto the iPhoto Trash icon, as you would an album. When you're asked if you're sure, click Delete or press the Return key.

- **File it away**. Drag it into an iPhoto folder (page 65) to keep it organized with the related albums and books.

- **Rename it**. Double-click its icon and then type away.

- **Edit it**. Click its icon and then change the bottom-of-screen controls.

Global Settings

As indicated by the preceding steps, you can make two kinds of changes to a saved slideshow: global ones (which affect all slides) and individual ones.

Most of the global options are hiding behind the Settings buttons, which summon the panel shown in Figure 6-9. Clicking the Themes and Music buttons call up panels, too.

The Themes panel

This is the same panel with the same 12 themes you saw before. If you decide the Snapshots theme just doesn't work for a slideshow of the high-school football game, then pick another theme here.

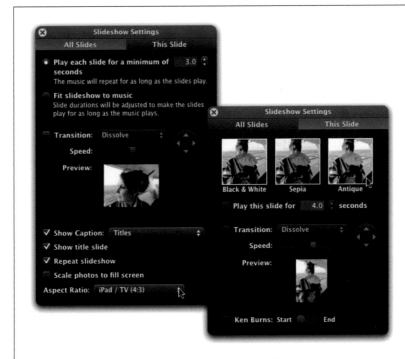

Figure 6-9:
Left: The Slideshow Settings panel's All Slides pane offers a few new options that you don't see when creating an instant slideshow. Everything in it is wired for a single purpose: to establish the standard settings for every slide in the show.

Right: Of course, you can override these settings on a slide-by-slide basis, if you'd like. The "This Slide" pane lets you change the color of individual slides to black & white, sepia, or antique, as well as the speed of a transition, and the amount of time an individual slide stays onscreen.

The Music Settings panel

The Music Settings panel should look familiar; it's identical to the panel shown in Figure 6-5. Here's where you choose the music to accompany your slideshow, as described on page 162.

The Slideshow Settings panel

The Settings button brings up a panel that only *seems* familiar (Figure 6-9). It's actually got two different tabs: All Slides and This Slide. As you can probably guess, the All Slides tab makes global changes across the whole show, while This Slide affects just the picture on the screen.

If you're using the Classic or Ken Burns theme, the All Slides pane contains many of the same options described earlier (transition style, slide duration, Ken Burns effect, choice of music track or playlist, options to show your photos' titles and ratings, and so on).

Note: The animated themes—Shatter, Sliding Panels, Scrapbook, and so on—handle their own transitions and have fewer options in the Slideshow Settings panel.

In this incarnation, though, you get a few new options. First, iPhoto wants to know how it should handle slideshows that aren't exactly the same length as the music you've selected for their soundtracks. Your options are "Play each slide for a minimum of __ seconds" (which loops the music as necessary to fit the slides) or "Fit slideshow to music" (plays the music only once, but squeezes or stretches the slides' time on the screen to fit the music).

Down at the bottom of the pane, you get an Aspect Ratio pop-up menu. Here, you can tell iPhoto what *shape* the screen will be.

Now, that may strike you at first as a singularly stupid statement. After all, doesn't the Mac know what shape its own screen is? But there's more to this story: Remember that you can build slideshows that aren't intended to be played on your screen.

You might want to export a slideshow to play on other people's screens, or even on their TV sets, by burning the slideshow to a DVD. That's why this pop-up menu offers four choices: This Screen; HDTV (16:9) for high-definition TV sets and other rectangular ones, iPad/TV (4:3) for iPads and standard squarish TV sets, or iPhone (3:2) for slideshows you plan to export to your nifty Apple smartphone.

In any case, the changes you make here affect *all* photos in the slideshow. Click the ✖ at the top left of the panel when you're done, confident in the knowledge that you can always override these settings for individual slides.

Individual-Slide Options

The All Slides pane of the Slideshow Settings panel offers plenty of control, but the changes you make there affect *every* slide in the show. But by clicking the panel's This Slide tab when you have a photo onscreen, iPhoto '11 gives you control over *individual* slides. For example:

POWER USERS' CLINIC

Cropping and Zooming

Here's a totally undocumented iPhoto feature: While creating a saved slideshow, you can choose to present only *part* of a photo, in effect cropping out portions of it, without actually touching the original.

To enlarge the photo (thus cropping out its outer margins), just drag the Zoom slider at the lower-left corner of the iPhoto window (you don't have to have any panels open to do it). Whatever photo size you create here is what will appear during the slideshow.

What you may not realize, though, is that you can also drag *inside* the picture itself to shift its position onscreen. Simply click within the main viewing area and *drag the image where you want it.*

Between these two techniques—sizing and sliding—you can display a very specific portion of the photo. (Heck, you could even present the photo *twice* in the same slideshow, revealing half of it the first time, half of it the next.)

Color options

Certain photos may have more power with special tint effects. Here, iPhoto lets you change the color of the selected photo to Black & White, Sepia (brownish, old-fashioned monochrome), or Antique, which lends a sort of faded, flattened look to the photo's colors.

Slide timing

As you know, the Slideshow Settings panel's All Slides pane (Figure 6-9, left) is where you specify how long you want each slide to remain onscreen—in general. But if you want to override that setting for a few particularly noteworthy shots, the This Slide pane (Figure 6-9, right) has the solution.

With the specially blessed photo on the screen before you, summon the Settings panel and click This Slide. Then use the "Play this slide for __ seconds" control to specify this slide's few seconds of fame.

Transition

The options in this pop-up menu are the different crossfade effects (Cube, Dissolve, and so on) that you can specify for the transition from one slide to another. (Whatever you choose here governs the transition *out* of the currently selected slide; every slideshow *begins* with a fade-in from black.)

Transition speed and direction

You can also control the speed of the transitions on a slide-by-slide basis, and even which direction the transition effect proceeds across the screen (for transition styles that offer a choice).

The Ken Burns checkbox

If you flip back a few pages, you'll be reminded that the Ken Burns effect is a graceful, panning, zooming effect that brings animation to the photos of your slideshow, so that they float and move instead of just lie there.

You'll also be reminded that when you apply the effect to an entire slideshow, you have no control over the pans and zooms. iPhoto might begin or end the pan too soon, so that the primary subject gets chopped off. Or maybe it zooms too fast, so that your viewers never get the chance to soak in the scene—or maybe it pans or zooms in the *wrong direction* for your creative intentions.

Fortunately, the Ken Burns controls located here let you adjust every aspect of the panning and zooming for one photo at a time. (Note: The settings you're about to make *override* whatever global Ken Burns setting you've made.) As you can see in Figure 6-10, it works like this:

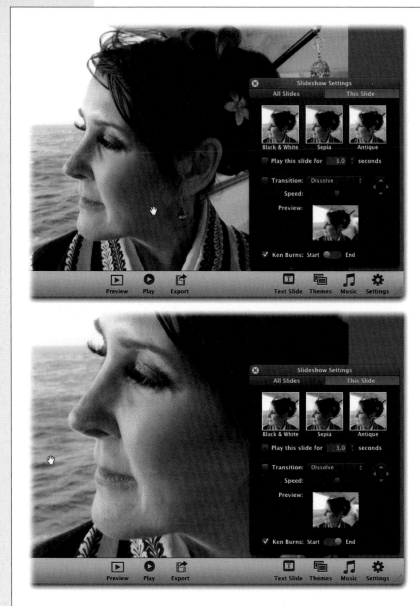

Figure 6-10:
The idea behind the Ken Burns effect is that you set the start and end points for the gradual zooming/panning effect. iPhoto, meanwhile, automatically supplies the in-between frames, producing a gradual shift from the first position to the second. In this case, the Ken Burns effect lets you save the "punch line" of this story-telling photo for the end of its time onscreen.

Top: Open the Slideshow Settings box and click the This Slide tab. Turn on the Ken Burns checkbox, and then click Start. Use the Zoom slider (lower left of the iPhoto toolbar) to magnify the photo, if you like. Once you've magnified it, you can drag inside the photo to reposition it inside the "frame" of your screen.

Bottom: Click End. Once again, use the Zoom slider, and then drag inside the photo, if you like, to specify the final degree of zoom and movement. In both shots here, you can see the tiny "grabbing hand" cursor that appears whenever your mouse wanders into the magnified-photo area.

1. **Select the photo. Click Settings→This Slide and turn on the Ken Burns checkbox at the bottom of the pane.**

   If more than one photo is selected, iPhoto applies the effect only to the first one.

2. **Click Start. Drag the Zoom slider (at the lower-left of iPhoto's toolbar) until the photo is as big as you want it at the *beginning* of its time onscreen. Drag inside the picture itself to adjust the photo's initial position.**

   In other words, you're setting up the photo the way it will first appear. Often, you won't want to do anything to it at all—you want it to start on the screen at its original size and then zoom in from there.

   But if you hope to create a zooming *out* effect, then drag Zoom slider to the right, magnifying the photo, and then drag the picture itself to center it properly (your cursor turns into a hand).

3. **Click End. Use the Zoom slider to set up the picture's final degree of magnification. Drag inside the photo to specify its final position.**

   You've just set the starting and ending conditions for the photo.

   Take a moment now to click the Preview button in the This Slide pane. The animated photo goes through its scheduled motion inside the window, letting you check the overall effect. Repeat steps 2 and 3 as necessary.

Tip: If you accidentally set the End position when you actually meant to set the Start position, then Option-click the word "Start." iPhoto graciously copies your End settings into the Start settings. Now both Start and End are the same, of course, but at least you can edit just the End—only one set of settings instead of two. (The same trick works in the other direction as well.)

Now that you've specified the beginning and ending positions of the photo, iPhoto interpolates, calculating each intermediate frame between the starting and ending points you've specified.

Click the Preview button in the This Slide pane to see the fully animated results of your programming.

Slideshow Tips

The following guidelines will help you build impressive slideshows that truly showcase your efforts as a digital photographer.

Picture Size

Choosing photos for your slideshow involves more than just picking the photos you like the best. You also have to make sure you've selected pictures that are the right size.

iPhoto always displays slideshow photos at full-screen dimensions—and on today's monitors, that means at least 1024 × 768 pixels. If your photos are smaller than that—because you cropped them or had your camera set to low-quality, say—then iPhoto stretches them to fill the screen, often with disastrously pixelated results.

Although iPhoto blows up images to fill the screen, it always does so proportionately, maintaining each photo's vertical-to-horizontal aspect ratio. As a result, photos often appear with vertical bars at the left and right edges when viewed on long rectangular screens like the Apple Cinema Display, the 17-inch iMac, and so on. To eliminate this effect, see "Scale Photos to Fill Screen" on page 169.

Determining the size of your photos

If you're not sure whether your photos are big enough to be slideshow material, just open the Info panel by clicking the little ❶ in the iPhoto toolbar and then look at the Size field near the panel's top left. You'll see something like "1600 × 1200." That's the width and height of the photo, measured in pixels.

As you might imagine, very small photos are horribly blocky and blurry when blown up to full-screen size. Very large ones look fine, but iPhoto takes longer to display them, and the crossfade transitions might not look smooth. For the best possible results, make your photos the same pixel size as your screen.

Here are a few other ways to make sure your slideshows look their best:

- Try to stick with photos whose proportions roughly match your screen. If you have a traditionally shaped screen, use photos with a 4:3 width-to-height ratio, just as they came from the camera. However, if you have a widescreen monitor (Cinema Display, 17-inch iMac, and so on), then photos cropped to 6:4 proportions are a closer fit.

FREQUENTLY ASKED QUESTION

Slideshow Smackdown: iPhoto vs. iMovie

I've read that iMovie makes a great slideshow program, too. Supposedly, I can import my photos, add music, and play it all back, full-screen, with cool cross-dissolves, just like you're saying here. Which program should I use?

The short answer: iPhoto for convenience, iMovie for control.

In iMovie, you can indeed import photos. Just as in iPhoto, you have individual control over their timing, application of the Ken Burns effect, and transitions between them.

But the soundtrack options are much more expansive in iMovie. Not only can you import music straight from a music CD (without having to use iTunes as an intermediary), but you can actually record narration into a microphone as the slideshow plays. And, of course, you have a full range of

title options, and credit-making and special-effects features at your disposal, too.

Still, iPhoto has charms of its own. Creating a slideshow is much less work in iPhoto, for one thing. If you want a slideshow to loop endlessly—playing on a laptop at somebody's wedding, for example, or at a tradeshow—iPhoto is also a much better bet. (iMovie can't loop.)

Remember, too, that iPhoto is beautifully integrated with your various albums. Whereas building an iMovie project is a serious, sit-down-and-work proposition that results in one polished slideshow, your Photo library has as many different slideshows as you have albums—all ready to go at any time.

If you don't have time to crop all your odd-sized or vertically oriented photos, then consider using the "Scale photos" feature described on page 169. It makes your pictures fill the screen nicely, although you risk cutting off important elements (like heads and feet).

- Preview images at full size before using them. You can't judge how sharp and bright an image is going to look based solely on its thumbnail.

- Keep the timing brief when setting the playing speed—maybe just a few seconds per photo. Better to have your friends wanting to see more of each photo than to have them bored, mentally rearranging their sock drawers as they wait for the show to advance to the next image. Remember, you can always pause a slideshow if someone wants a longer look at one picture.

- Consider the order of your photos. An effective slideshow should tell a story. You might want to start with a photo that establishes a location—an overall shot of a park, for example—and then follow it with closeups that reveal the details.

- If your viewers fall in love with what you've shown them, you have four options: (a) save the slideshow as a QuickTime movie that you can email them or burn onto a CD for their at-home enjoyment (Chapter 10); (b) turn the show into an interactive DVD using Apple's iDVD software (Chapter 11); (c) create a MobileMe slideshow (page 219); or (d) make your admirers buy their own Macs.

Tip: You can also export the slideshow as a QuickTime file perfectly formatted to play on an iPod, iPhone, iPad, or Apple TV (Chapter 10). In fact, the new Apple TV (the tiny black one) can see your iPhoto library and play saved slideshows, though it uses its own transitions.

Slideshows and iDVD

Instead of running a presentation directly from iPhoto, you can send your slideshow—music and all—from iPhoto to iDVD, Apple's simple DVD-authoring software. Using iDVD, you can transform the pictures from your album into an interactive slideshow that can be presented using any DVD player. (Just picture the family clicking through your photos on the big-screen TV in the den!)

Page 297 explains how to perform the iPhoto-to-iDVD conversion.

Making Prints

There's a lot to love about digital photos that remain digital. You can store thousands of them on a single DVD; you can send them anywhere on earth by email; and they won't wrinkle, curl, or yellow until your monitor does.

Sooner or later, though, most people want to get at least some of their photos on paper. You may want printouts to paste into your scrapbooks, to put in picture frames on the mantel, to use in homemade greeting cards, or to share with your Luddite friends who don't have computers.

With iPhoto, you can create such prints using your own printer. Or, for prints that look, feel, and smell like the kind you get from a photo-finishing store, you can transmit your digital files to Kodak Print Services, an online photo-processing service. In return, you receive an envelope of professionally printed photos on Kodak paper that are indistinguishable from their traditional counterparts.

This chapter explains how to use each of iPhoto's printing options, including the features that let you print greeting cards, contact sheets, and other special items from your digital photo collection. (Ordering greeting cards, postcards, calendars, and books is covered in Chapter 9.)

Making Your Own Prints

Using iPhoto to print your pictures is pretty easy. But making *great* prints—the kind that rival traditional film-based photos in their color and image quality—involves more than simply choosing the Print command.

One key factor, of course, is the printer itself. You need a good printer that can produce photo-quality color printouts. Fortunately, getting such a printer these days is pretty easy and inexpensive. Even some of the cheapo inkjet printers from Epson, HP, and Canon can produce amazingly good color images—and they cost less than $100. (Of course, what you spend on those expensive ink cartridges can easily double or triple the cost of the printer in a year.)

Tip: If you're really serious about producing photographically realistic printouts, consider buying a model that's specifically designed for photo printing, such as one of the printers in the Epson Stylus Photo series or the slightly more expensive Canon printers. What you're looking for is a printer that uses six, seven, or eight different colors of ink instead of the usual "inkjet four." The extra colors do wonders for the printer's ability to reproduce a wide range of colors on paper.

Even with the best printer, however, you can end up with disappointing results if you fail to consider at least three other important factors when trying to coax the best possible printouts from your digital photos. These factors include the resolution of your images, the settings on your printer, and your choice of paper.

Resolution and Shape

Resolution is the number of individual pixels squeezed into each inch of your digital photo, and therefore how large the individual pixels are in size. The basic rule is simple: The higher your photo's resolution, or *dpi* (dots per inch), the smaller the pixels become, and the sharper, clearer, and more detailed the printout will be. If the resolution is too low, the pixels will be large enough to see individually, so you'll end up with a printout that looks like it was made from Legos.

Low-resolution photos are responsible for more wasted printer ink and crumpled photo paper than any other printing snafu, so it pays to understand how to calculate a photo's dpi when you want to print it.

Calculating resolution

To calculate a photo's resolution, divide the horizontal or vertical size of the photo (measured in pixels) by the horizontal or vertical size of the print you want to make (usually measured in inches).

Suppose a photo measures 1524 × 1016 pixels. (How do you know? See Figure 7-1.) If you want a 4 × 6 print, you'll be printing at a resolution of 254 dpi (1524 pixels divided by 6 inches = 254 dpi), which will look fantastic on paper. (Photos printed on inkjet printers look their best when printed at a resolution of 200 dpi or higher.)

But if you try to print that same photo at 8 × 10, you'll get into trouble. By stretching those pixels across a larger print area, you're now printing at just 152 dpi—and you'll see a noticeable drop in image quality.

While it's important to print photos at a resolution of 200 to 300 dpi on an inkjet printer, there's really no benefit to printing at higher resolutions—600 dpi, 800 dpi, or more. It doesn't hurt anything to print at a higher resolution, but you probably won't notice any difference in the final printed photos, at least not on inkjet printers. Some inkjets can spray ink at finer resolutions—720 dpi, 1440 dpi, and so on—and using these highest settings produces very smooth, very fine printouts. But bumping the resolution of your *photos* higher than 300 dpi doesn't have any perceptible effect on their quality, and it'll just make your printer take longer to get the job done.

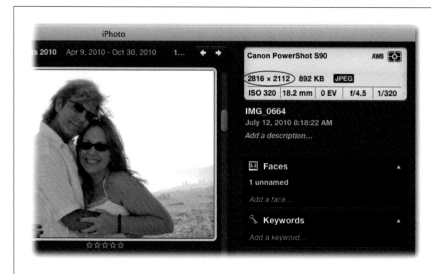

Figure 7-1:
To select the best size for a printout, you need to know a photo's size in pixels. iPhoto reveals this information in a convenient spot: at the top of the Info panel (circled).

Aspect ratio

You also have to think about your pictures' *aspect ratios*—their proportions. Most digital cameras produce photos with 4:3 proportions, which don't fit neatly onto standard photo paper (4 × 6 and so on). You can read more about this problem on page 131. (Just to make sure you're completely confused, some sizes of photo paper are measured *height by width*, whereas digital photos are measured *width by height*.)

If you're printing photos on letter-size paper, the printed images won't have standard Kodak dimensions. (They'll be, for example, 4 × 5.3.) You may not particularly care. But if you're printing onto, say, precut 4 × 6 photo paper (which you choose in the Print pane, explained next), you can avoid ugly white bands at the sides by first cropping your photos to standard print sizes.

Tweaking the Printer Settings

Just about every inkjet printer on earth comes with software that adjusts various print quality settings. Usually, you can find the controls for these settings right in the Print pane that appears when you choose File→Print. In iPhoto '11, you don't have to fiddle and fuss with additional menus or panels here. *This* version of the program knows that if you're printing in iPhoto, you're going to be making a photographic print, and it gives you an appropriate Print pane (Figure 7-2).

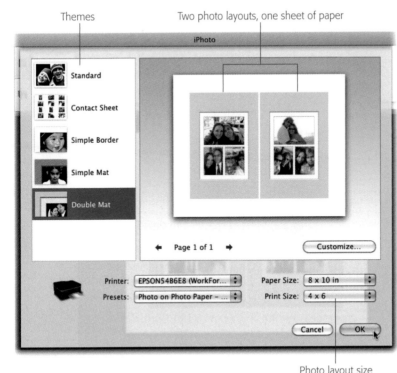

Themes

Two photo layouts, one sheet of paper

iPhoto

Standard

Contact Sheet

Simple Border

Simple Mat

Double Mat

← Page 1 of 1 →   Customize...

Printer: EPSON54B6E8 (WorkFor... ⬍)   Paper Size: 8 x 10 in ⬍
Presets: Photo on Photo Paper – ... ⬍   Print Size: 4 x 6 ⬍

Cancel   OK

Photo layout size

Figure 7-2:
iPhoto '11's incredibly helpful Print pane includes a clever twist: "mat" frames that you can print right onto the paper. Your savings: $25 and a trip to the frame store.

While you're here, note the relationship between Paper Size (each sheet) and Print Size (the prints within that sheet). In this example, the 8 × 10 paper is large enough to hold two 4 × 6 photo layouts per page.

Before you print, verify that you've got these settings right. On most printers, for example, you can choose from several different quality levels when printing, like Draft, Normal, Best, or Photo. There might also be a menu that lets you select the kind of paper you're using—plain, inkjet, glossy, and so on. You may also be able to select a combination of quality and paper options within the *same* menu, with items like "Photo on Photo Paper–Fine."

Choose the wrong settings, and you'll waste a lot of ink and paper. Even a top-of-the-line Epson photo printer churns out awful photo prints if you feed it plain paper when it's expecting high-quality glossy stock; you'll end up with a smudgy, soggy mess. So each time you print, make sure your printer is configured for the quality, resolution, and paper settings that you intend.

Paper Matters

When it comes to inkjet printing, paper is critical. Regular typing paper—the stuff you'd feed through a laser printer or copier—is too thin and absorbent to handle the amount of ink that gets sprayed on when you print a photo. You may end up with flat colors, slightly fuzzy images, and paper that's rippled and buckling from all the ink.

For really good prints, you need paper designed expressly for inkjets.

Most printers accommodate at least five grades of paper. Among them:

- **Plain paper**. The kind used in most photocopiers.

- **High-resolution paper**. A slightly heavier inkjet paper—not glossy, but with a silky-smooth white finish on one side.

- **Glossy photo paper**. A stiff, glossy paper resembling the paper that developed photos are printed on.

- **Matte photo paper**. A stiff, non-glossy stock.

- Most companies also offer an even more expensive **glossy** *film*, made of polyethylene rather than paper (which feels even more like traditional photographic paper).

These better photo papers cost much more than plain paper, of course. Glossy photo paper, for example, might run $25 for a box of 50 sheets, which means you'll be spending about 50 cents per 8 × 10 print—not including ink.

Still, by using good photo paper, you'll get much sharper printouts, more vivid colors, and results that look and feel like actual photographic prints. Besides, at sizes over 4 × 6 or so, making your own printouts is still less expensive than getting prints from the drugstore, even when you factor in printer cartridges and photo paper.

Tip: To save money, use your printer's Printing Utility to print its test page (usually a series of colored lines) on plain inkjet paper before printing any photos (this utility is typically found in your Applications folder). If the test print indicates a problem with ink or the print heads themselves, you'll know it before you feed the expensive glossy photo paper through your printer.

Printing from iPhoto, Step by Step

Here's the sequence for printing in iPhoto '11:

Phase 1: Choose photos to print

Just highlight the ones you want, using the techniques described on page 49.

You can also print a photo right from Edit view; the Print command is accessible in all of iPhoto's views.

When you're ready, choose File→Print, or press ⌘-P. The everything-you-need Print pane appears (Figure 7-2).

Note: In iPhoto '11, there is no longer a Print button on the toolbar.

As you examine this pane, it's important to understand the difference between a *photo layout* and a *page*.

Most people are used to printing one photo per sheet—for example, one photo on each 4 × 6 page. But in iPhoto '11, you can place several photos onto one 4 × 6 *photo layout*, and several layouts on each sheet of paper. For example, in Figure 7-2, each photo layout holds three pictures. And each 8 × 10 page holds two of those photo layouts.

No question about it: With great flexibility comes great complexity.

Phase 2: Choose a printing style (theme)

Here's another thing to consider: printing styles called *themes*, some of which permit colored borders or even captions.

Here are your options:

- **Standard**. You get no borders—just plain, unadorned photos, with optional captions and white, gray, or black margins.

- **Contact Sheet**. This means thumbnails—many of them—on each printed sheet. You control how many rows and columns appear, and what information appears beneath each thumbnail (date, name, camera model, shutter speed, and so on).

  The Contact Sheet option prints out a *grid* of photos, tiling as many as 120 pictures onto a single letter-size page (eight columns of 14 rows, for example).

  Photographers use contact sheets as a quick reference tool when organizing photos—a poor man's iPhoto, if you think about it. But this printing option is also handy in some other practical ways. For example, by printing several pictures side by side on the same page, you can easily make quality comparisons among them without using several sheets of paper (handy for showing friends or family so they can decide which ones they want you to print).

  You can also use contact sheet printing to make test prints, saving ink and paper. Sometimes a 2 × 3 print is all you need to determine if a picture is too dark or if its colors are wildly off when rendered by an inkjet printer. Don't make expensive full-page prints until you're sure you've adjusted your photo so that it will print out correctly.

- **Simple Border**. This puts up to four photos on each layout—or multiple copies of the same photo on each sheet, like school portrait packages. You can add captions and a white, gray, or black "frame" around the whole thing—even an oval one.

- **Simple Mat, Double Mat**. A mat, in the real framing biz, is a cardboard frame that's placed around a photo to give it more impact. iPhoto's clever twist is that it can print this mat directly onto the paper, saving you the hassle of cutting rectangles (and your finger) with an X-Acto knife.

  You get a choice of color (or, for Double Mat, a choice of two contrasting colors), as well as all the same layout options as Simple Border. You can also add a caption, as shown on page 188.

Click the theme you want on the left side of the Print pane. If you're printing more than one sheet (for example, more than one Standard, Border, or Mat picture), click the "Page 1 of 3" arrows to walk through the previews of each.

Phase 3: Choose print and paper sizes

At the bottom of the Print pane (Figure 7-2), specify what size photo paper you're putting into the printer, and what size you want each photo layout to be.

Most of the time, if you have a standard photo inkjet printer, these will be one and the same. You'll want 4 × 6 prints on 4 × 6 paper, for example. But as noted in Figure 7-2, if the paper size is much larger than the print size, you might be able to get more than one print (that is, photo layout) per sheet.

Tip: If you can't make the layout you want work with the paper size you've chosen, try picking a paper size that includes the word Borderless. That lets your printer know it's okay to print to the edges of the paper, if it's capable of edge-to-edge printing. For example, instead of choosing Letter Size, try 8 × 10 Borderless.

Phase 4: Adjust the layout

The themes iPhoto offers you are just starting points; you have many more options to choose from.

To see them, click Customize. You return to the main iPhoto window, where you land in the miniature page-layout view shown in Figure 7-3.

Tip: Until you either print or click Cancel, a new icon appears in your Source list, called Printing. While you're preparing your printout, you can click other Source-list icons and do other iPhoto work. You can return to your printout-in-waiting at any time by clicking that Printing icon.

You can also add new photos to the printout by dragging their thumbnails from other Events or albums right onto the Printing icon.

At the top of the window, you see the thumbnails of the photos you've selected for printing; a checkmark indicates a photo that you've already placed into a photo layout. (They all *start out* with checkmarks, but you might decide to remove a photo from a layout by dragging it out of its box.)

Note: The two tiny icons to the left of the thumbnails govern which thumbnails you see: thumbnails for the page layouts themselves, or thumbnails of the actual photos targeted for printing.

Photo thumbnails
Page thumbnails

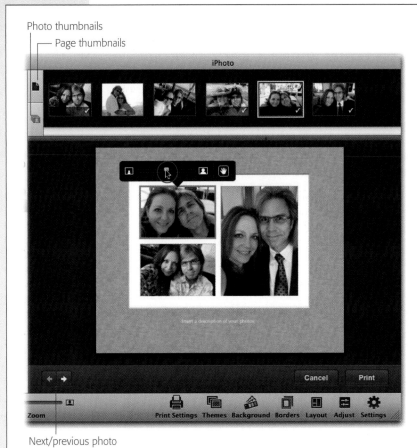

Next/previous photo

Figure 7-3:
In this mini layout view, use the toolbar buttons to change the theme, background color, border (mat) color, layout, and caption typeface and size.

Click a photo to make its Zoom slider appear, as shown here. Drag the slider (circled) to enlarge the photo; drag inside the photo to move it around within the frame. If you decide a photo needs a little color correction or sharpening, double-click it to open it in Edit view.

When viewing thumbnails (as shown here), you can drag a photo down into one of the rectangular placeholders in the page layout to replace whatever's there. You can even drag photos more than once, to get multiple copies (say, to cut out and give to friends).

Here, the buttons along the bottom of the window offer you hours of cosmetic tweaking opportunities (these options differ from theme to theme). For example:

- **Print Settings**. Click to return to the main Print pane shown in Figure 7-2.

- **Themes**. Choose a Standard, Simple Border, or Mat option (without *having* to go back to the Print pane).

- **Background**. Specify what color and texture you want to fill the margins of the paper, even for Standard layouts (see Figure 7-4).

- **Borders**. For all themes except Contact Sheet, you get a choice of border colors, thickness, and styles for the printed-on frame or mat, as shown in Figure 7-5.

- **Layout**. You can specify how many photos you want per page; whether you want horizontal (landscape) or vertical (portrait) orientation; and, for most themes, whether you want a caption to appear beneath the layout, so you can identify what you're printing.

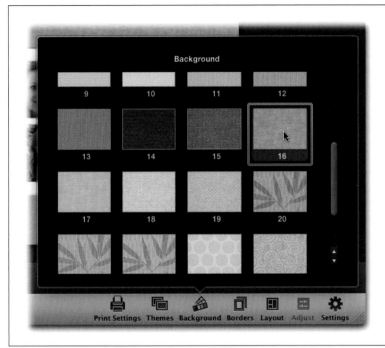

Figure 7-4:
If you choose the Simple Mat or Double Mat theme, iPhoto '11 gives you a whopping 26 background options for your printing pleasure.

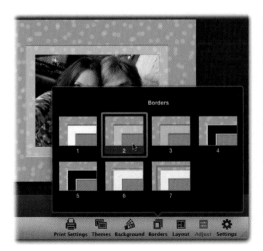

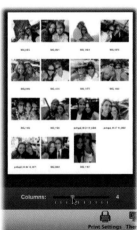

Figure 7-5:
Left: Your seven border options. The right combination of background and border makes for a wonderfully creative print.

Right: If you're creating a Contact Sheet, you don't get any border options. However, you do get a new Columns slider in the toolbar that lets you control how many columns of thumbnails appear on each page—and therefore how small the thumbnails are.

- **Adjust**. Single-click a photo in your layout to make the Adjust button available. When you click it, you get nearly the same Adjust panel described back on page 138 (Figure 7-6, top). The changes you make here don't have any effect on the actual photos in your library; they only affect this particular printed version.

- **Settings**. This button summons the pane shown in Figure 7-6, bottom, which contains an oddball assortment of miscellaneous commands. Here's where you can specify the type size and font for your captions; make crop marks appear on the printout (for ease of aligning if you plan to use a paper cutter); or turn on "Autoflow pages" (which makes the photos you selected pour themselves into a multi-photo layout automatically).

The most interesting control here is the Photos Per Page pop-up menu.

Tip: This pop-up menu is dimmed unless, in the Print pane (Figure 7-2), you've specified a page size large enough to hold more than one photo layout.

Ordinarily, iPhoto attempts to print as many photo layouts as possible on each sheet of paper; in other words, the factory setting is "Multiple photos per page." But if you don't want that paper-saving arrangement, you can choose "Single photo per page" instead. You'll get *one* photo layout per sheet, with a lot of white space.

Or, if you choose "Multiple of the same photo per page," you get that school photo-sampler effect (one 5 × 7, two wallet-size...).

Phase 5: Print

When the layout(s) look good, click the big Print button near the bottom-right of the iPhoto window. Only now do you see the more standard Print dialog box. Here's where you choose which printer you want, how many copies, and so on.

Finally, click the Print button (or press Return). Your printer scurries into action, printing your photos as you've requested.

Tip: The PDF button, a standard part of all Mac OS X Print dialog boxes, lets you save a printout-in-waiting as a PDF file instead of printing it on paper. It lets you convert any type of iPhoto printout to PDF. Click the button, choose "Save as PDF" from the pop-up menu, name the PDF in the Save dialog box, and then click Save. (Saving the file can take a while if you're converting several pages of photos into a PDF.)

Ordering Prints Online

Even if you don't have a high-quality color printer, traditional prints of your digital photos are only a few clicks away—if you have an Internet connection and you're willing to spend a little money, that is.

Thanks to a deal between Apple and Kodak, you can order prints directly from within iPhoto. After you select the size and quantity of the pictures you want printed, one click is all it takes to have iPhoto transmit your photos to Kodak Print Services and bill your credit card for the order. The rates range from 12 cents for a single 4 × 6 print to about $15 for a jumbo 20 × 30 poster. Within a couple of days, Kodak sends you finished photos printed on high-quality glossy photo paper.

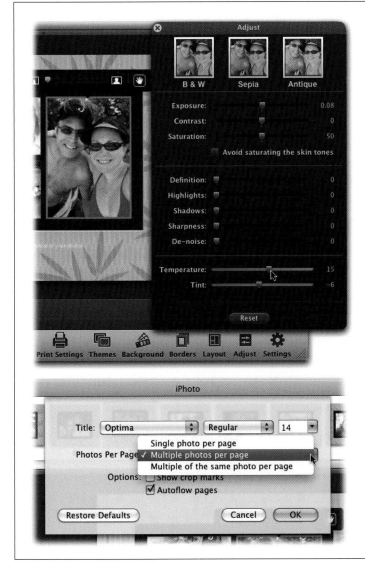

Figure 7-6:
Top: The Adjust panel in page-layout view is nearly the same as the one found in Edit view (though without a histogram). You can use it to fiddle with the image's exposure, color balance, and so on. You can also convert a photo to black and white, sepia, or antique by clicking one of the three buttons at the top (a great idea if the color in your photo is funky). None of this tweaking affects the original photos in your library.

Bottom: In this pane, you can make a few more miscellaneous tweaks to the layout, such as how many photos appear on each page, and adjust the caption typeface and size.

Here's how the print-buying process works:

1. **Select the photos you want to print.**

   Click an album to order prints of everything in it, or select specific photos.

Tip: If you plan to order prints, first crop your photos to the proper proportions (4 × 6, for example) using the Crop tool, as described in Chapter 5. Most digital cameras produce photos whose shape doesn't quite match standard photo-paper dimensions. If you send photos to Kodak uncropped, you're leaving it up to Kodak to decide which parts of your pictures to lop off to make them fit. (More than one Mac fan has opened the envelope to find loved ones missing the tops of their skulls.)

By cropping the pictures to photo-paper shape before you place the order, *you* decide which parts get eliminated. (You can always restore the photos to their original uncropped versions using iPhoto's "Revert to Original" command.)

---

2. **Choose File→Order Prints (or click the Share toolbar button and choose Order Prints).**

   Your Mac goes online to check in with the Kodak processing center (though in iPhoto '11 it doesn't say "Kodak" anymore). If the Mac can't make an Internet connection, then the Order Prints window, shown in Figure 7-7, doesn't open.

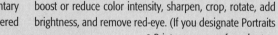

GEM IN THE ROUGH

Portraits & Prints

iPhoto's Layout pop-up menu offers some rudimentary *combination* templates like the portrait galleries delivered by professional photographers, but it doesn't offer much flexibility. You can't specify that you want more than four photos per sheet, for example.

Fortunately, a free companion program called Portraits & Prints nicely compensates for iPhoto's printing weaknesses (it's not an iPhoto plug-in; it's a completely separate program). You can download it from *www.tinyurl.com/printsportraits*.

The idea is that you drag selected photos directly out of the iPhoto window and into the Portraits & Prints window. There, you can

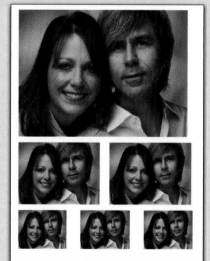

boost or reduce color intensity, sharpen, crop, rotate, add brightness, and remove red-eye. (If you designate Portraits & Prints as your preferred external editing program [page 122], then changes you make in Portraits & Prints will be reflected in iPhoto's thumbnails.)

But all that is just an appetizer for the main dish: a delicious variety of printing templates, like the one shown here. The program comes with several "portrait sets" that let you arrange different pictures at different sizes on the same sheet. You can even save your layouts as *catalogs*, so you can reuse them or reprint them at a later date.

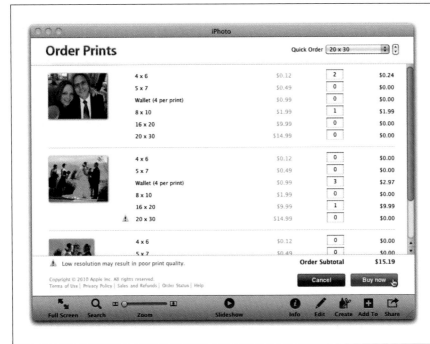

Figure 7-7:
The Order Prints window lets you order six different types of prints of your photos—from a set of four wallet-sized prints to mammoth 20 × 30 posters. Use the scroll bar on the right to skim through all the photos you've selected and specify how many copies of each one you want to order.

Note the yellow alert triangles next to certain print sizes. iPhoto is telling you the photo you're ordering is too low resolution for the size in question.

3. **Select the sizes and quantities you want.**

   If you want a 4 × 6 print or two of every photo, just use the Quick Order pop-up menu at the top of the window. Select a size and then use the up and down arrows to the right of the menu to choose your quantity.

   For more control over sizes and quantities of individual photos, then fill in the numbers individually for each photo, scrolling down through the list as necessary. The total cost of your order is updated as you make selections.

   As you order, pay heed to the alert icons (little yellow triangles) that may appear on certain lines of the order form (visible in Figure 7-7, bottom). These are iPhoto's standard warning symbols, declaring that certain photos don't have a high enough resolution to be printed at the specified sizes. A photo that looks great at 5 × 7 may look terrible as a 16 × 20 enlargement. Unless you're the kind of person who thrives on disappointment, *never* order prints in a size that's been flagged with a low-resolution alert.

Tip: You'll see the same warning icon when you print your own photos and order photo books, cards, or calendars (Chapter 9). As always, you have few attractive choices: You can order a smaller print, not order a print at all, or order the print and accept the lower quality that results.

---

4. **Click the "Buy now" button.**

   Another screen appears, showing the total for your order and various shipping methods.

5. **Click Check Out and sign in with your Apple ID, or create a new one.**

   If you already have an account to buy music and movies at the iTunes Store, then you don't need to set up a new Apple ID to buy photo prints. You can use the same name and password here; Apple will happily bill the same credit card.

   If you've never ordered anything from Apple, click "Create Apple ID now" to visit a series of screens where you surrender your identity and credit card info. You'll also see the option to turn on the "1-Click Ordering system," which is mandatory if you want to order prints. (All of this is a one-time task designed to save you time when you place subsequent orders.) For details on the process, see page 269. When the Summary screen finally appears, click Done to return to the Order Prints window.

   Either way, your photos are transferred, your credit card is billed, and you go sit by the mailbox.

A batch of 24 standard 4 × 6 snapshots costs about $3, plus shipping, which is probably less than what you'd pay for processing a roll of film at the local drugstore. (You also don't have to pay for the gas to get there or deal with the hassles of traffic and parking.)

Better yet, you get to print only the prints that you actually want. It's far more convenient than the drugstore method, and it's a handy way to send top-notch photo prints directly to friends and relatives who don't have computers. Furthermore, it's ideal for creating high-quality enlargements that would be impossible to print on the typical inkjet printer.

UP TO SPEED

How Low Is Too Low?

When you order photos online, the Order Prints form automatically warns you when a selected photo has a resolution that's too low to result in a good-quality print. But just what does Kodak consider too low? Here's the list of Kodak's official minimum resolution recommendations.

To order this size picture:	Your photo should be at least:
Wallet-sized	640 × 480 pixels
4 × 5	768 × 512 pixels
5 × 7	1152 × 768 pixels
8 × 10	1536 × 1024 pixels

These are *minimum* requirements, not suggested settings. Your photos will look better in print if you *exceed* these resolution settings.

For example, a 1536 × 1024 pixel photo printed at 8 × 10 inches meets Kodak's minimum recommendation but has an effective resolution of 153 × 128 dpi—a relatively low resolution for high-quality printing. A photo measuring 2200 × 1760 pixels, printed at the same size, would have a resolution of 220 dpi—and look much better on paper, with sharper detail and subtler variations in color.

Email, Web Galleries, and Network Sharing

Holding a beautifully rendered glossy color print created from your own digital image is a glorious feeling. But unless you have an uncle in the inkjet cartridge business, you could go broke printing your own photos. Ordering high-quality prints with iPhoto is terrific fun, too, but between printing and mailing, you'll spend a few days waiting on them to arrive.

For the discerning digital photographer who craves both instant gratification and economy, the solution is to put your photos *online*—by emailing them to others, posting them on the Web, or sharing them with other people on your home or office network.

All of this is particularly easy and satisfying in iPhoto, *especially* if you're a fan of Facebook or Flickr. And if you'd rather send electronic photos directly to your fan base (instead of requiring them to visit a website), you'll find that iPhoto '11's new graphical email themes are an unusual and attractive option. iPhoto even remembers each email you send, so you can always see when you sent which photos to whom.

Emailing Photos

Emailing from iPhoto is perfect for quickly sending off a single photo—or even a handful of photos—to friends, family, and coworkers. As you're about to learn, iPhoto '11 lets you do it in a gloriously graphical way. However, if you have a whole *batch* of photos to share (11 or more), consider using the web-publishing features described later in this chapter.

Using iPhoto's Mail Command

Previous versions of iPhoto handed your pictures off to your existing email program, where they appeared as file attachments. And you can still send your photos that way. The downside, of course, is that your recipients may not actually see the photos in the body of your message; they might have to open the attachments, which is a hassle for some (and beyond the technical skills of others).

That may be why Apple came up with iPhone '11's embedded-photo email feature, in which your photos are the body of the message, complete with captions, frames, and other graphic niceties. iPhoto even does the emailing itself, without having to open your email program.

Here's how the new embedded-email process works:

1. **Select the thumbnails of the photo(s) you want to email.**

    You can use any of the picture-selecting techniques described on page 49. (If you fail to select a thumbnail, you'll get an error message asking you to select a photo and try again.) You can choose up to 10 photos for a single email. If you want to email more than 10 photos, skip ahead to the section on dragging and dropping (page 203).

2. **Click the Share icon in the iPhoto toolbar; from the pop-up menu, choose Email.**

    When you click the Share button, the menu shown in Figure 8-1 (top) appears.

3. **Choose a theme.**

    Apple believes emailing your photos is an event worthy of graphics, descriptions, captions, and so on. You can choose among 10 designs themes in the Themes pane, shown in Figure 8-2:

    *   **Classic, Journal.** If you choose one of these no-nonsense themes, iPhoto inserts your photos into the email message without additional fanfare or extra graphics, just like in iPhoto '09. You see the phrase "Insert Text Here" by each photo, prompting you to add a caption. (If you don't add a caption, that spot appears blank in the recipient's email.) In Journal, you also see a spot to add a title for your photo email.

Tip: If you don't add a title before you click Send, iPhoto displays an error message letting you know you're about to include *placeholder text* with your email. But don't let iPhoto bully you—it's lying. If you don't add a title, that area appears blank (same with captions).

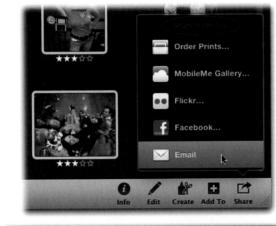

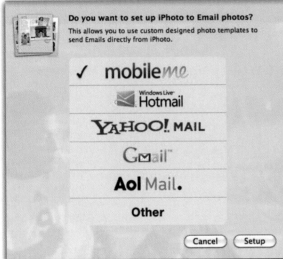

Figure 8-1:
Top: iPhoto '11 keeps track of how many photos you've selected for emailing and lists the number at the top of the Share menu (circled).

Bottom: If you've never used Mail (Apple's email program), you see this pane instead. Click the email provider you use and then click Setup. You're taken to another pane where you can enter your email address and password. Click Save.

- **Snapshots, Celebration**. These themes add a white border to each photo (like a Polaroid) and place them on a light-colored background, complete with drop shadows. In Snapshots, the background is light gray; you're prompted to add a message in a handwriting typeface, though you can change the typeface, size, and alignment using the pop-up menus that automatically appear (Figure 8-2). Celebration uses a light blue background and an embossed "card" complete with whimsical border and party hats; there's also a spot where you can add a message. Neither theme includes captions.

- **Corkboard**. Your message and photos are tacked onto a realistic-looking corkboard, as shown in Figure 8-2. The message area is on a piece of virtual graph paper, with your photos underneath in a filmstrip separated by white borders.

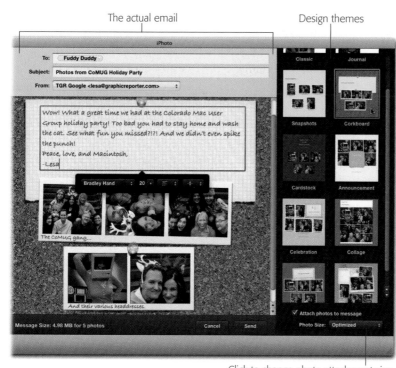

The actual email   Design themes

Click to change photo attachment size

Figure 8-2:
iPhoto '11's new design themes for email. To choose one, click in the Themes panel on the right. The left side of the window lets you fill in your email's missing blanks. The address field automatically pulls from OS X's Address Book and attempts to fill in the correct address once you start typing. As soon as you click within the message area, little pop-up menus appear that let you change the typeface, size, and alignment (both horizontal and vertical) of your message. This image shows the Corkboard theme, which gives you one captioning opportunity per photo strip.

- **Cardstock, Letterpress**. These sleek themes display your photos in rows of squares, surrounded by a thin border that looks like it was *pressed into* a textured background. In the Letterpress theme, a "card" containing a message area and today's date is perched atop the first row; in Cardstock, there's an area for this info below the photos. The two themes also differ in photo-border type and background color: In Cardstock, your photos are rimmed with a thin, light gray line and the background is bluish-gray; in Letterpress, the rims are wider and cream-colored, and the background is greenish-gray.

- **Announcement**. Similar to Cardstock and Letterpress, this theme displays slightly larger versions of your photos without borders. The images appear slightly inset into the background, and the message slot is on a rounded, "stitched" card, making it perfect for baby announcements.

- **Collage**. This theme truly showcases your photos—they're enlarged to fill the whole email. They're also placed side by side, just a few pixels apart, as a variety of rectangles. It's like the new Origami slideshow, minus the animation. There are no caption areas in this theme.

- **Postcard**. This fun theme adds borders and drop shadows to your photos, which appear "pasted" into a travel scrapbook page. A stamped postcard offers to hold your personal message and a coat-check tag automatically bears today's date. You can add a title to the largest photo, but that's it.

4. **Size and position your photos within their frames.**

   As with any project—a book, calendar, card (all discussed in Chapter 9), or print (Chapter 7)—you can resize and reposition your photos inside of each frame, as Figure 8-3 explains.

Tip: In most cases, you can stick with the Optimized size. It shrinks the photo files so that they transfer quickly via email, yet they're still large enough for your recipient to include in a slideshow. However, if your recipients might want to print the photos–and they have high-speed Internet connections, of course–then choose Actual Size instead. Doing so ensures enough pixels for printing at any size and resolution (see page 182 for more on resolution).

---

5. **Choose to attach photo(s) or not, and if so, choose the attachment size.**

   Once you're happy with your design and click Send, iPhoto converts the completed layout into a single JPEG image in the body of the message. But if "Attach photos to message" is turned on, iPhoto *also* compresses the photos into a single .zip file (which your recipient can double-click to open) and attaches it to the message.

Tip: If you've chosen a theme other than Classic or Journal, you can turn off the "Attach photos to message" checkbox. In that case, your recipient receives the JPEG of your design…and that's it. As you might imagine, this results in the smallest possible file size, making this option the most efficient for emailing.

---

iPhoto encourages you to send scaled-down versions of your photos, so it automatically sets that menu to **Optimized** (the resulting photo resolution falls between Medium and Large, as discussed below).

In most cases, Optimized works just fine—big enough for onscreen display, just not for printing. But the Photo Size menu gives you four additional choices:

- Choose **Small (Faster Downloading)** to keep your email attachments supersmall (320 × 240 pixels)—but only if you don't expect the recipient of your email to print the photo. (A photo this size can't produce a quality print any larger than a postage stamp.) On the other hand, your photos will consume less than 100 K apiece, making downloads quick and easy for those with dial-up connections. (For more about photo sizes, flip to page 202.)

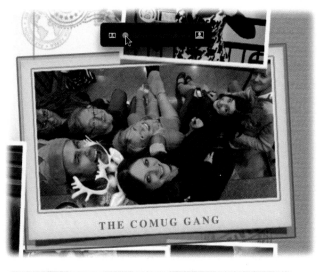

Figure 8-3:
Top: iPhoto lets you resize and reposition your photos inside the little frames. Click a photo once and then drag its zoom slider to the right to make it bigger, or to the left to make it smaller. To move the photo within the frame, click and drag it into place (your cursor turns into a tiny hand).

Bottom: Unless you tell it otherwise, iPhoto also attaches the original photo files to the outgoing message (the design arrives as a single JPEG file, and the photos arrive as an attached .zip file). Pick an attachment size from the Photo Size pop-up menu, or leave it set to Optimized.

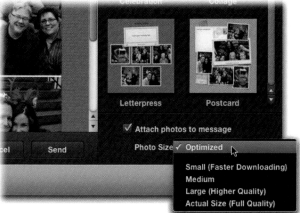

- Choosing **Medium** yields a file that will fill a nice chunk of your recipient's screen, with plenty of detail. It's even enough data to produce a slightly larger print—about 2 × 3 inches (640 × 480 pixels). Even so, the file size (and download time) remains reasonable; this setting can trim a 2 MB, 4-megapixel image down to an attachment of less than 150 K.

- The **Large (Higher Quality)** setting downsizes even your large photos to about 450 K, preserving enough pixels (1280 × 960) to make good 4 × 6 prints and completely fill the average person's screen. In general, send these sparingly. Even if your recipients have a cable modem or DSL, these big files may still overflow their email boxes.

- Despite all the cautions above, there may be times when a photo is worth sending at **Actual Size (Full Quality)**, like when you're submitting it for printing or publication. This works best when both you and the recipient have high-speed Internet connections and unlimited-capacity mail systems, as this option attaches a copy of your original photo at its original dimensions. (Most email services limit attachments to 20 megabytes.)

Note: iPhoto retains each picture's proportions when it resizes them. But if a picture doesn't have 4:3 proportions (maybe you cropped it, or maybe it came from a camera that wasn't set to create 4:3 photos), then it may wind up *smaller* than the indicated dimensions. In other words, think of the choices in the Size pop-up menu as meaning "this size or smaller."

---

6. **Include a personal message, caption, or title, if desired.**

   On the left side of the window is the actual email you'll send, and the body area is filled with text boxes you can customize; just click to change the text and use the little pop-up menus to change the typeface, size, and so on (see Figure 8-2). iPhoto automatically inserts the photo's Event or album name into the email's Subject line, though you can change it to anything you want.

7. **Type your recipient's email address into the "To:" box, and then click Send.**

   When you start typing an address, iPhoto looks to see if it matches an entry in OS X's Address Book and tries to fill it in for you. If you don't store your email addresses there, you can type any address you want into this field.

   As soon as you click the Send button, iPhoto processes your design and photos, converting the design to a single JPEG format and—if you told it to—resizing and compressing your photo attachments. (Behind the scenes, iPhoto uses Apple-Script to accomplish these tasks at warp speed.) Your photos are then sent on their merry way.

The second you click Send, iPhoto records the photo email in the Info panel. Select one of the included photos and then open the Info panel by clicking the Info button in the toolbar. If the photo was emailed from inside iPhoto, you see a new section called Sharing, shown in Figure 8-4.

Using Another Email Program

If you'd rather send photos as regular file attachments—as in older iPhoto versions, with no fancy graphics—you can tell iPhoto to hand them off to a program like Mail (the free email program that came with your copy of Mac OS X), America Online, Eudora, Entourage, or Outlook for the Mac. (To use any other email program, skip to the box on page 204.)

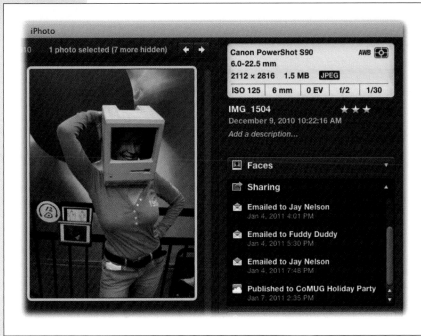

Figure 8-4:
Click to expand the Sharing section; you'll see a list of the photo emails that include the selected photo. Click an entry in the list to reopen that photo email so you can send it to someone else.

To set this up, choose iPhoto→Preferences (or press ⌘-comma), click General, and then choose the email program you want from the "Email photos using" pop-up menu. (If you have Outlook, but you don't see Outlook as a choice, choose Entourage instead.) For now on, when you choose Email from the Share menu, you'll get the dialog box shown in Figure 8-5.

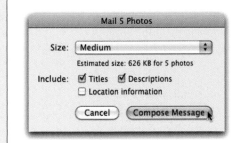

Figure 8-5:
The Mail Photo dialog box not only lets you choose the size of photo attachments, but it also keeps track of how many photos you've selected and estimates how large your attachments are going to be. You can also have the email message display any location (geotagging) information you've added to your photos (see Chapter 4), as well as their titles and descriptions.

Notes on photo size

The most important thing to understand about emailing photos with another program is this: *Full-size photos are usually too big to email.*

Suppose, for example, that you want to send three photos to some friends—terrific shots you captured with your 7-megapixel camera. First, a little math: A typical 7-megapixel shot consumes 3 megabytes of disk space. So sending along just three shots would make at least a 9-megabyte package.

Why is that bad? Let us count the ways:

- It will take you a long time to send.

- It will take your recipients a long time to download. During that time, the recipients must sit there, not even knowing what they're downloading. And when you're done hogging their time, they might not consider what you sent worth the wait.

- Even if they do open the pictures you sent, the average high-resolution shot is much too big for the screen. It does you no good to email somebody a 7-megapixel photo (for example, 3072 × 1728 pixels) when his monitor's maximum resolution is only 1280 × 800. If you're lucky, his graphics software will intelligently shrink the image to fit his screen; otherwise, he'll see only a gigantic nose filling his monitor. But you'll still have to contend with his irritation at having waited for so much superfluous resolution.

- The typical Internet account has a limited file-attachment size. If the attachment exceeds 5 MB or so, the message may bounce back or clog the mailbox. So your massive 9-megabyte photo package could push your hapless recipient's mailbox over its limit, meaning she'll miss out on important messages and be very, very angry.

Of course, it's all different when you use iPhoto. Instead of unquestioningly attaching a multi-megabyte graphic to an email message and sending off the whole bloated thing, it automatically offers you a scaled-down, reasonably sized version of your photo instead (though you can always send the photos at actual size, as described in the previous section). By taking advantage of this feature, your friends will savor the thrill of seeing your digital shots without enduring the agony of a half-hour email download.

The Drag-and-Drop Method

There are three situations in which you'd want to avoid iPhoto's Email command: When you want to send more than 10 photos, when you want to send the email to large groups of people, and when you want to retain the photo's original file format.

For example, iPhoto always converts photos into JPEG format when emailing them. So if you want to send Raw or Photoshop files, *don't* use the Email command. Instead, *drag* the thumbnails from iPhoto directly onto your email program's application icon (in the Dock, for example) to open a new message *and* attach them in one fell swoop.

Of course, both Raw and Photoshop files can be huge, and emailing huge files is a serious faux pas. However, keeping file sizes manageable depends on which email program you use. If you're using Apple Mail, you can use the Size pop-up menu at the bottom right of the message window to pick an appropriate size for your attachments. For any other email program, you'll want to export the photos first using the File→Export command, which offers you a choice of scaling options (discussed on page 202). When you're finished, drag the exported photos onto your email program's icon.

Publishing Photos on the Web

Putting your photos on the Web is the ultimate way to share them with the world. If the idea of allowing the vast throngs of the Internet-using public to browse, view, download, save, and print *your* photos sounds appealing, read on. It's amazingly easy to get your photos from iPhoto to the Internet.

Note: Publishing photos to the Web is not a substitute for backing them up. Chapter 13 has the scoop for creating a *real* backup plan.

Three Roads to Webdom

iPhoto actually provides three different web-publishing routes:

- **The easiest, most hands-off approach**. Publish your pictures to a Facebook page, Flickr account, or MobileMe Gallery. Anyone with a web browser can now admire your photography.

  Flickr.com, the world's most popular photo-sharing site, offers free basic accounts for anyone. You get a nice personal page to upload 300 megabytes' worth of photos every month. And if that's not enough, you can give Flickr $25 a year and upload as many photos as you want.

FREQUENTLY ASKED QUESTION

Using iPhoto with PowerMail, QuickMail Pro, MailSmith...

I don't use Apple Mail, America Online, Eudora, or Entourage. How can I get iPhoto to send my photos via Quick-Mail Pro? It's not listed as an option in iPhoto's Mail Preferences.

You're right. iPhoto's Preferences dialog box seems to know about no programs except America Online, Mail, Eudora, or Entourage. (The options at the bottom of don't have anything to do with the program you use to send and receive email; they pertain to email service providers only.)

There's a great workaround, though, thanks to the programming efforts of Simon Jacquier. Using his free utility, iPhoto Mailer Patcher, you can make iPhoto work obediently with MailSmith, PowerMail, QuickMail Pro, or even the ancient Claris Emailer. It replaces the Mail button on iPhoto's bottom-edge panel with the icon of your preferred email program. You can download iPhoto Mailer Patcher from *http://homepage.mac.com/jacksim/software*.

Facebook.com, on the other hand, has become *the* destination for people (500 million of them, and growing) to post news, details, and pictures of themselves and their friends online. The site offers photo-album space you can share with your Facebook friends—and the ability to email photo-album links to anyone, not just other Facebook members.

MobileMe, on the other hand, is Apple's $100-a-year suite of web services (or $60 a year if you buy from Amazon.com). It includes email accounts, secure file backup, address book and calendar synchronization (among Macs, PCs, and iPhones), website hosting—and Galleries. These are the most gorgeous photo presentations on the Web. And since you have iPhoto, publishing to a MobileMe account is literally a one-click affair. (See the box on page 224 for details on signing up.)

These kinds of online galleries show your photos to best advantage, big and clear. You can password-protect your pictures; permit people to download your full-size photos; and add new photos right from your cameraphone or email program.

Tip: Once you start publishing photos on Facebook, Flickr, or MobileMe, iPhoto keeps track of which photos went where. This proves handy when you can't remember where that photo of your latest facial piercing actually went. The box on page 217 has the scoop.

- **More effort, more design options**. Use iWeb, one of the other iLife programs. iPhoto can hand off any batch of photos to iWeb with only a couple of mouse clicks; from there, you can post them online with a single command.

- **For the experienced web page designer**. If you already have a website, you can use either of two approaches to generate Web pages (HTML documents): the Export command or the Share→iWeb command. You can upload these files, with the accompanying graphics, to your website, whether that's a MobileMe account or any other web-hosting service. (Most Internet accounts, including those provided by your phone or cable company, come with free space for web pages uploaded in this way.)

  This is the most labor-intensive route, but it offers much more flexibility to create sophisticated pages if you know how to work with HTML. It's also the route you should take if you hope to incorporate the resulting photo gallery into an existing website (that is, one in which the photos aren't the only attraction).

All of these methods are detailed in the following pages.

Flickr

Flickr.com is an insanely huge and busy international photo-sharing site; it's not uncommon for its members worldwide to upload 30,000 photos and videos a *minute*. The site recognizes geotagged photos and displays them on a map, so those pictures you so carefully pinpointed back in Chapter 4 take their location information with them.

iPhoto can send photos directly to your Flickr page. No more special add-on software needed, as in older iPhoto versions. All you need is a Flickr account.

To get one, visit *www.flickr.com* and sign up (you can also log in with your Google account, if you have one). If you're only a casual photographer, the free account will probably do you just fine; you can upload up to 300 megabytes of photos (15 megabytes each, max) and two 90-second video clips (up to 150 megabytes in size) a month. If you're serious about sharing, sign up for the $25-a-year Flickr Pro account. By going Pro, you can upload an unlimited number of photos per month and even post high-definition video clips to your Flickr page.

Either way, you're in for quite a ride. Flickr isn't just a place to post your photos on the Web for your friends and family to see, although it's great for that. It's also a place for photo fans to comment on your photos, link to one another's photo pages, search for photos by keyword (before visiting a place, for example), and so on.

Note: Flickr's privacy settings let you keep personal photos out of the public view. Through the site, you can set up lists of friends and family so that only the people you have placed on these lists can see specified sets of pictures. (Details at *www.flickr.com/help/faq.*)

One-Time Setup

Once you have your Flickr account, it's time to link it to iPhoto and then transfer some photos. Here's the one-time setup:

1. **In iPhoto, select some pictures that you want to share on Flickr.**

   You can select whole albums or choose individual photos in your library (see page 49).

2. **Click the Share button on the iPhoto toolbar; from the pop-up menu, choose Flickr.**

   iPhoto displays a message asking if you'd like to set it up to publish to your Flickr account. Click Set Up, as shown in Figure 8-6.

3. **Sign into your Flickr account.**

   iPhoto opens your web browser and asks for your Flickr user name and password. If you forgot to sign up for an account in your excitement about this whole Flickr thing, you can actually sign up here while on the Flickr website (if you've got a Google account, you can use that instead).

4. **Authorize your Flickr account to talk to iPhoto.**

   This is where you agree to let Flickr use its software to snag copies of your photos. Once you agree by clicking the *second* Next button, you get another screen confirming your choice. Click "Ok, I'll authorize it." Now you see a screen saying you can close the browser window and safely return to iPhoto (where the authorization pane disappears after a second or two).

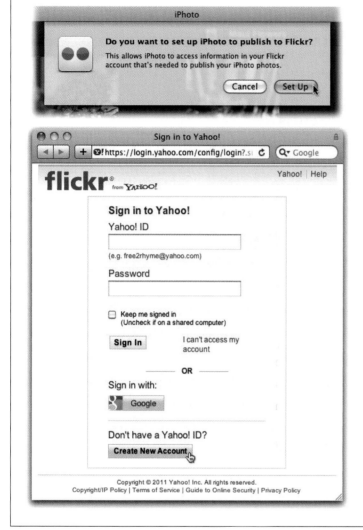

Figure 8-6:
Top: The first time you try to share your photos on Flickr, you're guided through a short setup process.

Bottom: iPhoto opens your web browser so you can log into your Flickr account or create a new one.

Posting to Flickr

Once your accounts are in order, you're ready to follow the more streamlined steps for sending pictures from iPhoto to Flicker:

1. **Click Share. From the pop-up menu, click Flickr again, and then click New Set or Photostream.**

   Figure 8-7 explains the difference between these options.

2. **An iPhoto pane appears, asking you privacy and file-size questions.**

Here, you can specify who will be allowed to view the pictures in the real world—You, Friends, Family, Family *and* Friends, or Anyone. You can also pick the size—Web, Optimized, or Actual—as shown in Figure 8-7. (To change your audience settings later on, log into *www.flickr.com*.)

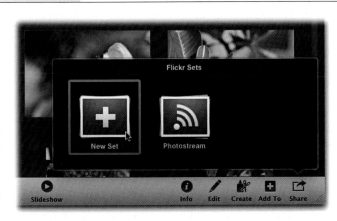

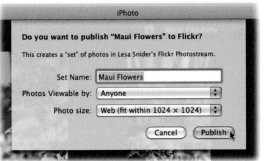

Figure 8-7:
Top: What iPhoto calls albums, Flickr calls sets, and you can create as many of them as you want. They're great for organizing images, especially if you plan to upload often. Alternatively, you can just publish photos straight into your Flickr photostream (think of it as a giant bucket that stores all your uploaded photos).

Bottom: Before it publishes the photos to your Flickr page, iPhoto wants to know what size to make them. Web and Optimized upload the fastest. Actual Size is available for Pro Flickr accounts only, and takes time if you have a lot of big shots to publish.

Note: Be aware that if you post your photos online at actual size, there's nothing to stop other people from downloading and printing them or otherwise passing them off as their own. If you worry about such things, scaling down your photos makes them less attractive to photo swipers.

3. **Click Publish.**

Using your Internet connection, iPhoto hands off the pictures to Flickr so that the world (or the subset of the world you've permitted) can see them. A status bar at the top right of the iPhoto window shows the program's progress. Depending on the number of photos you're uploading, this process can take awhile. (Let iPhoto finish publishing one set before you ask it to publish another; the program may crash otherwise.)

The name of your Flickr account now appears in the iPhoto Source list, under the Web heading, and any set or photos you've uploaded appear in the main viewing area like Events (see Figure 8-8).

Any keywords you've applied to your pictures in iPhoto (page 84) are converted into Flickr tags when you publish them on the site. So, if you've added the keywords *panda, National Zoo,* and *Washington DC* to all your panda pictures from that trip to the National Zoo, other Flickr members doing searches for photos tagged with *panda, National Zoo,* or *Washington DC* will see your pictures in their search results—if you've got your privacy settings configured to let anyone see your photos.

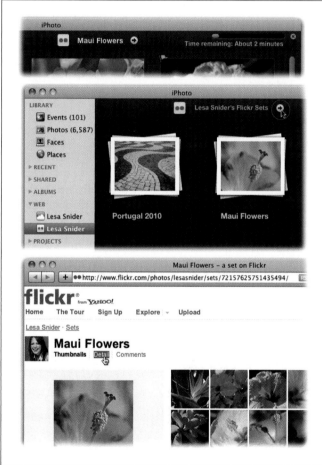

Figure 8-8:
Top: In the black bar at the top of your iPhoto window, a status bar lets you know how long it'll take to upload your photos (about 2 minutes, in this example).

Middle: Back in iPhoto, your Flickr account name appears over in the Source list. Give it a click to see all the photos and sets you've uploaded. They appear in the main viewing area, just like Events. Double-click a set's name to view its contents in iPhoto or click the right-pointing arrow (circled) to visit your Flickr web page.

Bottom: Behold, your Flickr page, where copies of your photos now reside.

Tip: If you change a Flickr set's name in iPhoto, it'll get updated on Flickr, too. (Just click your Flickr account in iPhoto's Source list, click the set in the main viewing area, and then type a new name; the name changes in iPhoto and Flickr.) It works the other way, too: Changing the set's name on Flickr also changes its name in iPhoto.

iPhoto Places on Flickr maps

If your photos are tagged with location information (Chapter 4), then your attention to detail is about to pay off. All the location data you embedded in your photos goes with them when they travel to Flickr's website.

Once the photos land on your Flickr page, and you double-click one of the photo thumbnails to visit its page, a small map appears to the photo's right, inviting visitors to see where the pictures were taken. When they do, a Yahoo map opens up in the browser, showing the spot based on the location information embedded in the picture. Figure 8-9 tells you how to add this info if it didn't travel with your photo.

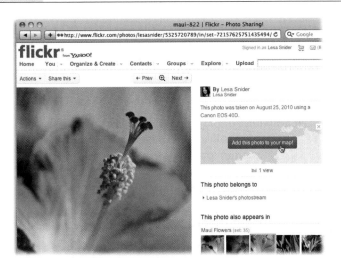

Figure 8-9:
Top: If you didn't geotag your photos before you sent them to Flickr, you can tag them on your Flickr map instead. Just click a thumbnail to see the photo on its own page and then click "Add this photo to your map" to its right.

Bottom: A larger map appears, where you can either type an address or drag the photo to a spot on the map. Then click the Save Location button. You can also map a bunch of photos at once. From your main Flickr page, click the You button in the navigation bar at the top and choose Your Sets. Next, click the Edit link beneath the set you want to change. Click the Map tab at the top of the resulting page, and then drag your photos from the strip at the bottom of the screen to the desired spots on the map.

There may be some occasions when you don't want this info out there on the Web—for example, location info could ruin your alibi or lead a stalker right to you. You can, of course, change your privacy settings to limit who can see your pictures, as described earlier in this section. (For more on Flickr's privacy settings, see *www .flickr.com/help/faq*.)

But if you don't feel like mucking around in your Flickr settings and you don't want to remove the location info from the photos, you can stop iPhoto from including it when it sends them to Flickr. Choose iPhoto→Preferences→Advanced. In the resulting pane, turn off "Include location information for published photos." (On the flip side, if you *want* your photos to include location info on Flickr but it's not happening, make sure that checkbox is turned *on*.)

While this stops iPhoto from automatically including location info, you can still add it to your Flickr map on a photo-by-photo basis, as described in Figure 8-9.

Tip: iPhoto and Flickr.com synchronize location information, too. If you add location info to published photos on Flickr, it magically appears on the photos in iPhoto (it's viewable in the Info panel). So if you do your geotagging on your Flickr page during slow moments at work, your efforts won't be in vain.

Adding more photos to published Flickr sets

Once you've published photos to a Flickr set, adding more photos to the set is easy: Just select the photos(s) you'd like to add and then choose Share→Flickr, as shown in Figure 8-10. Click the set you want to add the photos to. You see the privacy pane shown at the bottom of Figure 8-7 again. Click the Publish button.

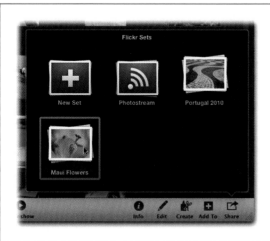

Figure 8-10:
After you've created a Flickr set, you can easily add more photos to it. However, iPhoto doesn't let you drag and drop them—you have to use the Share button on the toolbar or the Share menu.

You're not limited to viewing your own Flickr pictures in iPhoto, either. When you subscribe to other people's Flickr feeds (page 212), you can see their photos by clicking their album in the Subscriptions area of your Source list.

This syncing process goes two ways, by the way. When you upload a photo to this same set on Flickr (using Flickr's own uploading tools or your smartphone), small web-size copies of those same photos show up in your iPhoto library. This syncing happens automatically when you double-click a previously-published set inside iPhoto.

Note: Be sure to edit your photos before publishing them to Flickr. If you decide to edit (or re-edit) photos *after* they've been published, you may encounter trouble. As of this writing, double-clicking a published set after you've done some editing doesn't seem to replace those photos on Flickr. Fortunately, there's a solution.

If you want to edit one photo, delete it from your Flickr set in iPhoto *first* and then edit the image. Then follow the instructions above to add the photo back to the set.

If you want to edit a lot of published pictures, you can delete the whole set and then republish it. (In this case, it doesn't matter whether you do the editing before or after deleting the set in iPhoto.)

Deleting photos from Flickr

The old saying, "What goes up must come down" isn't exactly true here—with Flickr, it's more like, "What goes up must come down when you realize the photo is outdated, embarrassing, or no longer serves any purpose up there on the Web."

To remove individual pictures from an online Flickr set, click the Flickr icon in iPhoto's Source list and double-click the set you want to edit. Select the photos you want to zap and then press the Delete key. Flickr and iPhoto do a little dance, you see the progress bar at the top of your iPhoto window, and then the photos go *off*line. The originals, however, are still safe in your iPhoto library.

When deleting on the iPhoto end, you get the option to import any photos you added to the set *on the Flickr side* back into iPhoto. These aren't high-resolution versions, of course, just small web editions. Figure 8-11 describes yet another way to free your photos from Flickr.

Note: iPhoto '09 had a Share→Unpublish option, but it was removed in iPhoto '11.

Subscribing to Flickr feeds

Through the magic of RSS (really simple syndication), you can keep an eye on the pictures that your friends are uploading to their Flickr pages, right from the comfort of your own iPhoto window. All you need to do is *subscribe* to their Flickr feeds.

Suppose you want to see the travel photos that your Flickr buddy, who goes by the screen name "Retirement Rocks," uploads every week. Here's what you do:

1. **Get the address of the person's Flickr feed.**

   Visit your pal's Flickr collection on the Web and scroll down to the bottom of the page. Look for the 🔊 symbol with the line "Subscribe to Retirement Rock's photostream" next to it.

Control-click (or right-click) the ⊠ and then choose Copy Link Location from the shortcut menu. (The geoFeed link is the feed for photos that have embedded location information; the KML link shows photos tagged in the Google Earth program.)

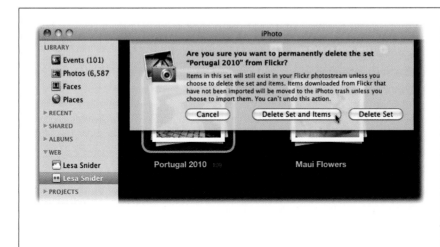

Figure 8-11:
You can delete a set from Flickr all at once. Select your Flickr account in iPhoto's Source list, click the offending set, and then press ⌘-Delete. A panel appears asking exactly what you'd like to delete. Click "Delete Set and Items" to get rid of the set and remove the photos from your photostream. To get rid of the set while leaving your photostream intact, click Delete Set instead.

2. **In iPhoto, choose File→"Subscribe to Photo Feed."**

   In the resulting pane, paste the feed's web address you just copied, and then click Subscribe.

3. **Admire the photos.**

   Under the Subscriptions heading in the iPhoto Source list, you now have an album called "Uploads from Retirement Rocks." Click the album icon to see his latest Flickr uploads in your iPhoto window, and try not to be too envious.

These are smallish web versions of the pictures, but at least you can still see them when you're not online. You can even drag the photos out of the iPhoto window to your desktop (say, to use as a new background), although they're not big enough to print very well.

Facebook

From its humble beginnings in 2004 as an online directory for Harvard students, Facebook has exploded into the world's most popular social-networking site, with more than 500 million members around the world. The concept is ingenious: You sign up for an account at *www.facebook.com*, create a "profile page" where you add résumé-like details, plus lists of your favorite books, movies, and quotes.

Through tools on Facebook, you link your profile to the profiles of your friends.

Once you've "friended" someone this way, you can see each other's profile pages and socialize in the virtual realm.

You can also upload pictures to photo albums on your profile page so your Facebook friends can see them. Once on Facebook, you can even "tag" a friend by name in those photos so you, your pal, and all the friends you *both* have can see those pictures.

With iPhoto '11, this whole photo-uploading part is a piece of cake. You can even upload videos to your "Wall" (your public bulletin-board page).

Once you have a Facebook account, you're ready to link it to iPhoto and transfer some photos:

1. **In iPhoto, select the photos you want to publish to Facebook.**

   You can select whole albums or arbitrary batches of photos (see page 49 for photo-gathering tips).

2. **Choose Share→Facebook.**

   Or, the long way: Click the Share button on the iPhoto toolbar; from the pop-up menu, choose Facebook.

3. **Sign into your Facebook account (Figure 8-12, top).**

   If you're not already logged in, you're asked to supply your Facebook user name and password. Facebook also prompts you for permission to communicate with iPhoto (if you don't have a Facebook account, you need to create one first at *www.facebook.com*).

4. **Choose where you want to put your photos on Facebook: in a new album, on your Wall, or in an existing album.**

   Obviously, Facebook needs to know *where* to upload your photos. Once iPhoto connects to your Facebook account, the Share menu displays the options shown in Figure 8-12 (bottom).

   To add photos to an existing album, click the album's thumbnail in the Share pane. iPhoto automatically uploads your photos to that album.

   If you want to create a *new* Facebook album, or publish the image(s) to your Wall, click the appropriate icon and then proceed to the next step.

Note: iPhoto lets you upload videos to your Facebook Wall, but not to Facebook albums.

---

5. **An iPhoto pane appears, asking you for more info.**

   If you clicked the Wall icon, iPhoto displays a box where you can type a comment that will appear with the photo.

   If you clicked the New Album icon, you see the pane shown in Figure 8-13, top, where you can give the album a name. Facebook also wants to know who can see the soon-to-be-uploaded photos: only the people you've personally accepted as Facebook friends, friends of those friends, or any Facebook member who meanders by.

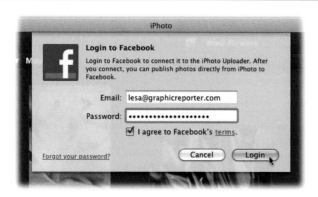

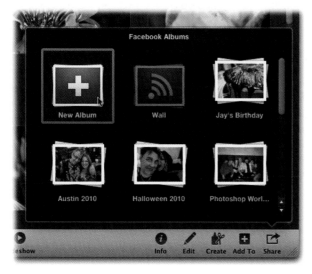

Figure 8-12:
Top: To upload your photos to Facebook, log into your Facebook account. After entering your email address and password, agree to Facebook's terms.

Bottom: Once you've logged in, the Share menu repopulates itself with the contents of your Facebook world (if you've posted a lot of photos, it'll take a moment or two). From here, you can add a new Facebook album, post the selected photos to your Facebook Wall, or plop them into an existing album.

6. **Click Publish.**

   Sit back as iPhoto passes the pictures over to Facebook. As before, it's best to let iPhoto finish publishing one set of photos before you start publishing another.

   In iPhoto's Source list, your Facebook account appears as a new entry under the Web heading (Figure 8-13, bottom).

Tip: You can also use iPhoto to change your Facebook profile picture. Page 218 tells you how.

At this point, you're ready to view your handiwork.

To see *all* your photos on your Facebook page, make sure your Facebook account is selected in the Source list. Then, in the black bar at the top of your iPhoto window, click the ➡ next to the "[Your Name]'s Facebook albums" heading (circled in Figure 8-13, bottom). To see *a single* Facebook album, double-click the album (they appear as stacks of photos, as shown in Figure 8-13 [bottom]), and then click the album link at the top of your iPhoto window.

Note: If there's more than one avid Facebooker uploading pictures through the same copy of iPhoto, then the Source list displays each member's Facebook account as a separate icon.

To change the name of an album you've published to Facebook from iPhoto, click its name and then enter a new one. The new name appears on Facebook when the album syncs, which happens when you double-click the album in iPhoto.

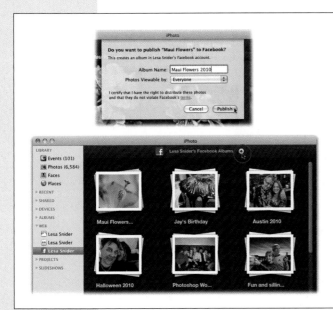

Figure 8-13:
Top: iPhoto lets you manage privacy options on a per-album basis, so you'll see this pane each time you upload photos to Facebook.

Bottom: Once you connect iPhoto to your Facebook account, you see a new icon in your Source list bearing your account's name. Click this icon to see all the albums you've ever published on Facebook, whether you used iPhoto to publish them or not. You can take a quick trip to your Facebook page by clicking the ➡ next to your Facebook account's name (circled).

Likewise, you can change the album's name on Facebook by clicking the Photos link on the left side of your profile page and then selecting the album you want to change. When the album opens to reveal all the pictures inside, scroll down to the bottom of the photos and click the Edit Album Info link. Enter something clever into the Album Name field and then click the Save Changes button.

Tip: You can use Facebook to share albums with people who aren't members. Click the Photos link on your profile page and open the album you want to share. At the very bottom of the page, you'll spot some light blue text that says, "Share this album with anyone by sending them this public link" with a web address underneath. Paste that link into an email message and send it off to invite one of the six people not yet on Facebook to see your photos.

Automatic photo-tagging in Facebook

Remember how much fun you had back in Chapter 4 getting iPhoto to recognize your friends with the grinding analytic power of Faces? If you took the time to add full names and email addresses to the snapshots on your Faces corkboard (shown on page 97), then tagging your Facebook friends in photos is pretty much a done deal.

Once you upload name-tagged photos to Facebook, friends you've identified in the pictures are also pinged with Facebook's own photo-tagging tool. In other words, if you've filled in Ralph's info on his Faces snapshot in iPhoto, Facebook blabs to all your mutual friends that you've just tagged Ralph in one of your pictures.

Depending on your Facebook settings, all 608 of your Facebook friends will spot a thumbnail of the newly Ralph-tagged photo and can click a link to see it at full size. If you're always tagging your pals on Facebook, iPhoto can save you a lot of time.

Note: If you know you've face-tagged someone on the iPhoto corkboard but the photo tags aren't show-ing up on Facebook, check the name and email address you entered in the Info panel (page 66). For every-thing to work, it has to match the name and email address the person uses for her Facebook account.

Add/delete photos from Facebook albums

Adding and deleting photos from your Facebook albums works exactly as it does with Flickr; see page 211. (Make sure you're deleting them from the Facebook icon and not from Photos view; deleting pictures from Photos deletes them from *iPhoto*.)

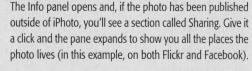

UP TO SPEED

The Info Panel Knows

Once you start publishing photos to Flickr, Facebook, and MobileMe, it can be tough to remember where each photo went. Sure, you can choose one of these services in your Source list and root around through sets or albums to see what's where, but there's a faster way: using the Info panel. In addition to showing you details about when, how, and where you took the photo, the Info panel also keeps track of what ser-vices you shared the photo with, and to whom you've sent photo emails (page 195).

To find out exactly where that photo of your latest tattoo ended up, select the photo in your library and then click the ❶ in the toolbar.

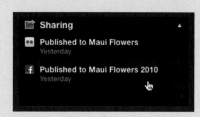

The Info panel opens and, if the photo has been published outside of iPhoto, you'll see a section called Sharing. Give it a click and the pane expands to show you all the places the photo lives (in this example, on both Flickr and Facebook).

If you need to quickly delete the tattoo shot from Facebook—in the hopes that Grandma hasn't yet seen it—click the Facebook icon in the Info panel. iPhoto opens the web page where the photo lives. There, you can cross your fingers and search for the service's Delete command. Or you can follow the instructions on page 71 for deleting the item within iPhoto.

As with Flickr, syncing is a two-way street between Facebook and iPhoto. If you move a photo into a different published Facebook album, add a picture to the album, or change album names and photo titles, iPhoto updates its own copies, too.

Changing your Facebook profile picture

New in iPhoto '11 is the ability to change your Facebook profile picture—the photo that appears at the top left of your profile page—*without* visiting Facebook on the Web.

Just select the photo you want to use and then click the Share button in your toolbar. Choose Facebook and the Share menu changes to include a new option: Profile Picture. Figure 8-14 explains the rest.

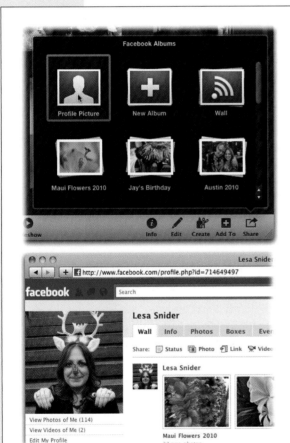

Figure 8-14:
Top: The Profile Picture option appears in the Share menu when you have just *one* photo selected. Give it a click and iPhoto asks you to confirm your choice. In the resulting message pane (not shown), click Set.

Bottom: iPhoto uploads your new mugshot to your Facebook account and sets it as your new profile picture. (Here, you can also see the new Maui Flowers album, which was uploaded back in Figure 8-12.)

The MobileMe Gallery

If you have a MobileMe account and a high-speed Internet connection, you're in for a real treat. iPhoto can publish your pictures to a gorgeous, interactive web-based Gallery—a delight for anyone who knows its web address (and who *also* has a high-speed connection).

As with Flickr and Facebook, publishing couldn't be simpler, and the steps are exactly the same:

1. **Choose the photos you want to publish.**

   You can click an album or an Event, or select a batch using the techniques described on page 49.

2. **Choose Share→MobileMe.**

   Or click the Share button on your toolbar; from the pop-up menu, choose MobileMe. Either way, iPhoto fetches your existing albums from your MobileMe account, and stuffs them inside the Share menu at the lower right part of your iPhoto window.

Note: If iPhoto doesn't yet know your MobileMe account information (it should, because you most likely entered it into your System Preferences when you first set up your Mac), a message pane offers you a Sign In button (in case you're already a member) and a Learn More button (in case you're not; see the box on page 224).

Choose whether to add your photos to an existing MobileMe album or create a new one. Once you make that decision, you see the message pane shown at the top of Figure 8-15.

3. **Specify who can see your pictures.**

   The "Album Viewable by" pop-up menu lets you specify who can see your photos. After all, not every picture in your life is appropriate for every rabble-rouser out there. (You know who you are, senators' children.)

   If you choose **Everyone**, then there are no restrictions on who can call up your photos. If you choose **Only Me**, then you've pretty much guaranteed that nobody sees your pictures unless they're sitting beside you.

   There is, fortunately, an in-between option. If you choose **Edit Names and Passwords**, you get the pane shown at the bottom of Figure 8-15, where you can create a name and password for this album. You can then distribute this name and password to friends and relatives to ensure that only the lucky few can get in.

Note: As the pane mentions, capitalization counts when you make up passwords; *fruitcake* and *Fruitcake* are two different things.

After you create a user name and password, click OK and you return to the Publish pane (Figure 8-15, top). Make sure the correct user name is visible in the "Album Viewable by" pop-up menu.

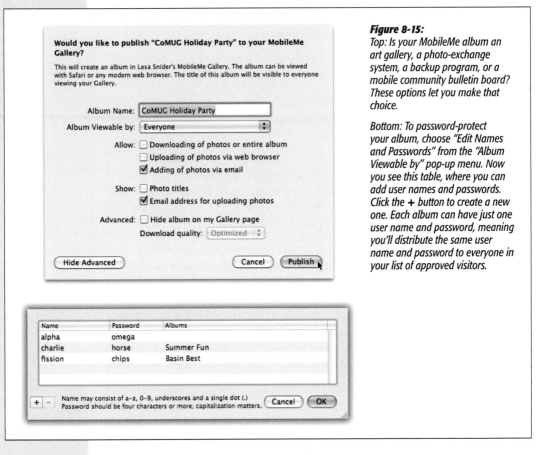

Figure 8-15:
Top: Is your MobileMe album an art gallery, a photo-exchange system, a backup program, or a mobile community bulletin board? These options let you make that choice.

Bottom: To password-protect your album, choose "Edit Names and Passwords" from the "Album Viewable by" pop-up menu. Now you see this table, where you can add user names and passwords. Click the + button to create a new one. Each album can have just one user name and password, meaning you'll distribute the same user name and password to everyone in your list of approved visitors.

4. **Adjust the other checkboxes to configure your Gallery.**

   "Allow: Downloading of photos or entire album" means that the Download button in the MobileMe Gallery will be available. Anyone who clicks it can download the full-size, full-resolution copy of that photo. If you're worried that people might try to make money off your masterful photographic work, don't turn this on.

   "Allow: Uploading of photos via web browser" is even more intriguing. It means that visitors to your Gallery can post photos of their own, adding to this online album, whether they're using Mac OS X or Windows. This is a great option for parties, as your guests can upload their own photos taken with their cameras to the Gallery you created. Details are on page 225.

It's important to note that iPhoto performs a *two-way sync* with your MobileMe Gallery. If you add photos to the published album, they show up on the Web automatically—and if someone *else* adds photos, they show up in the published album in *your* copy of iPhoto automatically! If you want to add the new photo to your iPhoto library—so it actually lives on your hard drive—drag it from the published album into the Photos or Events icon in your Source list.

Tip: You can upload photos from your iPhone directly to your MobileMe Gallery, too (assuming you've entered your MobileMe account information into your iPhone). In the Photo-viewing program on your iPhone, tap the Send icon, and then choose "Send to MobileMe." Enter a title and description for your photo (this part is optional), and then choose the Gallery you want it to go into. Click Publish and smile smugly at your technological prowess.

"Allow: Adding of photos via email" may be cooler yet. It lets anyone add photos by sending them to your Gallery's secret, unique email address. You won't discover the private email address until after you've published the Gallery. Once you do, you'll find it in the upper-right corner of the iPhoto window, as shown in Figure 8-16.

So how are would-be emailers supposed to know the secret address? Depends on how private you want to be.

If you turn on **"Show: Email address for uploading photos,"** then the MobileMe Gallery's email address appears in a message pane when visitors click the "Send to Album" button in the toolbar at the top of the web gallery itself. (It's one of the buttons barely visible in Figure 8-18.) If you leave that option turned off, then nobody will know the Gallery's email address…unless you email it to them.

"Show: Photo titles" means that the names of your pictures (as you've typed them in iPhoto) will appear on the Web.

Click the Show Advanced button in the left corner of the box to get to even more settings. Here, you can turn on the checkbox next to **"Hide album on my Gallery page"** if you want to publish this particular set of pictures—but keep them from showing up alongside all the other albums on your MobileMe Gallery page.

If you've turned on the checkbox that allows people to download copies of your photos, then the pop-up menu next to Download Quality is clickable. You can choose Optimized (smaller, faster, not as nice to print large) or Actual Size (the same resolution as what you originally uploaded).

5. Click the Publish button.

iPhoto sends your photos off to Webland and posts them in your Gallery. It can take quite awhile—a minute per picture, for example.

When it's all over, the iPhoto window looks like Figure 8-16. You'll notice a few changes:

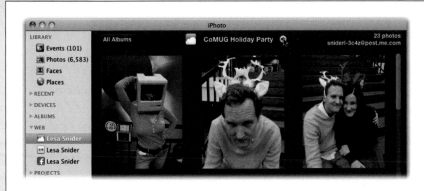

Figure 8-16:
Once iPhoto knows about your MobileMe account, you see a new icon in your Source list bearing the account holder's name.

- In the Source list under the Web heading, there's a new icon bearing your MobileMe account's name (iPhoto '09 used to list each album in the Source list individually). Click it to see every album you've ever published to your MobileMe Gallery.

  You can change what's in your album by adding, deleting, or editing the thumbnails inside each one. iPhoto publishes your changes automatically (you'll see a little status bar appear at the top right of this window when iPhoto is making changes).

- At the top of the iPhoto window, the name and email address of your Gallery appear. Click the ➡ next to the album's name to open the published version of the Gallery in your web browser.

- New in iPhoto '11 is the ability to change a Gallery's options from within the Info panel. Mouse down to your toolbar and click the Info button to reveal the options shown in Figure 8-17. Click Settings to reopen the pane shown in Figure 8-15 (top). When you're finished making changes, click Publish.

- iPhoto's Info panel is also home to the "Tell a Friend" button. Clicking it makes iPhoto generate a new outgoing email message, complete with viewing instructions. Figure 8-17 has the details.

Tip: If more than one person in your household uses MobileMe and your Mac, you can set up their accounts in iPhoto, too (iPhoto '11 just stacks them up in your Source list). If you turned on the "Allow: Adding of photos via email" option, you'll also see your Gallery's secret email address at the album's top right in iPhoto. To see all of your MobileMe albums in iPhoto, click the All Albums button at the top left of the main photo-viewing area (or press ⌘-left arrow).

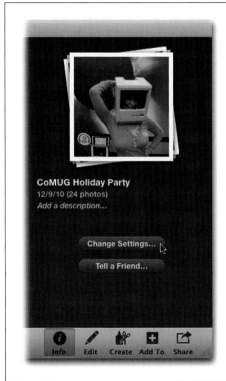

Note: Syncing changes to published albums is supposed to be an automatic affair in iPhoto '11, but it doesn't always work. If the changes you make in iPhoto to an album or its settings don't make it onto the Web, you have little choice but to delete the album and republish it: Select the album in iPhoto and press ⌘-Delete (iPhoto asks if you're sure you want to delete the album). Then republish it as described earlier in this section and your album should be right as rain.

Using MobileMe Gallery

Once your fans arrive at the web address you've given them, they're in for a rollicking good time. They can walk through your little art show using one of the four, super-slick slideshows shown in Figure 8-18:

- **Grid** is the standard layout. Your photos appear as thumbnails, which you can click for a larger view.

- **Mosaic** offers a "table of contents" of thumbnails on the right side; click one to see that photo at full (or at least fuller) size in the middle of the window. The advantage here is that you don't lose sight of the full photo array; you can jump among them without proceeding in sequence.

- **Carousel** is a lot like Cover Flow (in Mac OS X, your iPhone, iPad, or iPod). This show, too, lets you keep track of where you are in the stack of pictures. As you drag the horizontal scroll bar (or drag the photos themselves), the photos fly past, enlarging to a decent size as they pass the center point.

- **Slideshow**, of course, is a traditional slideshow, where your visitor doesn't have to do anything but sit back and watch as the pictures parade across the screen, complete with crossfades between them. (A control bar with Download, Previous, Next, Pause, and Exit Full Screen buttons is available, however, when a little more interactivity is desired. Wiggle the mouse to make it appear.)

There are some handy buttons across the top of your Gallery page, too (visible, though tiny, at top left in Figure 8-18):

- **Download**. If you've given permission in the album's settings, visitors can download the full-resolution photos to their own hard drives. This is a great way to supply your pictures to other people, anywhere in the world, who might want to print them—without dealing with the hassles and file-size limits of email.

UP TO SPEED

Getting a MobileMe Account

MobileMe, Apple's subscription online service, provides everything you need to put a collection of your photos online—and on your network. Unfortunately, the service isn't free. A membership will set you back $100 per year (it's much less from Amazon).

The good news is that Mac OS X makes it incredibly easy to sign up for an account, and a two-month trial account is free. (There are a few limitations on the trial account; it grants you 20 MB of iDisk space instead of 20 gigabytes, for example.) If you don't already have an account, here's how you get one:

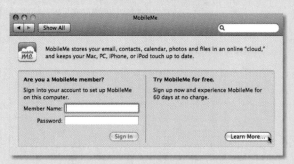

Choose →System Preferences, and then click the MobileMe icon (it looks like a little cloud). Next, click Learn More under the "Try MobileMe for free" heading.

Now you go online, where your web browser opens the MobileMe home page. Click the Free Trial button to summon the sign-up screen. Fill in your name and address, make up an account name and password, and, if you like, turn off the checkbox that invites you to receive junk email.

You're also asked to make up a question and answer (such as, "First grade teacher's name?" and "Flanders"). If you ever forget your password, the MobileMe software will help you—provided you can answer this question correctly. Click Continue.

An account summary screen now appears; print it or save it. On the next screen, the system offers to send an email message to your friends letting them know about your new email address (which is *whatever-name-you-chose@me.com*).

The final step is to return to the MobileMe pane of System Preferences and fill in the account name and password you just created. You're now ready to use your MobileMe account.

- **Subscribe**. This option lets you see someone else's MobileMe Gallery. See page 226 for details.

- **Upload**. Your public can click this button to upload new photos to your Gallery, if you've permitted it; when they do, they'll see the message pane shown in Figure 8-19. Once they prove they're human, they click Choose Files. Next, they find and highlight their *own* photos to upload, and then click Select. The files are automatically uploaded and posted on your Gallery. This kind of photo sharing is incredibly handy for parties, graduations, and weddings.

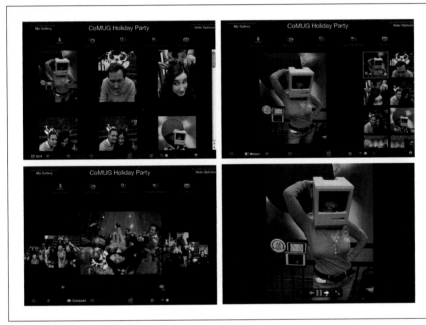

Figure 8-18:
Your finished web gallery at work. Clockwise from top left: Grid, Mosaic, Slideshow, and Carousel presentation modes.

Note: Uploaded photos show up in the published album in iPhoto, but they don't yet live in your iPhoto library. In fact, they bear a little symbol at the bottom left of the thumbnail letting you know that they only live online (it looks like a tiny, white ➘). To add an uploaded photo to your library, drag the photo from the album onto your Events or Photos icon in the Source list.

- **Send to Album**. Others can click this button to reveal the Gallery's private email address, if you've permitted emailing photos.

- **Tell a Friend**. Click to send a link to your Gallery to someone else by email. Spread the word!

- At the bottom of the window, the four **Color** buttons let viewers change the background color of the Gallery: Black, dark gray, light gray, or white. Finally, the Size slider at the lower right controls the thumbnail size in Grid and Mosaic views.

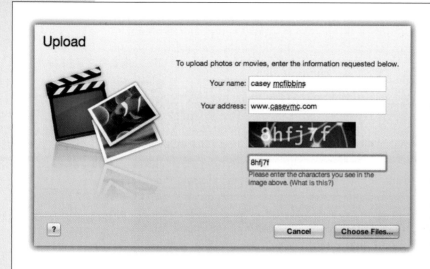

Figure 8-19:
If you permit upload-
ing, your visitors will
see an Upload button
at the top of your
Gallery. Clicking it
produces this pane,
where uploaders can
enter a name and
email address. They
must also type in the
distorted characters
in the middle to prove
they're human, and
not one of those
spam-generating
software robots
that cruise the Web
wreaking havoc.

Deleting Your MobileMe Albums

It's easy to find out how many albums you've published to your MobileMe Gallery: Just click the MobileMe icon in your Source list; they're listed right there in the iPhoto viewing area.

They're very easy to take down, too, once they've outlived their usefulness. To delete a published album, click its name and then press ⌘-Delete (the ⌘ key addition is new in iPhoto '11).

If your album contains photos that were synced to your copy of iPhoto from the Gallery (for example, photos submitted by other people), a message appears to warn you that those pictures are about to be obliterated. (It also gives you an "Import photos to your library before deleting this album" checkbox.)

Then, it disappears, not only from your Source list, but also from the Web and from any subscribers' copies of iPhoto. And you reclaim that much of your MobileMe storage space.

Subscribing to Published Albums

If your fans have iPhoto '08 or later, they can *subscribe* to your MobileMe Gallery. That means that if you make changes to the Gallery—adding or removing pictures, say—those changes are soon thereafter reflected in the iPhoto libraries of your subscribers. Photo-feed subscriptions are a fantastic way for grandparents and other interested parties to keep up with the photos of your life, with zero effort on their part and very little on yours.

You can subscribe to someone's iPhoto feed in two ways. Both of them require that you know the Gallery's web address, as sent to you by its creator:

- **Visit the album's web page on the MobileMe Gallery**. There, click the Subscribe button and you're given the choice of opening the feed in your favorite feed-reading program (for example, NetNewsWire or Safari) or in iPhoto. Choose iPhoto and then click OK. Back in iPhoto, you'll see a message pane asking if you're *sure* you want to subscribe to this photo feed; click Subscribe.

- **In iPhoto, choose File→"Subscribe to Photo Feed."** In the resulting box, paste the Gallery's address, and then click Subscribe.

Once you've subscribed to someone's MobileMe Gallery, a new icon appears in your Source list under a new heading: "Subscriptions." When you click it, the main Photos view changes to show you the latest pictures from that Gallery. (It can take awhile for the photos to appear the first time you subscribe, though. Best not to sit there waiting for it; go do something else and come back later.)

iPhoto '11 doesn't check the Gallery to see if there are changes until you click the ↻ button next to the Gallery's name. And there's no longer a Preference setting to make iPhoto automatically check for updates, either.

FREQUENTLY ASKED QUESTION

Photocasting, R.I.P.

What happened to photocasting?

Photocasting was a hot new feature of iPhoto 6. But in iPhoto '08, it was replaced by the .Mac Web Gallery photo feed, which has *now* been replaced by the MobileMe feed.

Photocasting was a direct pipe from your copy of iPhoto into somebody else's. You could "publish" an album (baby pictures, for example); they could "subscribe" to it (grandparents, let's say). Whenever you made changes to that album—you added more photos, for example—the grandparents saw the changes in their own copies of iPhoto.

They could also drag your photos into their own copies of iPhoto—the full-resolution originals.

So why is it gone? Maybe not enough people used it, or maybe Apple wants to push sales of its MobileMe accounts (required for the Gallery feature).

If you upgraded to iPhoto '11, any albums you had photocast continue to work. But their web address (URL) has changed, and it's up to you to notify everyone who subscribed to them. (To find the new URL, click the album in the Source list; the URL appears at the top of the window. Your fans should choose File→"Subscribe to Photo Feed," and then paste in this new address.) And you can't create *new* photocasts.

If you have a MobileMe account, you can also change your Photocast albums into web galleries, described in this chapter; people with iPhoto '08 can still subscribe to your photos and, if you permit it, download them or even add their own pictures.

Here's how: Select the Photocast album in your Source list, and then click Unpublish on the toolbar. When that button changes to say MobileMe, click it; next, survey the publishing options, and then publish away.

---

iPhoto to iWeb

Here it is—the second-easiest way to publish your photos on the Web. Your photos end up on a handsome-looking web page in just a few quick steps, with far more design freedom than the web galleries give you.

1. **In iPhoto, select the photos you want to put on the Web, or click the album that contains them.**

   The selection can be one you've dragged pictures into, a smart album, the Last Import album, a year album, and so on. Or use the selection techniques described on page 49 to isolate a bunch of photos within an album.

Note: The iWeb photo-gallery template can't handle more than 99 photos per web page. If you want to publish more than that, you'll have to create a series of separate pages.

---

2. **Choose Share→iWeb→Photo Page.**

   If you choose Share→iWeb→Blog instead, you'll create a different sort of web page—not so much an art gallery as a daily journal page, with spaces where you can type up comments about your pictures. The steps are exactly the same as described here, except that you should begin by selecting, at most, three photos.

   When you open iWeb for the first time, you're asked to sign into or create a MobileMe account. To bypass it, click No Thanks. Once you're in iWeb, you can set it up to publish to your own website instead, as described in the Note on page 229.

   After a moment, iWeb appears.

3. **Choose from the list of templates (color/design schemes).**

   When you click a template, the window immediately displays a mock-up of your finished web page (Figure 8-20), displaying the thumbnails in whatever order they appeared in iPhoto.

4. **Edit the page title, subtitle, and individual photo titles.**

   Don't be concerned by the presence of all the Latin ("Lorem ipsum dolor amet..."); that's just placeholder text. Drag your cursor through it and type new stuff to replace it.

   If you don't bother changing the photo names, iPhoto will simply use whatever titles the photos have in the program itself.

5. **Edit the design of the photo grid, if you like.**

   Click any photo thumbnail. Now you see the floating panel of options shown in Figure 8-20. You can control how many columns appear, how many lines you want for each caption, and so on.

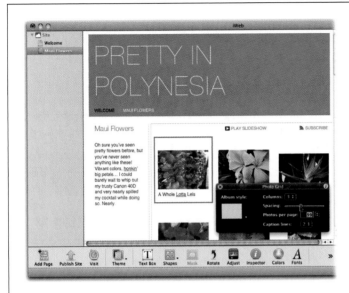

Figure 8-20:
In iWeb, iPhoto shows you what your yet-to-be-published web page is going to look like. iWeb '11's new theme Fine Line is shown here.

To adjust the layout, click any photo to open the Photo Grid panel. There, you can adjust the thumbnail spacing, number of columns, photos per page, and so on.

6. **Click Publish Site (shown at lower left in Figure 8-20).**

   This is the big moment: iPhoto connects to the MobileMe website, scales down your photos to a reasonable size, and then transfers them to the server. This magic requires, of course, that you already have a MobileMe account, and that you've entered your account name and password. It can also take a *very* long time.

   When the uploading process is complete, as indicated by the alert dialog box, you can go to the page and see your results.

Note: You don't *have* to have a MobileMe account to use iWeb. If you maintain your own website, for example, click the site's name on the left side of the iWeb window and the Site Publishing Settings pane appears. From the "Publish to" pop menu, choose FTP Server or Local Folder.

If you include larger photos in your web page, iPhoto automatically scales them down to reasonably sized JPEG files so that they can be more easily loaded and displayed in a web browser. If you want your web pages to include *exact* copies of your original photos—regardless of size or file format—use the Export option described on page 314.

What you get when you're done

When you see what you've created with iWeb, you'll be impressed: It's a professional-looking, stylishly titled web page with thumbnails neatly arranged in a grid. Clicking a thumbnail opens an enlarged version of the picture in its own window; clicking the Start Slideshow button creates a full-window, beautiful slideshow complete with Previous and Next buttons and—when you move the cursor to the top of the window—even a little thumbnail browser. You can return to your main index page at any time by closing the slideshow window.

Tip: In the web addresses of your MobileMe-hosted websites (for example, *http://me.com/casey/Site/MauiVacation.html*), capitalization counts—a point not to be forgotten when you share the site's address with friends. If you type one of these addresses into a web browser with incorrect capitalization, you'll get only a "missing page" message.

Then again, maybe it's better to send your friends a much shorter, easier-to-remember address. You can convert long addresses into shorter ones using a free URL-redirection service. At *www.tinyurl.com*, for example, you convert *http://me.com/gladys/Site/pickles.html* into *http://tinyurl.com/5k9q5b*, or you can enter a custom blurb after the "com." (You can do your own shopping for similar services by searching Google for "free URL redirection.")

Editing or deleting the web page

Within iWeb, make your changes (delete photos or add them using the Media Browser, rearrange them, rename them, and so on) and then click the Publish Site button again at the bottom of the screen. iWeb sets about updating the gallery online.

To delete a photo-gallery page, click its name in iWeb's left-side panel (the Site Organizer), and then press the Delete key (or Control-click the site's name and choose Delete from the shortcut menu). Next, click Publish Site in the toolbar; this step tells the program, "OK, make the online version of my site match what I now have in iWeb."

Deleting a photo page like this also deletes all of the online photo files, which frees up space on your iDisk.

FREQUENTLY ASKED QUESTION

Where Did All the Photos Go?

When iWeb transfers my photos to the MobileMe website, where are they going?

Everything gets stored on your iDisk, the virtual disk that comes with your MobileMe account. (Your iDisk looks and behaves like a miniature hard drive, but it's really just a privately reserved chunk of space on one of Apple's secure servers.)

The HTML pages generated by iWeb automatically go in the Web→Sites→iWeb folder on your iDisk. (In fact, if you know how to use a web page creation program like Dreamweaver, you can make changes to your web pages by editing these documents.)

The photos themselves get dumped into folders called Images within that iWeb folder on the iDisk.

Exporting iPhoto Web Pages

If you already have your own website, you don't need MobileMe or iWeb to create an online photo album. Instead, you can use iPhoto's Export command to generate HTML pages that you can upload to any web server. You're still saving a lot of time and effort—and you still get a handy thumbnail gallery page.

The web pages you export directly from iPhoto don't include any fancy designs or themed graphics. In fact, they're kind of stark; just take a look at Figure 8-21.

This is the best method if you plan to post the pages you create to a website of your own—especially if you plan on tinkering with the resulting HTML pages yourself.

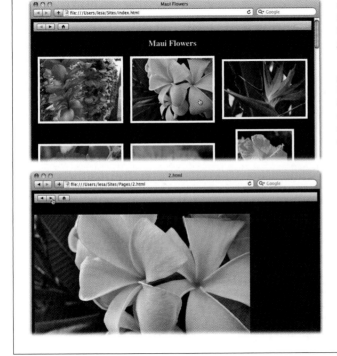

Figure 8-21:
Here's what a web page exported straight from iPhoto looks like (top). Just click any photo to see a larger version of it (bottom).

The no-frills design is functional, but not particularly elegant. The only thing you can control is the number of photos per row, the text and background colors, and whether or not the photos' titles or descriptions are displayed. On the other hand, the HTML code behind this page is 100 percent editable.

Preparing the Export

Here are the basic web-exporting steps:

1. **In iPhoto, select the photos you want to include on the web pages.**

   The Export command puts no limit on the number of photos you can export to web pages in one burst. Select as many photos as you want; iPhoto will generate as many pages as needed to accommodate all the pictures in your specified grid. (If you don't select any photos, iPhoto assumes you want to export all the photos in the current album, including the Library or the Last Import album.)

2. **Choose File→Export, or press Shift-⌘-E.**

   The Export dialog box appears.

3. **Click the Web Page tab.**

   You see the dialog box shown in Figure 8-22.

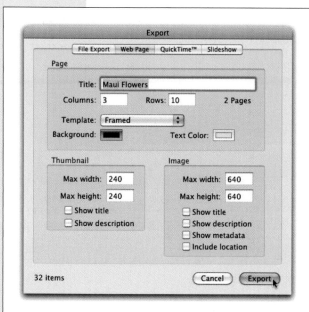

Figure 8-22:
As you change the size of the thumbnails or the grid, the number of pages generated to handle the images changes. The page count, based on your current settings, appears just to the right of the Rows field. The total count of the photos you're about to export appears in the lower-left corner of the window.

The Template pop-up menu offers to put a little frame around each thumbnail. And if you turn on the "Show metadata" checkbox, when someone clicks a thumbnail to open the full-size photo, the camera, shutter, aperture, exposure, and other photographic data appear for analysis and admiration. And you can turn on the "Include location" checkbox to provide the location information in geotagged pictures.

4. **Set the Page attributes, including the title, grid size, and background.**

   The title you set here will appear in the title bar of each exported web page, and as a header in the page itself.

Tip: For maximum compatibility with the world's computers and operating systems—if you're trying to get a lot of international visitors to check out your photos—use all lowercase letters and no spaces.

Use the Columns and Rows boxes to specify how many thumbnails you want to appear across and down your "index" page. (The little "2 pages" indicator tells you how many pages this particular index gallery requires.)

If you'd like a background page color other than white, click the rectangular swatch next to the word "Background" and follow the instructions in Figure 8-23. You can also pick a color for the text that appears on each page by clicking the Text Color swatch.

You can even choose a background *picture* instead of a solid background color. To make it so, click the Image Palettes button at the top of the Color Picker.

Then, from the pop-up menu near the bottom of the window, choose "New from File" to select the graphics file on your hard drive. Be considerate of your audience, however. A background graphic makes your pages take longer to load, and a busy background pattern can be very distracting.

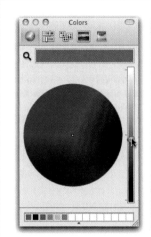 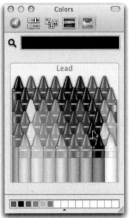

Figure 8-23:
Left: Drag the right-side slider all the way up to see the spectrum of colors available to you. Drag downward to view darker colors.

Right: Alternatively, click one of the other color-picking buttons at the top of the dialog box. The crayon picker delights with both ease of use and creative color names, like Lead.

5. **Specify how big you want the thumbnail images to be, and choose a size for the enlargements that appear when you click a thumbnail.**

   The sizes iPhoto proposes are fine *if* all your photos are horizontal (that is, in landscape orientation). If some are wide and some are tall, however, you're better off specifying *square* dimensions for both the thumbnails and the enlarged photos—240 × 240 for the thumbnails and 640 × 640 for the biggies, for example.

6. **Turn on the various checkboxes, as desired.**

   Show title draws upon the titles you've assigned in iPhoto, centering each picture's name underneath its thumbnail. The larger version of each picture will also bear this name when it opens into its own window.

   Turning on **Show description** displays any text you've typed into the Description field for each picture in iPhoto. Depending on which checkboxes you turn on, you can have the description appear under each thumbnail, under each larger image, or both.

   Show metadata will display reams of photographic data (shutter speed, aperture, flash status, and so on) beneath each larger image.

   Finally, **Include location** lets the photo take along any geotags showing where it was taken. If you have privacy concerns, it's best to leave this one turned off.

7. **Click Export.**

   The Save dialog box appears.

8. **Choose a folder to hold the export files (or, by clicking New Folder, create one) and then click OK.**

    The export process gets under way.

Examining the Results

When iPhoto is done exporting, you end up with a series of HTML documents and JPEG images—the building blocks of your website-to-be. A number of these icons automatically inherit the name of the *folder* into which you've saved them. If you export the files into a folder named "Tahiti," for example, you'll see something like Figure 8-24:

*   **Tahiti.html.** This is the main HTML page, containing the first thumbnails in the series that you exported. It's the home page, the index page, and the starting point for the exported pages.

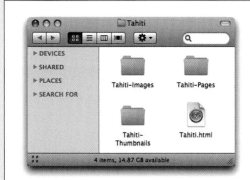

Figure 8-24:
This is what a website looks like before it's on the Internet. All the pieces are here, filed exactly where the home page (called, in this example, Tahiti.html) can find them.

*   **Page1.html, Page2.html...** You see these only if you exported enough photos to require more than one page of thumbnails—that is, if iPhoto required *multiple* "home" pages.

*   **Tahiti-Thumbnails.** This folder holds the actual thumbnail graphics that appear on each of the index pages.

*   **Tahiti-Pages.** This folder contains the HTML documents (named Image1.html, Image2.html, Image3.html, and so on) that open when you click the thumbnails on the index pages.

*   **Tahiti-Images.** This folder houses the larger JPEG versions of your photos. Yes, these are the *graphics* that appear on the Image.html pages.

Tip: Some web servers require that the home page of your site be called *index.html*. To force your exported website to use this name for the main HTML page, save your exported pages into a folder called "index." Now the home page will have the correct name (*index.html*) and all the other image and page files will be properly linked to it. (After exporting, feel free to rename the folder. Naming it "index" was necessary only during the exporting process.)

Once you've created these pages, it's up to you to figure out how to post them on the Internet where the world can see them. To do that, you'll have to upload all the exported files to a web server, using an FTP program like the free RBrowser, available from *www.rbrowser.com*. For a more robust program, check out Transmit or Fetch. They're available from the Mac App Store for about $30 each. (The Mac App Store appears in your Dock if you're running Mac OS X 10.6.6 or later.)

Enhancing iPhoto's HTML

If you know how to work with HTML code, you don't have to accept the unremarkable web pages exported by iPhoto. You're free to tear into them with a full-blown web authoring program like Adobe Dreamweaver or the free KompoZer (*www.kompozer.net*) to add your own formatting, headers, footers, and other graphics. Heck, even Microsoft Word lets you open and edit HTML documents—plenty of power for changing iPhoto's layout, reformatting the text, or adding your own page elements.

If you're a hard-core HTML coder, you can also open the files in a text editor like BBEdit or even TextEdit to tweak the code directly. With a few quick changes, you can make your iPhoto-generated web pages look more sophisticated and less generic. Here are some of the changes you might want to consider making:

- Change font faces and sizes.
- Change the alignment of titles.
- Add a footer with your contact information and email address.
- Add *metadata* tags (keywords) to the page header so that search engines can locate and categorize your pages.
- Insert links to your other websites or relevant sites on the Web.

Photo Sharing on the Network

One of the coolest features of iTunes is the way you can "publish" certain playlists on your home or office network so that other people in the same building can listen to your tunes. Why shouldn't iPhoto be able to do the same thing with pictures?

In fact, it can. Here's how it works.

For this example, suppose that you're the master shutterbug who has all the cool shots. On your Mac, choose iPhoto→Preferences and click Sharing. Turn on "Share my photos" (Figure 8-25).

You might be tempted to turn on "Share entire library" so that no crumb of your artistry will go unappreciated—but don't. Even the fastest Macs on the fastest networks will grind to a halt if you try to share even a medium-sized photo library. You are, after all, attempting to cram gigabytes of data through your network to the other Macs. It's far more practical to turn on the checkboxes for the individual albums you want to share, as shown in Figure 8-25.

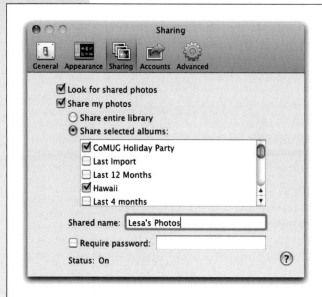

Figure 8-25:
If you turn on "Share entire library," you make all your pictures available to others on the network—and doom your fans to a lifetime of waiting while gray empty boxes fill their iPhoto screens.

Alternatively, click "Share selected albums" and then select the individual albums that you want to make public. Either way, turning on Sharing makes only photos available on the network—not movie clips.

Unless you also turn on "Require password" (and make up a password), everyone on the network with iPhoto 4 or higher can see your shared pictures.

Finally, close the Preferences window.

At this point, other people on your network will see *your* albums show up in *their* Source lists, above the list of their own albums; see Figure 8-26. (Or at least they will if they have "Look for shared photos" turned on in their iPhoto Preferences.)

Note: If you're lucky enough to own an Apple TV—the newer and smaller black version—your iPhoto library will be visible to it, too.

As you may know, when you share iTunes music over a network, other people can only *listen* to your songs—they can't actually *have* them. (The large, well-built lawyers of American record companies have made sure of that.)

But iPhoto is another story. Nobody's going to issue you a summons for freely distributing your own photos. So once you've jacked into somebody else's iPhoto pictures via the network, feel free to drag them into your own iPhoto albums, thereby copying them onto your own Mac. Now you can edit them, print them, and otherwise treat them like your own photos.

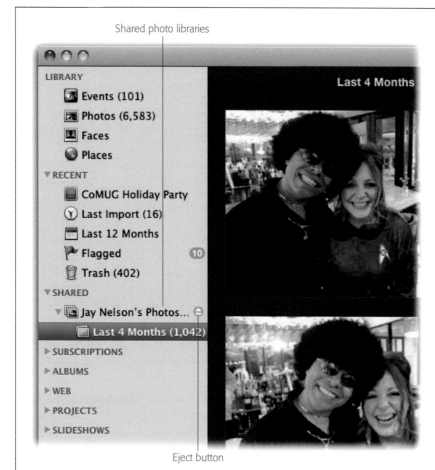

Shared photo libraries

Eject button

Figure 8-26:
You can't delete or edit the photos you've summoned from some other Mac. But you can drag them into your own albums (or your own library) to copy them. The Shared category appears in your Source list only if iPhoto detects at least one shared iPhoto collection on the network. When you've had enough, click the ⊖ button to eject the shared library—the flippy triangle, the list of albums, and the ⊖ button itself disappear. The names of shared collections (like "Jay Nelson's Library" in this example) remain on the screen, in case you want to bring them back for another look later.

Photo Sharing Across Accounts

Mac OS X is designed from the ground up to be a *multiple-user* operating system. You can set up Mac OS X with individual *user accounts* so that everyone has to log in. When the Mac starts up, in other words, you have to click your account name and type a password before you can start using it.

Upon doing so, you discover the Macintosh universe just as you left it, including *your* icons on the desktop, Dock configuration, desktop picture, screensaver, web browser bookmarks, email account, fonts, startup programs, and so on. This accounts feature adds both convenience and security. As you can imagine, this feature is a big deal in schools, businesses, and families.

It also means that each account holder has a separate iPhoto Library folder. (Remember, it lives inside your own Home folder.) The photos *you* import into iPhoto are accessible only to you, not to anyone else who might log in. If you and your spouse each log into Mac OS X with a different account, you each get your own Photo Library—and neither of you has access to the other's pictures in iPhoto.

But what if the two of you *want* to share the same photos? Ordinarily, you'd be stuck, since iPhoto can't make its library available to more than a single user. You could transfer the photos by CD or by setting up a .Mac photo gallery, of course, but here are two easier solutions to this common conundrum.

Easy Way: Share Your Library

iPhoto's sharing feature isn't just useful for sharing photos across the network. It's equally good at sharing photos between *accounts* on the same Mac.

To make this work, iPhoto has to be running in the account that will be sharing the pictures. And you have to turn on Fast User Switching. To find this checkbox, choose →System Preferences, and then click the Accounts icon (it looks like two head-and-shoulders silhouettes). Click the golden padlock at the bottom left of the dialog box and enter your password (if you have one). Next, click the Login Options button at the bottom of the account list on the left. Turn on "Show fast user switching menu as" and pick an option from the pop-up menu to its right.

Now you're ready. Log in as, say, Dad, and share some albums.

Now Mom chooses her name from the little Fast User Switching menu at the upper-right corner of the screen, thereby switching to her own account (and shoving Dad's to the background). She'll find that Dad's albums show up in her copy of iPhoto, exactly as shown in Figure 8-27 (provided both users are logged in). She can copy whichever pictures she likes into her own albums.

Geeky Way: Move the Library

The problem with the Share Your Library method is that you wind up with *copies* of the pictures. In some situations, you may want to work on exactly the same set of pictures. You want, in other words, to share the *same iPhoto library*.

What will trip up any normal person's attempt to share an iPhoto library is a little thing called *permissions*. That term refers to the insanely complex web of invisible Unix codes that keep your files and folders out of the hands of other account holders, and vice versa.

One easy way to sidestep this problem is to put the iPhoto library on an external hard drive that both Macs can access. However, the two of you can't access the same library at the same time.

If that's not possible, then here's a more elaborate method that requires the assistance of a piece of free software.

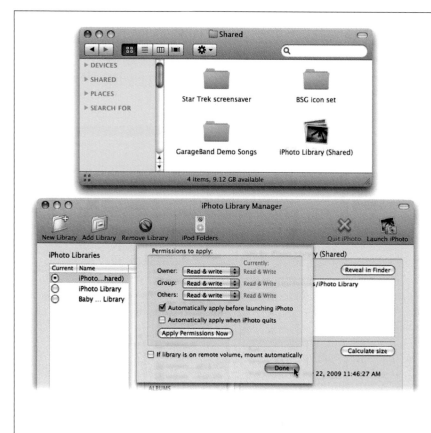

Figure 8-27:
*Top: To share your
photo library with
other user-account
holders on your Mac,
start by moving its
folder into your Mac's
Shared folder. Here,
the library is named
"iPhoto Library
(Shared)."*

*Bottom: Now add the
shared library to the
list of iPhoto libraries
in iPhoto Library
Manager by clicking
Add Library at the top
of the window and
navigating to that
Shared folder.*

*Set the "iPhoto
Library (Shared)"
folder's three pop-up
menus to "Read &
write," as shown
here, and then click
Done. Finally, turn on
the shared library's
checkmark, and then
click Launch iPhoto.*

First, put your photo library somewhere where every account holder has access to it.
Next, change the library's permissions from "mine" to "everyone's." Then quit iPhoto
and follow this drill:

1. **In the Finder, drag your iPhoto Library icon into the Shared folder.**

   Your iPhoto Library contains all your pictures (and all the information associated with them, like albums, comments, and so on). It's probably sitting, at this
   moment, in your Home→Pictures folder. To move it, you'll probably have to
   open two Finder windows side by side, so you can see your starting and ending
   points at the same time.

   Your destination is the Shared folder, which is in your Macintosh HD→Users
   folder. Drag the iPhoto Library into the Shared folder.

   You've done most of the setup. Now comes a step that each account holder must
   take individually. Suppose, for example, that you're now Mom.

2. **Log into your account. Don't open iPhoto yet; open iPhoto Library Manager instead.**

   The gloriously useful (and wonderfully free) iPhoto Library Manager program is described at length in Chapter 13. (Download it from *www.fatcatsoftware.com*.)

3. **Click the Add Library button. Navigate to the Macintosh HD→Users→Shared folder, click the iPhoto Library, and then click Open.**

   Now the shared photo library appears in iPhoto Library Manager's list of libraries, as shown in Figure 8-27 (bottom). Make sure it's highlighted.

4. **Click Options. Set all three pop-up menus to "Read & write," as shown in Figure 8-27 (bottom). Also turn on "Automatically apply before launching iPhoto," then click Done.**

   You've just made Dad's iPhoto Library folder your own. And every time you open iPhoto (from within iPhoto Library Manager, that is), those pesky permission bits will be automatically set to give you ownership for this editing session.

5. **Select iPhoto Library in the list at left, and then click Launch iPhoto.**

   Incredibly, iPhoto opens up that iPhoto library in your account—even if it wasn't yours to begin with. You're free to edit the photos. And you won't have to repeat any of these steps, either; from now on, just opening iPhoto (from within iPhoto Library Manager) takes you straight to the pictures.

   Better yet, each family member (or rather, account holder) can set things up the same way for themselves, by repeating steps 2 through 5. (Only one person can actually have the library open for editing at a time, though.)

Books, Calendars, and Cards

At first, gift-giving is fun. During those first 10, 20, or 40 birthdays, anniversaries, graduations, Valentine's Days, Christmases, and so on, you might actually *enjoy* picking out a present, buying it, wrapping it, and delivering it.

After a certain point, however, gift-giving becomes exhausting. What the heck do you get your dad after you've already given him birthday and holiday presents for 15 or 35 years?

If you have iPhoto, you've got an ironclad, perennial answer. The program's Book feature lets you design and order (via the Internet) a gorgeous, professionally bound photo book, printed at a real bindery and shipped to the recipient in a slipcover. Your photos are printed on glossy, acid-free paper, at 300 dots per inch, complete with captions, if you like. It's a handsome, emotionally powerful gift *guaranteed* never to wind up in the attic, at a garage sale, or on eBay.

These books ($30 and up) are amazing keepsakes to leave out on your coffee table—the same idea as most families' photo albums, but infinitely classier and longer lasting (and not much more expensive).

Since iPhoto's debut, in fact, the self-publishing business has expanded. You can now create equally great-looking calendars (covering any year, or any group of months that works for you), postcards, and new in iPhoto '11, *letterpress* greeting cards (cards that have inked designs pressed into the paper). Your projects arrive beautifully wrapped in elegant, Apple logoed envelopes that are a sight to behold in and of themselves.

Fortunately for you, the designing and ordering tools are the same for all of these photo-publishing categories. And in iPhoto '11, the whole process is easier and more visually pleasing than ever (see Figure 9-1). This chapter begins with a tour of the book-making process and follows up with calendars and cards.

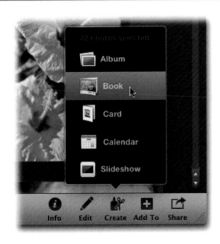

Figure 9-1:
Once you've gotten a book, calendar, or card under your belt, Full Screen view reveals the world's coolest project bookshelf. Click a project and iPhoto illuminates it with a built-in shelf light. Hover your mouse over the project to see its details.

Phase 1: Pick the Pix

The hardest part of the whole book-creation process is winnowing your photos to the ones you want to include. Many a shutterbug eagerly sits down to create his very first published photo book—and winds up with one that's 98 pages long (and well over $100).

In most of Apple's ready-made book designs, each page of your photo book can hold a maximum of six or seven pictures. Older book designs called Catalog and Yearbook, which could hold up to 32 tiny pictures per page in a grid, are gone. No great loss, really; at that size, your pictures didn't exactly sing. The whole thing more closely resembled, well, a catalog or a yearbook.

Even the six-per-page limit in most themes doesn't necessarily mean you'll get 120 photos into a 20-page book, however. The more pictures you add to a page, the smaller they have to be, and therefore the less impact they have. The best-looking books generally have varying numbers of pictures per page—one, four, three, two, whatever. In general, the number of pictures you'll fit in a 20-page book may be much lower—50, for example.

Either way, sifting through your brilliant pictures and choosing the most important few can be an excruciating experience, especially if you and a collaborator are trying to work together. ("You can't get rid of that one! It's adorable!" "But honey, we've already got 139 pictures in here!" "I don't care. I *love* that one.")

You can choose the photos for inclusion in your book using any selection method you like. You can open an Event, pick and choose among your entire library (page 49), or file them in an album as a starting point. You can even select a *group* of albums that you want included, all together, in one book.

If you opt to start from an album, take this opportunity to set up a preliminary photo *sequence*. Drag the pictures around in the album to determine a rough order. You'll have plenty of opportunity to rearrange the pictures on each page later in the process, but the big slide-viewer-like screen of an album makes the process easier. Take special care to place the two most sensational or important photos first and last. They'll be the ones on the cover and the last page of the book; if you're making a hardbound book (which includes a paper dust jacket), then you need special photos for the inside front and back flaps and back cover, too.

Phase 2: Publishing Options

Once you've selected an album or a batch of photos, click the Create button in the iPhoto toolbar and then choose Book from the resulting menu (Figure 9-2). You can also choose File→New→Book.

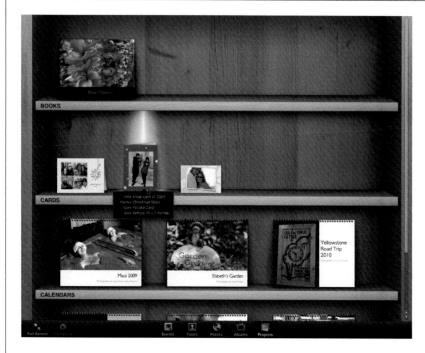

Figure 9-2:
You can use the new Create menu to begin any project discussed in this chapter.

Creating a project is a fantastic excuse to use Full Screen view. Just click the Full Screen button at the bottom left of your toolbar and you'll have more room to work.

Your screen changes into a giant desktop where you can specify *exactly* what you want your book to look like. It's crawling with important design options, explained next.

Book Type

The Book Type buttons, shown open in Figure 9-3, let you specify whether you want to publish your book as a hardbound volume (classier and more durable, but more expensive); as a paperback; or with a wire spiral binding. You also have a choice of book sizes for each option:

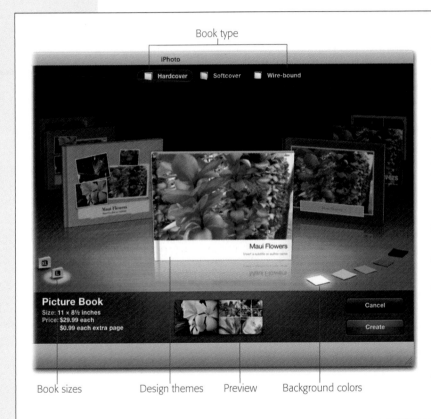

Book type

Book sizes   Design themes   Preview   Background colors

Figure 9-3:
iPhoto '11's new project-design workspace is both gorgeous and easy to use. You can change these settings later, even after you've started laying out your book pages. But if you have the confidence to make these decisions now, you'll save time, effort, and (if you want captions for your photos) possibly a lot of typing.

As you scroll through the designs (either by pressing the ◄ and ► keys or by swiping a finger across your Magic Mouse or Magic Trackpad), the bottom of the window reveals a thumbnail preview of what your book would look like if you chose that style.

- **Hardcover.** Your choices are 11 × 8.5 inches (large) or 13 × 10 (extra large).

Note: In iPhoto versions of old ('08 and earlier), you'd specify whether you wanted your hardbound book to have single-sided or double-sided pages. (Softcover and wire-bound books have always been printed on both sides of the page.) These days you don't make that decision; hardcover books are all double-sided now.

- **Softcover.** Choose between 11 × 8.5 (large), which feels the slickest and most formal; 8 × 6 (medium), which is more portable; and 3.5 × 2.525 (small), the smallest option of any book type.

   This last option gives you a tiny, wallet-size flipbook, with one photo filling each page, edge to edge. You have to order these in sets of three (for a total of $12), which suggests that Apple thinks of them as spontaneous giveaways to relatives, wedding guests, business clients, and so on. In any case, they're absolutely adorable (the booklets, not the business clients).

- **Wire-bound**. These books are available in 11 × 8.5 (large) or 8 × 6 (medium) only.

Theme Choices

And now, the main event: choosing a *theme*—a canned design, including typography and color scheme—for the cover and pages of your book. The carousel in the center of your iPhoto '11 window contains 18 professionally designed page templates, each dedicated to presenting your photos in a unique way.

Apple's photobook themes offer a variety of dynamic visual styles intended to pop your photos off the page. Some are designed to cover even the background of the page with textures, shadows, passport stamps, ripped-out clippings, and other photorealistic simulations.

Here's a brief description of each theme:

- **Picture Book, Photo Essay**. The motto for these designs could be "maximum photos, minimum margins." There's little room for text and captions (save for on the book jacket), and the photos stretch gloriously from one edge of the page to the other—a *full bleed*, as publishers say.

  These dramatic designs can be emotionally compelling in the extreme. You can opt to have a single caption appear at the bottom or on the sides of a page (no matter how many photos—from one to 16—appear on it). But the absence of text and minimization of white space seems to make the photos speak—if not shout—for themselves. (Plenty of people start out believing that captions will be necessary. But once they start typing "Billy doing a belly flop" or "Dad in repose," they realize they're just restating the obvious.)

  The Photo Essay theme, new in iPhoto '11, is nearly the same in design, but it contains page layouts that can hold 1–12 photos and has a variety of roomier caption areas. It also has a more serious feel to it, which is sure to please even the most discerning photographer.

  You can also add map pages to either theme for custom cartography. (Remember all those photos you geotagged back in Chapter 4? There's another benefit on the horizon.) There are six map options in Picture Book and one in Photo Essay.

Tip: Keeping in mind that the book is published horizontally, in landscape mode, will help you maximize page coverage. For example, on pages with only one photo, a horizontal shot looks best, since it'll fill the page, edge to edge. On pages with two photos, two vertical (portrait-mode) shots look best; they'll appear side by side, filling the page top to bottom.

- **Journal.** Also new in iPhoto '11, this theme pairs bordered photos with full-page beauties, and includes a variety of captioning options. It has six different map layouts, with page designs that can accommodate up to 16 photos. You can choose among eight background colors, or use another photo as a page background instead.

- **Travel, Asian Travel, Old World Travel, Tropical Travel**. These festive themes—the latter three of which are new in iPhoto '11—make your photos look like they've been taped into a scrapbook, usually at a slight angle to the page (some seem to have been built from 25 smaller ones, all assembled into one larger mosaic image). Five color choices are available for a variety of textured backgrounds, along with six different map layouts. (The texturing is a hoax, of course—the paper is the same acid-free, shiny stuff of every iPhoto book; it's just *printed* to look like it's textured.) Adding captions to the pages is optional; if you want them, they'll appear on strips that look like they've been ripped, jagged edge and all, from a piece of stationery.

  Overall, the effect is casual and friendly—not what you'd submit to *National Geographic* as your photographic portfolio, of course, but great as a cheerful memento of a trip or vacation.

- **Simple Border, Line Border, Textured Border**. These three are all variations on (ahem) a theme. They differ only in the kind of border that appears around each photo.

  The Border designs are characterized by plenty of "white space" (margins around each photo and each page); crisp 90-degree lines (no photos cocked at an angle); and up to four photos per page. A caption can appear at the bottom of each page, if you like. And you can choose the background color you want for the page itself.

- **Snapshots**. This layout goes for that scrapbook-done-in-a-hurry look. All the photos, up to six per page, are slightly askew and often overlapping. They all have white margins, as though they're bordered prints from the 1970s.

- **Modern Lines**. Each page can have up to four photos on it, with plenty of white margin, plus fine gray "modern lines" that separate the pictures. You can add a one-line caption to the bottom of each page, or leave the pages text-free.

- **Formal**. Think "wedding" or "graduation." When you order this book, the photos are printed to look like they've been mounted on fancy album pages. You can choose, for each page, either a textured or untextured gray background; up to six photos can occupy a page. You'll have the chance to add a short caption to the bottom of each page.

- **Watercolor**. "Watercolor," in this case, refers to the page backgrounds, which appear in gentle, two-toned pastel colors. This time, you can choose to have your photos "mounted" on the pages either slightly askew, for an informal look, or neatly parallel to the page edges. Note, though, that this design doesn't offer an option for photo captions, so you'll have to let the pictures tell the story.

- **Contemporary**. The page backgrounds are gray or white, the photos are all clean and square to the page, and captions, if you want them, appear in light gray, modern type. The maximum number of photos on a page is three, ensuring that they remain large enough to make a bold statement. Clearly, though, Apple is hoping that you'll choose only one maximum-impact photo per page; it offers you four different "white-space" treatments for one-photo pages.

- **Folio**. This design is among the most powerful of the bunch, primarily because of the glossy jet-black page backgrounds. (You can also choose plain white.) It looks really cool.

  This template must have been some designer's pet project, because it's the only one that offers special layout designs for a title page, About page, and explanatory-text page, all done up in great-looking fonts in white, gray, and black. Caption space is also provided.

- **Family Album**. OK, now Apple's officially gone nuts with printing pages to look like they're physical scrapbook pages. In this design, photos look like they've been affixed to the page using every conceivable method: attached using "photo corners," taped into photo montages made up of 25 smaller images, licked like giant postage stamps with perforated edges, fastened by inserting their corners into little slits in the page, or even inserted into one of those school-photo binders with an oval opening so your charming face peers out. Up to six pictures can occupy a page; a page caption is optional.

- **Crayon**. Here's another design where the pages are photographically printed to look like they're textured paper. For each page, you can choose either a photos-mounted-askew layout or—get this—a straight layout in which each photo has a frame "drawn" around it with a crayon. And to keep with that Crayola-ish theme, you can choose from any of six background colors for each page.

  You can place up to six photos on a page. You're offered the opportunity to include a caption at the bottom of each page.

The buttons in the bottom-left corner of the window let you choose the book's size (different sizes are available for book types, as mentioned on page 244). Once you pick a size, the area below the buttons fills you in on the details of the options you've selected, including the maximum number of pages, dimensions, and, oh yeah…the price. The buttons near the bottom right of the window look like little sheets of paper; they let you pick the background color of your book (though you can always change it later in the creation process).

Once you've settled on a design theme for your book, your initial spate of decision-making is mercifully complete. Click Create.

Phase 3: Design the Pages

Two things now happen. First, a new icon appears in your Source list under the Projects heading, representing the book layout you're about to create. You can work with it as you would other kinds of Source-list icons. For example, you rename it by double-clicking, file it in a folder by dragging it there, delete it by dragging it to the iPhoto Trash, and so on.

Note: If you're used to some older iPhoto version, then the book icon in your Source list is a happy bit of news. It means that a book is no longer tied to an album. Therefore, rearranging or reassigning photos in the original album no longer wreaks havoc with the book design that's associated with it.

Second, you see the miniature page-layout program shown in Figure 9-4, displaying thumbnails of the individual pages after iPhoto automatically fills them with photos. This is called All Pages view.

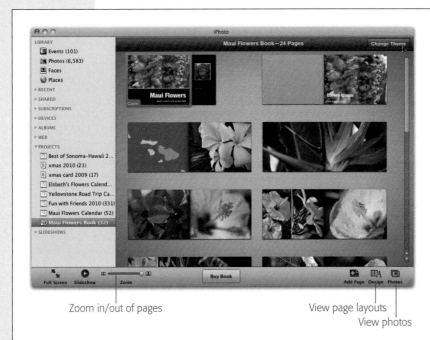

Figure 9-4:
Behold, iPhoto's miniature page-layout program in All Pages view. You can always revisit your choice of theme—or even book type—by clicking the Change Theme button in the upper right.

You can drag pages to reorder them, and use the slider at the bottom left to make the pages bigger or smaller. The buttons at the bottom right let you add pages, view different layout designs for each page, or see all the photos you selected for your project.

Zoom in/out of pages

View page layouts

View photos

Once you've selected an album and a theme, the most time-consuming phase begins: designing the individual pages.

Note: If you change themes after you've started designing pages, you'll lose most or all of your customization when iPhoto flows your photos into the new theme. A workaround is to duplicate your original project before changing themes; to do that, Control-click (right-click) its Source icon and choose Duplicate. That way, you can safeguard your page-design work on the other theme.

You may be surprised to see your pages already filled with photos. iPhoto 11's Autoflow feature automatically places your photos into the pages in chronological order, according to the dates they were shot. No doubt, it's a fast and easy way to lay out the pages of your book, but of course you may not agree with iPhoto's choices. It may clump that prizewinning shot of you and William Shatner on the same page as three less-impressive photos.

On the other hand, you can always touch up the layout afterward, accepting *most* of iPhoto's design but punching it up where necessary, as described on the following pages.

Note: If you don't want your photos automatically placed, you can clear them by opening the Photos panel (described next) and clicking the Clear Placed Photos button. Now you're free to place them manually, as discussed on page 254.

Open a Page

As soon as you pick a theme, you see miniature previews of the pages in your book; this is All Pages view. The first ones represent the cover, the inside flap (for hard-cover books), and an Introduction page. When you double-click one of the page thumbnails, a larger working version of that page appears in the main editing area (called Single Page view). To go back to viewing all your pages, click All Pages at the top left of the main viewing area or press ⌘-left arrow.

From there, when you click the button labeled Photos in the bottom right of the iPhoto window (it looks like a tiny stack of photos), the Photos panel opens on the right side of your screen, revealing a scrolling parade of the *photos* you've selected for inclusion in your project (Figure 9-5). A checkmark on a thumbnail indicates that either you or iPhoto has placed that photo onto one of your pages.

Note: You can't change the order of thumbnails in the Photos panel. If you want your photos to appear in an arrangement other than chronological, create an album first and reorder the photos there before starting your book project.

Choose a Page Layout

If you flip through your book, you can see that iPhoto has cheerfully suggested varying the number of photos per page. Depending on the theme, you may see two-per-page on the first page, a big bold one on the next, a set of four on the next, and so on.

If you approve of these photos-per-page proposals, great. You can go to work choosing which photos to put on each page, as described in the next section.

Sooner or later, though, there will come a time when you want three related photos to appear on a page that currently holds only two. That's the purpose of the Design panel shown in Figure 9-6, which shows you the different page designs that Apple has created to fit the number of photos you select.

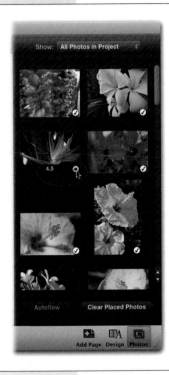

Figure 9-5:
iPhoto '11's new Photos panel shows you the pictures in your project. You can use the Show pop-up menu at the top to switch between viewing all the photos in your project or only the ones that are placed on page, or jump to the Recent items in your Source list, such as the last viewed Event, Last Import, and so on.

Checkmarks on the thumbnails indicate that the photo is being used in your book. If you point to a thumbnail, iPhoto displays a little number at the bottom indicating what page(s) it lives on. To visit that page, click the ➡ to its right (circled).

Note: After you double-click a page to enter Single Page view—and before you've clicked to select a photo on the page—a little pop-up menu appears so that you can switch layouts and backgrounds *without* opening the Design panel.

The first page in your book *must* be the cover, so selecting it produces precious few options in the Design panel. For a hardcover book, the cover appears on the glossy dust jacket. The cover of the actual book inside the dust jacket displays only the title of the book, embossed into the suede-like material.

You have a choice of cover layouts depending on the number of photos you pick from the Layout pop-up menu (anywhere between 1 and 6). For example, you're usually offered a choice of one huge photo (and no text), a big photo with a title beneath, or several smaller photos plus a title.

For the rest of your pages, the Layout menu gives you design choices aplenty:

- **1 Photo, 2 Photos, 3 Photos...** These items let you specify how many photos appear on the selected page. iPhoto automatically arranges them according to its own internal sense of symmetry. (Some themes offer up to 16 photos per page.)

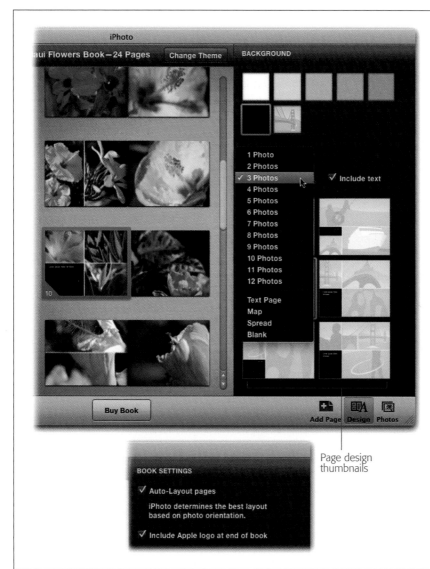

Figure 9-6:
Top: Click a page in All Pages view, and then click the Design button to reveal the new Design panel. Here, you can specify the background color for certain page designs (front and back cover, flaps, and pages that allow captions), as well as how many photos you want on any given page.

The Layout menu shows the different page designs for that photo quantity. Both the number of photos and layout menus change according to the page type you've chosen on the left. (You get fewer options for bonus page types like Cover and Introduction.)

Bottom: If you don't have any pages selected, the Design panel changes to show global project options, like the Book Settings shown here.

Page design
thumbnails

Use these options to create a pleasing overall layout for the book and to give it variety. Follow a page with one big photo with a page of four smaller ones, for example.

You can also use these options to fit the number of photos you have to the length of your book. If you have lots of pictures and don't want to go over the 20-page minimum, then choose higher picture counts for most pages. Conversely, if iPhoto warns you that you have blank pages at the end of your book, then spread your photos out by putting just one or two photos on some pages.

- **Text Page**. Satisfy your inner author by adding a text page to your book. In most themes, this special page design (which used to be named Introduction) has no photos at all. It's just a big set of text boxes that you can type (or paste) into. Here's where you can let the audience know about the trip, the company, or the family; tell the story behind the book; praise the book's lucky recipient; scare off intellectual-property thieves with impressive-sounding copyright notices; and so on.

Tip: A Text Page doesn't have to be the first page of the book after the cover. Truth is, you can turn *any* page into a Text Page. Such pages make terrific section dividers.

They're especially useful in designs where no text accompanies the photos. In this case, a Text Page can set the scene and explain the following (uncaptioned) pages of pictures.

- **Map**. Although the Travel theme goes to town with map styles, you can add an *actual* map page to any theme. (A map can't be on a book's cover or dust jacket, however.) Location information doesn't have to be embedded in the pictures if you want to add a map, but if you've got geotagged photos in the mix, the map page automatically displays *that* area of the world.

  You can fine-tune your map in a variety of ways, like dragging the map image around within the page until it shows the area you want. You can also double-click the map to enlarge it and then summon *more* design options by clicking the map again. A slider appears at the top of the map, which lets you adjust the size of the area on display, and a Location section where you can plot additional places on the map, as shown in Figure 9-7.

Tip: Maps are a great way to illustrate the route of a cross-country trip or multi-destination vacation. To add "Indiana Jones"-style lines linking each location on the journey, choose Curved from the Lines pop-up menu (you can change line style or turn them off). Locations are linked in the order they appear in the Places list. So if you need to change the order of the lines connecting each place, drag the location name to the correct spot on the list.

  A variety of checkboxes let you show or hide titles and text, display location names, enhance the map's look with textures and shadows, or even display a compass on the page. Control-click (or right-click) the map to get a shortcut menu full of other options (Figure 9-7), such as highlighting the region with a soft white glow and centering the map on your marked location. Changing the line style, or returning to the journey's starting point are here, too. And if you want to start over, choose Restore Default Map in the shortcut menu or click the Reset Map button in the Design panel.

- **Spread**. New in iPhoto '11, this layout spreads (hence the name) your photos across two full pages in a variety of designs that make the photos fill each page. It's a great way to showcase your most beautiful photos, and to break up pages that include captions. You can choose to add text, though that can cause iPhoto to decrease the size of your photos.

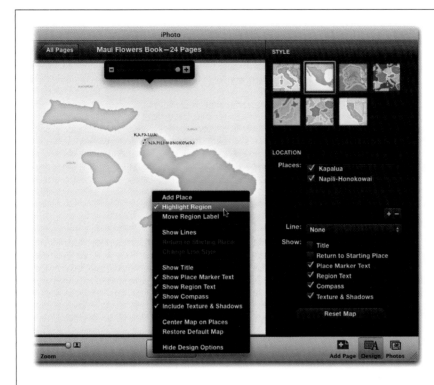

Figure 9-7:
After adding a Map page, the customization begins. Double-click the map to enlarge it and enter Single Page view, and then click it again to reveal even more design options. Here you can choose from a variety of map styles at the top of the Design panel, and plot new points by clicking the + button in the Places list. (To delete a location, select it and click the − button.)

Control-clicking (or right-clicking) the map brings up a shortcut menu of other options.

- **Blank**. Here's another way to separate sections of your book: Use an empty page. Well, empty of *pictures*, anyway; most of the new iPhoto '11 themes still offer a choice of "look" for a blank page, such as a choice of color or simulated page texture.

Once you've chosen how *many* photos you want on a page, iPhoto displays thumbnail representations of the page designs available to you (labeled in Figure 9-7). If you choose "3 Photos," for example, the thumbnails offer you a few different arrangements of those three photos—big one on top, two down the side, or whatever. Click one to select it.

Doubling the Cover Photo

I want to use my cover photo as one of the pages in the book, just like they do in real coffee-table books. How do I do it?

No big deal. In iPhoto '11, you can use a single photo on as many different book pages as you like.

In other words, just because a thumbnail has a checkmark (meaning that you've already used it) doesn't mean you can't use it again.

Lay Out the Book

The key to understanding iPhoto's book-layout mode is realizing that pages and photos are *draggable*. Dragging is the key to all kinds of book-design fun.

In fact, between dragging photos and using a handful of menu commands, you can perform every conceivable kind of photo- and page-manipulation trick.

Note: The view you're in determines what's draggable at any given time. For example, in All Pages view, you can drag the pages themselves—left, right, up, or down—to rearrange them. However, to drag and drop photos—between pages or between the Photos panel and a page—you must first double-click a page to enter Single Page view.

Ways to manipulate photos

Once you double-click a page to enter Single Page view, you can move photos around in the following ways (see Figure 9-8 for a summary):

- **Swap two photos on the same page (or two-page spread)** by dragging one directly on top of the other. When the existing picture sprouts a colored border, let go of the mouse button; the two pictures swap places.

- **Move a photo to a different page of the book** by dragging it from the main layout area onto a different page thumbnail.

- **Remove a photo from a page** by clicking its icon and then pressing the Delete key. The checkmark on its icon in the Photos panel disappears.

- **Remove a photo from the book altogether** by clicking its icon in the Photos panel and then pressing the Delete key. It disappears from both the layout and the Photos panel, although the actual photo is still in your library.

- **Add a photo to a page** by dragging it out of the Photos panel onto a *blank* spot of the page. iPhoto automatically increases the number of photos on that page, even changing the Layout pop-up menu to match.

Note: You can't create a layout that doesn't exist using this technique. If there are three photos on a page, and you add a fourth, iPhoto switches to the next *available* layout, which might be one with six photos.

- **Swap in a photo** by dragging it out of the Photos panel *onto* a photo that's already on a page of your book. iPhoto swaps the two (see Figure 9-8, bottom).

- **Add new pictures to the Photos panel** by dragging them onto the book's icon in the Source list. For example, you can click any Event, album, smart album, slideshow, or the Library icon to see what photos are inside—and then drag the good ones onto your book icon to add them to your project.

  Once they've arrived in the Photos panel, you can drag them onto individual pages as described above.

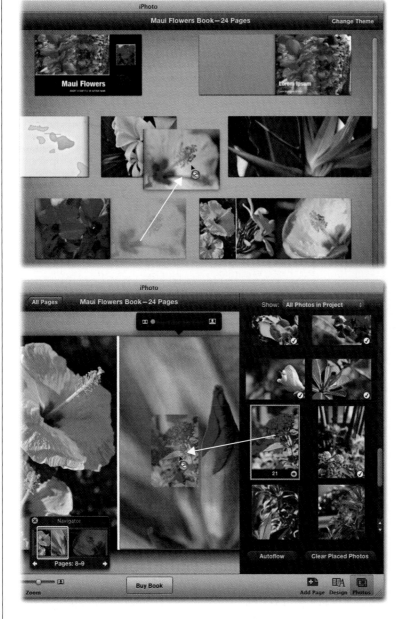

Figure 9-8:
iPhoto's book-layout mode is crawling with tricks that let you move photos around, add them to pages, remove them, and so on.

The fun begins when you understand the difference between All Pages view (top), where you can rearrange the pages in your book—as shown here with a white arrow—and Single Page view (bottom), where you can rearrange the photos on your pages and swap in new pictures from the Photos panel (also shown).

In Single Page view, you can use the slider in iPhoto's toolbar to zoom in or out of the page you're working on, which can be handy when you're editing captions at small type sizes. (The slider above the photo changes its size on the page.)

You can use the tiny arrows in the Navigator panel (shown here at bottom left) to move between pages while you're in Single Page view. If you've got a Magic Mouse or Magic Trackpad, you can use one-finger gesturing to move from page to page, or to move around within a single page while you're zoomed in.

- **Enlarge or crop a picture**, right there on the page, by clicking it. A tiny Zoom slider appears above the photo, which you can use to magnify the picture or shift it inside its boundary "frame" (Figure 9-9, top left). This trick is helpful when you want to call attention to one part of the photo, or to crop a photo for book-layout purposes without actually editing the original.

Tip: You may be startled to discover that iPhoto does a fairly smart job about placing photos within their little confined placeholders when you zoom in. That's face recognition at work—it tries to avoid lopping off people's faces.

- **Change how photos are stacked** by Control-clicking it (or right-clicking) an image and, from the shortcut menu, choosing "Move to Front" or "Send to Back." Figure 9-10 reveals all.

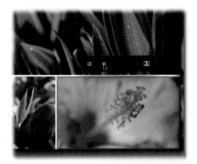
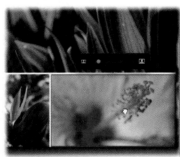
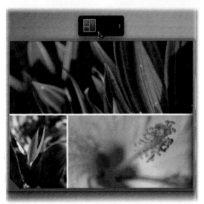

Figure 9-9:
Top left: Single-click a photo to make its Zoom slider appear (the blue border lets you know the photo is active). Drag the slider to the right to enlarge the photo within its rectangular frame.

Top right: At this point, you can drag inside the photo to adjust its position within its frame. None of this affects the actual photo (as using the cropping tool would). You're just changing the relationship between the photo and its boundary rectangle on the page template.

Bottom: By clicking an empty area in the woodgrain background while in Single Pages view, you select the whole page and summon this handy pop-up menu. Click it to change layouts and backgrounds without having to open the Design panel.

- **Edit a photo** by double-clicking it in Single Page view. In a flash, iPhoto's book-layout mode disappears, and you find yourself in Edit mode, described in Chapter 5. (You can also Control-click [right-click] a photo and choose Edit Photo from its shortcut menu.)

When you're finished editing, click the button at the top left of your editing window that's labeled with the name of the book you were tweaking (for example, "Maui Flowers Book"). Poof! You return to the book-layout mode, with your changes intact.

Note: None of these edits affect the original photos, though. In essence, you can edit the same photos in different ways in every single book or project—all without touching the originals.

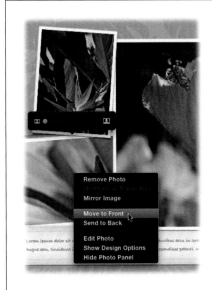
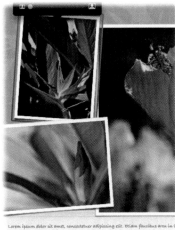

Figure 9-10:
In some book themes—like Tropical Travel, shown here—photos have been "tossed" onto the page so they overlap slightly. In the rare event that an important part of a photo is covered up by another, you can rearrange their front-to-back order using the shortcut menu shown at left. Here, the lower-left photo (left) is being slipped on top of the bigger photo (right).

Ways to manipulate pages

Photos aren't the only ones having fun. In All Pages view, you can drag and manipulate the pages themselves, too (just click the All Pages button near the top left of your window or press ⌘-left arrow):

- **Move pages around within the book** by dragging their thumbnails horizontally in the main viewing area (you saw this back in Figure 9-8, top).

- **Remove a page from the book** by clicking its icon and then pressing the Delete key. (iPhoto asks if you're sure you know what you're doing.) iPhoto lets you delete only one page at a time, no matter how many you select. So to delete a two-page spread, for example, you have to delete each page individually.

  Note that removing a page never removes any *pictures* from the book. You're just removing the checkmark from that photo's thumbnail in the Photos panel. But removing a page *does* vaporize any captions you've typed in.

- **Insert a new page into the book** by clicking the Add Page button in the toolbar. Before you go nuts with it, though, note that iPhoto inserts the new page *after* the currently selected page. It's helpful, therefore, to begin by first clicking the desired thumbnail in All Pages view, as shown in Figure 9-11.

Note: iPhoto books require an even number of pages. If you delete a page and end up with an odd number instead, iPhoto will add a blank page automatically to restore its even-numbered balance. (The minimum number of pages for a book is 20.)

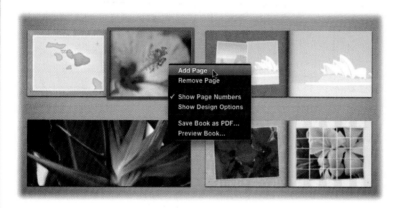

Figure 9-11:
You can Control-click (or right-click) a blank spot on any page and, from the shortcut menu, choose Add Page or Remove Page. (If you Control-click a photo, you get a different menu [shown on page 257].)

Light gray placeholders appear on the new pages, ready to fill. iPhoto decides how many photos should go on the new page, but you can change that number using the techniques discussed earlier.

Layout strategies

Sometimes chronological order is the natural sequence for your photos, especially for memento books of trips, parties, weddings, and so on. Of course, nothing's stopping you from cheating a bit—rearranging certain scenes—for greater impact and variety.

As you drag your pictures into order, consider these effects:

- Intersperse group shots with solo portraits, scenery with people shots, or vertical photos with horizontal ones.
- On multiple-photo pages, exploit the direction your subjects face. On a three-picture page, for example, you could arrange the people in the photos so that they're all looking roughly toward the center of the page, for a feeling of inclusion. You might put a father looking upward to a shot of his son diving on a photo higher on the page, or siblings back-to-back facing outward, signifying competition.
- Group similar shots together on a page.

Backgrounds, Borders, and Effects

Some themes let you choose the background color of the pages, and others let you tweak photo or caption borders. However, all themes let you apply certain effects to your photos right here in book-layout mode.

To change any of the above, first double-click a page to enter Single Page view, and then click the Design button in the toolbar to open the Design panel. Any background options appear at the top of the panel. You may have only two choices (like black or white), or you may have a half-dozen options (a range of pastels, say), depending on the theme you've chosen. Most intriguingly, you can use one of your *photos* as a background, and then adjust its transparency so that it forms a faded image behind the placed photos. Figure 9-12 has the details.

Tip: You can also click an empty area in the woodgrain background while in Single Page view and use the Layout pop-up menu that appears to change backgrounds. Unfortunately, this trick doesn't work for photo or text borders or for photo effects.

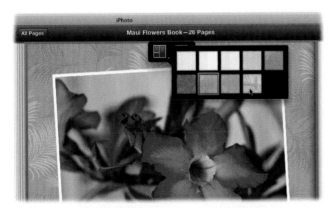

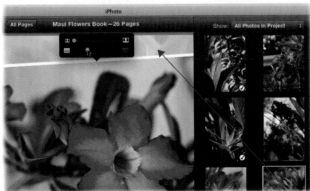

Figure 9-12:

Top: To install a picture as a photographic backdrop, choose the final background option (the one with the Golden Gate Bridge on it) in the design pop-up menu, as shown here, or in the Design panel. Then open the Photos panel (if it's not open already) by clicking the Photos button in the toolbar, and then drag the photo you want onto a blank spot of the gray background. Sunsets, sandy beaches, cobblestones, and so on, can work well for book backgrounds.

Bottom: The controls shown here automatically appear. Use the top slider to adjust the crop and position of the background photo; use the bottom slider to change its transparency (drag left to make it more see-through). The idea is that a background photo should be fainter and subtler than the foreground shots.

If you really want to get creative, try using the same shot as both background and foreground. By enlarging the background shot and decreasing its transparency, you can create some neat effects.

If the theme you've chosen doesn't allow a background change, it may still offer the chance to change the photo or text area's borders, and it most certainly gives you the opportunity to apply a black-and-white, sepia, or antique color effect to any photo on your page. Figure 9-13 has more.

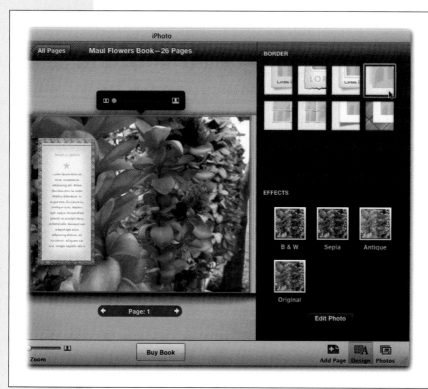

Figure 9-13:
When you're in Single Page view, you can click any photo and then open the Design panel to see its Border and Effects options. A single click on one of the thumbnail previews makes it so.

Making Your Photos Shape Up

iPhoto's design templates operate on the simple premise that all of your photos have a 4:3 aspect ratio. That is, the long and short sides of the photo are in four-to-three proportion (four inches by three inches, for example).

In most cases, that's what you already have, since those are the standard proportions of typical digital photos. If all your pictures are in 4:3 (or 3:4) proportion, they'll fit neatly and beautifully into the page-layout slots iPhoto provides for them.

But not all photos have a 4:3 ratio. You may have cropped a photo into some other shape. Or you may have a camera that can take pictures in the newfangled 16:9 ratio (like a high-definition TV screen), or the more traditional 3:2 film dimension, which work better as 4 × 6 prints.

When these photos land in one of iPhoto's page designs, the program tries to save you the humiliation of misaligned photos. Rather than leave unsightly strips of white along certain edges (therefore producing photos that aren't aligned with one another), iPhoto automatically blows up miscropped photos so they perfectly fill the 4:3 space allotted to them. Figure 9-14 shows the effect.

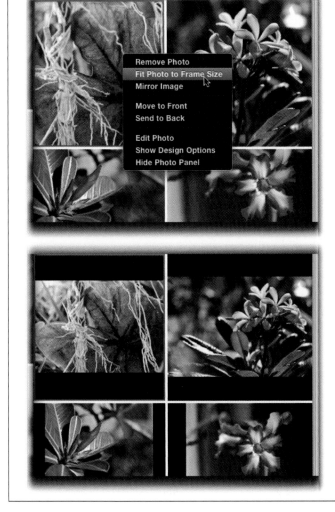

Figure 9-14:
Top: When you first start working on a book, the photos all look nice together—they nestle side by side. Every now and then, however, you may be disheartened to find that iPhoto is lopping off something it shouldn't.

Bottom: If you Control-click a photo and choose "Fit Photo to Frame Size," you'll discover that the problem is a photo that doesn't have 4:3 proportions (on this page, that's all four of them). iPhoto thought it was doing you a favor by blowing them up enough to fill the 4:3 box. Now you get ugly black or white gaps, but, hey, at least you're seeing the entire photo.

Unfortunately, this solution isn't always ideal. Sometimes, in the process of enlarging a nonstandard photo to fill its 4:3 space, iPhoto winds up lopping off an important part of the picture.

In that case, you have two alternatives. First, you can use the "Fit Photo to Frame Size" command described in Figure 9-14. Second, you can crop your non-4:3 photos using the Constrain pop-up menu (page 132) set to "4 × 3 (Book)." This way, *you* get to decide which parts of the photo get lopped off. (Or just use the adjustment technique shown in Figure 9-9.)

Page Limits

iPhoto books can have anywhere from 20 to 100 double-sided pages (in other words, 10 to 50 actual sheets of paper between the covers). Of course, if you really have more than 100 pages' worth of pictures, there's nothing to stop you from creating multiple books. (*Our Trip to East Texas, Vol. XI*, anyone?)

Hiding Page Numbers

Don't be alarmed if iPhoto puts page numbers on the corners of your book pages— that's strictly a function of the theme you've chosen (some have numbering, some don't). In any case, you never have to worry about a page number winding up superimposed on one of your pictures. A picture *always* takes priority, covering up the page number.

Even so, if it turns out that your theme *does* put numbers on your pages and you feel that they're intruding on the mood your book creates, you can eliminate them in the following ways:

- In All Pages view, click an empty area of the main viewing area's woodgrain background to make sure no pages are selected, and then click the Design button on the toolbar. The Design panel opens to reveal Book Settings, and you'll see a "Show page numbers" checkbox that you can turn off.

- As a shortcut, you can also Control-click (or right-click) anywhere in the main viewing area of All Pages view and, from the shortcut menu that appears, choose Show Page Numbers to turn it on or off.

Phase 4: Edit the Titles and Captions

Depending on the theme and page-layout templates you've chosen, iPhoto may offer you any of several kinds of text boxes that you can fill with titles, explanations, and captions by typing or pasting (Figure 9-15):

- **The book title**. This box appears on the book's cover. If it's a hardbound book, it's actually foil-stamped into the cover material; it also appears on the dust jacket.

    When you first create a book, iPhoto proposes the *album's* name as the book name, but you're welcome to change it.

    A second text box, set with slightly smaller type formatting, appears below the title. Use it for a subtitle: the date, "A Trip Down Memory Lane," "Happy Birthday Aunt Enid," "A Little Something for the Insurance Company," or whatever.

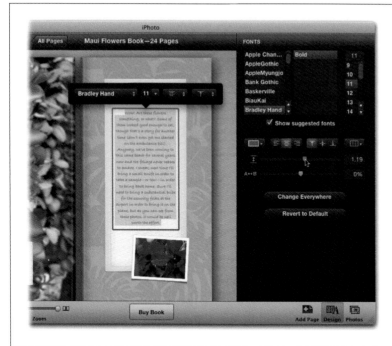

Figure 9-15:
In iPhoto '11, few themes let you type captions for individual photos. Instead, you get caption boxes for entire pages. Text boxes also appear on the inside dust-jacket flap (shown here), on Text Pages, and so on.

As soon as you click to edit the text, a little pop-up menu of fonts, sizes, and alignment controls appears. For even more power, click the Design button in your toolbar to open the Fonts panel, where you have a full arsenal of typographic controls. You can even alter the space between lines of text, as shown here. To make your changes affect all the text in the book, click Change Everywhere, a new and glorious option in iPhoto '11.

- **The dust jacket**. If you order a hardbound book, you've got that glossy dust jacket to consider. You can type up marketing blather or other descriptive material to appear on the inside front cover flap, just like on a book at Barnes & Noble. You're also allowed a couple of lines of text on the back cover, which can be the same as the title and subtitle, but doesn't have to be.

- **Captions**. Apple really, really doesn't want you adding a caption to *each photo*. Every theme lets you caption an *entire page*, but only the Folio theme lets you caption each photo—and it limits you to two photos per page, max.

- **Text Page, About, Contact**. Most themes let you add Text Pages, though the Folio theme, intended as a showcase for photographers to display their best work, offers two additional text-page options. As you learned earlier, Text Pages are striking, simple, title-plus-text-block affairs that let you describe the book, chapter, or photo grouping. The About layout is the same thing, but it offers one big title and one subtitle in addition to the text block. Finally, Contact is filled with places to list your phone number, website, email address, and so on—along with the contact info for your agent.

Editing Text

In general, editing text on your book pages is straightforward. First, open a page in Single Page view, and then:

- Click inside a text box to activate the insertion-point cursor, so you can begin typing. Zoom in on the page (using the Zoom slider at lower left) and scroll it, if necessary, so the type is large enough to see and edit. Click outside a text box—on another part of the page, for example—to finish the editing.

- You can select text and then use the Edit menu's Cut, Copy, and Paste commands to transfer text from box to box.

- You can also move selected text *within* a text box by dragging it and dropping it. The trick is to hold down the mouse button for a moment before dragging. Add the Option key to make a copy of the selected text instead of moving it.

- Double-click a word, or triple-click a paragraph, to neatly highlight it.

- Press Control-right arrow or Control-left arrow to make the insertion point jump to the beginning or end of the line.

- To make typographically proper quotation marks (curly like "this" instead of like "this"), press Option-[and Shift-Option-[, respectively. And to make a true long dash—like this—instead of two hyphens, press Shift-Option-hyphen.

Check Your Spelling

Taking the time to perfect your book's text is extremely important. A misspelling or typo you make here will haunt you—and amuse the book's recipient—forever.

As in a word processor, you can ask iPhoto to check your spelling in several ways:

- **Show spelling and grammar**. Perhaps the safest way to ensure your book doesn't include embarrassing spelling or grammatical mistakes, click inside a text block or highlight a word (or several) and then choose Edit→Spelling→"Show Spelling and Grammar" (or Control-click the text box and choose the same command from the resulting shortcut menu). The standard Mac OS X "Spelling and Grammar" dialog box appears, which lets you fix or ignore potential problems. This command's keyboard shortcut is ⌘-colon (:).

- **Check spelling**. This command does exactly the same thing, though without checking grammar (and without the dialog box). Click inside a text block or highlight a word (or many), and then choose Edit→Spelling→Check Spelling (⌘-semicolon). If the word is misspelled, in iPhoto's opinion, then a red dotted line appears under it. Proceed as shown in Figure 9-16.

- **Check as you type**. The trouble with the spelling commands described above is that they operate on only a single, tiny text block at a time. To check your entire photo book, you have to click inside each title or caption and invoke the spelling command again. There's no way to have iPhoto sweep through your entire book at once.

  Your eyes might widen in excitement, therefore, when you spot the Edit→Spelling→Check Spelling While Typing command, which is turned on straight from the factory. It makes iPhoto flag words it doesn't recognize *as you type them*.

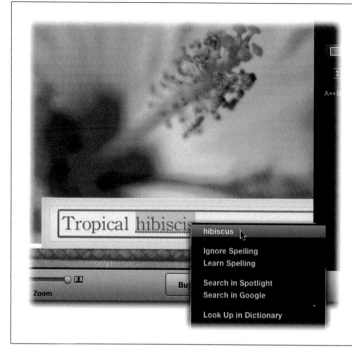

Figure 9-16:
Control-click (or right-click) any word that's underlined with a red dotted line. If the resulting shortcut menu contains the correct spelling, choose it.

Otherwise, if the word in your text box is fine as it is, click either Ignore Spelling ("Stop underlining this, iPhoto. It's a word I want spelled this way, so let's go on") or Learn Spelling ("This name or word is not only correctly spelled, but it's also one that I may use again. Add it to my Mac OS X dictionary so you'll never flag it again.").

Sure enough, whenever you type a word that's not in iPhoto's dictionary, iPhoto adds a colorful dashed underline. (Technically, it underlines any word not in the *Mac OS X* dictionary, since you're actually using the standard Mac OS X spelling checker—the same one that watches over you in Mac OS X's Mail program, for example.)

To correct a misspelling that iPhoto has found in this way, Control-click (or right-click) it; a shortcut menu appears. Now proceed as shown in Figure 9-16.

- **Check grammar with spelling**. This feature, new in iPhoto '11, is an automatic version of the first item in this list. If iPhoto thinks you've made a spelling or grammatical mistake, it underlines the offending word(s) or phrase(s) in red. To turn it on, choose Edit→Spelling→Check Grammar With Spelling.

- **Correct spelling automatically**. Also new in iPhoto '11 is the ability to let the program fix your mistakes automatically. If you harbor an enormous amount of trust in iPhoto's dictionary, take a deep breath and choose Edit→Spelling→Correct Spelling Automatically.

Listen to Your Book

Unfortunately, even a spell checker won't find missing words or really awkward writing. For those situations, what you really want is for iPhoto to *read your text boxes aloud* to you.

No problem: Just highlight some text by dragging over it, and then Control-click (or right-click) the highlighted area. The same shortcut menu shown in Figure 9-16 appears, containing the Speech submenu. From it, you can choose Start Speaking and Stop Speaking, which makes iPhoto start and stop reading the selected text aloud. It uses whatever voice you've selected in Mac OS X's System Preferences→Speech settings.

Phase 5: Preview Your Masterpiece

Ordering a professionally bound book is, needless to say, quite a commitment. Before blowing a bunch of money on a one-shot deal, you'd be wise to proofread and inspect it from every possible angle.

Print It

As any proofreader can tell you, looking over a book on paper is a sure way to discover errors that somehow elude detection onscreen. That's why it's a smart idea to print out your own, low-tech edition of your book at home before beaming it away to Apple's bindery.

MEMORY LANE

Goodbye, Yellow Exclamation Points

As you worked on your project designs in previous versions of iPhoto, you may have encountered dreaded yellow triangle exclamation points. They appeared on photos or individual pages of your book or calendar.

They showed up when at least one of your photos didn't have enough resolution (enough pixels) to reproduce well in the finished book.

But in iPhoto '11, that's all changed. The only time you'll spot a yellow triangle warning is on the order screen when you're purchasing prints (shown on page 193).

Apple says that its photo-enlargement technology has gotten so good, your pictures will look fabulous regardless of their resolution. Plus, Apple also figures you're shooting with a camera that's at least 3 megapixels (which includes the iPhone 3GS), so you'll have enough pixels to produce a nice print. (A 3-megapixel device can produce a high-quality 8 × 10 print, and decent quality 10 × 13.)

Bottom line: Unless you're placing photos in your project that you've snatched from the Web or received in an email—at a greatly reduced size—you don't have anything to worry about.

That said, if the photo looks really blurry after it's placed in your project, it'll print blurry, too (Even Apple's photo-enlargement technology can't work miracles).

In that case, the easiest solution is to shrink the photo on its page. And the simplest way to do *that* is to increase the number of pictures on that page. Or, if your page design has places that hold both large and small photos, you can drag the problem photo onto one of the smaller photos, swapping the large and small positions.

Finally, if nothing has worked so far, then your only options are to eliminate the photo from your book, or to cross your fingers and order the book anyway.

While you're in Book mode, choose File→Print. After the standard Mac OS X Print dialog box appears, fire up your printer, and then click Print when you're ready. The result may not be wire-bound and printed on acid-free paper, but it's a tantalizing preview of the real thing—and a convenient way to give the book one final look.

Slideshow It

Here's a feature that might not seem to make much sense at first: After you're finished designing a book, you can *play* it—as a slideshow. Just click the ▶ button at the bottom of the screen.

When you click that button, the screen goes black. Depending on the complexity of your book's layout, it may take iPhoto a minute or two to compose itself and generate the slideshow. Once the show starts in glorious full-screen mode, it comes up in the Classic slideshow theme (page 160). To change the music or transitions, wiggle the mouse to get to the full-screen toolbar and then click the Music or Settings icons.

Once you're satisfied, the show kicks in, displaying the cover of your book before moving on to each individual page, one at a time. (This is probably one of the easier ways to get a book turned into a movie.)

Viewing your book as a slideshow is primarily a proofreading technique. It presents each page at life size, or even larger than life, without the distractions of menus or other iPhoto window elements, so you can get one last, loving look before you place the order.

But book slideshows are also kind of cool for another reason: They present a more varied look at your photos than a regular slideshow. That is, your photos appear in page groupings, with captions, groupings, and backgrounds that there'd otherwise be no way to create in a slideshow.

Turn It into a PDF File

You've almost certainly encountered PDF (Portable Document Format) files before. Many a software manual, Read Me file, and downloadable "white paper" come in this format. When you create a PDF document of your own, and then send it off electronically to a friend, it appears to the recipient *exactly* as it did on your screen, complete with the same fonts, colors, page design, and other elements. They get to see all of this even if they don't *have* the fonts or the software you used to create the document. PDF files open on Mac, Windows, and even Linux machines—and you can even search the text inside them.

If you suspect other people might want to have a look at your photo book before it goes to be printed—or if they'd just like to have a copy of their own—a PDF file makes a convenient package (plus you can show it off on your iPad).

Here's how to create a PDF file:

1. With your book design on the screen in front of you, choose File→Print.

   The Print dialog box appears.

2. Click the "Save as PDF" button, if you have one, or choose "Save PDF" from the PDF pop-up button.

   The Save sheet appears.

3. Type a name for the file, choose a folder location for it, and then click Save.

   Your PDF file is ready to distribute. (Fortunately, the recipients will be able to correct the rotation within Adobe Acrobat using its View→Rotate Counter-clockwise command, or within Preview using the Tools→Rotate commands.)

Tip: You can also create a PDF by using the book-creation shortcut menu. Just Control-click (or right-click) an empty spot in the woodgrain background in either All Pages or Single Page view, and then choose "Save Book as PDF" from the shortcut menu. Give your PDF a name in the resulting dialog box and click Save.

If you want to *see* the PDF first, choose "Preview Book" from the shortcut menu instead to open an unsaved version in Mac OS X's Preview program. To capture the PDF on your hard drive, choose File→Save As.

Phase 6: Send the Book to the Bindery

When you think your book is ready for birth, click the big Buy Book button in the toolbar.

After several minutes of converting your screen design into an Internet-transmittable file, iPhoto offers you a screen like the one shown in Figure 9-17.

Note: iPhoto '11 no longer offers you a choice of cover color for hardcover books. That's because the cover is actually a reprint of the dust jacket. Slick!

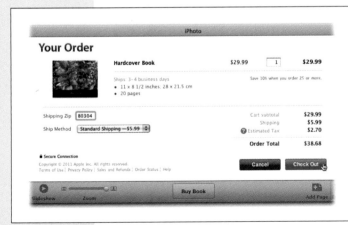

Figure 9-17:
You're ready to pull the trigger! Here's where you choose a quantity and recipient.

You won't be allowed to complete your order, though, until you've signed up for an Apple account, which you'll enjoy using over and over again to order books and stuff from the Apple online stores. The next section explains how to do that.

That is, assuming you don't get any of iPhoto's prepublication warnings first—namely, that you haven't filled in all the default text boxes, like the title and subtitle; that some of your text boxes or photos bear the yellow-triangle low-resolution warning (see the box on page 266); that your book is "incomplete" (you didn't fill in all the gray placeholder rectangles with pictures); and so on.

At this stage, your tasks are largely administrative.

- **Inspect the charges**. If you've gone beyond the basic 20 pages, you'll see that you're about to be charged between 30 cents and $1 per additional page, depending on the book type.

- **Indicate the quantity**. You can order multiple copies of the same book. Indeed, after you've spent so much time on a gift book for someone else, you may well be tempted to order yourself a copy.

- **Enter the Zip code where you want it sent**. The book doesn't have to come to you; it can go anywhere. Though in order for iPhoto to calculate the proper sales tax, it needs to know the destination Zip code.

- **From the Ship Method pop-up menu, indicate how you want the finished book shipped**. For U.S. orders, Standard shipping takes about four days and costs $6. Express means overnight or second-day shipping (depending on when you place the order) and costs $15. An additional book sent to the same address costs another $1 for Standard shipping, $2 for Express.

Note: You can order books if you live in Europe, Japan, or North America, but Apple offers shipping only to people in your own region.

Your Apple ID

You can't actually order a book until you've signed up for an Apple account.

However, you may well already have an Apple account if, say, you've ever bought something from an online Apple store or the iTunes Store. Whether you have or not, ordering your first iPhoto book requires completing some electronic paperwork, like this:

1. **Adjust the fields in the Your Order window (Figure 9-17) as explained above, and then click Check Out.**

2. **On the Sign In screen that appears, either enter your Apple account info or click the "Create Apple ID now" link.**

   If you already have an Apple account, enter your Apple ID and account password in the Returning Customer fields. (An Apple ID is your email address; it's your MobileMe address, if you have one.)

   When you're finished, click Sign In and skip to step 3.

If you've never established an Apple account, then click "Create Apple ID now," and enjoy a whirlwind tour through Apple's account-signup screens. You'll be asked to provide your contact info and credit-card number, make up a password, and indicate whether you want to receive Apple junk mail. You'll also be offered the chance to set up a number of addresses for people you may want books shipped to.

Click Continue and you wind up right where you started: at the Your Order screen. This time, however, the controls at the bottom are "live" and operational.

3. **Click Check Out.**

   You've already stored your credit card information, so there's nothing to do now but wait for your Mac to upload the book. After a few minutes, you'll see a confirmation message.

4. **From the Ship To pop-up menu on the next screen, choose the lucky recipient of your book.**

   If it's you, choose Myself. If not, you can choose Add New Address from this pop-up menu.

5. **Click Done, and then go about your life for a few days, holding your breath until the book arrives.**

   When it does, you'll certainly be impressed. The photos are printed on Indigo digital presses (fancy, digital, four-color offset machines). The book itself is classy, it's handsome…and it smells really good!

WORKAROUND WORKSHOP

Secrets of the Apple Book-Publishing Empire

It's no secret that when you order prints of your photos via the Internet, Kodak makes the prints. But neither temptation nor torture will persuade Apple to reveal who makes the gorgeous iPhoto books.

It didn't take long for Mac fans on the Internet, however, to discover some astonishing similarities between iPhoto books and the books created by a firm called MyPublisher .com. The pricing, timing, and books themselves are all identical. (When asked if it's Apple's publishing partner, MyPublisher.com says, "We don't discuss our partner relationships," which means "Yes.")

iPhoto-generated books are more elegantly designed than the ones you build yourself at MyPublisher.com (or anywhere

else, for that matter). And it's certainly easier to upload books directly from iPhoto, rather than to upload photo files one at a time using your web browser.

Still, you should know that building your books directly at MyPublisher.com offers greater design freedom than iPhoto does. You have a wider choice of cover colors and materials (even leather), you can add borders around the pages, and you have much more flexibility over the placement of photos and text.

In fact, it's easy to get carried away with these options and produce something absolutely ghastly, which is probably why Apple chose to limit your options. This way, you simply can't go wrong.

Photo Calendars

Custom-made photo books? Old hat, dude. Nowadays, the kids at school are buzzing about the other custom stuff you can order: calendars, greeting cards, and postcards. (Mugs and bumper stickers will have to wait for iPhoto '12 or '13. In the meantime, you can order them from *www.cafepress.com*.)

The calendars are absolutely beautiful—and, in iPhoto '11, they're honkin' big (10.4 × 13 inches). As shown in Figure 9-18, each calendar is wire-bound, with a big Picture of the Month (or Pictures of the Month) above the month grid. You can customize each calendar with text, titles, national holidays, events imported from your own iCal calendar, and even little thumbnail photos on the date squares.

If you've ever designed an iPhoto book, designing an iPhoto calendar will give you an overwhelming sense of déjà vu. The calendar-design module is identical to the book-design module (and the card-design module, and so on). However, since you're usually dealing with 12 calendar pages instead of 20 book pages, they don't take as long to assemble (and what great holiday gifts they make!).

Anyway, here's the drill:

Phase 1: Choose the Photos

Pick out pictures for the cover photo, the "picture of the month" photos, and any pictures you want to drag onto individual date squares. You can select an Event, a full album, several albums, or any group of thumbnails in the viewing area.

Phase 2: Choose the Calendar's Design

Click the Create button on the iPhoto toolbar, and then choose Calendar.

iPhoto's main viewing area changes to display miniature calendar designs in a carousel (Figure 9-18, top). These are the calendar design *themes*, which are just like the book themes described earlier in this chapter. Once again, scroll through the themes—either by pressing the ◄ and ► keys or by swiping a finger across your Magic Mouse or Magic Trackpad—to see what the finished calendar will look like in the little preview thumbnail at the bottom of the window. The designs differ in photo spacing, the size of the numbers marking the dates, the availability of captions, and so on.

Display the theme you want, and then click Create. Now the dialog box shown at bottom in Figure 9-18 appears; here's where you can set up your calendar. For example, you can specify what period you want the calendar to cover.

The "Show national holidays" pop-up menu lets you fill your calendar with important holidays. The United States dates include things like Valentine's Day, Lincoln's Birthday, and Thanksgiving; the French dates include Whit Sunday, Assumption Day, and Bastille Day (in English); and the Malaysian holidays are along the lines of Merdeka, Awal Ramadan, and Yang Di-Pertua of Sarawak's Birthday. (But you knew that.)

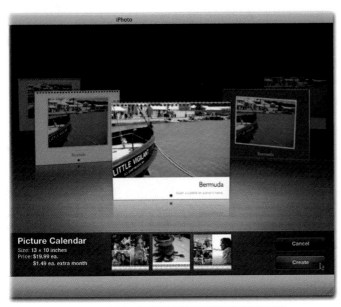

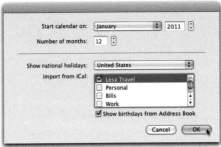

Figure 9-18:
Top: All the calendar themes are, well, designs for calendars. The differences among them have to do with date sizes, photo placement, and background pattern.

Bottom: As indicated by the "Start calendar on" controls, your calendar doesn't have to start with January, and it can include up to 24 months (two years).

As for "Import from iCal," you can turn on the checkboxes individually for each calendar (that is, category) that you've set up in iCal: Work, Social, Home, Star Trek Conventions, whatever.

Finally, if you keep your calendar in iCal (the calendar program in your Applications folder), you can choose to have those events appear on your new photo calendar (Figure 9-18, bottom).

As a bonus, you can turn on "Show birthdays from Address Book." That's a reference to the Mac OS X address-book program, which—along with names, addresses, and phone numbers—has a space to record each person's birthday. Incorporating them into your *printed* calendar means that you'll never forget a loved one's (or even a liked one's) special day.

Tip: This isn't the only chance you'll have to adjust these settings. You can return to them at any time— when you're moving to Malaysia, for example, and want to change the holidays—by following the instructions in Figure 9-19.

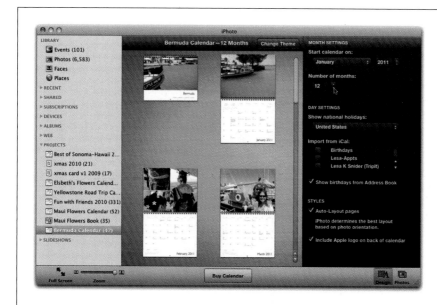

Figure 9-19:
If you're working on your calendar project in All Pages view and you don't have any pages selected, you can return to the calendar's settings by clicking the Design button in the toolbar.

You can rearrange the pages of your calendar in this view, too; just click and drag the pages into place.

When you're finished setting things up, click OK; you arrive in iPhoto '11's new calendar-design workspace, which looks like a big desktop (Figure 9-19). A new icon appears in your Source list, representing the calendar you're creating; you can file it into a folder, rename it, or trash it just as you would a slideshow or a book.

Now you're ready for the really fun part: arranging photos on your calendar pages.

Phase 3: Design the Pages

Each page "spread" of the calendar shows a month grid on the lower page (below the spiral binding) and a "photo of the month" on the upper page. iPhoto automatically populates your pages with photos and lovingly places them in chronological order according to when they were taken. However, once you've double-clicked a page to enter Single Page view, you can replace iPhoto's choices with your own, as Figure 9-20 explains.

The design controls here work exactly the same way as they do when you're designing a book. You can click a photo to reveal its zoom slider and then move the photo around within its frame by clicking and dragging (your cursor turns into a tiny hand).

Use the Zoom slider in the toolbar to make individual pages bigger as you're working on them. Once you zoom in, the Navigator appears (Figure 9-20, lower left), which lets you move around on the current page, or jump to other pages by clicking the arrows. (You can also move around by swiping your finger across the top of your Magic Mouse or Magic Trackpad.)

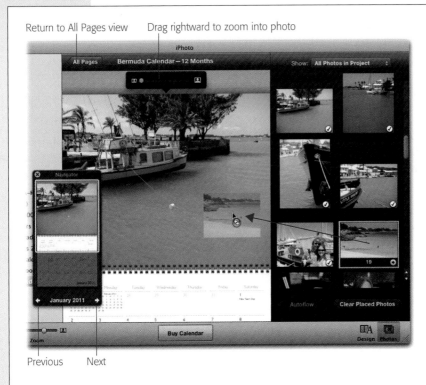

Return to All Pages view   Drag rightward to zoom into photo

Previous   Next

Figure 9-20:
If you click the tool-bar's Photos button while in Single Page view, you open the Photos panel, where you can see thumb-nails of the pictures you've selected for inclusion. To replace a photo, drag it from the Photos panel onto the photo frame, as shown here.

See the little number 19 on the photo's thumbnail? That's the calendar page it's used on; click the ➡ to the number's right to hop to that page. But why does it say 19 when your calendar has 12 months? Because iPhoto counts each calendar page as 2, beginning with the first month (it excludes the front and back covers), so a 1-year calendar has 24 pages.

Tip: If you're not a fan of iPhoto'sAutoflow feature, and you'd rather place all the photos onto the calendar pages yourself, click the Clear Placed Photos button at the bottom of the Photos panel (shown in Figure 9-20). The photos will be replaced with gray boxes into which you can drag new photos.

In Single Page view, you drag pictures into the photo boxes exactly the way you do when you're designing photo books. If you don't see the photo you want in the Pho-tos panel, you can add it to your calendar project in a couple of ways. Once you've located the photo in your library:

- Select it and then click the Add To button in your toolbar; from the pop-up menu, choose Calendar.

- Select the photo and drag it onto your calendar project in the Source list.

Either way, the photo lands in your Photos panel, ready to be dragged onto a calendar page.

Speaking of placing photos, choose one really good shot to grace the front; this is what the recipient (even if it's you) is going to see when first unwrapping the calendar. You'll want to repeat the photo elsewhere in your calendar in order to fully enjoy it, though.

And of course you'll want to illustrate each month with an especially appropriate photo—or more than one. Click the Design button to open the Design panel and use the Layout pop-up menu to choose 2 Photos, 3 Photos, or whatever; some themes let you place as many as seven pictures above the spiral binding.

There's one other place you can put photos that might not have occurred to you: dragging photos onto the *individual date squares* of your calendar, as demonstrated in Figure 9-21 (left). You can put people's faces on their birthday squares, for example, or vacation shots on the dates when you took them.

Tip: Once you've dropped a picture onto a calendar square, it's hard to get rid of. The only way to delete it is to drag it *off* the calendar and back *into the Photos panel*. It's weird, but it works.

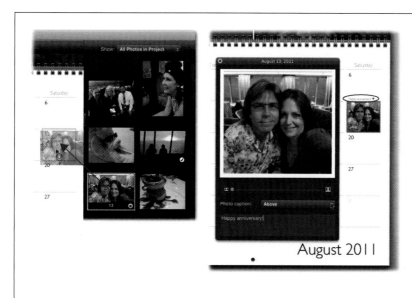

Figure 9-21:
After you drag an image from the Photos panel onto a date square (left), you can click the photo in the calendar to display a handy panel (right). You can use the panel's slider to enlarge the picture within its little box or drag inside the picture to reposition it in the frame.

To add a caption, choose a location from the "Photo caption" pop-up menu and then type your text. Since the photo fills the entire date square—hiding the date itself—captions have to live outside the square: above it, below it, or to its left or right.

Tip: You can edit photos right on the calendar-page layouts, just as you can edit photos in book layouts: Once you're in Single Page view, double-click a photo to enter Edit mode (or Control-click [right-click] the image and choose Edit Photo from the shortcut menu). The changes you make here don't affect the original photo in your library.

When you're finished editing a particular month, if you *haven't* used the toolbar's Zoom slider to enlarge the page, you can move on to the next month by clicking one of the white arrows that appear on either side of the page's name ("August 2011," for example) beneath your calendar. If you *have* zoomed in, you won't see the page name or the arrows. Instead, you see the handy Navigator shown in Figure 9-20; just use the arrows at the bottom of it to, well, *navigate* to the month you want to mess with.

Phase 4: Edit the Text

Once your calendar is photographically compelling, you can finish it off with titles, captions, and other text.

The cover, for example, offers both a main title and—in most themes—a subtitle. Click the placeholder words to select and replace them with new text of your own.

You can also single-click any date square to open up a caption box where you can type important events (like "Robin's Graduation" or "Company Picnic"; see Figure 9-22). If the date has a photo on it, you need to choose a location from the Caption pop-up menu, as described in the previous section.

Tip: Once the caption box is open, you don't have to close it and reopen it for another date. Each time you click a square on the calendar, the caption box automatically changes to show its text contents. (This trick also applies to the photo box shown in Figure 9-21.)

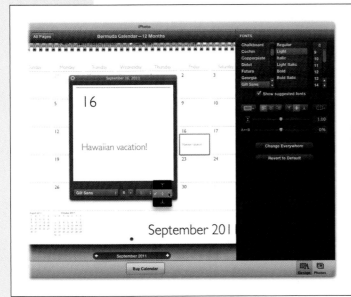

Figure 9-22:
Click any date square to open this caption box.

iPhoto really wants to center your text vertically within the square, so you need to click a spot near the middle of the caption box to get the blinking insertion point. To change the vertical alignment—say, to make your text appear at the top or bottom of the square—you can use the little pop-up menu shown here.

Just as with books, you can change the font formatting—either globally (for all pages) or for just some selected text:

- To change the font globally, click the Design button in the toolbar. In the resulting panel, specify the fonts and sizes you want and then click Change Everywhere. (If you decide that Apple's original font assignments were actually better than what you've come up with, click "Revert to Default.")

- To change the formatting of a single word or sentence, highlight it by dragging across it and then use the formatting pop-up menu that appears. (If you'd rather use the Design panel's controls, you can do that too.)

Phase 5: Order the Calendar

When you've said to yourself, "I'm [your name here], and I approve of this calendar," then click the Buy Calendar button on your toolbar.

If you've left any gray boxes empty (without putting your photos into them), or if any caption placeholders are still empty, an error message appears. You won't be able to order the calendar without filling the gray boxes, although leaving captions empty is OK. (The calendar will simply print without any text there—not even the dummy placeholder text.)

After a moment, your Mac connects to the Internet, and you see the Your Order screen. It looks and works just like the Your Order screen for books (Figure 9-17), except that the pricing is a little different. A 12-month calendar costs $20. Each additional month adds another $1.50 to the price, though there is a 10% discount if you order 25 or more at a time.

Assuming you're all signed up as a certified Apple customer (page 269), all you have to do is specify how many copies you want, where you want them shipped, and via which method (Standard or Express). Click Check Out, and mark off the very few days on your old calendar as you wait for the new one to arrive.

Greeting Cards and Postcards

Why stop at books and calendars? iPhoto also offers gorgeous greeting-card and postcard designs (Figure 9-23). These items are professionally printed using your own photographic material, they look great, and they don't cost an arm and a leg.

Note: New in iPhoto '11 is the ability to create *letterpress* cards, which have inked designs pressed into beautifully textured paper. They're spectacular—but they cost $3 each.

---

1. **In your iPhoto collection, select the photo(s) you want to use in your card. Then click Create button in the toolbar; from the pop-up menu, choose Card.**

   iPhoto's familiar themes carousel appears, this time showing card designs (Figure 9-23).

Tip: It's best to start with several photos—some card themes can hold up to seven pictures!

---

2. **From the menu at the top, choose a card type: Letterpress, Folded, or Flat. Then use the arrow keys to display the design you want.**

   iPhoto offers 27 different designs for Letterpress cards, and 54 designs for Folded or Flat. They include holiday-themed cards (including Easter, Valentine's Day, and Halloween), thank-you notes, baby announcements, birthday cards, invitations, and so on.

3. **If you're making a letterpress card (which has fewer customization options), click Create. If you're making a folded or flat card, use the icons labeled in Figure 9-23 to choose a layout and background color for your card, and then click Create.**

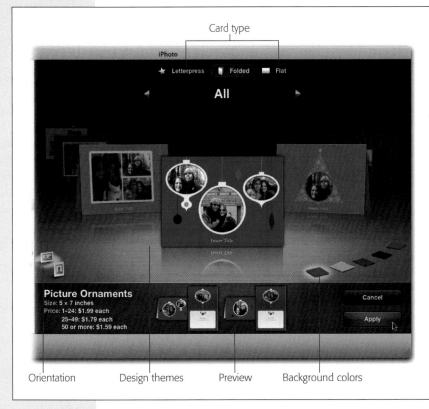

Card type

Figure 9-23:
Choose a card type from the top of the window; the various design themes appear below.

As of this writing, there are 27 Letterpress themes. If you choose Folded or Flat (think postcard), you get a whopping 54 themes fit for every card-sending opportunity you can imagine.

If you've read about how to design and order books or calendars, this section's description of the card-ordering process will feel like déjà vu all over again—only simpler, because you have fewer pages to deal with.

Orientation   Design themes   Preview   Background colors

You arrive in the now-familiar iPhoto page-design screen (technically it's Single Page view), where you can adjust the photo, card background, and text (see Figure 9-24). You'll see two rectangles here: the inside and outside (of a greeting card) or front and back (of a postcard).

A new icon appears in your Source list, too, representing your card-in-progress.

4. **Adjust the photo(s).**

   If you single-click a photo, you enter the picture-adjustment mode described on page 256, where you can drag the slider to enlarge the photo, or drag the picture to adjust its position inside the frame. Double-click the photo to open it in Edit mode.

You can also replace the photo. If you had the foresight to choose several candidates in step 1, then simply open the Photos panel (click the Photos button in the toolbar), and then drag thumbnails directly into the card's photo frames to try them out.

If you didn't think ahead, all is not lost. Click the album that contains the photos you want to try as alternatives, and then drag their thumbnails onto the card's icon in the Source list.

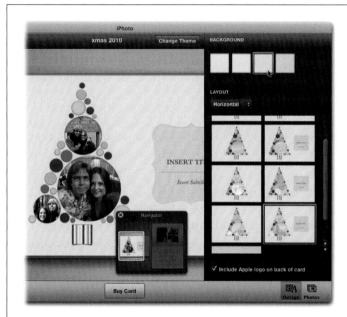

Figure 9-24:
Depending on what's selected, you'll see different options in the Design panel. With the card selected, you get a choice of color schemes (and, in some designs, patterns) for the background and interior of the card. You also get a choice of layouts, as shown here. (The little Navigator shows you which part of the card you're viewing.)

If you have a photo selected, you see Effects buttons offering to convert your photo to black and white, sepia, or antique.

5. **Open the Design panel to adjust the card's background color and layout.**

   Click the Design button in your toolbar to see alternative layouts and color schemes, as shown in Figure 9-24.

   The contents of the Design panel change depending on whether you've clicked the front of the card, the inside/back, or a photo itself. For the front, you get alternative layouts of text and photo (like adding the option to type a caption on the front of the card, or round the corners of the photo). If you've clicked the back of a Flat card, then you get to choose a standard mailable postcard back (with lines where you can write in a name and address, for example), or a nonmailable design that looks more like the inside of a greeting card.

   The Layout pop-up menus and Background options for greeting cards varies based on which theme you choose; Holiday/Events cards have the most options. The Orientation pop-up menu lets you specify whether this card is folded at the top or the left side (Horizontal or Vertical, respectively). The Photos pop-up menu lets you pick how many photos you want to include. And if you click a photo, you get the option to apply a black-and-white, sepia, or antique color effect to it.

6. **Edit the text.**

   Single-click any bit of placeholder text to open its text box for editing. (It's generally uncool to send out baby-announcement cards bearing the legend, "Insert a name here.")

Tip: Don't forget that you can zoom in on any part of your card by dragging the slider in the toolbar, which is helpful when you're adding text.

You can also edit the type styles and fonts, exactly as described on page 263.

7. **Order the card.**

   When the card looks good, click Buy Card. Your Mac goes online, and the Your Order screen appears. Here you'll discover that you're allowed to buy cards individually (you don't have to buy, say, 12 in a box—thanks, Apple!). But of course, you can buy in bulk if you like.

   Letterpress and Folded cards are 5 × 7 inches, come with matching envelopes, and cost $3 and $2 each, respectively. For quantities of 25 or more Folded cards, you get a 10% discount; for 50 or more, you get 20% off. (Unfortunately, there are no discounts for Letterpress cards, no matter how many you order.)

   Postcards are 4 × 6, also come with matching envelopes, and cost $1.50 each. Here again, they cost less if you order 25 or more ($1.29), and even less in quantities above 50 ($1).

As you can see, these cards are cheap enough and amazing enough that you should consider making them part of your everyday arsenal of social graces. After all, you're living in an era where very few other people can pull off such a thing—and you'll be the one who gets credited with the computer savvy, design prowess, and thoughtfulness to actually put a card in the mail.

iPhoto Goes to the Movies

As Chapter 6 makes clear, once you select your images and choose the music to go with them, iPhoto orchestrates the production and presents it live on your Mac's screen as a slideshow. Which is great—as long as everyone in your social circle lives within six feet of your screen.

The day will come when you want friends and family who live a little farther away to be able to see your slideshows. That's the beauty of QuickTime, a portable multimedia container built into every Mac. Even if the recipient uses a Windows PC—hey, every family has its black sheep—your photos will meet their public; QuickTime movies play just as well on HPs and Dells as they do on iMacs and MacBooks.

iPhoto '11 makes it easier than ever to convert those photos into mini-movies. A Slideshow Export option lets you save your slideshows to QuickTime movie files that play flawlessly on iPads, iPods, iPhones, Apple TVs, and other video-watching gadgets. If you want something smaller and simpler, you can also export your photos to a standalone QuickTime movie. In either case, you'll then have a file on your hard drive that you can email to other people (including Windows people), post on your web page or MobileMe Gallery for downloading, burning onto a CD, and so on.

Note: iPhoto '11 lets you view and trim video clips. Skip ahead to page 292 to learn how.

Before You Export the Slideshow

You have two ways to convert your masterpiece to a video file: Slideshow Export and QuickTime Export, both described in this chapter. But no matter which method you choose, before you send your "slideshow movie" to hapless relatives who'll have to endure downloading it over a dial-up connection, make sure it's worth watching in the first place.

Perfect the Slideshow

As you review your presentation, place the pictures into the proper sequence, remembering that you won't be there to verbally "set up" the slideshow and comment as it plays. Ask yourself, "If I knew nothing about this subject, would this show make sense to me?"

You might decide that your presentation could use a few more descriptive images to better tell the story. If that's the case, go back through your master photo library and look for pictures of recognizable landmarks and signs. Put one or two at the beginning of the show to set the stage. For example, if your slideshow is about a vacation in Washington, D.C., then you might want to open with a picture of the Capitol, the White House, or the Lincoln Memorial.

Tip: If you don't have any suitable opening shots in your library, or even if you do, another option is to begin your show with a few words of text, like opening credits. You can let iPhoto do the job, or, for something more elaborate, you can create a JPEG graphic containing the text in a program like Pages or Photoshop Elements. (Make sure this graphic matches the pixel dimensions of your slideshow, as described in the following section.) Then drag the file right into your slideshow album, placing it first in the sequence. You've got yourself an opening title screen!

Which photos make the cut

If you're used to the slideshow feature described in Chapter 6, then the method for specifying which photos are exported to your QuickTime movie might throw you:

- If *one* thumbnail is selected, that's all you'll get in the finished QuickTime movie—the world's shortest slideshow. (This is the part that might throw you: An iPhoto slideshow would begin with that one selected photo and then move on from there, showing you all the rest of the photos in the album.)

- If *several* thumbnails are selected, only they make it into the slideshow movie.

- If *no* thumbnails are selected, the entire album's worth of photos wind up in the show.

When you're ready to convert your presentation to a movie, you need to make yet another decision: Do you want to do it the easy way, or the way that gives you more control?

Two Ways to Make Movies

Older versions of iPhoto offered just one way to export your photos as a slideshow: Export a basic QuickTime movie. You can still do that—and that method has its advantages, namely smaller file size. But in addition to the time-honored Quick-Time export, iPhoto '11 gives you an even easier way: Slideshow Export.

The Slideshow Export feature lets you convert your instant and saved slideshows into custom-sized QuickTime movies designed to look good on specific screens, like an iPhone or an iPad. And these easy-to-save clips even retain the fancy theme animations, music, and other settings of an iPhoto slideshow, described back in Chapter 6.

To use Slideshow Export, all you need is…*a slideshow.*

Exporting an Instant Slideshow

That instant slideshow is up on your Mac's screen now, full of great freshly uploaded pictures of the kids. And you *really* want to take a copy of it with you on your iPad before you have to leave for the airport in a few hours. Here's what to do:

1. **Choose File→Export (or press Shift-⌘-E).**

   The Export dialog box appears on your screen (Figure 10-1).

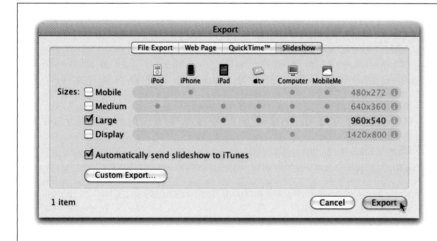

Figure 10-1:
The Slideshow Export option—updated in iPhoto '11—takes the guesswork out of getting the right settings. Based on what you (or your recipient) will use for movie-watching, choose the size of your exported slideshow on the left. The box shows you what the resolution will be and what gadgets the video works best with.

Tip: For iPod, iPad, or iPhone transfer, turn on the Export dialog box's option to send the movie to the iTunes library.

2. **Click the Slideshow tab and see Figure 10-1.**

   You now have another choice to make: what you want to play the slideshow *on*—TV, computer screen, iPhone, or whatever. Here, iPhoto politely takes all the guesswork out of the settings you need for that slideshow to look good on an iPad. The box even shows you what preconfigured sizes work best on which screens. Here's the rundown:

- **Mobile**. With a resolution of 480 × 300 pixels, this size is good for iPhones, iPod Touches, and uploading to a MobileMe Gallery (page 219). This setting also makes a smallish file to watch on a computer.

- **Medium**. If you have an iPad or an Apple TV hooked up to your widescreen set, this is the smallest export size you should consider. The 640 × 400 resolution looks good on a computer or MobileMe Gallery (but takes a little longer to upload). It's also the one to choose if you plan to copy the slideshow to your iPod to play there—or pipe up to a pal's TV set after you connect the two boxes with an iPod AV cable.

- **Large**. At 864 × 540 pixels, this size looks even better on an iPad, Apple TV, computer, or MobileMe player—but makes for a bigger file hogging up space somewhere.

- **Display**. If you want a slideshow that looks great on a Cinema Display or other large screen, go for this 1280 × 800 pixel option. Just be prepared for a hefty file.

Note: If you want precise control over things like audio and video compression settings, click Custom Export and then click the Options button. Those settings are for AV Club members who really like to bang around under the hood of a video file.

---

3. **Send the file to iTunes (or not).**

   If you want to send the exported file right into iTunes for easy syncing to an iPad, iPod Touch, or iPhone, turn on "Automatically send slideshow to iTunes." If you don't want the file in iTunes, turn off the box; the exported file lands in Home→Pictures→iPhoto Slideshows.

4. **Click Export.**

   iPhoto exports the slideshow as a QuickTime-friendly *.m4v* file. The export process may take several minutes. (Motion-heavy themes like Shatter take longer to export than, say, a straightforward Classic slideshow.) If you opted to send the file to iTunes, then iPhoto kicks the exported slideshow into the Movies area of your iTunes library. From there, it's one quick sync to Podville.

Exporting a Saved Slideshow

That masterpiece of a slideshow you spent all weekend slaving over—one of the *saved* slideshows described on page 170—is easy to export. In fact, it's even easier than exporting an instant slideshow:

1. **In the Slideshow area of the iPhoto Source list, select the chosen production.**

   The saved creation appears in the iPhoto window.

2. **Click the big, fat Export button on the iPhoto toolbar, shown in Figure 10-2.**

The button takes you right to the settings shown in Figure 10-1, though this time they appear in a pane. Follow steps 2 through 4 in the previous section to export your saved Slideshow to the chosen format.

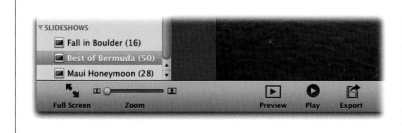

Figure 10-2:
Exporting a saved slideshow doesn't get any easier than this. Just select the show in the Source list and then click the Export button on the toolbar. You don't even have to root around in menus to find an export option (although File→Export works, too).

That's it. Copy that file onto an iPod, burn it to a disc (page 326), or do whatever you want with it.

Tip: With all the music and animations, exported slideshows can be pretty big—35 megabytes or more for a 40-slide show with all the bells and whistles. That's too big to email, but there are other ways of getting it to your friends over the Internet. For one, you can use the file-transfer feature of instant-messaging programs like iChat or AIM to send the file from your Mac to your recipient's computer.

Or if you have a MobileMe account, you can drag the file to your iDisk and then, at me.com, click the Share Files button to send a message to a friend. The message contains a link for your pal to directly download the file from your iDisk—no muss, no fuss.

Exporting a QuickTime Movie

The two slideshow-exporting tricks described on the previous pages are so easy, the manual effort of the older "Save as QuickTime" command might seem obsolete. Unfortunately, all of the special effects and fancy graphics in iPhoto's slideshow themes have two drawbacks: They take a lot of time to export, and they create huge files that are too big to email.

If that's a problem, you can ditch all those preformatted slideshows and, instead, simply save an album or a selected bunch of photos as a humble set of moving pictures. Simple QuickTime movies can be as small as a megabyte and much easier to send around the Internet to friends. You can even add a little music to perk things up.

Here are the steps involved in creating this older, simpler sort of slideshow movie:

Step 1: Choose QuickTime

Select an album, a group of photos, or all the photos in a saved slideshow, and then choose File→Export. The Export dialog box shown back in Figure 10-1 appears. Click the QuickTime tab, where you have some important decisions to make (Figure 10-3).

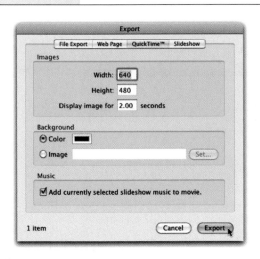

Figure 10-3:
Here's the Export dialog box with the QuickTime tab selected. This is the air lock, the womb, the last time you'll be able to affect your movie before it's born.

You're free to change these dimensions, however. If the movie will be played back from a hard drive, you may want to crank up the dimensions closer to the size of the screen itself; 800 × 600 is a safe bet if you're not sure of the size. Remember, though, you have to leave some room for the QuickTime Player controls so that your audience can start and stop the movie.

Step 2: Choose the Movie Dimensions

Specifying the width and height for your movie affects not only how big it is on the screen during playback, but also its file size, which may become an issue if you plan to email the movie to other people. iPhoto generally proposes 640 × 480 pixels. That's an ideal size: big enough for people to see some detail in the photo, but usually small enough to send, in compressed form, by email.

Proportion considerations

All of these suggestions assume, by the way, that your photos' dimensions are in a 4:3 ratio, the way they come from most cameras. That way, they'll fit nicely into the standard QuickTime playback window.

But there's nothing to stop you from typing other numbers into the Width and Height boxes. If most of the shots are vertical, for example, you'll want to reverse the proposed dimensions so that they're 480 × 640, resulting in a taller, thinner playback window.

Size considerations

As you choose dimensions, bear in mind that they also determine the *file size* of the resulting QuickTime movie. That's not much of an issue if you plan to play the movie from a CD, DVD, or hard drive. (And in that case, you might want to generate your movie from a saved slideshow instead, as described on page 170.) But if you plan to send the movie by email or post it on a web page, watch out for ballooning file sizes that will slow dial-up sufferers to a crawl.

For example, an 18-slide movie with an MP3 music soundtrack would take up 3.1 MB on your hard drive (at 640 × 480 pixels)—and at least that much in your recipients' email inboxes. Scaling it down to half that size in each dimension (320 × 240) would shave off about a third, resulting in a 2.4 MB file.

You could eliminate the soundtrack, which would shrink the movie to a mere 350 K—but who wants a silent movie?

Fortunately, there's a middle road. It involves some work in iTunes and a slight reduction in sound quality, but reducing the file size of the music track can result in substantial file shrinkage. See the box below details.

Step 3: Choose the Seconds per Photo

How many seconds do you want each picture to remain on the screen before the next one appears? You specify this number using the "Display image for __ seconds" box in the QuickTime Export dialog box.

POWER USERS' CLINIC

Musical Liposuction

If you're struggling with the size of a QuickTime movie slideshow that's too big for emailing, consider shrinking the size of the music track. By cutting its *bit rate* (a measure of its sound quality) from 192 to 128 kbps, for example, the file size for a hypothetical 320 × 240 pixel movie would shrink from 2.1 MB to 1.5 MB—and most people playing the movie over typical computer speakers wouldn't hear the difference.

This kind of surgery requires iTunes, the music-management software that comes with every Mac.

Start by choosing iTunes→Preferences. In the Preferences dialog box, click General, and then click the Import Settings button. From the Import Using pop-up menu, choose MP3 Encoder. Then, from the Setting pop-up menu, choose, for example, "Good Quality (128 kbps)." (A lower Custom number will result in even smaller files, although the sound quality may suffer.) Click OK to close the dialog box.

Now highlight the track you want to add to your slideshow, and then choose Advanced→Create MP3 Version.

iTunes creates a copy of the song that has the new, lower sample rate (quality setting). The song's name appears in your iTunes Music Library list just below the original. (You might want to rename it to differentiate it from the original, higher-quality song by highlighting it and then choosing File→Get Info. Click Info in the resulting dialog box.)

Now return to iPhoto. Click the album you're going to import, click the ▶ icon in the iPhoto toolbar, click the Music tab, and finally select your new resampled song from the list of titles in the dialog box. Click Save Settings.

When you export the slideshow to QuickTime, you'll find that it's much more svelte, but the music sounds practically identical to the puffier version.

Step 4: Choose the Background Colors

The color or image you choose in the Background section of the dialog box will appear as the first and last frames of the export. It will also fill in the margins of the frame when a vertically oriented or oddly proportioned picture appears.

Solid colors

To specify a solid color, click the color swatch next to the Color button. The color picker described in the figure on page 233 appears.

Generally speaking, white, light gray, or black makes the best background. Black is particularly good if you want to present your slideshow in full-screen mode, which turns the Mac into a virtual movie screen and makes the borders between your movie and the screen indistinguishable.

Background graphics

If you click the Image radio button and then the Set button next to it, you can navigate your hard drive in search of a *graphics* file to use as the slideshow background. This is where a graphics program like Photoshop Elements or GraphicConverter comes in handy. By designing a picture there (in dimensions that match your movie) and exporting it as a JPEG file, you have complete freedom to control the kind of "movie screen" your QuickTime slideshow will have.

Step 5: Export the Movie

Having specified the dimensions, frame rate, music, and background for your movie, there's nothing left but to click the Export button in the dialog box. You'll be asked to specify a name and folder location for the movie (Figure 10-4), and then click Save (the suffix *.mov* at the end of the name is added automatically). After a moment of computing, iPhoto returns to its main screen.

Press ⌘-H to hide iPhoto; then navigate to the folder you specified and double-click the movie to play it in QuickTime Player, the movie-playing program that comes with every Mac. When the movie opens, click the Play button (the triangle) or simply press the space bar to enjoy your newly packaged slideshow (Figure 10-5).

Whenever playback is stopped, you can "walk" through the slides manually by pressing the right arrow key twice (for the next photo) or the left arrow key once (for the previous one).

Tip: Even Windows PC users can enjoy your QuickTime movies—if they visit *www.apple.com/quicktime/download* to download the free QuickTime Player program for Windows.

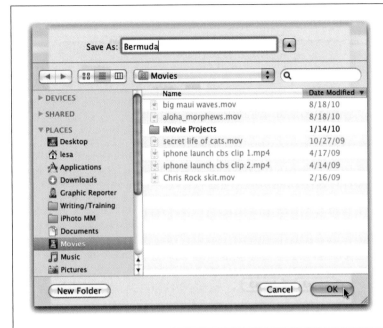

Figure 10-4:
You may spend a lot of time creating your saved slideshow movie, but it won't take you long to configure the Export dialog box. Your options are limited here. Clearly, the iPhoto engineers figured that at this point, you'd spent quite enough time making artistic decisions.

Once iPhoto finishes its work, you have your slideshow intact as a QuickTime file with its transitions, effects, and music. It's really quite astounding.

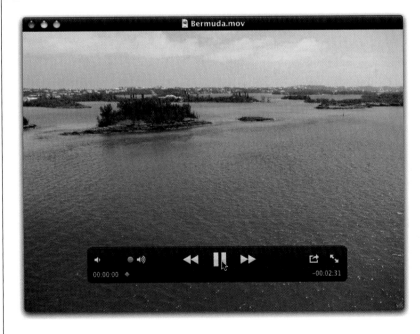

Figure 10-5:
Once you're in Quick-Time Player, you can control the playback of the slideshow in a number of ways. If you don't feel like clicking and dragging onscreen controls, the arrow keys adjust the volume (up and down) or step through the photos one at a time (right and left).

Fun with QuickTime Player X

QuickTime Player is, well, just a player, but it does have some additional features worth noting:

- **Play movies in full-screen mode**. QuickTime Player X can play full-screen videos—no menu bar, Dock, window edges, or other distracting elements. In effect, it turns your laptop screen into a portable theater. Choose View→Enter Full Screen (or press ⌘-F).

Note: Apple discontinued QuickTime Pro—the $30 upgrade that offered more powerful editing features—after version 7. (If you owned it before upgrading to Snow Leopard, you may still find it in your Macintosh HD→Applications→Utilities folder.) Then again, you may as well use iMovie, which you already own.

- **Record video and audio**. You can record your own video or audio in Quick-Time Player X, using the built-in camera on your Mac, a USB webcam, or a camcorder connected via FireWire. You can record audio with your Mac's built-in microphone, or an external mic or musical instrument connected via USB.

  Choose File→New Movie Recording or New Audio Recording. In the resulting preview window, pick one of the input sources described above, choose a quality, and then click the Record button. When you're finished, click the Record button again. You'll find the new movie waiting in your Movies folder (inside your Home folder).

- **Share movies to iTunes, MobileMe, and YouTube**. The Share menu lets you choose a variety of ways to, well, share your movie. Choose iTunes to convert your flick into a suitable format for iTunes, iPads, iPods, iPhones, and Apple TVs. The MobileMe Gallery option optimizes it for the Web and uploads it to your gallery (obviously, you need a MobileMe account).

  Choosing YouTube optimizes your masterpiece for the popular video-sharing website and uploads it (your YouTube account and password are required). To send a movie to YouTube, it must be *less* than 15 minutes long and *smaller* than 32 gigabytes.

Note: If you *do* upload your movie to YouTube, they may strip out your soundtrack if it's copyrighted. Check out GarageBand, part of your iLife suite, for creating your own copyright-free music soundtrack.

- **Shorten your flicks**. QuickTime Player X lets you trim off excess footage, as explained next. It's also great for combining or editing down the little movies that iPhoto downloads from your digital camera.

Tip: iPhoto '11 also lets you trim video clips. Page 292 shows you how.

Shorten Your Movie

QuickTime Player X lets you trim footage from the beginning or end of your movie…and that's it. No more cutting, copying, or pasting footage wherever you'd like. The good news is that it's a simpler process than ever before.

Choose Edit→Trim, and then proceed as shown in Figure 10-6.

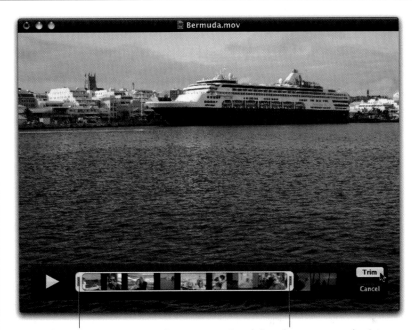

Drag rightward to set your start point   Drag leftward to set your end point

Figure 10-6:
Trimming your movie is easier than ever in QuickTime Player X. A thin red line (called the playhead) represents where you currently are in your movie. You can drag the playhead to find the bits of the movie that you want to get rid of.

Drag the yellow sliders inward to indicate the footage you want to keep. When you're finished, click the yellow Trim button.

Exporting Edited Movies

After you've finished working on a movie, you can send it back out into the world by choosing File→Save As. At this point, you can specify a new name for your edited masterpiece and choose either the original or a new size option from the Format pop-up menu.

If you choose "Save for Web," you'll see the options shown in Figure 10-7.

Once you've stored the new version on your hard drive, you can drag it back into iPhoto.

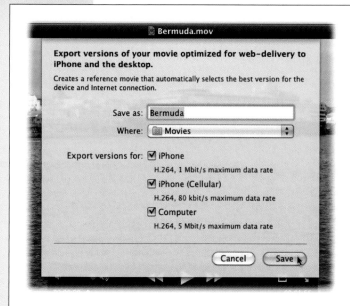

Figure 10-7:
The "Save for Web" option produces a very tiny file that contains no footage at all; it's like an alias of the movie you edited. It works only as long as the original movie remains on your drive.

Movies from Your Camera

Digital-camera movies were once a novelty that few people cared about. Today, though, they've become a convenient way to record video without lugging around a camcorder. Current digicams can capture movies with standard (640 × 480) or even high-definition resolution, TV smoothness (30 frames per second), and sound. Most smartphones (including the iPhone) can capture high-quality video, too.

When you import your movies into iPhoto, the program cheerfully adds those video files to your library, denoted by a little camcorder icon and a duration indicator. And while previous versions of iPhoto didn't provide any tools to edit the video or even to watch it, iPhoto '11 is more than happy to let you do both.

Playing Digital Movies in iPhoto

To play a movie that's found its way into iPhoto, double-click its thumbnail. (Or, if the thumbnail is highlighted already, press the space bar.) The movie immediately expands to fill your screen and begins to play.

That might seem like an obvious behavior, but it took Apple years to achieve it. Until iPhoto '11 came along, double-clicking an imported movie meant coffee-break time, because you had to wait for a different program to open (QuickTime Player) before you could view the movie. Now it all happens right in one place.

After a moment, the control bar vanishes; this minimalist design works great when all you want to see is your movie. In fact, if you move your mouse away while the movie is playing, the control bar fades away, leaving nothing but your movie. When you move your mouse, the controls reappear. The controls are explained in Figure 10-8, but the main thing is this: Hit the space bar to pause or resume playback.

When you've had enough, double-click the movie to collapse it back into thumbnail form.

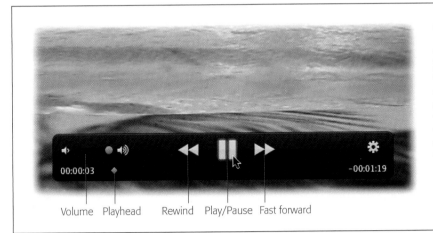

Figure 10-8:
The volume slider controls the sound of your movie independently of the volume setting on your computer (click the ◀ icon to mute the video). Next, the typical play/pause, fast-forward, and rewind buttons.

Volume   Playhead   Rewind   Play/Pause   Fast forward

Tip: The ✿ button harbors a pop-up menu that lets you view the movie at its original size or blown up to window size, and holds the Trim and Reset Trim commands, described next.

Editing Digital-Camera Movies in iPhoto

To trim the dead air off a movie, right there in iPhoto, follow these steps:

1. **Double-click the movie's thumbnail.**

   You can also select the video's thumbnail and then press the space bar. Either way, the movie starts playing.

2. **From the ✿ pop-up menu, choose Trim.**

   Yellow handles appear at the beginning and end of the video's scroll bar. Your job now is to isolate the part of the movie you want to keep.

3. **Drag the yellow sliders left or right to designate the new start and end points of your movie, and then click the Trim button (Figure 10-9).**

   iPhoto trims your movie. Now you can show it to people without subjecting them to the 30 seconds of fumbling at the beginning and end of the shot.

   The changes aren't permanent, though. You can always restore the original full-length director's cut by clicking that ✿ icon and choosing Reset Trim from the pop-up menu.

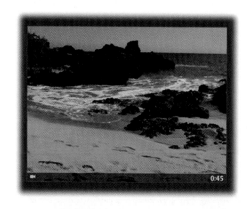

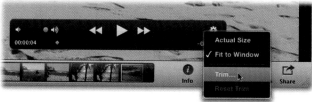

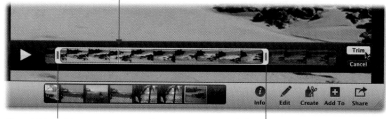

Playhead

Drag rightward to set your start point   Drag leftward to set your end point

Figure 10-9:
Top: Videos are marked with a tiny camcorder icon at the bottom left of their thumbnails. The number on the right side represents the movie's length.

Middle: Click the ✿ icon to reveal the Action menu.

Bottom: When you've positioned the yellow sliders just right, click the Trim button.

You can also move around within your movie by swiping a finger across the top of your Magic Mouse or Magic Trackpad.

Editing Movies in iMovie

For more editing power, you can open iMovie (the video-editing component of your iLife suite). In the Event Library at the left side of the window (choose Window→Event Library if you don't see it), click iPhoto Videos. Drag the clip you want right into iMovie's Project area.

The end.

All right, there's a *little* more to it—like learning how to *use* iMovie—but that's a different book. (*iMovie '11 & iDVD: The Missing Manual*, to be exact.) The point here is that you can incorporate movies from iPhoto's library in whatever iMovie project you have open, ready to edit as you would any other clips.

Tip: Want a great way to organize your camera's movies all at once? Create a new smart album, as described in Chapter 2. Set it up so that the pop-up menus and text boxes in the New Smart Album dialog box say "Photo," "is," and "Movie." You'll always find all your movies safely collected in this self-updating smart album.

Burning a Slideshow Movie CD or DVD

If your slideshow lasts more than a minute or two, it's probably too big to send to people by email. Luckily, you've got an alternative: Burn them a CD or DVD. Here's how the process goes:

1. **Prepare your exported movie.**

   Since file size isn't as much of an issue, you can make your slideshow dimensions 640 × 480, 720 × 480, 800 × 600, or any other size that fits on the computer screen. There's no need to throttle down the music quality, either.

2. **Put a blank CD or DVD in your burner.**

   A few seconds after you insert the disc, a message asks what you want to do with the blank disc. Choose "Open in Finder" and click OK.

   Now the disc's icon appears on your desktop as Untitled CD or Untitled DVD. You can rename it by clicking its name and then typing away.

3. **Drag the movie(s) onto the disc's icon.**

   These are, of course, the slideshow movies you've exported from iPhoto or the video clips from your digital camera.

4. **Click once on the disc icon and then choose File→Burn [the disc's name].**

   A confirmation dialog box appears (Figure 10-10).

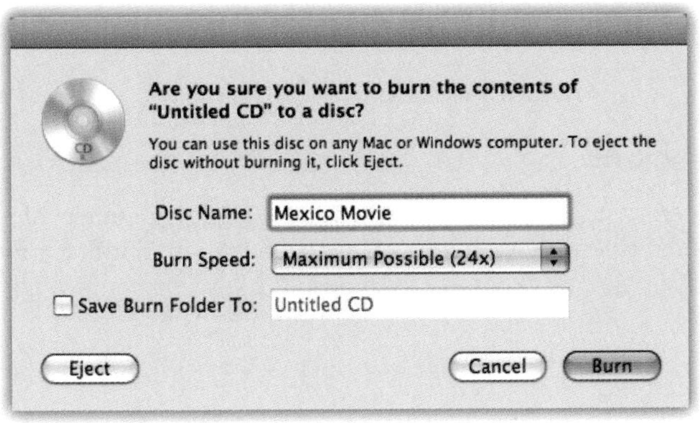

Figure 10-10:
You have one last chance to change your mind before you burn the disc. If everything's a go, then click Burn.

5. **Edit the disc's name, and then click Burn.**

   The Mac saves the movies onto the CD or DVD.

When the process is complete, eject the disc. It'll play equally well on Mac OS 9, Mac OS X, and Windows computers that have QuickTime Player installed.

Another approach: In the Finder, choose File→New Burn Folder. A new folder called Burn Folder appears on your desktop. Name it anything you want, and then drag your movies inside. Now open the folder and click the Burn button in the upper-right corner. The Mac asks for a blank CD or DVD and then walks you through the process of burning it.

Slideshow Movies on the Web

Chapter 8 offers complete details for posting individual photos on the Web. But with just a few adjustments to the instructions, you can just as easily post your slideshow movies on the Web, too, complete with music.

If you maintain your own website, you can upload the movie as you would any graphic. Create a link to it in the same way, and your movie will start to play in your visitors' web browsers when they click that link.

But if you have a MobileMe account, posting the movie is even easier, and you can do it from within iPhoto '11 without resorting to iMovie. In fact, the process works exactly the same for movies as it does for photos, as described in Chapter 8 (page 219).

You can also share movies on Flickr and your Facebook Wall (though you can't post them to a Facebook album).

Note: In order to share a movie to MobileMe, Flickr, or Facebook, you have to click the movie's thumbnail first. In other words, you need to be in full view, where the movie is playable and trimmable.

---

iDVD Slideshows

Let's face it: Most of the methods iPhoto gives you to show off your prize photos are geek techniques like sending them by email, posting them on a web page, turning them into a desktop picture, and so on. All these methods involve making your audience sit, hunched and uncomfortable, around a *computer* screen.

Now imagine seating them, instead, in front of the big-screen TV in the family room, turning down the lights, cranking up the surround sound, and grabbing the DVD remote to show off the latest family photos. And just think how cool it would be to send photo DVDs to family and friends who live far away!

Thanks to iDVD, part of Apple's iLife suite, you can create DVD-based slideshows from your photo collection, complete with soundtracks, navigational menus, and screens just like the DVDs you rent from Netflix.

This chapter covers the basics of how to bring your photos from iPhoto to iDVD and how to customize, preview, and burn your slideshows once you've exported them to iDVD.

The iDVD Slideshow

You don't actually need iPhoto to create a slideshow in iDVD. By itself, iDVD has all the tools you need to create interactive DVDs that include movies and soundtracks as well as slideshows.

But using iPhoto can save you a lot of time and trouble. You can use iPhoto to preview, edit, and organize all your photos into albums first. Then, once your photos are arranged into neatly organized albums, you can hand them off to iDVD with just one click, which converts them into a DVD-readable format. iDVD also hooks up all the navigational links and menus needed to present your show. Sweet!

Creating an iDVD Slideshow

Creating a DVD of your own photos entails choosing the photos that you've organized in iPhoto, selecting a theme, building menus, and configuring the settings that determine how your slideshow will look and operate. Finally, you can preview the entire DVD (without actually burning a disc) to test the navigation, pacing, and other settings. When the whole thing looks right, you burn the final disc.

You can begin in either of two ways: from iPhoto or from iDVD. The following pages walk you through both methods.

Starting in iPhoto

As mentioned above, beginning your odyssey in iPhoto saves you a few steps:

1. **Select the photos you want to turn into a slideshow.**

   You can select a random batch of individual photos using the selection tricks you learned back on page 49, or you can select just about anything in the Source list—an album, smart album, the Last 12 Months icon, or whatever. If you want to include an entire Event in your slideshow, click Events in the Source list and then click the Event's thumbnail.

   Note: You can even select multiple albums in your Source list to send to iDVD all at once. However, if you're sending a saved slideshow from iPhoto to iDVD, you can't select anything else; if you do, you'll get an error message over in iDVD. If you try to select two slideshows, the "Send to iDVD" menu command becomes grayed out and unclickable.

   If you select a slideshow icon (a saved slideshow, as explained on page 284), you'll commit the entire slideshow, complete with transition effects and music, to DVD. Once it's in iDVD, you can't make changes to the slides or music, but you can rearrange the slide order.

   Remember that if your photos aren't in the same aspect ratio as the screen they'll be viewed on, then they'll wind up flanked by black bars (either on the top or sides of your photo). The fix is to create a saved slideshow in iPhoto and then open the Slideshow Settings panel as described on page 165. In the panel's All Slides pane, turn on "Scale photos to fill screen" and choose HDTV from the Aspect Ratio pop-up menu. The downside is that vertical shots will *also* be enlarged to fill the screen, which may cause important bits to dangle offscreen (though you can always reposition what's showing in that particular slide by using the technique described in the box on page 174).

2. **Choose Share→iDVD (Figure 11-1).**

   This is the big hand-off. iDVD opens up a standard presentation window, shown in Figure 11-2. The names of your selected albums are listed as menu items that can be "clicked" with the DVD's remote control.

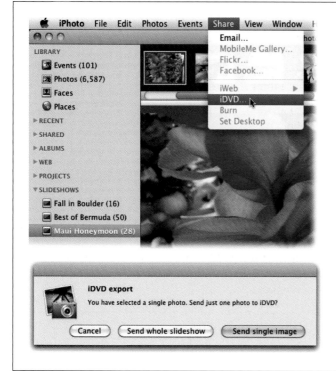

Figure 11-1:

Top: You can hand a project, album(s), video clip(s), or a slideshow off to iDVD by choosing Share→iDVD. (For reasons known only to Apple, this option isn't available from the Share button in the iPhoto toolbar.)

Bottom: If you're sending a slideshow to iDVD and happen to have a slide selected when you choose Share→iDVD, you see this message, which politely asks if you'd like to send the whole slideshow to iDVD instead. Click "Send whole slideshow;" iPhoto sends you on your way.

Tip: The first menu item is the name of the iDVD theme (in Figure 11-2, that's Revolution Main), which, happily, you can also edit.

Technically, at this point, your slideshow is ready to meet its public. If you're looking for some instant gratification, click the ▶ button at the bottom of the window to flip iDVD into Preview mode. Then click the name of your album as it appears on the DVD menu to start the show. (Use the iDVD remote control shown in Figure 11-8 to stop, pause, or rewind the show in progress.)

To really make the finished show your own, though, you'll want to spend some quality time adding custom touches. If that's got you salivating, skip ahead to "Customizing the Show" on page 301.

Starting in iDVD

You can also start building a show right in iDVD. To see how, click the program's Media button, and at the top of the panel that appears, click Photos (see Figure 11-3). You now see a tiny iPhoto window, right there in iDVD, complete with thumbnails of your photos (and movie clips), your Source list, and even a Search box.

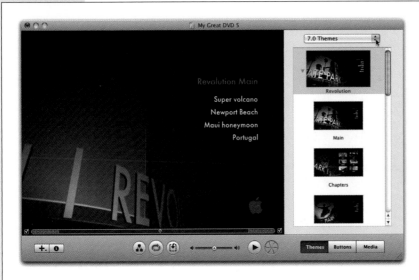

Figure 11-2:
The name of each exported album appears on the main menu page in iDVD. Single-click a menu item to select it and, after a pause, click it again to edit its typeface and size. Double-click an item to open iDVD's editing window where you can see the included photos and change their order (as discussed later in this chapter). Read on to learn how to change the menu screen's design scheme.

Each album you drag out of the list and onto the main iDVD stage area becomes another menu item that your audience members will be able to click with their remotes. (If the album won't "stick" and bounces back to the Source list, it's because that menu screen is too full. iDVD doesn't like menu screens with more than 12 items.)

Tip: You can also drag photos, or folders full of them, right off your Finder desktop and onto iDVD's main menu screen to add them as slideshows. Also, iDVD used to squawk if you tried to add a folder or album containing more than 99 photos, but that's not the case anymore.

If you've selected some music to accompany the slideshow of that album in iPhoto, then iDVD remembers, and plays it automatically when you play the DVD slideshow.

To assign different music, double-click the name of your slideshow to reveal the Slideshow Editor shown in Figure 11-4. Click Audio at the top of the Media panel and survey your iTunes collection. When you find a song or playlist that seems right, drag its name onto the little square Audio well, also shown in Figure 11-4.

Click the Return button to go back to the menu-design page.

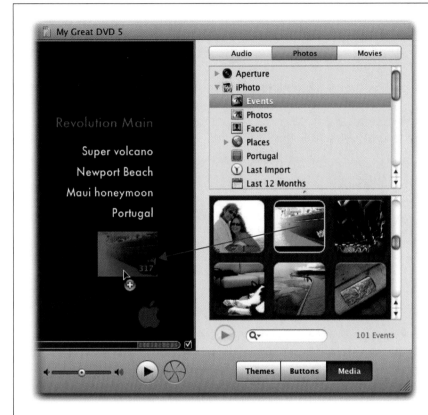

Figure 11-3:
Look familiar? Yep, it's your Source list from iPhoto. (You can also access Aperture, Apple's pro-level photo editor.)

All the hard work you've done in iPhoto orienting your photos and organizing them into albums pays off now, when you're designing your DVD. You can use the Search box at the bottom to find photos by name or keyword.

Even your iPhoto movie clips appear here. That's incredibly handy, because you can use movie clips in iDVD in so many ways—as filler for a drop zone, as a menu background, or as even as a standalone movie on the DVD.

Customizing the Show

iDVD provides an impressive number of options for customizing the look, feel, and sound of your slideshow, including its overall design scheme. Here's how to add a personal touch:

1. **Choose a theme.**

   Click the Themes button at the bottom of the iDVD window to reveal the list of ready-to-use visual themes that you can apply to your slideshow. Click a theme to apply it to your DVD's main-menu screen.

2. **Add your own background graphics, if you like.**

   You can drag a photo into any theme's background. (Click Media, then Photos, and then drag a picture's thumbnail directly onto any blank area of the main menu screen.) Some let you drop a photo into more interesting, animated *regions* of the background called *drop zones*, as described in Figure 11-5.

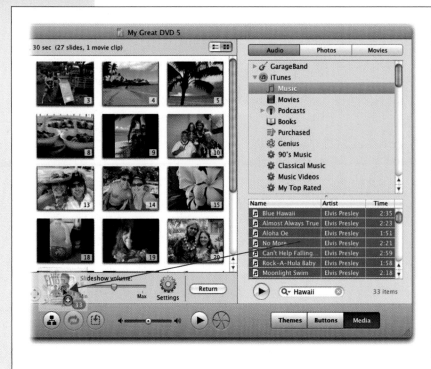

Figure 11-4:
In the Media panel, click the Audio button to see your entire list of iTunes music—in fact, you even see your playlists here. If you don't see the music you want, you can type a word in the Search box toward the bottom to locate those songs ("Hawaii" was entered here).

To avoid the dreaded music-ending-too-soon syndrome, you can drag an entire playlist into the little Audio well beneath the slide display. Your DVD will play one song after another according to the playlist.

3. **Add, remove, and reorder your pictures.**

   When you bring albums into iDVD from iPhoto, your photos arrive in the same sequence as they appeared within their iPhoto albums. Once you're in iDVD, however, you can change the order of these photos, remove them from the show, or add others.

Tip: Movies can be part of your slideshows, too; just drag them right into your slideshow among your photos. During playback, they play in sequence.

To edit a slideshow in this way, double-click its title on the DVD menu page ("Maui honeymoon" in Figure 11-5, for example).

The slideshow editing window shown in Figure 11-6 appears. Here, you can also set up other options, like switching between automatic and manual advancing of photos, selecting a different soundtrack, and adding navigation buttons to a slideshow.

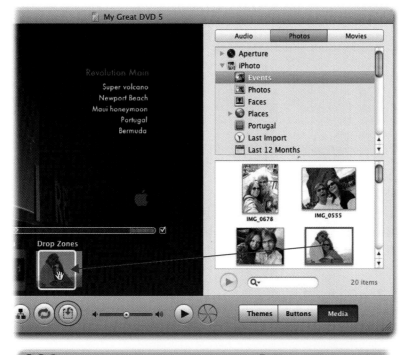

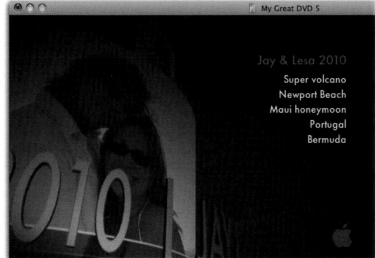

Figure 11-5:
Top: In this animated main-menu screen (the standard theme, called Revolution), the words of the title and the photo on the cylinder rotate. The photo on the cylinder is a "drop zone," an area that you can fill with a photo or movie of your choosing.

To activate a drop zone, click it once and its edges turn into black and yellow stripes. Click the Media button, click the Photos or Movies button, and then drag the item you want directly into the drop zone. If the drop zone is moving too fast, click the Edit Drop Zones button in iDVD's toolbar (circled), and an icon for each available drop zone appears (the number of drop zones depends on the theme). Click the Edit Drop Zones button again when you're finished.

Bottom: Once you add a photo or movie to the drop zone, you'll see it appear on the DVD menu, as shown here. How cool is that? Don't forget to change the theme's name, too, or else the DVD recipient will have a heck of a time trying to figure out what "Revolution Main" means.

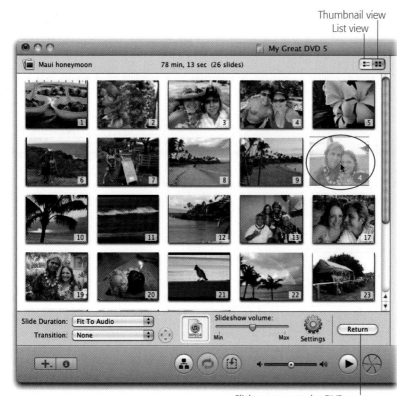

Thumbnail view
List view

Figure 11-6:
Changing the sequence of slides involves little more than dragging them around on this "light table." As in iPhoto, you can select multiple slides at once and then drag them en masse, as shown here (the number of photos you're dragging appears in red).

Don't miss the tiny icon at the top-right corner of the window. It switches to a list view that still lets you drag photos up or down to rearrange them.

Click Return to go back to your main-menu design screen.

Click to return to the DVD menu

You can rearrange the slides by dragging them (the other slides scoot aside to make room), delete selected slides by pressing the Delete key, or add more pictures by dragging new photos into your slideshow from the Media panel or your Mac's desktop.

Then, of course, there are the controls in the iDVD toolbar near the bottom of the window. They offer a great deal of control over your show. For example:

- **Slide Duration** lets you specify how much time each slide spends onscreen before the next one appears: 1, 3, 5, or 10 seconds, or Manual. Manual means that your audience will have to press the Next button on the remote control to change pictures.

  Then there's the "Fit to Audio" option, which appears in the Slide Duration pop-up menu only after you've added a sound file to your slideshow. In this case, iDVD determines the timing of your slides automatically—by dividing the length of the soundtrack by the number of slides in your show. For example, if the song is 60 seconds long and the show has 20 slides, each slide will sit on the screen for 3 seconds.

- **Transition** lets you specify any of several graceful transition effects—Dissolve, Cube, and so on—to govern how one slide morphs into the next. Whatever transition you specify here affects all slides in the show.

- **Slideshow volume**, of course, governs the overall audio level.

Five more controls pop up when you click the toolbar's Settings icon, as shown in Figure 11-7:

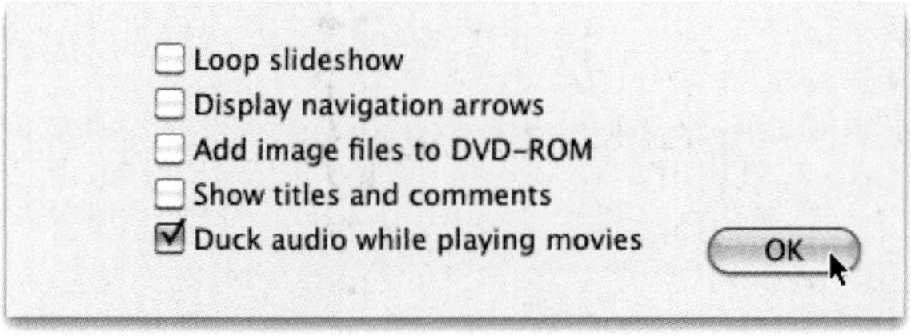

Figure 11-7:
When you click the Settings button on the iDVD toolbar, this handy menu appears.

- **Loop slideshow** makes the slideshow repeat endlessly.

- **Display navigation arrows** adds Previous and Next navigation arrows to the screen as your slideshow plays. Your audience can click these buttons with their remote controls to move back and forth in your slideshow.

  The arrows aren't technically necessary, of course. If you set your slides to advance automatically, you won't need navigation arrows. And even if you set up the slideshow for manual advance, your audience can always press the arrow buttons on their DVD remote to advance the slides. But if you think they need a visual crutch, this option is here.

- **Add image files to DVD-ROM** is an interesting one. When iDVD creates a slideshow, it scales all of your photos to 640 × 480 pixels. That's ideal for a standard television screen, which can't display any resolution higher than that.

  But if you intend to distribute your DVD to somebody who's computer savvy, you may want to give them the original, full-resolution photos. They won't see these photos when they insert the disc into a DVD player. But when they insert your DVD into their computers, they'll see a folder filled with the original, high-res photos, suitable for printing, using as desktop background, paying you for (ha!), and so on. (You've created a disc that's both a DVD-video disc and a DVD-ROM.)

- **Show titles and comments** means that any text you've added to your photos in iPhoto (their names or descriptions) will also appear on the screen during DVD playback. You can edit them right in iDVD.

- **Duck audio while playing movies** lets music in a video clip override the DVD's own soundtrack. Straight from the factory, this option is turned on.

4. **Add more slideshows, if you like.**

If you're making a "Family Photos 2011" DVD, for instance, you might create a separate slideshow called Holidays. To do that, click the **+** button in the main iDVD window; from the pop-up menu, choose Add Submenu. iDVD adds a menu item on the main screen that reads "My Submenu." Click it once to change the name to something clever like "Holiday photos," and then double-click it to open your secondary, empty menu page. Now you can drag all the holiday-related albums onto it from the mini-iPhoto browser shown in Figure 11-3.

You can return to the main DVD menu by clicking the Return button near the middle of the iDVD window.

Previewing the DVD

Your last step before burning a disc is to *test* your DVD presentation to check navigation, timing, photo sequences, and so on.

1. **Click the ▶ button.**

iDVD switches into Preview mode, which simulates how your disc will behave when inserted into a DVD player. This is a great chance to put your DVD-in-waiting through its paces before wasting a blank disc.

2. **Use the iDVD remote control to click your menu buttons, stop, pause, or re-wind the show in progress (Figure 11-8).**

3. **Click the Exit button on the remote when you're finished.**

When everything in the DVD looks good, you're ready to master your disc. Insert a blank disc in your SuperDrive and then click the Burn button (just to the right of the Play button, as shown in Figure 11-9).

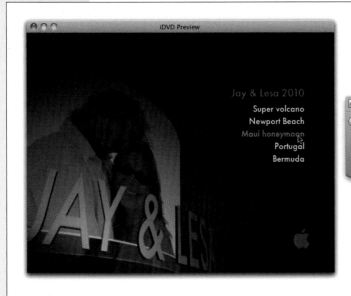

Figure 11-8:
When you put iDVD in Preview mode (by clicking the Play button), a small remote control panel appears next to the main window. It works just like your real DVD player's remote control. You can pause, rewind, or fast-forward slideshows. Clicking the Menu button takes you out of a slideshow and back to the DVD's main menu, where you can select other slideshows or movies to view.

Extra Credit: Self-Playing Slideshows

As you work on your DVD's menu structure, iDVD builds a handy map behind the scenes. You can use it to add or delete DVD elements, and you can double-click one of the icons to open the corresponding menu, movie, or slideshow.

To view the map, just click the Map button in the iDVD toolbar (Figure 11-9), and the element you were working on appears with colored highlighting. (Click the Map button again to return to the DVD menu screen.)

But the map is more than just a pretty navigational aid. It also makes possible a self-playing slideshow, one that plays automatically when the DVD is inserted, before your viewers even touch their remote controls.

Once you've got the Photos list open in the Media panel, as shown in Figure 11-9, you can drag an entire iPhoto album onto the AutoPlay icon. Alternatively, in the Customize panel (identified in Figure 11-9), you can click and ⌘-click just the photos you want, and then drag them en masse onto the AutoPlay icon. In fact, you can even drag photos—as a group or in a folder—right from your desktop onto this icon.

To control how long your still image remains on the screen, or how quickly your autoplay slideshow plays, double-click the AutoPlay tile. You arrive at the slideshow editor shown in Figure 11-6, where you can adjust the timing, transition, and even the audio that plays behind the pictures.

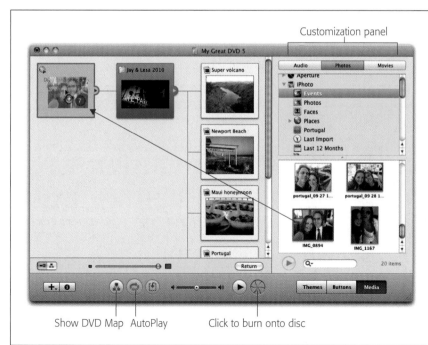

Customization panel

Show DVD Map   AutoPlay   Click to burn onto disc

Figure 11-9:
Map view is most useful when you're creating a complex DVD with nested menu screens, like the ones you might rent from Netflix.

But for slideshow purposes, its most useful feature is the AutoPlay icon. Any pictures or albums you drag onto this tile begin to play automatically when you insert the DVD into a DVD player—no remote-control fussing required.

If you decide to replace your autoplay material, just drag new stuff right onto it. Or, to eliminate the autoplay segment, drag it *off* the AutoPlay tile (it disappears in a little puff of cartoon smoke).

You can design a project that way for the benefit of, for example, technophobic DVD novices whose pupils dilate just contemplating using a remote control. They can just insert your autoplay-only DVD and sit back on the couch as the pictures flash by automatically.

It's even possible to create a DVD that consists *only* of autoplay material, a slideshow that repeats endlessly during, say, your cocktail reception—no menu screen ever appears. Just highlight the AutoPlay tile and then choose Advanced→"Loop slideshow" and poof! You've got yourself a self-running, self-repeating slideshow of digital photos that plays on a TV at a party or wedding reception (and your computing prowess will be the envy of every family member or friend who sees it). The DVD will loop endlessly—or at least until it occurs to someone in your audience to press the Menu or Title button on the remote. The Menu button redisplays the previous menu screen; the Title button causes a return to the main menu.

Tip: To learn more about iDVD, pick up a copy of *iMovie '11 & iDVD: The Missing Manual.*

Screensavers, AppleScript, and Automator

You've assembled libraries of digital images, sent heart-touching moments to friends and family via email, published your recent vacation pics on the Web, authored a QuickTime movie or two, and even boosted the stock price of Canon and Epson single-handedly through your consumption of inkjet printer cartridges. What more could there be?

Plenty. This chapter covers iPhoto's final repertoire of photo stunts, like turning your photos into one of the best screensavers that's ever floated across a computer monitor, plastering one particularly delicious shot across your desktop, calling upon AppleScript to automate photo-related chores for you, and harnessing iPhoto's partnership with Automator. (This chapter's alternate title: "Miscellaneous iPhoto Stunts that Didn't Really Fit in the Outline.")

Building a Custom Screensaver

Mac OS X's screensaver feature is so good, it's pushed more than one Windows person over the edge into making the switch to Mac OS X. When this screensaver kicks in (after several minutes of inactivity on your part), your Mac's screen becomes a personal movie theater. The effect is something like a slideshow, except that the pictures don't simply appear one after another and sit there on the screen. Instead, they're much more animated. They slide gently across the screen, zooming in or out, smoothly dissolving from one to the next.

Mac OS X comes equipped with a few photo collections that look great with this treatment: forests, space shots, and so on. But let the rabble use those canned screensavers. You, a digital master, can use your own photos as screensaver material.

Meet the Screensaver

Your entire iPhoto world—everything in your Source list, plus Faces and Places info (Chapter 4)—is accessible within your Mac's System Preferences and, therefore, available as an instant screensaver. Just imagine the possibilities! If you've taken the time to tag your photos with Faces info, you can create a screensaver of Mom and Dad's entire life to play at their 50th wedding anniversary luau in seconds, *without* opening iPhoto. Having a dinner party and want to show off photos from Portugal? If they're geotagged, your screensaver is ready and waiting for you.

Note: If you've got dual monitors—or a monitor plugged into a laptop—you see *different* photos on each monitor as the screensaver plays. Sweet!

Choose ☀→System Preferences; then click the Desktop & Screen Saver icon. You've opened the window shown in Figure 12-1. Click the Screen Saver tab near the top, and then scroll down to the iPhoto album of your choice. Click it to see, in the Preview area, what it will look like. The box on page 312 has more on customizing your screensaver.

Tip: Horizontal shots fill your monitor better than vertical ones—the verticals have fat black bars on either side to fill the empty space. However, if you change the screensaver's Display Style to Collage (as shown in Figure 12-1), the black bars disappear.

One-Click Desktop Backdrop

iPhoto's desktop-image feature is the best way to drive home the point that photos of your children (or dog, or mother, or self) are the most beautiful in the world. You pick one spectacular shot to replace the standard Mac OS X swirling blue desktop pattern or outer-space photo. It's like refrigerator art on steroids.

Creating wallpaper in iPhoto is so easy that you could change the picture every day—and you may well want to. In iPhoto, click a thumbnail, and then choose Share→Set Desktop. Even though the iPhoto window is probably filling your screen, the change happens instantly behind it. Your desktop is now filled with the picture you picked.

Note: If you choose *several* thumbnails or an album, iPhoto assumes that you intend to make Mac OS X *rotate* among your selected photos, displaying a new one every few minutes on your desktop throughout the day.

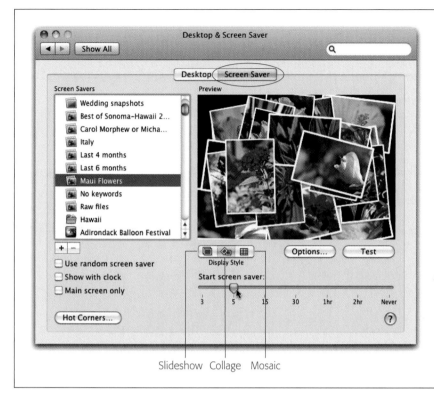

Figure 12-1:
All of your iPhoto albums are listed in the Screen Saver panel of the Desktop & Screen Saver window. Just pick the one you want to use as a screen-saver and your Mac turns your photos into a smooth, full-screen slideshow.

Here, the Display Style is set to Collage, in which your photos don white borders and appear to float down onto your desktop, one by one, into a big stack.

Slideshow Collage Mosaic

Note: Scroll far enough through the Screen Savers list and you'll discover all of your smart albums, Events, Facebook, Flickr, MobileMe, Faces, and Places albums, too. If you've ever used Aperture (Apple's pro-level photo editor), you see all of its albums at the very bottom of this list.

Just three bits of advice. First, choose a picture that's as big as your screen (at least 1024 × 768 pixels, for example, which is smaller than photos taken on your *iPhone*). Otherwise, Mac OS X will stretch it to fit, distorting the photo in the process. If you're *really* fussy, you can even crop the photo first to the exact measurements of the screen; in fact, the first command in iPhoto's Constrain pop-up menu (page 132) lists the exact dimensions of your screen, so you can crop the designated photo (or a copy of it) to fit precisely.

Second, horizontal shots work much better than vertical ones; iPhoto blows up vertical shots to fit the width of the screen, potentially chopping off the heads and feet of your loved ones.

Screensaver Basics

You don't *technically* need a screensaver to protect your monitor from burn-in. Today's flat-panel screens never burn in, and even the latest CRT monitors wouldn't burn an image into the screen unless you left them on continuously for two years.

No, screensavers today are solely about entertainment (or privacy).

In Mac OS X's Desktop & Screen Saver window (Figure 12-1), when you click a module's name in the Screen Savers list, you see a mini version of it playing in the Preview area.

You can control when your screensaver takes over your monitor using the "Start screen saver" slider. It lets you specify when the screensaver kicks in (after what period of keyboard or mouse inactivity).

When you click the Hot Corners button, you're presented with a pane than lets you turn each corner of your monitor into a hot spot. Whenever you roll your cursor into that corner, the screensaver either turns on instantly (great when you happen to be shopping on eBay at the moment your boss walks by) or stays off permanently (for when you're reading on-screen or watching a movie). For example, you can use two corners for controlling the screensaver and the other two to activate Exposé (Mac OS X's window-hiding feature).

In any case, pressing any key or clicking the mouse always removes the screensaver from your screen and takes you back to whatever you were doing.

The Options button reveals the additional settings shown here, some of which are very useful. (Make sure you have the Slideshow Display Style selected to see all these options.) Turn off "Crop slides to fill screen," for example, if you want your Mac to show each photo, edge to edge (even if it has to use black bars to fill the rest of your monitor, as shown in the preview here); otherwise, it enlarges each photo to fill the screen, often lopping off body parts in the process. (If "Crop slides" is on, then you can also turn on "Keep slides centered" to prevent your Mac from panning across each photo.)

And turning off "Zoom back and forth," of course, eliminates the majestic, cinematic zooming in and out of successive photos that makes the screensaver look so darned cool.

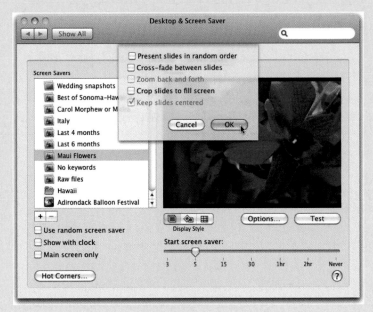

Finally, if a photo doesn't precisely match the screen's proportions, note the pop-up menu shown at the top of Figure 12-2. It lets you specify how you want the discrepancy handled. Here are your choices:

- **Fill Screen**. This option enlarges or reduces the image so that it fills every inch of the desktop, and in most cases, it does a good job. But if the image is small, the low-resolution stretching can look awful. Conversely, if the image is large and its dimensions don't precisely match your screen's, parts get chopped off. This option never distorts the picture, as the Stretch option (below) does.

- **Fit to Screen**. This setting centers the photo neatly on the screen, at whatever size fits. It doesn't fill the entire background; instead, it sits right smack in the center of the monitor. Of course, this arrangement may leave a swath of empty border all the way around it. As a remedy, Apple provides a color-swatch button next to the pop-up menu. When you click it, the Color Picker appears, so you can specify a color for the "frame" around the photo.

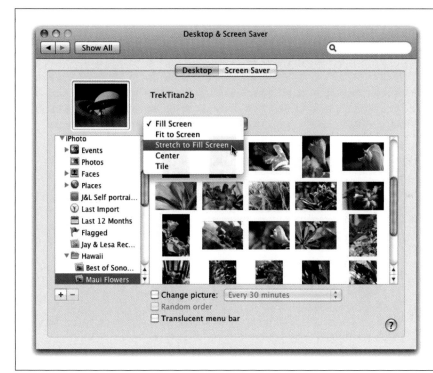

Figure 12-2:
If your photo doesn't fit the screen perfectly, choose a different option from the pop-up menu in the Desktop & Screen Saver window. In most cases, though, the factory setting of Fill Screen works just fine.

While you're in the Desktop & Screen Saver window, you might notice that all of your iPhoto albums are listed below the collection of images that came with your Mac. You can navigate through those albums to find a new desktop image.

- **Stretch to Fill Screen**. Use this option at your peril, since it makes your picture fit the screen exactly, come hell or high water. Unfortunately, larger pictures may be squished vertically or horizontally as necessary, and small pictures are drastically blown up and squished, usually with grisly results.

- **Center**. This one is basically the same as "Fit to Screen," except that it shows your picture at full size. If the picture is larger than the screen, you see only the middle; the edges get chopped off where they extend beyond your screen.

- **Tile**. This option makes your picture repeat over and over until the multiple images fill the entire monitor. (If your picture is larger than the screen, no such tiling takes place. You see only the top center chunk of the image.)

And one last thing: If public outcry demands that you return your desktop to one of the standard system backdrops, open System Preferences, and then click the Desktop & Screen Saver icon. There, click the Desktop button if necessary, choose Apple in the list at the left of the window, and then take your pick.

Exporting and Converting Pictures

The whole point of iPhoto is to provide a central location for every photo in your world, but that doesn't mean they're locked in there forever. You'll be pleased to know that it's as easy to take pictures *out* of iPhoto as it is to put them in. Liberating a photo from iPhoto can be useful in situations like these:

- You're creating a web page outside of iPhoto and you need a photo in a certain size and format.
- You shot a bunch of 10-megapixel photos but you're running out of disk space, and you wish they were all 6-megapixel shots instead. (They'd still have plenty of resolution, but not so much wasted space.)
- You're going to submit some prize-winning photos to a newspaper or magazine, and the publication requires TIFF-format photos, not iPhoto's standard JPEG format.
- Somebody else on your network loves one of your pictures and would like to use it as a desktop background on *that* machine.
- You want to set a few of the photos free so you can copy them *back* onto the camera's memory card. (Some people use their digicams as much for *showing* pictures to their friends as for *taking* them.)
- You want to send a batch of pictures on a CD or DVD to someone.

Exporting by Dragging

It's amazingly easy to export photos from iPhoto: Just drag their thumbnails out of the photo viewing area and onto the desktop (or onto a folder, or into a window on the desktop), as shown in Figure 12-3. After a moment, their icons appear.

The drag-and-drop method has enormous virtue in its simplicity and speed. It does not, however, grant you much flexibility. It produces JPEG files only, at the original camera resolution, with the camera's own cryptic naming scheme (unless you renamed them in iPhoto, of course).

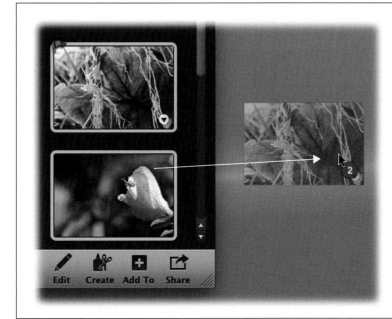

Figure 12-3:
*The drag-and-drop technique
produces full-size JPEG files, exactly as they appear in iPhoto.
Their names, however, might
not be particularly user-friendly.
If you haven't renamed your
photos yet (page 67), then a
picture named IMG_5197.jpg
will wind up on the desktop.*

Exporting by Dialog Box

To gain control over the dimensions, names, and file formats of the exported graphics, use the Export command. After selecting a picture, a group of pictures, or an
album, you can invoke this command by choosing File→Export (or pressing Shift-
⌘-E).

The highly useful Export dialog box appears, as shown in Figure 12-4. Click the File
Export tab, if it's not already active, and then make the following decisions:

Tip: If you want to email a few photos, don't bother with the Export dialog box; use iPhoto's new Email
command instead. Page 195 has the scoop.

File format

You can use the Kind pop-up menu to specify the file format of the photo(s) you're
about to export. Here are your options:

- **Original**. iPhoto exports the photo in whatever format it was in when you imported it. If the picture came from a digital camera, for example, it's usually a
  JPEG.

  If your camera captured the photo in Raw format (page 151), though, the Original
  option is even more valuable. It lets you export the original Raw file so that you

can, for example, work with it in a more sophisticated editor like Adobe Camera Raw, which comes with Photoshop and Photoshop Elements. (The exported file doesn't contain any edits you've made to that photo, however.)

- **Current.** This option exports the file format your photo is currently in. For example, if you imported a Raw image and then edited it, it will be exported as a JPEG.

- **JPEG.** This abbreviation stands for Joint Photographic Experts Group (that's the group of geeks who came up with this format). The JPEG format is, of course, the most popular format for photos on the Internet (and in iPhoto), thanks to its wide range of colors and small file size.

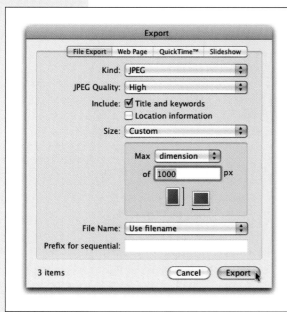

Figure 12-4:
The Export dialog box gives you control over the file format, names, and dimensions of the pictures you're about to extract from iPhoto. You can also include the photo's map coordinates by turning on the Location Information checkbox. The number of photos you're about to export appears in the lower-left corner of the box.

You can even tell iPhoto to use whatever names you gave your pictures, instead of the original, incomprehensible file names bestowed by your camera. To do so, choose "Use title" from the File Name pop-up menu.

And don't miss the Custom option in the Size pop-up menu. This option lets you export scaled-down versions of your photos, de-megapixeling them for web pages, desktop pictures, folder-window pictures, and so on.

Note: If you choose JPEG, you can also use the JPEG Quality pop-up menu to specify a quality level (High, Medium, and so on), with the understanding that the file gets bigger as the quality increases.

- **TIFF.** These files (whose abbreviation is short for Tagged Image File Format) are something like JPEG without the "lossy" compression. That is, they maintain every bit of quality available in the original photograph, but usually take up much more disk space (or memory-card space) as a result. TIFF is a good choice if quality is more important than portability (like when the photo is destined for print).

- **PNG.** This format (Portable Network Graphics) was designed to replace the GIF format on the Web. (The company that came up with the algorithms behind the GIF format exercised its legal muscle...long story.)

Whereas GIF graphics generally don't make good photos because they're limited to 256 colors, PNG is a good choice for photos (except the variation called *PNG-8*, which is just as limited as GIF). The resulting files are smaller than TIFF images, yet don't exhibit any compression-related quality loss à la JPEGs. Not all graphics programs and web browsers recognize this relatively new format, but the big ones—including iPhoto, GraphicConverter, Photoshop, and most recent browser versions—all do.

Titles and keywords

iPhoto maintains two names for each photo: its *original file name*, as it appears in the Finder, and its *iPhoto title*, the one you may have typed in while working in the program.

If you turn on "Title and keywords" (available with JPEG or TIFF formats only), then each exported file has the name you gave it in iPhoto. It also has, stored invisibly, any keywords you assigned to it (page 84). That's a big deal, because it means that (a) you'll be able to find it on your Mac with a Spotlight search, and (b) if you import it into another iPhoto library, it remembers the keywords you gave it.

Size options

Remember that although digital-camera graphics files may not always have enough resolution for prints, they generally have far *too much* resolution for displaying onscreen.

Using these controls, you can depixelize your photos, shrinking them down to something more manageable.

Your choices are **Small** (320 × 240 pixels, suitable for emailing or web pages visited by dial-up victims); **Medium** (640 × 480, good for email or websites again); **Large** (1280 × 960, nice for slideshows); **Full Size** (whatever the photo is now, best for printing); and **Custom**.

If you choose Custom, you get the curious controls shown in Figure 12-4, where a Max pop-up menu lets you specify the maximum pixel measurement for each photo's height, width, or both. Why didn't Apple just offer you Height and Width boxes? Because the exported photos might have all different proportions, so saying, "Export these at 800 × 600" wouldn't always make sense. This way, you're specifying the *maximum* dimensions on one side or both.

File Name

From this pop-up menu, specify how you want the exported files to be named:

- **Use title**. The exported files are named whatever you named them within iPhoto.
- **Use filename**. The exported files bear their original, underlying names given to them by your camera, like DSC_0192.jpg or IMG_4821.JPG.
- **Sequential**. The files will be named Bad Hair Day 1, Bad Hair Day 2, and so on. (In the "Prefix for sequential" box, type *Bad Hair Day* or whatever you like.)

- **Album name with number**. This option tells iPhoto to name your exported photos according to their album name and sequence within that album. So if an exported photo is the fourth picture in the first row of an album titled Maui Flowers, iPhoto will call the exported file "Maui Flowers–04.jpg." Because *you* determine the order within an album (by dragging), this is the only option that lets you control the numbering of the exported result.

Plug-Ins and Add-Ons

On one thing, friends and foes of Apple can all agree: iPhoto is no Photoshop. iPhoto was deliberately designed to be simple and streamlined, although it's picking up more power with each new version.

Yet Apple thoughtfully left the back door open. Other programmers are free to write add-ons and plug-ins—software modules that contribute additional features, lend new flexibility, and goose up the power of iPhoto.

And yet, with great power comes great complexity—in this case, power and complexity that Apple chose to omit. But at least this plug-in arrangement means that nobody can blame *Apple* for junking up iPhoto with extra features. After all, *you're* the one who installed them.

A few of the most important plug-ins and accessory programs are described in the relevant chapters of this book:

- **Duplicate Annihilator** (see the box on page 153) determines whether you have any duplicate photos in your iPhoto library, and gives you several options for dealing with them.

- **iPhoto Library Manager** (page 240) lets you create and manage multiple iPhoto libraries.

- **Keyword Manager** (see the Tip on page 90) is designed to lend flexibility to the way iPhoto handles keywords.

- **Portraits & Prints** (see the box on page 192) expands iPhoto's printing features and lets you create a multi-photo layout on a single sheet of paper for printing.

As the popularity of iPhoto grows, new add-ons and plug-ins will surely sprout up like roses in your macro lens. It's worthwhile trolling the MacUpdate (*www.macupdate.com*) and Version Tracker *(www.versiontracker.com/macosx)* websites from time to time *to see what's available*. Search for *iPhoto*; you'll be surprised at the number of goodies waiting for you to try.

AppleScript Tricks

AppleScript is the famous Macintosh *scripting language*—a software robot that you can program to perform certain repetitive or tedious tasks for you.

iPhoto is fully *scriptable*, meaning that AppleScript gurus can manipulate it by remote control with AppleScripts that they create. (It even works with Automator, the program in Mac OS X that makes programming even easier than using AppleScript; see the following section.)

But even if you're not an AppleScript programmer yourself, this is still good news, because you're perfectly welcome to exploit the ready-made, prewritten AppleScripts that other people come up with. You can find them by Googling *iPhoto AppleScripts*.

Automator Tricks

If you use your Mac long enough, you're bound to start repeating certain tasks over and over again. Automator is a program that lets you teach your Mac what to do, step by step, by assembling a series of instructions called *actions* (each is a single, specific task). You can make your Mac perform super complex tasks by assembling a variety of pre-recorded actions into a specific order in Automator. To trigger the task, you can click Automator's Run button ▶ or you can save the task as a genuine, double-clickable, standalone application. Either way, your Mac faithfully runs each action one at a time, one right after the other.

As it turns out, Automator works great with iPhoto. By following "recipes" that you find online—or the sample described here—you can add all kinds of new, timesaving features to iPhoto and your Mac.

The Lay of the Land

To open Automator, visit your Applications folder and give its icon a swift double-click. You should see something like Figure 12-5, starring these key elements:

Tip: To see all of Automator's ready-made actions for iPhoto, type *iPhoto* into the Search box at the top left of the program's window.

Template pane

The Template pane (Figure 12-5, top) shows you the different things you can create in Automator. (If you single-click an icon, its description appears at the bottom of the pane.) For example, to combine several actions into a single complex task, choose Workflow; to create an action that automatically runs when you drop files onto it, choose Application; to create an action that's available within the Service menu of many Mac OS X programs, choose Service; and so on.

Library list

Automator's Library list shows you all the items on your Mac that can be controlled by Automator actions: Calendar, Contacts, Files & Folders, and so on. When you click to make a selection, the Action list to its right shows you every action (command) that the chosen item understands. When you find an action you want to use in your workflow, drag it to the right into the large Workflow pane to begin building and customizing your new software robot.

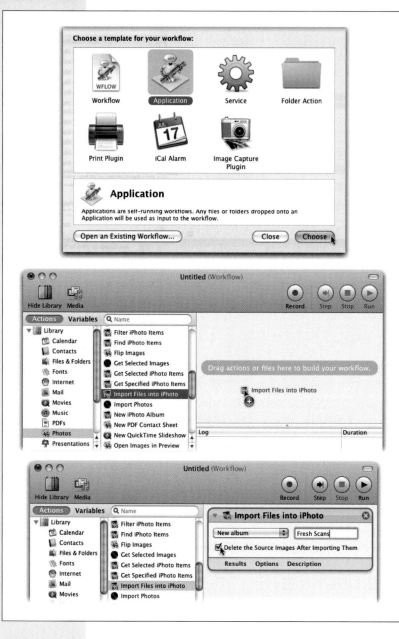

Figure 12-5:
Top: You can choose what you want to create—and how you'll trigger it—in this template pane, which opens when you first start the program. (You can reopen it later by choosing File→New.) To create a task that you can trigger by dropping files or folders onto an icon, choose Application.

Middle: Narrow down the action options by choosing what kind of task you want Automator to perform. In this case, choose Photos in the far left column. Then, locate a specific action in the second column and double-click the action's name or drag it into the column on the right to tweak its settings.

Bottom: By choosing "Import Files into iPhoto" and adjusting the settings as shown here, you can have Automator fetch the files you just scanned and plop them into iPhoto, saving you the steps of creating a new iPhoto album, importing the files into it, and then deleting the originals from your hard drive. To trigger the task, scan all your files, stick them in a folder and then drop that folder onto the application icon. If you do a lot of scanning, this could be a huge timesaver.

Action list

This list (which doesn't have a heading—it's to the right of the Library list) shows you the contents of whatever categories you've selected in the Library list. If, for example, you selected Photos in the Library list, the Action list would show you all the photo-related actions available on your Mac. To build your own workflow (or customize one that already exists), you drag actions *from* the Action list into the Workflow pane, as shown in Figure 12-5 (middle). (Double-clicking an action does the same thing as dragging it.)

Workflow pane

You can think of the Workflow pane as Automator's kitchen. This is where you put your actions in whatever order you want, set any action-specific preferences, and fry them all up in a pan.

But the Workflow pane is also where you see how the information from one action gets piped into another, creating a stream of information. That's how the Workflow pane differentiates Automator from the dozens of nonvisual, programming-based automation tools out there.

When you drag an action out of the Action list and into the Workflow pane, any sur-rounding actions scoot aside to make room for it. When you let go of the mouse, the action you dragged materializes right there in the Workflow pane.

Tip: If you select an action in the Action list and press Return, Automator automatically inserts that action at the bottom of the Workflow pane.

Saving your Task

Once you're finished creating your little Automator robot, you need to save it by choosing File→Save As. Give your new task a name, and then click the File Format pop-up menu.

Choose Workflow if you'll trigger the task from within Automator by clicking its Run button (see Figure 12-5), or choose Application to create an icon that triggers the task when you drop files *onto* it.

Tip: If you picked Application in the Template pane, you can choose File→Save instead. In that case, Automator already knows *what* you want to save; you just need to give it a name and tell it where to put the new application on your hard drive.

The Auto Import Folder

If you know where to look, you'll find that Apple *secretly* included an Automator folder action into your copy of iPhoto. That's right, it's sitting on your hard drive waiting to be discovered. It's a folder called Auto Import.

The beauty of this magic folder is that you can park it on your desktop. As you go about your week, you can drag photo files into it. Then, the next time you open iPhoto, they'll be imported automatically.

How is this useful? In so many ways:

- As you add more photos, iPhoto takes longer and longer to open. When you know iPhoto is going to take 30 seconds to open, and you just have a couple of photos to import, it scarcely seems worth sitting through the startup process. But thanks to the Auto Import folder, you can add photos throughout your day, a couple at a time or whatever, without ever waiting for iPhoto to open up. When you finally have some time to really work, *then* you can open iPhoto, and *then* it will grab the photos you've scheduled for importing.

- You can park different "Add to iPhoto" folders on your desktop, one for each iPhoto *library* (page 29). When iPhoto opens, it's smart enough to import only the photos from the correct Auto Import folder for the library you're using.

- When you're in a hurry, you can insert your camera's memory card into your Mac, look over the photos right there in the Finder, and copy only the worthwhile ones to your Mac—by dropping them into the Auto Import folder. There, they're safe and ready to be imported into iPhoto, but meanwhile you haven't wasted any time waiting for iPhoto to open and close.

Here's how to set up the Auto Import folder:

1. **Locate your iPhoto library in your Home→Pictures folder.**

   As you learned back in Chapter 1, this is where your iPhoto library lives unless you moved it somewhere else. (See page 29 for more on iPhoto libraries.)

2. **Control-click (or right-click) the iPhoto Library icon; from the shortcut menu, choose Show Package Contents (Figure 12-6, top).**

   A new Finder window opens showing everything that's inside the iPhoto Library package.

3. **Locate the folder named Auto Import. ⌘-Option drag it to your desktop (Figure 12-6, bottom).**

   You've hit paydirt! This is the folder action Apple snuck into your copy of iPhoto without telling you. Holding down the ⌘ and Option keys forces your Mac to create an *alias* of the folder (a shortcut to the real one). The alias has a little curved arrow on its bottom-left corner.

From now on, whenever you want to schedule some pictures for iPhoto importing, drag them onto the Auto Import icon on your desktop. The next time iPhoto opens, you'll see it flip automatically into Importing mode and slurp those photos in. After the import is complete, you'll notice that the Auto Import folder is empty once again.

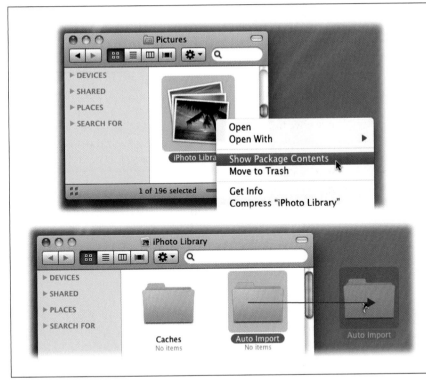

Figure 12-6:
If iPhoto is running, the files you drop onto the Auto Import folder are added to your library immediately. If iPhoto isn't running, the files are added the next time you launch the program.

Once you've created the Auto Import alias, you can rename it anything you want. A good choice might be "Add to iPhoto."

iPhoto File Management

For years, true iPhoto fans experienced the heartache of iPhoto Overload—the syndrome in which the program gets too full of photos, winds up gasping for RAM, and acts as if you've slathered it with a thick coat of molasses. And for years, true iPhoto fans have adopted an array of countermeasures to keep the speed up, including splitting the Photo library into several smaller chunks.

Now that iPhoto can manage 250,000 pictures per library, such drastic measures aren't generally necessary.

Nonetheless, learning how iPhoto manages its library files is still a worthy pursuit. It's the key to swapping photo libraries, burning them to CD or DVD, transferring them to other machines, and merging them together.

About iPhoto Discs

iPhoto discs are CDs or DVDs that you can create in iPhoto to archive your entire library—or any selected portion of it—with just a few mouse clicks.

The beauty of iPhoto's Burn command is that it exports much more than just the photos themselves to a disc. It also copies the thumbnails, titles, keywords, comments, ratings, and all the other important data about your iPhoto library. Burning this valuable information to disc lets you do all sorts of useful things:

- Make a backup of your whole photo collection for safekeeping.
- Transfer specific photos, albums, or a whole iPhoto library to another Mac without losing your keywords, descriptions, ratings, and titles.
- Share discs with other iPhoto fans so that your friends and family can view your photo albums in their own copies of iPhoto.

- Offload photos to CD or DVD as your photo collection grows, to keep your current iPhoto library at a trim, manageable size.

- Merge separate libraries (such as the one on your laptop and the one on your iMac) into a single master iPhoto library.

Note: One thing an iPhoto disc is *not* good for is sharing your photos with somebody who doesn't have iPhoto! An iPhoto disc is designed *exclusively* for transferring pictures into another copy of iPhoto. If you want to create a CD or DVD that can be read by a Windows machine or by a photo-processing company, you'll need to use the File→Export command discussed in Chapter 8 (page 314).

Burning an iPhoto CD or DVD

All you need to create an iPhoto disc is a Mac and a blank disc.

1. **Select the photos that you want to include on the disc.**

   You can hand-select your photos using the techniques you learned back on page 49, click a Source list icon (Event, album, book, or slideshow), or click the Photos icon to burn your entire photo collection.

   In any case, the photo-viewing area should now be showing the photos you want to save onto a disc.

2. **Choose Share→Burn.**

   A dialog box appears, prompting you to insert a blank disc. Pop in the disc and after a few moments, the dialog box vanishes. Be sure to use a CD-RW (a disc that you can burn info onto multiple times), or a blank CD-R or DVD-R.

3. **Check the size of your selection to make sure it will fit.**

   Take a look at the disc info at the bottom of the iPhoto window, as shown in Figure 13-1; the little graph shows you how much of the disc will be filled up. If the set of photos you want to burn is smaller than 650 or 700 megabytes (for a CD), 4.3 gigabytes (for a DVD), or 8 gigs (for a dual-layer DVD), then you're good to go. You can burn the whole thing onto a single disc.

   If your photo collection is larger than that, however, it's not going to fit. You'll have to split your backup operation across multiple discs. Select whatever number of photo albums or individual pictures *will* fit on a single disc, using the indicator shown in Figure 13-1 as your guide. (Also shown in the figure: the Name box, where you can name the disc you're about to burn.)

   For example, you might decide to copy the 2009 folder onto one disk, the 2010 folder onto another, and so on, using the calendar feature (page 81) to round up your photos by year.

   After burning one disc, select the next set of photos, and then burn another CD or DVD. Burn as many discs as needed to contain your entire collection

---

of photos. If and when you ever need to restore your photos from the multiple discs, you'll be able to merge them back together into a single iPhoto library using the technique described in "Merging Photo Libraries" on page 334.

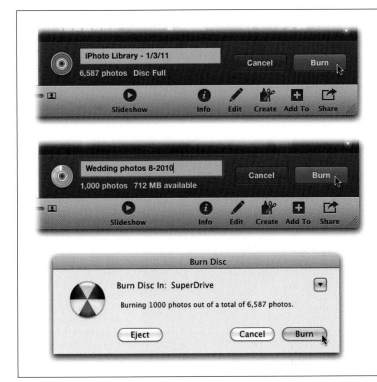

Figure 13-1:
Top: Once you've clicked Share→Burn and inserted a blank disc, inspect the bottom of your screen to see how close you are to filling the disc. The indicator icon updates itself as you select or deselect photos and albums. If your photos won't all fit on the disc, the little disc icon turns red (as shown here), and when you click Burn you'll get a message saying there's not enough space on the disc.

Middle: Keep deselecting photos, albums, or Events until the disc icon turns green. Feel free to take this opportunity to give your disc a custom name, too.

Bottom: If all is well, however, you get this message instead. Click Burn and sit back to enjoy the fruits of your Mac's laser.

4. **Click the Burn button.**

   As discussed in Figure 13-1, you'll either get a "not enough space" message or a "Burn Disc" message. If you get the latter, you're ready to proceed.

5. **Click Burn.**

   First, iPhoto makes a *disk image*—a sort of pretend disc on your hard drive that serves as a temporary holding area for the photos that will be burned. Next, iPhoto copies the photos from your iPhoto Library to the disk image.

   Finally, the real burning begins. When the process is done, your Mac spits out the finished CD or DVD, ready to use, bearing whatever name you gave it.

Tip: You can safely bail out of the disc-creating process by clicking the Cancel button when the progress dialog box first appears (when your Mac is creating the disk image discussed in step 5 above).

But don't click Stop once the Burning dialog box appears. At that point, your disk drive is already busy etching data onto the disc itself. Clicking Stop brings the burning to a screeching halt, leaving you with a partially burned, nonfunctioning disc (and no, they really don't work well as coasters).

What you get

The finished iPhoto disc contains not just your photos, but a clone of your iPhoto library as well. In other words, this disc includes all the thumbnails, keywords, comments, ratings, photo album information—even the unedited original versions of your photos that iPhoto keeps secretly tucked away.

If you want to view the contents of your finished disc in iPhoto, pop it back into the drive. If iPhoto isn't running, your Mac opens it automatically.

Moments later, the icon for the CD or DVD appears in the Source list of the iPhoto window, as shown in Figure 13-2. If you click the disc's icon, the photos it contains appear in the photo-viewing area, just as if they were stored in your library.

You can't make changes to them, of course—that's the thing about CDs and DVDs. But you can copy them into your own albums and make changes to the copies.

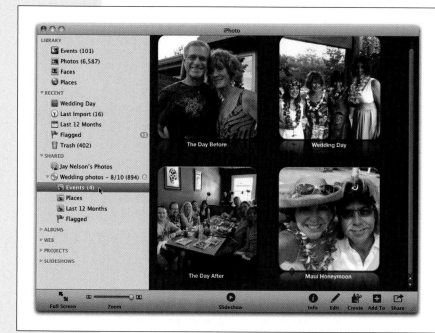

Figure 13-2:
Pop an iPhoto CD or DVD into your Mac and it appears right along with your albums in iPhoto, under the Shared heading. Click the disc icon or one of the disc's album icons to display the photos it contains (Events is selected here).

In essence, iPhoto is giving you access to two different libraries at once—the active photo library on your Mac's hard drive and a second library on the disc.

When Not to Burn

The Burn command is great for creating quick backups, archiving portions of your library, or transferring photos to another Mac. But it's definitely *not* the best way to share your photos with Windows folks, or even other Mac folks still stubbornly clinging to Mac OS 9.

Think about it: Burning an iPhoto disc automatically organizes your photos into a series of numerically named subfolders inside an iPhoto library, surrounded by scads of special data files like *.attr* files, *Library.cache*, and *Dir.data*. All of this makes perfect sense to iPhoto but is mostly meaningless to anyone—or, rather, any computer—that doesn't have iPhoto. A Windows person or a photo-processing company, for example, would have to dig through folder after folder on your iPhoto CD to find and open your photos.

So if the destination of your CD or DVD isn't another iPhoto nut, *don't* use the Burn command. Instead, export the photos using the File→Export option described in Chapter 8 (page 314). The pictures won't have any ratings, comments, keywords, and so on, but they'll be organized in a way that's much easier for the non-iPhoto world to navigate.

iPhoto Backups

Unfortunately, bad things can happen to digital photos. They can be accidentally deleted with a slip of your pinkie. They can become mysteriously corrupted and subsequently unopenable. They can get mangled by a crashed hard drive and be lost forever. Losing one-of-a-kind family photos can be extremely painful—and in some documented cases, even marriage-threatening. So if you value your digital photos (and your relationships), you should back them up regularly, perhaps after each major batch of new photos joins your collection, and certainly before upgrading iPhoto when a new version comes out.

If you're using Mac OS X 10.5 or later and its Time Machine feature, then you can safely skip this section. You're already covered, as your entire machine is constantly backed up, as discussed on page 20.

If you have a MobileMe account and you're using its Backup program, you can use its canned iLife backup template to make sure that all your photos, movies, and music are backed up. (Of course, the standard MobileMe account offers only 20 gigabytes of storage space, although you can buy more.)

But you can also back up your stuff manually, as the following sections explain.

Backing Up to CD or DVD

The most convenient do-it-yourself way to back up your iPhoto library—a small one, anyway—is to archive it onto a blank CD or DVD using iPhoto's Burn command, as described on the previous pages. If anything bad ever happens to your photo collection, you'll be able to restore your library from the backup discs, with all your thumbnails, keywords, comments, and other tidbits intact.

To restore your photo collection from such a backup, see "Merging Photo Libraries" on page 334.

Backing Up to a Hard Drive

One of iPhoto's main jobs is to keep all your photos together in *one* place—one icon that's easy to copy to a backup disk of any kind.

That all-important icon is the *iPhoto Library*, which resides inside the Pictures folder of the Home folder that bears your name. If your user name (the short name you use to log into Mac OS X) is *Casey*, then the full path to your iPhoto Library file from your main hard drive window drive is Macintosh HD→Users→Casey→Pictures→iPhoto Library.

As described in Chapter 2, the iPhoto library contains not just your photos, but also a huge assortment of additional elements, including:

- All the thumbnail images in the iPhoto window.

- The original, safety copies of photos you've edited in iPhoto or an external editor.

- Various data files that keep track of your iPhoto keywords, comments, ratings, and photo albums.

To prepare for a disaster, you should back up *all* these components.

To perform a complete backup, quit iPhoto and then copy the entire iPhoto Library icon to another location. Copying it to a different hard drive—to another hard drive or another Mac via the network—is the best solution. (Copying it to another folder on the *same* disk means you'll lose both the original iPhoto library and its backup if, say, your hard drive crashes or your computer is hit by an asteroid.)

Note: Of course, you can also back up your photos by dragging their thumbnails out of the iPhoto window and into a folder or disk on your desktop, once you've dragged the iPhoto window to one side.

Unfortunately, this method doesn't preserve your keywords, comments, album organization, or any other information you've created in iPhoto. If something bad happens to your iPhoto Library, then you'll have to import the original photos again and reorganize them from scratch.

Managing Photo Libraries

iPhoto can comfortably manage around 250,000 photos in a single collection, give or take a few thousand, depending on your Mac model and how much memory it has.

But for some people, 250,000 pictures is a bit unwieldy. It makes them nervous to keep that many eggs in a single basket. They wish they could break up the library into several smaller, easier-to-manage, easier-to-back-up chunks.

If that's your situation, then you can archive some of the photos to CD or DVD using the Burn command described earlier, and then *delete* the archived photos from your library to shrink it down in size. For example, you might choose to archive older photos, or albums you rarely use.

Note: Remember, archiving photos to disc using the Burn command doesn't automatically remove them from iPhoto; you have to do that part yourself. If you don't, your library won't get any smaller. Just make sure that the CD or DVD you've burned works properly before deleting your original photos from iPhoto.

---

iPhoto Disk Images

The one disadvantage of the abovementioned offload-to-disc technique is that it takes a big hunk of your photo collection *offline*, so that you can no longer get to it easily. If you suddenly need a set of photos that you've already archived, for example, you have to hunt down the right disc. That could be a problem if you happen to be on the road in New York and need the photos you left on a DVD in San Francisco.

Here's a brilliant solution to that disc-management problem: Turn your iPhoto discs into *disk image files* on your hard drive.

Open Disk Utility (which sits in your Applications→Utilities folder); then insert the iPhoto CD or DVD you've burned. In the left pane of the Disk Utility window, click the disc's icon (see Figure 13-3).

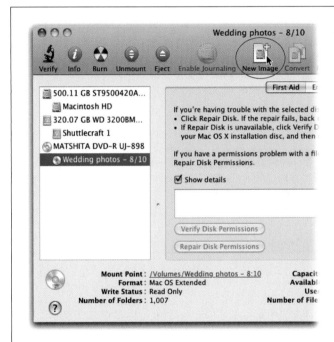

Figure 13-3:
Be sure to click the CD or DVD icon bearing a plain-English name, like "iPhoto Library" or "Wedding photos" as shown here (it's usually the last one listed). Don't click the icon bearing your CD burner's name, like "MATSHITA DVD-R."

Then choose File→New→"Disk Image from [Disc Name]," or click the New Image button in the toolbar at the top of the window (circled in Figure 13-3). In the resulting Save As dialog box, you can type a name for the disk image you're about to create. You can even password-protect it by choosing "128-bit AES" from the Encryption pop-up menu. Next, choose a location for the disk image, such as your desktop, and then click Save.

You've just created a disk image file whose name ends with .dmg. It's a "virtual CD" that you can keep on your hard drive at all times. When you want to view its contents in iPhoto, double-click the .dmg icon. You'll see its contents appear in the form of a

CD icon in the iPhoto Source list, just as though you'd inserted the original iPhoto disc.

You can spin off numerous chunks of your iPhoto collection this way, and "mount" as many of them simultaneously as you like—a spectacular way to manage tens of thousands of photos, chunk by chunk, without having to deal with a clumsy collection of discs.

Multiple iPhoto Libraries

Now that iPhoto can hold 250,000 photos per library, there's not as much need to split it into separate libraries as there once was. Still, there are two good reasons why you might want to consider it:

- Splitting your collection into several libraries may make iPhoto run faster, especially during scrolling, because there are fewer photos in it. (Fortunately, iPhoto '11 is noticeably faster than previous versions.)

- You can keep different types of collections or projects separate. You might want to maintain a Home library for personal use, for example, and a Work library for images that pertain to your business. Or you can start a new library every other year.

Creating new libraries

iPhoto provides a built-in tool for creating fresh libraries and switching among several of them:

1. **Quit iPhoto.**

   You're going to do the next step in the Finder.

2. **While pressing the Option key, open iPhoto again.**

   When iPhoto starts up, it senses that you're up to something. It offers you the chance to create a new library, or to choose an existing one (Figure 13-4).

3. **Click Create New. In the following dialog box, type a name for the new library (*Wedding Photo Library* or whatever), and then click Save.**

   You're offered not only the chance to create a new library, but also to choose a location for it if it's not your regularly scheduled Pictures folder.

   When iPhoto finishes opening, all remnants of your old iPhoto library are gone. You're left with a blank window, ready to import photos.

Using this technique, you can spawn as many new photo libraries as you need. You can archive the old libraries on CD or DVD, move them to another Mac, or just keep them somewhere on your hard drive so that you can swap any one of them back in whenever you need it.

As for *how* you swap them back in, you have two options: Apple's way and an easier way.

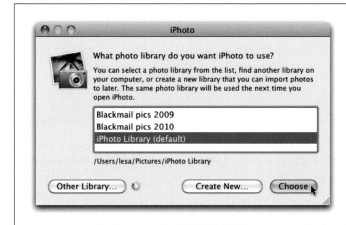

Figure 13-4:
If you open iPhoto while holding down the Option key, the program invites you to pick which library you want to open or to create a new one. If your goal is to start a fresh library for the new year, click Create New and give it a name.

To pick an existing library, either double-click it in the list or click once to select it and then click Choose.

Swapping libraries (Apple's method)

Once you've built yourself at least two iPhoto libraries, you can use the same Option-key trick (see step 2 above) to switch between them. When the dialog box in Figure 13-4 appears, select the library you want to open in the list, and then click Choose. (If you don't see the library you want, then click Other Library and hunt it down on your hard drive.)

When iPhoto finishes reopening, you'll find the new set of photos in place.

Swapping libraries (automatic method)

If that Option-key business sounds a little disorienting, you're not alone. Brian Webster, a self-proclaimed computer nerd, thought the same thing—but *he* decided to do something about it. He wrote iPhoto Library Manager, a free program that streamlines the creation and swapping of iPhoto libraries (see Figure 13-5). Waste no time in downloading it from Brian's site at *www.fatcatsoftware.com/iplm*.

The beauty of this program is that it offers a tidy list of all your libraries; you can switch among them with two quick clicks.

Here are a few pointers for using iPhoto Library Manager:

- The program doesn't just activate *existing* iPhoto libraries; it can also create new libraries for you. Just click the New Library button in the toolbar, choose a location and name for the library, and then click OK.

- You still have to quit and relaunch iPhoto for a change in libraries to take effect. Conveniently, iPhoto Library Manager includes Quit iPhoto and Launch iPhoto buttons in its toolbar.

Tip: You can also switch libraries using the pop-up menu from iPhoto Library Manager's Dock icon.

- iPhoto Library Manager is fully AppleScriptable. If you're handy with writing AppleScript scripts (discussed in Chapter 12), then you can write one that swaps your various libraries automatically with a double-click.

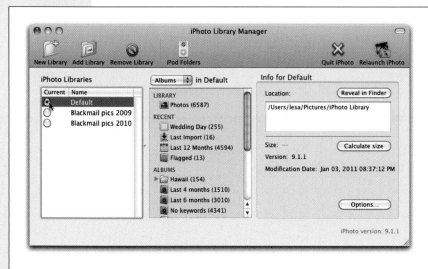

Figure 13-5:
iPhoto Library Manager lets you switch among as many different iPhoto libraries as you want. Select a library from the list on the left and the middle column shows its albums and other details. To view the photos in iPhoto, select a library and click Launch iPhoto (or Relaunch iPhoto). The program is free, though $20 unlocks even more advanced features, as discussed in the next section.

Merging Photo Libraries

You've just arrived home from your photo safari of deepest Kenya. You're jet-lagged and dusty, but your MacBook Pro is bursting at the seams with fresh photo meat. You can't wait to transfer the new pictures into your main iPhoto library—you know, the one on your Mac Pro Core Quad with 20 gigs of RAM and a 60-inch Apple IMAX Display.

Or, less dramatically, suppose you've just upgraded to iPhoto '11. You're thrilled that you can fit 250,000 pictures into a single library—but you still have six old iPhoto 5 library folders containing about 10,000 pictures each.

In both cases, you have the same problem: How are you supposed to merge the libraries into a single, unified one?

How Not to Do It

You certainly can combine the *photos* of two Macs' photo libraries—just export them from one (File→Export) and then import them into the other (File→"Import to Library"). As a result, however, you lose all of your album organization, comments, and keywords.

Your next instinct might be: "Hey, I know! I'll just drag the iPhoto Library icon from computer number 1 into the iPhoto window of computer number 2!"

Big mistake. You'll end up importing not only the photos, but also the original versions of any photos that you edited. You'll wind up with duplicates or triplicates of every photo in the viewing area, in one enormous, unmanageable, uncategorized, sloshing library. (At least iPhoto '11 is smart enough not to import all the thumbnail images, as older iPhoto versions did.)

You could also use iPhoto CDs or DVDs as intermediaries, but that's time-consuming and uses up blank discs.

The Good Way

The only *sane* way to merge libraries is to use iPhoto Library Manager, described above. For $20, you can unlock some features that aren't available in the free version—including a miraculously simple Merge Libraries command.

All you have to do is choose File→Merge Libraries. In the resulting dialog box, turn on the checkboxes of the libraries you want to merge, and proceed as shown in Figure 13-6.

Note: iPhoto Library Manager's merging process preserves all keywords, ratings, photo titles, albums, and editing you've done. However, it doesn't maintain books, calendars, saved slideshows, or smart albums.

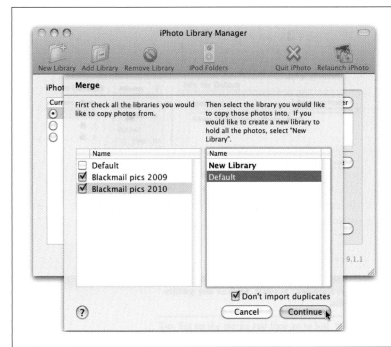

Figure 13-6:
Turn on the checkboxes of the libraries you want to combine in the column on the left.

To combine them into a new library, leave New Library selected in the right column.

Or, to add them to an existing library (like your Default library), select the existing library on the right and then click Continue—and walk away (or go to bed, because it can take awhile).

Beyond iPhoto

Depending on how massive your collection of digital photos grows and how you use it, you may find yourself wanting more file-management power than iPhoto offers. Maybe you wish you could organize 500,000 photos in a single catalog, without having to swap photo libraries or load archive DVDs. Or maybe you have a small network, and you'd like a system that lets a whole workgroup share a library of photos simultaneously.

To enjoy such features, you'll have to move beyond iPhoto into the world of *digital asset management*, which means spending a little money. Programs like Adobe Photoshop Lightroom ($300, *www.adobe.com/lightroom*), Apple's own Aperture ($200), Extensis Portfolio Standalone ($200, *www.extensis.com*), Canto Cumulus ($100, *www.canto.com*), and Microsoft Expression Media (formerly iView MediaPro, $200, *www.microsoft.com/expression*) are terrific programs for someone who wants to take the next step up, as shown in Figure 13-7. (These companies offer free trial versions on their websites.)

Here are a few of the stunts some of these more advanced programs can do that iPhoto can't:

- Create custom fields to store any other kind of information you want about your files—dates, prices, web addresses, and so on.
- Track graphics files stored in any location on a network, not just in a specific folder.
- Catalog not just photos, but other file types, too: QuarkXPress and InDesign documents, QuickTime movies, sound files, PowerPoint slides, and so on.
- Share a catalog of images with dozens of other people over a network.
- Customize the fonts, colors, and borders of the thumbnail view.
- Create catalogs that can be read on both Macs and Windows PCs.
- Display previews of "offline" photo files that aren't actually on your Mac at the moment (they're on CDs or DVDs on your shelf, for example).

Some of the features in this list were obviously developed with professionals in mind, like graphic designers and studio photographers. But this kind of program is worth considering if your photo collection—and your passion for digital photography—one day outgrows iPhoto.

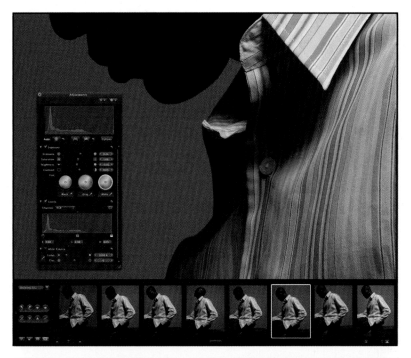

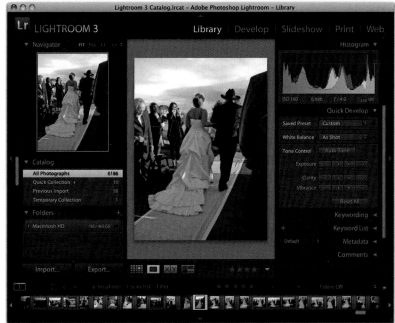

Figure 13-7:
Aperture is one of several programs that do what iPhoto does—and a lot more besides.

Top: Here, for example, is Aperture's version of full-screen editing mode. One key difference: When you make changes, Aperture doesn't duplicate the photo file (and use up disk space), as iPhoto does. It just remembers which changes you've applied, and can undo them in any sequence.

What's also nice about Aperture is that it works well with iMovie. For example, it seamlessly imports iMovie libraries, complete with albums, keywords, ratings, and so on.

Bottom: Adobe Photoshop Lightroom is Aperture's archrival. Among other features, it can upload changed galleries directly to the Web, without requiring an FTP program.

Troubleshooting

i Photo isn't just a Mac OS X program—it's a *Cocoa* Mac OS X program, meaning that it was written exclusively for Mac OS X. As a result, it should, in theory, be one of the most rock-solid programs under the sun.

Still, iPhoto does have its vulnerabilities. Many of these shortcomings stem from the fact that iPhoto works under the supervision of a lot of cooks, since it has to interact with plug-ins, connect to printers, talk to web servers, and cope with an array of file corruptions.

If trouble strikes, keep hands and feet inside the tram at all times—and consult the following collection of problems, solutions, questions, and answers.

The Most Important Advice in This Chapter

Apple's traditional practice is to release a new version of iPhoto (and iMovie, and iDVD…) that's got some bugs and glitches—and then, just when public outcry reaches fever pitch a couple of weeks later, send out a .0.1 update that cleans up most of the problems.

Spare yourself the headache: Update your copy to 9.1.1 (or whatever the latest version is)! To do that right now, choose iPhoto→Check for Updates.

Importing, Upgrading, and Opening

Getting photos into iPhoto is supposed to be one of the most effortless parts of the process. Remember, Steve Jobs promised that iPhoto would forever banish the "chain of pain" from digital photography. And yet…

"Unable to upgrade this photo library"

There may be locked files somewhere inside your iPhoto library. If something's locked, iPhoto can't very well convert it to the '11 format.

Trouble is, there can be hundreds of thousands of files in an iPhoto library. How are you supposed to find the one file that's somehow gotten locked?

The quickest way is to type out a Unix command. Don't worry, it won't bite.

Open your Applications→Utilities folder, and then double-click Terminal. The strange, graphics-free, all-text command console may look alien and weird, but you'll witness its power in just a moment.

Type this, exactly as it appears here:

```
sudo chflags -R nouchg
```

—and add a space at the end (after "nouchg"). Don't press Return yet.

Now switch to the Finder. Open your Pictures folder and drag your iPhoto Library icon right *into* the Terminal window. Now the command looks something like this:

```
sudo chflags -R nouchg /Users/Casey/Pictures/iPhoto\ Library/
```

Press Return to issue the command. Mac OS X asks for your account password, to prove that you know what you're doing. Type it, press Return, and your problem should be solved.

iPhoto doesn't recognize my camera.

iPhoto generally "sees" any recent camera model, even iPhones and photos saved on an iPod Touch. If you don't see the Import screen (Chapter 1) even though the camera most assuredly is connected, then try these steps in order:

- Make sure the camera is turned on. Check the USB cable at both ends.

- Try plugging the camera into a different USB port.

- Some models don't see the computer until you switch them into a special "PC" mode, using the Mode dial. Check to see if your camera's in that category.

- Try turning on the camera *after* connecting its USB cable to the Mac.

- Turn the camera off, then on again, while it's plugged in.

- If iPhoto absolutely won't notice its digital companion, then use a memory-card reader, as described on page 17, or the SD card slot on the left side of newer MacBook Pros.

iPhoto crashes when I try to import.

This problem is most likely to crop up when you're bringing pictures in from your hard drive or another disk. Here are the possibilities:

- The culprit is usually a single corrupted file. Try a test: Import only half the photos in the batch. If nothing bad happens, then split the remaining photos in half again and import *them*. Keep going until you've isolated the offending file.

- Consider the graphics program you're using to save the files. It's conceivable that its version of JPEG or TIFF doesn't jibe perfectly with iPhoto's. (This scenario is most likely to occur right after you've upgraded either your graphics program or iPhoto itself.)

  To test this possibility, open a handful of images in a different editing program, save them, and then try the import again. If they work, then you might have a temporary compatibility problem. Check the editing program's website for updates and troubleshooting information.

- Some JPEGs that were originally saved in Mac OS 9 won't import into iPhoto. Try opening and resaving these images in a native Mac OS X editor like Photoshop. Speaking of Photoshop, it has an excellent batch-processing tool that can automatically process mountains of images while you go grab some lunch.

Tip: Can't afford hundreds of dollars for full Photoshop? Try the free online version, Photoshop Express, at *www.photoshop.com*. You can do most basic photo-editing tasks and even store up to 2 gigabytes of pix. Photoshop Elements—the consumer version of Photoshop—is another good option. It's amazingly powerful and costs less than $100.

Finally, a reminder, just in case you think iPhoto is acting up: iPhoto imports Raw files—but not from all camera models. For details, see the Note on page 24.

iPhoto crashes when I try to empty the Trash.

Open iPhoto while pressing ⌘ and Option; in the dialog box shown in Figure A-2 (page 346), turn on "Rebuild the photos' small thumbnails," and then click Rebuild.

iPhoto won't import images from my video camera.

Most modern digital camcorders can store your still images on a memory card instead of DV tape. If you're having a hard time importing these stills into iPhoto with a direct camera connection, try these tricks:

- Take out the tape cassette before connecting the camcorder to your Mac.

- Try copying the files directly from the memory card to your hard drive with a memory-card reader. Once the images are on your hard drive, you should be able to import them into iPhoto.

Exporting

Clearly, "Easy come, easy go" doesn't always apply to photos.

After I upgraded iPhoto to the latest version, my Export button became disabled.

This problem is usually caused by outdated plug-ins. If you have any older plug-ins, such as an outdated version of the Toast Titanium export plug-in, disable them, and then relaunch iPhoto to see whether that solves the problem.

Note: In Mac OS X 10.5 (Leopard) and earlier, you could turn plug-ins on or off using iPhoto's File→Get Info window. In Mac OS X 10.6 (Snow Leopard) and later, you have to *remove* the plug-in from iPhoto instead.

Here's how to disable your plug-ins:

1. **Quit iPhoto. Then, in the Finder, Control-click (right-click) the iPhoto application icon and choose Show Package Contents.**

   Your Mac opens a window containing a folder called Contents (Figure A-1).

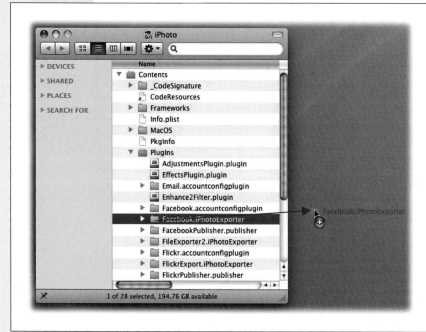

Figure A-1:
To remove a plug-in, just drag it out of the PlugIns folder, as shown here.

You may be surprised to discover that a number of iPhoto's "built-in" features are actually plug-ins written by Apple's programmers. Most of them are responsible for familiar printing and exporting options. Any others should be turned off in times of troubleshooting. (If you can't remember which plug-ins you've installed yourself, then reinstall iPhoto.)

2. **In the resulting window, open the Contents→PlugIns folder.**

   A complete list of the plug-ins you currently have loaded appears, represented by easily removable icons and folders.

3. **Locate the non-Apple plug-ins that you suspect might be causing the problem, and drag them onto your desktop (or anywhere outside the iPhoto folder).**

Now launch iPhoto and test the Export function. If the technology gods are smiling, the function should work now. All that's left is to figure out which *one* of the plug-ins was causing your headaches.

To find out, quit iPhoto. Using the steps above, reinstate your plug-ins one by one (by dragging them back into the PlugIns folder) until you find the offending software.

Once you locate the culprit, delete it. You may also want to check the website of the offending plug-in for an updated version.

Printing

Printing has its share of frustrations and wasted paper, but checking a few settings can solve some common problems:

I can't print more than one photo per page. It seems like a waste to use a whole sheet of paper for one 4 × 6 print.

Check the following:

- Have you, in fact, selected a paper size that's larger than the prints you want on it? (See Figure 7-2 back on page 184.)

- Have you entered the photo-layout mode (page 187), clicked Settings, and then turned on "Multiple photos per page?"

My picture doesn't fit right on 4 × 6, 5 × 7, or 8 × 10 inch paper.

Most digital cameras produce photos in a 4:3 width-to-height ratio. Unfortunately, those dimensions don't fit neatly into any of the standard print sizes.

The solution: Crop the photos first, using the appropriate print size in the Constrain pop-up menu (see page 132).

Editing and Sharing

There's not much that can go wrong here, but when it does, it *really* goes wrong.

iPhoto crashes when I double-click a thumbnail to edit it.

You probably changed a photo file's name in the Finder—in the iPhoto Library package, behind the program's back. iPhoto hates this! Only grief can follow.

Sometimes, too, a corrupted picture file will make iPhoto crash when you try to edit it. To locate the scrambled file in the Finder, Control-click (or right-click) its thumbnail; from the shortcut menu, choose Show Original File. Open the file in another graphics program, use its File→Save As command to replace the corrupted picture file, and then try again in iPhoto.

iPhoto won't let me use an external graphics program when I double-click a thumbnail.

Choose iPhoto→Preferences, and then click the Advanced button. Check the "Edit Photos" pop-up menu to make sure that the external program's name is selected. (If not, click "In application," and then choose the program you want to use.)

Also make sure that your external editing program still *exists*. You might have upgraded to a newer version of that program, one whose file name is slightly different from the version you originally specified in iPhoto.

Faces really stinks at identifying the people in my pictures!

To get Faces more skilled at matching up names to the folks in your photos, you need to help it along by *training* it. If Faces hasn't identified someone you *know* is in your library, then open up the photo (or photos) with the poor nameless soul, click the Info button on the toolbar, and then click the Faces icon to expand that section. Click "Add a face" and then proceed as shown on page 98. Manually naming the face, however, doesn't do much for iPhoto's face-recognition algorithm—it's your *confirming* results in the automatic face-recognition roundup that helps Faces learn.

So click Faces in the Source list, open that person's snapshot on the corkboard, and then click the Confirm Name button in the toolbar. Scroll down to the "may also be in the photos below" list, and start confirming or rejecting the suggestions (page 99) so Faces gets more practice in *correctly* identifying your buddies.

Published pictures I re-edit in iPhoto aren't updating on my free Flickr page.

Sometimes there's a breakdown in communication: between heads of state, management and labor, and even iPhoto and Flickr. Fortunately, that last one is the easiest to solve. In iPhoto, delete the misbehaving photo(s) from your Flickr album. Then make your edits or changes to the pictures (if you haven't already), and then publish the photos to Flickr again, as described on page 207. If you have only one picture in the Flickr album, delete the whole album from the iPhoto Source list, fix the picture in iPhoto, and then republish the photo to Flickr as a brand-new album.

I've messed up a photo while editing it, and now it's ruined!

Highlight the file's thumbnail and then choose Photos→"Revert to Original." iPhoto restores your photo to its original state, drawing on a backup it has secretly kept.

General Questions

Finally, here's a handful of general—although perfectly terrifying—troubles.

iPhoto's wigging out!

If the program "unexpectedly quits," well, that's life. It happens. This is Mac OS X, though, so you can generally open the program right back up again and pick up where you left off.

If the flakiness is becoming really severe, try logging out (choose ➞Log Out) and logging back in again. And if the problem persists, see the data-purging steps on page 346.

I don't see my other Mac's shared photos over the network.

Chapter 8 covers network photo sharing in detail. If you're having trouble making it work, here's your checklist:

- Make sure you've turned on "Look for shared photos" in the Sharing pane of iPhoto's Preferences.

- Is the Mac that's sharing the photos turned on and awake? Is iPhoto running on it, and does it have photo sharing turned on? Is it on the same network subnet (network branch)?

- Do the photo-sharing Macs both have iPhoto 4 or later installed?

I can't delete a photo!

You may be trying to delete a photo right out of a smart album. That's a no-no.

There's only one workaround: Find the same photo in the iPhoto Library by heading to the Source list and clicking an icon in the Library heading—Events, Photos, the Last Import or the Last 12 Months icon—and then delete it from there.

I deleted a photo, but it's back again!

You probably deleted it from an album (or book, calendar, card, or slideshow). These are all only *aliases*, or *pointers*, to the actual photo in your library. Just removing a thumbnail from an album doesn't touch the original.

All my pictures are gone!

Somebody probably moved, renamed, or fooled with your iPhoto Library icon. That's a bad, bad idea.

If it's just been moved or renamed, then find it again using your Mac's search feature (Spotlight, for example). Drag it back into your Pictures folder, if you like. In any case, the important step is to open iPhoto while pressing the Option key. When the dialog box shown on page 346 appears, show iPhoto where your library folder is now. (If that solution doesn't work, read on.)

All my pictures are still gone! (or)
My thumbnails are all gray rectangles! (or)
I'm having some other crisis!

The still-missing-pictures syndrome and the gray-rectangle thumbnails are only two of several oddities that may strike with all the infrequency—and pain—of lightning. Maybe iPhoto is trying to import phantom photos. Maybe it's stuck at the "Loading photos…" screen forever. Maybe the photos just don't look right. There's a long list, in fact, of rare but mystifying glitches that can arise.

What your copy of iPhoto needs is a big thwack upside the head, also known as a major data purge.

You may not need to perform all of the following steps. But if you follow them all, at least you'll know you did everything possible to make things right. Perform these steps in order; after each one, check to see if the problem is gone.

- **If you haven't already done so, upgrade to the very latest version of iPhoto**. For example, the 9.1 update was hot on the heels of iPhoto 9.0 (also known as iPhoto '11, of course).

- **Rebuild the iPhoto library and fix its permissions**. To do that, quit iPhoto. Then reopen it, pressing the Option and ⌘ keys as you do so.

  The dialog box shown in Figure A-2 appears; it offers six different repair techniques. For best results, turn on all of them. (Or, to save time, try the second checkbox only if the other ones, which are faster, don't solve the problem.)

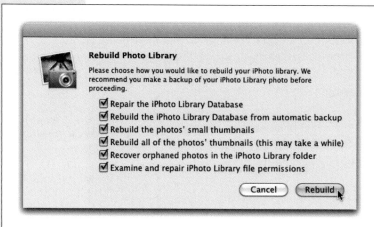

Figure A-2:
These maintenance procedures solve all kinds of iPhoto library corruptions. Sometimes you'll be instructed to use only one of the checkboxes to save time. If you're really desperate, turn on all six.

Once you click the Rebuild button, iPhoto works its way through each album and each photo, inspecting it for damage, repairing it if possible, and finally presenting you with your new, cleaned-up library. This can take a *very* long time, but it usually works.

- **Throw away the iPhoto preference file**. Here we are in the age of Mac OS X, and we're still throwing away preference files?

  Absolutely. A corrupted preference file can still bewilder the program that depends on it.

  Open your Home→Library→Preferences folder, where you'll find neatly labeled preference files for all of the programs you use. In this case, trash the file called com.apple.iPhoto.plist.

The next time you run iPhoto, it will build itself a brand-new preference file that, if you're lucky, lacks whatever corruption was causing your problems.

- **Import the library into itself**. If, after all these steps, some or all of your photos are still missing, try this radical step. Create a new, empty iPhoto library (page 332). Then drag the older, troubled library folder right from the Finder into the empty iPhoto window. The program imports all of the graphics it finds (except the thumbnails, which you don't want anyway).

  You lose all your keywords, Event names, comments, albums, folders, books, saved slideshows, and so on. And you might wind up with duplicates (the edited and unedited versions of the pictures). But if any photos were in the old library but somehow unaccounted for, they'll magically reappear.

- **Just find the pix yourself**. If none of these steps restored your missing photos, all is not lost. Unless you somehow opened your Home→Pictures folder and, while sleepwalking, manually *threw away* your iPhoto Library folder, then your pictures are still there, somewhere, on your hard drive.

  Use Spotlight or the Find command to search for them, as shown in Figure A-3.

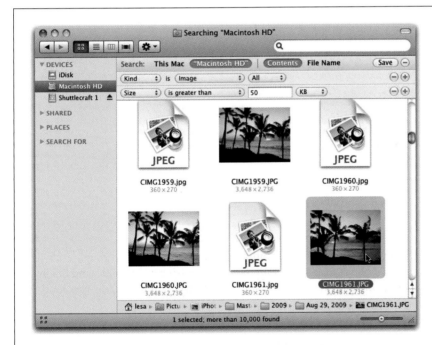

Figure A-3:
Search for images (or file extensions .JPG or .JPEG) with file sizes greater than, say, 50 K (to avoid rounding up all of the little thumbnail representations; it's the actual photos you want).

The results may include thousands of photos. But in this desperate state, you may be grateful that you can either (a) click one to see where it's hiding, or (b) select all of them, drag them into a new, empty iPhoto library, and begin the process of sorting out the mess.

Where to Go from Here

Your Mac, your trusty digital camera, and this book are all you need to *begin* enjoying the art and science of modern photography. But as your skills increase and your interests broaden, you may want to explore new techniques, add equipment, and learn from people who've become just as obsessed as you. Here's a tasty menu of resources to help you along the way.

iPhoto and the Web

- **Apple's iPhoto support page** (*www.apple.com/iphoto*) features the latest product information, QuickTime tutorials, FAQ (frequently asked questions) lists, camera and printer compatibility charts, and links to discussion forums where other iPhoto users share knowledge and lend helping hands. There's even a feedback form that goes directly to Apple. In fact, each piece of feedback is read personally by top-level Apple executives. (Just a little joke there.)

- **VersionTracker** (*www.versiontracker.com*) is a massive database that tracks, and provides links to, all the latest software for Mac OS X, including the cool iPhoto add-ons described in this book.

- **O'Reilly's Mac DevCenter** (*www.macdevcenter.com*) features the latest Mac software techniques for power users and programmers.

Digital Photo Equipment Online

- **Imaging-Resource** (*www.imaging-resource.com*) offers equipment reviews, price comparisons, and forums, all dedicated to putting the right digital camera in your hands.

- **Digital Photography Review** (*www.dpreview.com*) is similar: It offers news, reviews, buying guides, photo galleries, and forums. It's a must-visit site for the digicam nut.

- **Digital Camera Resource** (*www.dcresource.com*) is just what it says: a comprehensive resource page comparing the latest in digital cameras.

- **Photo.net** (*www.photo.net*) offers industry news, galleries, shopping, travel, critique, and community sharing.

- **Photo District News** (*www.pdnonline.com*) covers trends on the photography industry, news, and camera reviews, plus RSS feeds to keep you updated on the go.

When it comes to time to buy, you can't beat your local camera store for service (some stores offer training, too). Camera gear is almost always cheaper online, though. At *www.shopping.com*, for example, you can find a price roundup of all the online shops selling a particular camera. (To avoid being scammed, look for Shopping .com's *smart buy* badge, which indicates the best price at a highly rated store.)

Show Your Pictures

Nothing beats Flickr.com, Facebook.com, and MobileMe for easily posting your pictures online, straight from iPhoto (Chapter 8). But there are alternatives:

- **Photobucket** (*www.photobucket.com*) offers its members Web space for 10,000 photos—free. The photo-sharing site groups submitted photos into categories like "Funny Signs" and "Black & White" for easy browsing on its home page and features one-click posting to sites like Facebook, Blogger, TypePad, and MySpace.

- **SmugMug** (*www.smugmug.com*) is another popular site for creating beautiful and secure photo galleries (special programming blocks visitors from Control-clicking to save images to their desktops). If you spring for the pro version, you can generate some extra income by selling your photos as files, prints, and photo products (you get to set the pricing). If you want to start an online photography business, this site is worth checking out. Pricing ranges from $40 to $150 a year.

- **Fotki.com** (*www.fotki.com*) is similar—it, too, is a thriving online community of photo fans who share their work online—but the free account is unlimited. Chime in with your shots, or just check out what everyone else is shooting.

Online Instruction

- **KelbyTraining.com** (*www.kelbytraining.com*) is relatively new to the online training realm, though it features some of the best instructors in the world. It offers a multitude of streaming videos on all aspects of photography, along with related software (Photoshop, Photoshop Elements, Lightroom, and so on). Unlimited subscriptions are available for $25 a month or $200 a year.

- **Lynda.com** (*www.lynda.com*) is another video-training company that's been around for years. Here you'll find all manner of instruction on the basics of digital photography, using iPhoto, and a lot more. Subscriptions range from $25 a month to $375 a year.

- **ShortCourses.com** (*www.shortcourses.com*) offers short courses (no surprise there) in digital photography techniques and how to use the latest equipment.

Online Printing

- **Mpix** (*www.mpix.com*) is a wonderfully friendly online service that provides very high-quality prints, books, greeting cards, and anything else that a photo can be attractively printed on. This lab is regarded very highly by photo pros all over the world.

- **Shutterfly** (*www.shutterfly.com*) is another alternative to iPhoto's built-in photo-ordering system. It's Mac OS X-friendly and highly reviewed (at least by *Macworld*).

- **American Greetings PhotoWorks** (*www.photoworks.com*) is another Mac OS X-friendly photo printing site that's also received high marks for quality.

Books

David Pogue's Digital Photography: The Missing Manual (O'Reilly) offers expert advice from the moment you start shopping for a digital camera to producing your own stunning shots—with plenty of nuts-and-bolts instruction on lighting, composition, and choosing the best camera settings along the way.

The Digital Photography Book by Scott Kelby (Peachpit Press) contains all kinds of wonderful advice on taking better pictures and choosing essential gear, along with tips and tricks for setting up simple lighting yourself.

Understanding Exposure by Bryan Peterson (Amphoto Books) is another great guide. To get the most out of your camera, you have to understand exposure, a confusing concept; but this book makes it crystal clear through text and beautiful imagery. If you're passionate about photography or just want to get a little more serious, this book is an essential and enjoyable read.

Digital Photography Companion by Derrick Story (O'Reilly) is a handy, on-the-go digital-photo reference that fits nicely in your camera bag.

The Moment It Clicks by Joe McNally (New Riders Press) is a visually attractive photography book that gives you unique insight into the realm of one of the world's best shooters.

Take Your Best Shot by Tim Grey (O'Reilly) dives into the digital darkroom, covering the fundamentals of camera hardware as well as more advanced topics like color management and optimizing images.

Index

Colophon

iPhoto '11: The Missing Manual was composited in Adobe InDesign CS4 by Nellie McKesson.

The cover of this book is based on a series design originally created by David Freedman and modified by Mike Kohnke, Karen Montgomery, and Fitch (*www.fitch.com*). Back cover design, dog illustration, and color selection by Fitch.

David Futato designed the interior layout, based on a series design by Phil Simpson. The text font is Adobe Minion; the heading font is Adobe Formata Condensed; and the code font is LucasFont's TheSans Mono Condensed. The illustrations that appear in the book were produced by Lesa Snider using Adobe Photoshop and Illustrator CS5.

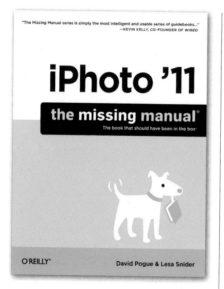
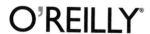